Selected Titles in This Series

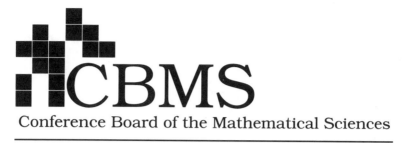

Conference Board of the Mathematical Sciences

Issues in Mathematics Education

Volume 7

Research in Collegiate Mathematics Education. III

Alan H. Schoenfeld
Jim Kaput
Ed Dubinsky
Editors

Thomas Dick, *Managing Editor*

American Mathematical Society
Providence, Rhode Island
in cooperation with
Mathematical Association of America
Washington, D. C.

1991 *Mathematics Subject Classification.* Primary 00-XX, 92-XX.

ISBN 0-8218-0882-6
ISSN 1047-398X

CONTENTS

PREFACE

Welcome to the third volume of *Research in Collegiate Mathematics Education (RCME III)*. For an introduction to the series of volumes see the preface to *RCME I*, which appeared in this *CBMS* series in 1994; for a general introduction to the field of research in undergraduate mathematics education see the first chapter in that volume, by Alan Schoenfeld. In this preface we focus on providing brief introductions to the papers that appear in this volume.

In the three years since we began this enterprise, we have tried to have these volumes grow with the field, reflecting the broad spectrum of work done by researchers concerned with collegiate mathematics education. In journal-like fashion, we consider papers independently and publish those that we think reflect or advance the state of the art. Nevertheless, it still makes sense to structure the collection of papers that have been accepted, for purposes of coherence and to introduce the content and methodological issues they deal with.

In Volumes I and II we established the tradition of bringing each volume to a close with an article focusing on open questions in the field and/or suggestions for future research. Volume I presented Lynn Steen's "Twenty Questions for Research on Undergraduate Mathematics Education," an attempt to "define the challenge and frame the debate" concerning the role of education research in the mathematics enterprise. In Volume II we printed a list of 18 questions raised at the first Oberwolfach conference in Undergraduate Mathematics Education that was held in the Fall of 1995. These are a combination of 18 research and curriculum questions that have no special status other than that after several hours of discussion 24 people at a conference agreed that they are important. In this volume we close with a paper by Annie and John Selden that presents a set of questions that arose during the first annual Conference on Research in Collegiate Mathematics Education held at Central Michigan University, September 5–8, 1996.

The eight papers that comprise the core of this volume can be seen as falling naturally into three sets. The first set contains three papers that focus, in different ways, on the same undergraduate course in mathematical problem solving. The second set also contains three papers, each of which highlights different ways to examine student understanding. The third set contains two reports on how students think about, and try to deal with, the idea of proof in mathematics.

A PROBLEM SOLVING COURSE

This is an unusual series of three papers, each focused on aspects of a problem solving course taught for many years by Alan Schoenfeld and widely reported upon by him and his colleagues. The unusual and highly reflexive nature of the set deserves some explanation. We first received a paper by Abraham Arcavi, Cathy Kessel, Luciano Meira, and Jack Smith, each of whom concentrated on a particular aspect of the classroom activity and Schoenfeld's teaching. While this long four-part paper was in review (a review directed by Kaput and Dubinsky, entirely independently of Schoenfeld) we received a paper by Manuel Santos-Trigo, who likewise analyzed an aspect of the course. All these authors had sat in on the course and/or had analyzed classroom videotapes, transcripts and field notes taken during two offerings of the course (Arcavi et al. in 1990, Santos in 1994). Arcavi et al.'s overall intent was to document and explain the workings of the course's beginnings at a fine level of detail, while at the same time providing sufficient theoretical underpinning to hold the detail together in a principled, explanatory way. Santos deals with related issues, covering more of the course. After receiving positive external reviews that recommended the publication of the two papers contingent upon revisions, and while the two papers were being revised, Schoenfeld was invited to write a response paper in which he reflected on what the others were saying about his teaching. He chose to do so by reviewing the details of their analyses from the perspective of his current work, which is aimed at developing an explicit model of teaching that is intended to explain the real-time decision-making by teachers in terms of their beliefs, knowledge, goals and specific classroom situations. We present the papers in the order of what they cover: Arcavi et al. focusing on the beginning of the course, Santos discussing aspects of the course as a whole, and Schoenfeld in response to both.

This set of papers is intended to provide a close look at a particular example of "good practice," a highly refined course and pedagogical approach that over the years seems to succeed in teaching powerful problem solving skills. It is not intended to be construed as the only form of good practice, or even as a model for everyone to emulate; many other instructors have their own successful ways of teaching their version of problem solving. We hope, however, that these papers are seen as being of value for substantive and methodological reasons. They examine a good practice in fine-grained detail, exploring how real-time classroom decision-making is related to the instructor's knowledge, goals and beliefs about problem solving, and suggesting how it may be taught and learned. Moreover, they serve as case studies in how to document and analyze classroom situations.

Classroom practice, both good and bad, merely seems to happen—somewhat like the weather. While it is often discussed in general and even passionate terms, and people struggle to measure its outcomes, it is seldom examined in a detailed way, where claims are explicitly linked to events, and a coherent explanatory story is put together. Our ultimate goal for studies of this type is that they lead to a new level of analytic explicitness regarding the varieties of classroom practice that will help expose the underpinnings of good teaching so that more of us can achieve it more easily and routinely.

METHODOLOGICAL PLURALISM

Marilyn Carlson applies a combination of quantitative and qualitative methods to the study of understanding the function concept. Carlson has designed a written examination that helps her in the selection of students for more extensive (and time-consuming) follow-up interviews. Written examinations can be administered to large numbers of students, providing "large n" data and enough information about individual students to sort them into rough equivalence classes regarding some aspects of their mathematical understandings. One can then interview representatives from those classes, reducing the interviews to a manageable number while still exploring a wide range of student understandings. Also, the interviews provide an opportunity for triangulation on the findings from the written exam—that is, for seeing whether what the students do in interviews corresponds to the inferences one can draw from their written work. Aside from the question of methodology are Carlson's findings. She considered high performing students across a range of undergraduate levels from those taking college algebra to students beginning graduate work in mathematics. Unfortunately, she finds that difficulties in developing a powerful function concept occur at all levels and are even seen in our brightest students. One thing this paper does is point to the complexity of the concept, and the multiple sets of understandings one must develop in coming to grips with it. It also shows that, in spite of the tremendous amount of research on understanding the function concept and the important improvements in pedagogy that it has led to, much still remains to be done. As Carlson concludes from the study, "an individual's view of the function concept evolves over a period of many years and requires an effort of 'sense making' to understand and orchestrate individual function components to work in concert."

David Meel used a similarly pluralistic methodology to analyze students' understandings of selected calculus concepts (limit, derivative, and integral) by students in a third-semester honors calculus class. But there are important differences in the way Meel analyzed his data. While Carlson's selection criteria for student interviews were grounded in the "at-a-point vs. across-time" perspective of Steve Monk as well as the APOS Theory of the RUMEC group, Meel employed a specific model of understanding developed by Pirie and Kieren, together with standard statistical methods, to largely direct his analysis of the data. While addressing broader issues of conceptual understanding in general, Meel is also

concerned with a more focused issue: the study of the relative effects of two very
different pedagogical approaches to calculus, a reformed course called *Calculus
& Mathematica* and the traditional calculus course. Meel compares students from
these courses in terms of how well they can perform calculations, their problem-
solving ability, and their level of conceptual understanding. The results of the
comparison are mixed. Meel finds no serious differences between the two groups
in their overall performance on the written instrument and in particular with
respect to the differentiation concept, procedurally-oriented items and text-and-
pictorial items. He does, however find that the students taking a traditional
course performed significantly better on the limit concept, conceptually-oriented
items, and on text-only items. On the problem-solving interviews, however, he
finds that the *Calculus& Mathematica* students tended to be more flexible and
were more successful in solving problems. In additional interviews which he calls
"understanding interviews" he finds little difference between the two groups.
Moreover, he finds serious inadequacies in both groups with respect to understanding the limit and differentiation concepts, although they did much better
with integration. Meel's overall conclusion seems to be a concern with whether
"either curriculum satisfied the needs of these honors calculus students."

The methodological challenges faced by Alvin Baranchik and Barry Cherkas
were very different indeed. The question they faced was this. Suppose you have
available a widely used standardized test for elementary algebra—in their case
the College Entrance Examination Board's *Elementary Algebra Skills Test*. The
test uses multiple choice items, and reports the number of items the student has
gotten correct. What kinds of inferences can you draw about students' understandings, if you look at the full pattern of their responses to the test? Baranchik
and Cherkas had experts evaluate responses to the test items (including "dis-
tracter" items) for clues to possible understandings, and they assigned partial
credit for such partial understandings; they also used statistical techniques to
identify components of algebraic skills from patterns of responses to the items.
The two methods agreed, and provided some predictive power. The bottom line
of the study: "Genuine partial understanding, which is relevant to student performance and is missed by number correct scoring alone, can be inferred from
students' selections of certain incorrect alternatives."

PROOFS IN MATHEMATICS

In this invited foundational paper Guershon Harel and Larry Sowder provide
a distinctly psychological framework (although informed by historical, philosophical and cultural analyses) for examining students' understanding of proof.
The paper was developed as part of the first author's NSF funded research on
students' understanding, production and appreciation of mathematical proofs,
ultimately focusing on mathematics majors as the target population. Building on
a literature review, Harel and Sowder look closely at what constitutes evidence
in the eye of the student rather than in the eye of the instructor or curriculum
writer, and they expose deep differences that help to explain the historical failure

of most students to learn the hows and whys of mathematical proof. Their main strategy is as follows: to characterize students' cognitive schemes of proof—how students understand proof, evidence and justification; to document how these schemes are reflected in the behavior of college students working in different domains and at different levels; to show how these schemes develop over time and experience among mathematics majors; and to offer principles for instruction that help facilitate appropriate development. They examine evidence taken from a series of teaching experiments executed by the first author in Number Theory, Geometry, introductory and advanced Linear Algebra, and a case study of a precocious junior high school student taking Geometry and Calculus at the university level. The paper is not about how to teach proof, or about comparative methods (Method A versus Method B). Instead, by closely examining student behaviors and responses to a variety of teaching experiments, it tries to construct a systematic cognitivist way of understanding how students understand and learn how to prove mathematical assertions. The resulting system of *External-Conviction*, *Empirical* and *Analytic Proof Schemes*, each with several interconnected sub-schemes, is not simple (we would have every reason to be suspicious if it were), but it is consistent with a substantial body of episodic evidence garnered from the teaching experiments. The lengthy series of episodes taken from the teaching experiments illustrate each type of proof scheme that they describe and relate it to the work of others in the field. However, as the authors note, they do not regard their typology as the last word on the subject. Rather, it should be seen as a starting point that will need refinement and data from many other sources as well as more sequenced teaching experiments to examine the longer term development of these schemes. Nonetheless, they suggest how we might begin to examine how existing practices foster certain weaknesses, how instructors can recognize and interpret their students' proof behaviors, and how alternative practices and curricula might build more powerful schemes.

David Gibson takes a more focused look at one aspect of how students develop proofs and what teaching can do to help. Rather than consider the whole question of proofs as did Harel and Sowder, Gibson looks at the method of using diagrams in the course of proving a statement in mathematics. He conducted interviews of 12 students who had just completed a first course in analysis, discussing with them the proofs they gave on three separate homework problems. Gibson describes what students use diagrams for, how these diagrams might help students, and why they seemed to help. He found four things students used diagrams for and analyzes the interviews to find out something about the how and the why. Gibson finds that diagrams were used to help students understand given information. The diagrams seemed to appeal to students' natural thinking, partly because the diagrams were concrete and reduced mental load. Students used diagrams to judge the truthfulness of statements. Diagrams helped students apply their criteria for truth; and this was because the diagrams corresponded to the students' criteria. Making discoveries was stimulated by diagrams. They helped students obtain ideas more readily, and the students reported that diagrams corresponded to their understanding of information, were alterable and reduced mental burden. Finally, diagrams were used to write out ideas. They helped link the student's ideas to verbal and symbolic representation. Again, this was because diagrams were seen to correspond to ideas and reduce mental load. Gibson argues that information of this sort could be helpful to teachers in planning their pedagogy for helping students learn to make proofs.

QUESTIONS

At a 1996 conference that was organized by the Research in Undergraduate Mathematics Education Community (RUMEC) and sponsored by the Exxon Educational Foundation, a number of research questions emerged out of the presentation and discussion of research reports. John and Annie Selden selected some of those questions and organized them for presentation here. Open questions are the heart of a research enterprise. Among the various ways in which we can decide what is an important problem to work on or evaluate a piece of research is to look for problems that others have raised, have worked on, and would like to see progress on. It is a way of making more objective judgments and raising the quality levels of the work that we do. The Seldens worked to identify the questions that people were interested in. They selected a total of 30 questions, which they organized in four categories: questions about the nature of mathematics and its teaching and learning; questions (which could be refined for) research; questions about RUME and how one does it; and questions asked by practitioners (college mathematics teachers) to members of the research community. It is certainly the case that we can watch our field grow and mature by observing an increasing concern with trying to solve problems that others are posing.

Alan Schoenfeld
Jim Kaput
Ed Dubinsky

CBMS Issues in Mathematics Education
Volume **7**, 1998

Teaching Mathematical Problem Solving: An Analysis of an Emergent Classroom Community

ABRAHAM ARCAVI, CATHY KESSEL,
LUCIANO MEIRA, AND JOHN P. SMITH III

INTRODUCTION

Toward the end of the semester I assigned the following .... As usual, the class broke into groups to work on the problem. One group became the staunch defenders of one conjecture, while a second group lobbied for another. The two groups argued somewhat heatedly, with the rest of the class following the discussion. Finally, one group prevailed, on what struck me as solid mathematical grounds. As is my habit, I did not reveal this but made my usual comment: "OK, you seem to have done as much with this as you can. Shall I try to pull things together?" One of the students replied, "Don't bother. We got it." The class agreed. (Schoenfeld, 1994, pp. 63–64)

This paper is the product of a long and enjoyable collaboration that began in 1990, in Berkeley, California, and continued over six years and four continents (thanks to e-mail). Each major section was individually developed and thus has a single author, though all of us critiqued each section. The *Introduction* and the *Concluding Discussion* reflect our shared views, and each of us had some part in writing them. However, Abraham Arcavi, Luciano Meira, and Jack Smith would like to thank Cathy Kessel who composed these sections with unusual editorial care and wisdom.

The authors thank the editors, Ed Dubinsky and Jim Kaput; the reviewers, Barbara Pence, Beth Warren, and one anonymous reviewer; and members of the Functions Group, Ilana Horn, Andrew Iszak, Sue Magidson, and Natasha Speer, for their help in improving the successive versions of this article.

We owe special thanks to Alan Schoenfeld. This article would not have been possible without his cooperation. It is not easy to be the subject of any analysis, let alone one so prolonged. Schoenfeld not only cooperated with us, but did so with grace, tolerance, and generosity.

© 1998 American Mathematical Society

Two main goals of Alan Schoenfeld's problem solving course are illustrated by this anecdote: That the class function as a "mathematical community" advancing and defending conjectures and proofs on mathematical grounds, and that the locus of authority be the "mathematical community," not the teacher (Schoenfeld, 1994, p. 65). Such incidents are not common in undergraduate mathematics classes, whether they are composed of elite mathematics majors or students struggling through their first calculus course. All too often students seem passive, disengaged, and untroubled by contradictions in their work.

After twelve or more years of schooling, most undergraduates have well-developed expectations for mathematics classes based on their many experiences of listening, taking notes, and learning procedures to solve standard problems. In order to establish his "classroom community," Schoenfeld must convey his nonstandard expectations for behavior and at the same time convince his students that he knows what he's talking about, that his course is of value, and that heuristics as well as formalism are essential parts of doing mathematics. In other words, Schoenfeld must renegotiate the "didactic contract" (Brousseau, 1986) with his students. This contract includes, among other things, teachers' and students' understandings of what is to be expected in the classroom: "What assistance can the students reasonably expect from the teacher; what assistance can the students seek from each other; what level of explanation is the teacher obliged to provide; what questions can the teacher reasonably ask; what form of response will be considered satisfactory" (Clarke, 1995 April).

Schoenfeld's situation is an instance of a more general problem: If a course differs radically from students' previous courses, how can its instructor convince students that the course is worthwhile and convey expectations for classroom behavior? This problem is often encountered by those who teach first-year undergraduate courses. It is also faced by teachers of reformed calculus courses (Cipra, 1995; Culotta, 1992; University of Michigan, 1993). Students are uncomfortable with changed teaching and expectations. At some universities this discomfort has brought calculus reform to a halt (Cipra, 1995, p. 19).

Like Schoenfeld, some instructors have solved the problem of how to establish desired classroom norms. Others have noted it, but not yet developed a solution. Those new to teaching may not be aware the problem exists. We think that our description of Schoenfeld's solution will be of interest to people in each of these categories and present this account, not as a prescription to be followed, but as an example that might illuminate aspects of the difficult task of mathematics teaching.

We also hope to suggest an analytic way in which to talk about teaching and attempt to make salient considerations that are sometimes overlooked. Instead of describing selected incidents from the class or characterizing Schoenfeld's "teaching style," we focus on making sense of all the teaching actions at the beginning of the course, describing actions in detail as well as providing a rationale. Our account offers a method of description as well as the description itself.

In the fall of 1990, Schoenfeld taught his undergraduate course Mathematical Problem Solving in the mathematics department of the University of California at Berkeley. The course is designed to provide students with an introduction to what it means to think mathematically. It is an elective course. The prerequisite is one semester of calculus or consent of instructor.

In order to build an empirical base for his own in-depth analysis of the course, Schoenfeld asked the first author (who had already attended this class at Berkeley in 1987) to videotape each of the 29 two-hour class meetings. The first author attended and videotaped each class session, and the other three authors also attended numerous class sessions. All four authors were members of Schoenfeld's research group[1] at the time, and they became interested in the same question: How does Schoenfeld create a classroom community of problem solvers in which undergraduates learn to think and do mathematics?

This question shapes our analysis. We focus on the initial stages of the community, using the videotape records of the first two class sessions as the principal data. Other data include the remaining 27 videotapes, interviews with students after the class ended, audiotaped discussions with Schoenfeld, and Schoenfeld's writings. To understand the emergence of this community, we examine how Schoenfeld understood and made the connections between his mathematics classroom and the professional community of practicing mathematicians; how he stated and enacted his expectations for student participation; how he introduced students to desired forms of mathematical discourse and activity; and how he introduced heuristics in the context of specific problems.

At this point it is important to delimit the scope of this paper.

- It is not our intention to describe, compare, or ignore the design and implementation of successful mathematics classroom practices. We believe that there are many such practices, but we decided to concentrate on this one because we were fortunate enough to observe, analyze, and discuss it in depth. We hope this example will encourage other researchers to offer similarly detailed accounts of mathematics teaching and learning.

- We do not analyze the success of the course. This has been documented: Students learn to use heuristics successfully (Schoenfeld, 1982; 1985) and the class becomes a "mathematical community" (Schoenfeld 1989a; 1991; 1992a; 1992b; 1994).

- We do not provide an analysis of how the classroom evolved over the semester, how students participated, how they learned, how they changed from being rather silent to being very involved. We decided to focus on Schoenfeld's teaching at the very beginning for two main reasons: first, the analyses suggest some very interesting and counter-intuitive findings about the initial stages of such a class; and second, if continued through

---

[1]Schoenfeld's research group, the Functions Group at the University of California at Berkeley, has been involved since 1985 in a series of research and development studies of mathematical teaching and learning.

the remaining 54 hours of tape, the analyses would result in a long book rather than a long article.

As one might expect, data in the form of videotapes and interviews require methods of analysis different from those used to examine data that are more uniform and manageable. Our analytic method, often known as microanalysis, has roots in cognitive science and ethnography. Schoenfeld, Smith, and Arcavi (1993) describe it as striving "for explanations that are both locally and globally consistent, acounting for as much observed detail as possible and not contradicting any other related explanations." (For general discussion of this method, see Schoenfeld, 1988; Schoenfeld, Smith, & Arcavi, 1993; Schoenfeld, 1992b. For discussion of related methods in the analysis of teaching, see Schoenfeld et al., 1992; Schoenfeld, Minstrell, & van Zee, 1996 April.)

After our initial collaborative analysis of the first two videotapes, each author selected instructional segments from those tapes to analyze in detail. Each analysis was discussed with the other authors. The results are the four main sections of this article. Though we share a common interest in mathematics education, our backgrounds are different enough for us to provide a multilayered view of the class. Arcavi has a Master's degree in mathematics and a Ph.D. in mathematics education. He has taught secondary school mathematics for 10 years, in teacher education programs for 10 years, and has been involved in curriculum development and research on mathematics teaching and learning for the past 15 years. Meira has a Master's degree in cognitive psychology and a Ph.D. in mathematics education. He has teaching experience at the elementary, secondary and tertiary levels, and has been involved in research on mathematics teaching and learning for the past ten years. Smith taught upper elementary, middle, and high school mathematics for 6 years, with a B.A. in mathematics before obtaining a Ph.D. in educational psychology. His research centers on detailed analyses of student understanding and learning of precollege mathematics. Kessel has a Ph.D. in mathematics, taught lower and upper division undergraduate courses as a teaching assistant, lecturer, and assistant professor for 14 years, and works as a researcher in mathematics education.

In the first of these sections, *An Overview of the Problem Solving Course*, Arcavi provides a general description of the goals, curriculum, and pedagogy of the course, as well as some background on the 1990 class. In the second section *Presenting and Doing Mathematics: An Introduction to Heuristics*, Meira analyzes how mathematical problem solving was first discussed and enacted. Central to this analysis are the distinctions among *doing* mathematics, *presenting* mathematics, and *presenting how to do* mathematics, which Meira uses to examine the complex relationships among professional mathematics, school mathematics, and Schoenfeld's course. Smith's section *Making the Case for Heuristics: Authority and Direction in the Inscribed Square*, focuses on the solution to the second problem of the course, analyzing how heuristics were introduced and how the students' work with them was managed. His emphasis on the role of Schoenfeld's leadership and authority in the early days of the class, shows how complex and counterintuitive the initiation of a classroom community can be. In *Practicing Mathematical Communication: Using Heuristics with the Magic Square*, Kessel discusses the third problem of the course, focusing on Schoenfeld's use of traditional and non-traditional mathematical language and discourse. Smith's and Kessel's sections discuss different aspects of the complex interplay between teacher authority and communal judgment, and between traditional and non-traditional elements of Schoenfeld's pedagogy. In the *Concluding Discussion* we summarize what we consider to be the most important issues arising from these analyses and offer some implications.

AN OVERVIEW OF THE PROBLEM SOLVING COURSE
Abraham Arcavi

This section describes Schoenfeld's problem solving course, providing the context and background for the analysis of the following sections. The description includes his professional background, his goals for the course, the basic characteristics of the "classroom culture" he wants to create in order to achieve them, the curriculum and pedagogy, and some details about the 1990 class. The description is based on our observations of the 1987 and 1990 classes, on personal dialogues with Schoenfeld, and his written accounts (Schoenfeld, 1983; 1985; 1988; 1989a; 1991; 1994).

Background and goals

Schoenfeld's conceptualization, design and teaching of his course draw upon three distinct but related fields: mathematics, cognitive science, and college teaching. As a member of the mathematical community, he has examined the nature of his own mathematical activity and the practices of the discipline itself (Schoenfeld, 1983; 1985; 1991; 1994). His participation in that professional practice is directly reflected in his goals for his course. As a cognitive scientist, he has conducted extensive research on the nature of mathematical problem solving and thinking (Schoenfeld, 1985; 1987; 1992; Schoenfeld, Smith, & Arcavi, 1993). This research has provided detailed models of successful (and unsuccessful) problem solving which have directly influenced his teaching practice. As a teacher of college mathematics, he designed the problem solving course, taught, evaluated, and revised it over a period of more than 15 years (Schoenfeld, 1983; 1985; 1991; 1994).

Though most students who take the course are among the successes of the mathematics education system, they begin the course with very different expectations and practices from those envisioned by Schoenfeld. In the area of problem solving, students' past experiences in mathematics consist mostly of generating "the answer" to problems by applying procedures for manipulating numerical and symbolic expressions. They have learned to view the professor (and/or the textbook) as the sole authorities in the classroom and to defer to this external judgment on most issues. They have developed an ability to "master" facts and procedures for exams which are the accepted evidence of their mathematical competence. However, given problems out of context they may well not know when to apply those facts and procedures. Moreover, as Schoenfeld (1994, p. 43) notes, "For most of them, doing mathematics has meant studying material and working tasks set by others, with little or no opportunity for invention or sustained investigations."

A major goal of Schoenfeld's problem solving course is to provide his students with the opportunity to engage in doing mathematics by creating and supporting a "classroom culture" in which students *can* solve problems given out of context, judge the validity of their solutions without appealing to an external authority, and have the opportunity for invention and sustained investigations. These aspects of the course are consistent with those of the mathematical community.

Characteristics of the "classroom culture"

The task of creating and nurturing the "mathematics classroom culture" in which students will have the experience of doing mathematics, has the following characteristics.

Development of a mathematical point of view. According to Schoenfeld, doing mathematics is more than acquiring the primary tools (e.g., facts and procedures) and deploying them thoughtfully in solving problems. It involves looking at the world with "mathematical spectacles" in a wide variety of problem situations— using mathematics to symbolize, abstract, model, prove or disprove conjectures; perceiving connections across problems and results; and creating knowledge that is new to oneself or to the community. The search for and discussion of solutions to problems is not the only focus of the activity. Problems should also serve as springboards for generalization (or specialization), to establish connections between mathematical domains, to reveal mathematical structure, and to pose new problems.

Emphasis on processes as well as on results. While emphasizing and honoring results that are new to the class, Schoenfeld gives greater priority to the reasoning processes that generated the results. Results that students cannot explain, regardless of their correctness, power, or appeal, are not valued. Tricks, results proven elsewhere ("we proved in Math 127 that ... "), and "rabbits pulled out of hats," are dismissed in favor of presentations of accessible and non-technical mathematical arguments that presume only what is known by all members of the community. Explanations of how ideas are generated are highly valued, even when they do not produce solutions.

Communication. Students' mathematical activity takes place in an inherently social milieu, where they work as individuals, as members of small groups and as participants in whole-class activities. The classroom setting encourages and supports various levels of oral and written mathematical communication:

from expressions of raw ideas, suggestions, intuitions, or insights to top-level descriptions of mathematical arguments and also final, polished, and airtight mathematical presentations. Students are encouraged to evaluate, question, and criticize each other's suggestions and work, in both small-group and whole-class activities. Schoenfeld plays a strong role in shaping this communication, ensuring that students criticize the mathematics rather than each other (Schoenfeld, 1994).

Leadership and authority. As the established leader of this community, Schoenfeld's task requires both a detailed overall design and a continual day-to-day shaping. He sets the top-level goals, selects the initial problems, directs students' work on those problems, models desirable mathematical actions and dispositions, and consults with individuals and groups of students. He states his goals openly and explicitly relates them to specific teaching actions and decisions. However, his intention is to gradually transfer the locus of authority and community leadership from himself to the students as they become more comfortable with him and the class. He starts by deferring to students in evaluating the validity of proposed solutions. He asks them to question and challenge any hidden or explicit parts of mathematical arguments that are unconvincing, unclear, or based on implicit knowledge not shared by the whole class. Schoenfeld leads the class towards assuming responsibility for safeguarding standards, for what can be accepted as "basic" shared knowledge and for the completeness, coherence, and conviction of mathematical arguments. He does so by asking very direct questions and by providing initial modeling of desirable actions.

Though he expects students to play a substantial role in setting the mathematical agenda, in presenting their thinking, and in evaluating each others' arguments, he reserves the right to encourage the class in certain directions and not others. He describes this as follows:

I know what fruitful directions are that students are likely to [engage in], or can be nudged into, and on the basis of my general sense of what's mathematically valuable, I'm going to try, without letting the students know it, to nudge the conversation in the direction of things which I consider important, giving enough latitude to go where they think it's right. It's clear that that works in the sense that, in a number of classes they've discovered mathematics which I didn't know, it was good mathematics ... on the other hand, I am nudging away from things that are frivolous, not necessarily dead ends (because dead ends can be profitable), and I try to do that in a way which is not terribly overt, but someone who really understands the mathematics and the goals for my class can clearly pick that up. (From an audiotaped conversation with Schoenfeld about his course, May, 1991)

Reflective mathematical practice. Learning to solve problems and think mathematically requires continuous reflection on the nature of that activity. Questions that Schoenfeld first asks of students almost routinely, are intended to play a central role in developing that reflective capability. For example, Schoenfeld has shown that skillful mathematical problem solving includes the development of a critical attitude toward mathematical argument: "Is this airtight?," "Does it convince me, a friend, an enemy?" (Mason, Burton, & Stacey, 1982; Schoenfeld, 1994), "Am I done with this problem?" Other questions help to develop the mathematical point of view: "How could this have been done in another way?," "How can this result be generalized?," "Is this result similar to another we have seen?" and so on.

Later in the course, Schoenfeld also devotes time to develop what he calls "executive control of students' solution attempts." Briefly stated, control is "a category of behavior [which] deals with the way individuals use the information potentially at their disposal. It focuses on major decisions about what to do in a problem, decisions that in and of themselves may 'make or break' an attempt to solve a problem. Behaviors of interest include making plans, selecting goals and subgoals, monitoring and assessing solutions as they evolve, and revising or abandoning plans when the assessments indicate that such actions should be taken" (Schoenfeld, 1985, p. 27). Schoenfeld nurtures this behavior by asking students the following questions while they work: (1) "What are you doing?," (2) "Why are you doing it?," and (3) "How does it help you?" (Schoenfeld, 1985; 1988; 1992a). Schoenfeld suggests that these kinds of questions are slowly internalized and become an integral part of the students' doing mathematics.

Curriculum

The curriculum of the course consists of a collection of carefully chosen problems, drawn from a wide variety of mathematical domains—including number theory, Euclidean constructions, cryptarithmetic, calculus, algebra, and probability. Problems are presented to students on sheets distributed in class. In general, each problem sheet does not have more than one or two problems from the same mathematical domain.

This aspect of the curriculum addresses one of the main course goals: That students learn how to solve problems out of context. In traditional courses, problems and exercises are often sequenced in such a way that students can easily find solution techniques. Thus problems are perceived as mere opportunities to exercise a pre-established and known technique. Schoenfeld deliberately chooses not to sequence problems from the same mathematical domain consecutively. On the contrary, whenever he feels a technique or a solution strategy is understood, he changes the type of problem, even giving examples in which the thoughtless application of a recently "mastered" technique can lead to error or nowhere. Thus the sequencing of the problems is consonant with his intention to teach students to approach problems as professionals do, namely without having explicit cues about the techniques to be used. Because of that, to a casual observer, it may seem that the design of the course has discontinuities and lacks coherence: a result reached in one class session may not be recalled or invoked until three or four sessions later when the result is relevant, useful, or connected with the issues discussed.

Since Schoenfeld is not constrained to "covering" a predetermined amount of content, he can afford to allocate time flexibly so that work and discussion can yield the maximum mathematical profit. Problems which can be solved in minutes with traditional "show and tell" teaching are worked on and discussed as long as they have mathematical substance, fulfilling one of the main course goals: That students have the opportunity for invention and sustained investigations.

What are problems and how are they chosen? Are there any criteria for good problems? Schoenfeld regards problems as demanding, non-routine and interesting mathematical tasks, which students want and like to solve, and for which they lack readily accessible means to achieve a solution (Schoenfeld, 1985; 1989a). Problems selected for the course must satisfy five main criteria (Schoenfeld, 1994).

- Without being trivial, problems should be accessible to a wide range of students on the basis of their prior knowledge, and should not require a lot of machinery and/or vocabulary.
- Problems must be solvable, or at least approachable, in more than one way. Alternative solution paths can illustrate the richness of the mathematics, and may reveal connections among different areas of mathematics.
- Problems should illustrate important mathematical ideas, either in terms of the content or the solution strategies.
- Problem solutions should be constructible without tricks.
- Problems should serve as first steps towards mathematical explorations, they should be extensible and generalizable; namely, when solved, they can serve as springboards for further explorations and problem posing.

A main topic in Schoenfeld's curriculum is, as already implied, *heuristics*— "rules of thumb for successful problem solving, general suggestions that help an individual to understand a problem better or to make progress towards its solution" (Schoenfeld, 1985, p. 23). Commonly used heuristics include: exploiting analogies, examining special cases, arguing by contradiction, working backwards, decomposing and recombining, exploiting related problems, generalizing and specializing, and relaxing conditions in the problem (see Pólya, 1973 for a more complete list). The rationale for teaching heuristics is clear: expert problem solvers develop and rely on these strategies to make progress on difficult problems. Thus if heuristics can be taught, they may help students become better problem solvers. Indeed, this hypothesis (among others) led Schoenfeld to develop the course.

Researchers in mathematics education have not found it easy to teach heuristics in the classroom (e.g., Lester, Garofalo, & Kroll, 1989). Schoenfeld has himself experienced difficulty at the college level. In his early work teaching problem solving, he identified three main complications in the task of teaching heuristics (Schoenfeld, 1985).

- *The specificity problem.* If heuristics are presented in their most general (and useful) form, students will be unable to apply them; if they are given in more context-specific forms, their number explodes and only some can be taught.
- *The implementation problem.* Applying heuristics requires many steps, and therefore creates many opportunities for students to make fatal errors.
- *The resource problem.* To be successful, students must know both the appropriate heuristics and the mathematics required to solve the problem.

In his continuing development and revision of the course, Schoenfeld has had to address each of these problems. A major goal of this paper is to understand his approach.

Effect

Schoenfeld has discussed the course many times (see [Schoenfeld 1983; 1985; 1988; 1989a; 1991; 1994] for the most substantive discussions). Some accounts have been descriptive introductions built around vignettes: rich snapshots of the class working on particular problems, such as the magic square (Schoenfeld, 1989a; 1991) or Pythagorean triples (Schoenfeld 1988; 1991; 1994). These accounts suggest that his students are engaged in more productive sorts of mathematical thinking and activity than are typical of most undergraduates.

Students work collaboratively in groups with or without Schoenfeld's presence —indicating engagement and commitment to the enterprise. They stop looking to him to evaluate the validity of their arguments, turning instead to their peers. They produce results that are new to them, surprising and interesting to Schoenfeld, and occasionally publishable (Schoenfeld, 1989b). And most important, they learn to use heuristics effectively over a range of problems, considering, pursuing, and monitoring multiple approaches.

Schoenfeld examined students' problem solving performance before and after the course using measures which ranged from paper-and-pencil tests to analyses of problem-solving protocols (see Chapters 7, 8, 9, and 10 of Schoenfeld, 1985). His results showed that students who completed the course (1) used a variety of heuristics effectively to solve challenging problems; (2) had a better sense of how to proceed and were less likely to "plunge in" with the first approach that came to mind; (3) saw through the surface features to the deeper mathematical structure of problems; and (4) used heuristics to solve problems unlike those they had worked previously in the course.

On the first day of class, Schoenfeld described one of the measures he used in his analysis:

> I gave an in-class final, and there were three parts to the final exam. The first part was problems like the problems we solved in class. No surprise, you expect people to do well on those. The second part was problems that could be solved by the methods that we used in class—but ones for

which if you looked at them you couldn't recognize that they had obvious features similar to the ones that we'd studied in class. So yes, you had the tools and techniques, but you had to be pretty clever about recognizing that they were appropriate. And, the class did pretty well on those too. Part three of the final exam ... There's a collection of books called the *Hungarian Problem Books* which have some of the nastiest mathematical problems known to man and woman. I went through those, and as soon as I found a problem I couldn't make any sense of, whatsoever, I put it on the final. (I know that makes you feel good.) [Laughter from class, Schoenfeld smiles.] The class did spectacularly well, and actually wound up solving some problems I didn't ... .

Pedagogy

In the versions of the course we observed (1987 and 1990), the class was organized into six principal modes: lectures, reflective presentations, student presentations, small-group work, whole-class discussions, and individual work. In the first two class sessions all six modes occurred, although not exactly in the same proportions as throughout the semester. On the first day of the course Schoenfeld described these modes to the students:

> Most days I'm going to walk in ... and hand out a bunch of problems. I've got enough here to probably keep us busy for two days or so. And what you're seeing here is unusual, because you won't be seated in rows watching me talk. Instead you're going to break into groups of three or four or five, and work on problems together. As you're working on them, I'll circulate through the room, occasionally make comments about the kinds of things you're doing, respond to questions from you. But, by and large, I'll just nudge you to keep working on the problems.

> Then at some point I'll call us to order as a group, and we'll start discussing the things that you've done, and talk about the things that you've pushed and why; what's been successful, what hasn't. I'll mention a variety of specific mathematical techniques as we go through the problems. Many of the problems are chosen so that they illustrate useful techniques. So you'll work on one for a while; may or may not make some progress; and then we'll talk about it. And as we talk about it what I'll do is indicate some of the problem solving strategies that I know, and that are in the literature, that might help you make progress on this problem, and progress on other problems.

Lectures. In contrast with most college classrooms, the lecture mode occurred relatively infrequently. When Schoenfeld lectured, the lecture segments were relatively short and oriented toward particular goals: to provide background on mathematical resources needed to make progress (e.g., mathematical induction), to introduce heuristics, and to describe his goals for the class. He did not generally present his own solutions to problems, except on the occasion that an important solution was not developed by the class. Because his lecture segments were short, pointed, and related to activities in other modes, many of the traditional effects of the lecture—e.g., student passivity and disengagement—were not evident. (More details are provided throughout the following sections by Meira, Smith and Kessel.)

Reflective presentations. In this mode, Schoenfeld presented mathematical commentaries to the class, interpreting segments of activity just completed and highlighting important aspects. We characterize them as "reflective" because they directed students' attention to mathematically significant features of either Schoenfeld's or his students' actions. They differed from lectures because they engaged students as participants. They were unlike whole-class discussions because Schoenfeld pursued specific goals and directly controlled the flow. Reflective presentations took quite different forms: e.g. modeling a problem solution to illustrate a particular heuristic, to demonstrate a specific mathematical point, or to highlight executive control in problem solving; recounting, and highlighting aspects of students' presentations of their solutions; conducting "post-mortem" reviews of complete problem solutions (see Schoenfeld, 1983 for a specific example). Like lectures, they all involved significant forms of teaching by telling; i.e., substantive insertions of content into the classroom discourse (Ball & Chazan, 1994), but occurred in the broader context of problem solving. They provided students with a clear view of the reflective mathematical practices of a skilled mathematician, an opportunity that is absent from many college classrooms.

Student presentations. At appropriate junctures, students were invited to present their solutions to assigned problems. During these presentations, Schoenfeld avoided giving immediate verbal feedback and non-verbal evaluations of student success, though students initially expected such judgments (see Smith's analysis of the inscribed square problem). With a blank "poker-face" he usually addressed the class with one of the following questions: "What do you guys think?," "Does the class buy this argument?," or "Are you convinced?" These questions were routinely posed after each presentation to signal that students should not wait for an external authoritative judgment. Student presentations also provided opportunities to work on issues of mathematical exposition and communication; such as top-level descriptions of an argument vs. more polished and detailed versions, comparing formal/symbolic and informal presentations, contrasting convincing arguments with "hand-waving."

Small-group work. About 30% of each class was devoted to work in small groups of two to four students. Its purpose was to provide a stable and continuous context for students to engage collectively in problem solving. In the best of cases, this collaborative work generated negotiation among the members of the group about approaches to pursue, allowed each student to calibrate his/her own understanding of the mathematics involved with the other group members, and promoted the disposition to listen to and learn from peers. In this mode,

Schoenfeld played the role of "traveling consultant" and critic.

Whole-class discussions. After an individual presentation or small-group work, Schoenfeld often engaged the class in collective discussion. Sometimes the class attempted to solve a problem as a whole group, and, as in the small-group work, Schoenfeld usually avoided immediate evaluation of the usefulness of the approach suggested by students, even when the approach could lead to a dead end. This mode had several purposes: it allowed all students to listen to each other's questions, comments, and solution attempts. As students started to feel more comfortable with the class, it slowly became a forum in which they could openly voice misunderstandings and/or requests for mathematical resources invoked by some and lacked by others. There were occasions later in the course in which the whole-class discussion also dealt with issues of mathematical elegance and aesthetics.

Individual work. Students had many opportunities to work individually before, within, and after some of the modes described above. However, individual work was the main mode for homework assignments, and the two take-home exams, on which students worked for about two weeks with the promise of not consulting each other. Individual work consisted not only in solving problems, it also included, as mentioned above, preparation for communication of results, either to a small group, the whole class, or (in the case of the written take-home exams) the teacher.

Students received specific guidelines about exams and grading. On the first day of class Schoenfeld told the students:

> [A] week or two into the class I'll give you the opportunity to write out a problem or two for me so that I can get a sense of the kind of writing you do, and give you some feedback on the kind of writing I expect. The first main thing we do is: about half-way through the course I'll give you a two-week take-home. It'll consist of about ten problems and they will occupy you for a long time. But you'll make progress on them and you'll do reasonably well on them. And then, the final. Again, the department formally requires me to give an in-class final, so I usually wind up giving a one-problem in-class final to meet the rules and regulations. That's about ten percent of the final exam grade. The rest of it is another take-home that you'll have two weeks to work on. There are some funny rules, which are that:

> What counts is not simply the answer, what counts is doing mathematics. And that means, among other things, if you can find two different ways to solve a problem, you'll get twice as much credit for it. If you can extend the problem and generalize it and make it your own, you'll get even more. The bottom line is, I'd like to have you doing some mathematics and I will do everything I can—including using grading—as a device for having you do that.

The 1990 class

Students

Mathematical Problem Solving, listed in the university catalog as Math 67, is not a required course for any major. The course prerequisite is one semester of calculus or consent of instructor.

The students in the first two classes had a wide range of mathematical backgrounds (see Table 1). For example, Jeff,[2] a history major, had taken one semester of calculus three years ago, and Diane, a genetics major, had taken the calculus sequence. In contrast, Mitch was a graduate student in computer science, and Jesús, a fourth year applied math major.

In the first week, the "traffic" in and out of the class was relatively heavy; students were shopping for classes and adjusting their schedules. The university catalog had also listed the course as beginning one hour later than it did, thus adding to the traffic. Thirteen students attended all or part of the first session. Three new students entered in the second session.

The eight students who completed the course were all enrolled for credit. Six were majors (or intended majors) in mathematics or computer science. Only one of these students (Jeff) had a major outside of science, mathematics, and engineering. Only one was female. The group comprised four European Americans, two Asian Americans, and two Hispanics.

Brief overviews of the first two class sessions

Session #1. For the first twenty minutes Schoenfeld introduced the course: its history, its basic mechanics, the grading system (a complete transcript is given in Appendix A). He then distributed the first set of problems and asked students to start working on them in groups. For the next twenty minutes most groups worked mainly on the first two problems: finding the sum of the telescoping series and inscribing a square in an arbitrary triangle. Forty minutes into the class, Schoenfeld called the class back and, for about twenty-five minutes, he discussed the telescoping series problem. This discussion is analyzed in detail in Meira's section.

The students then went back to work in their small groups, and Schoenfeld moved around the class monitoring the work of each group. He discovered that some groups did not fully understand the written statement of the inscribed square problem, so he explained the distinction between showing that the required square exists and giving a construction. Approximately one hour and twenty-five minutes into the session, Schoenfeld again called the class back to a whole-class discussion of this problem which was interrupted when the class period ended. Students left class with instructions to think about the problem at home.

---

[2]All students are referred to by pseudonyms.

TABLE 1. Background of Students Participating in Sessions 1 and 2

Student	Origin of Interest; Entry	Background
Austin	Saw description in the catalog Looking for such a course "for years" Entered at start of Session 2	Third-year computer science major Calculus sequence, discrete math Audited one class of Putnam* course
Devon	Saw description in the catalog Entered at start of Session 1	Third-year student with interests in math and computer science; part-time: Math 67 only course; older student, recent transfer to UCB
Don	Saw description in the catalog Entered at start of Session 1	Math major; Calculus sequence plus 4 upper division courses
Jeff	Saw description in the catalog Entered at start of Session 1	Fourth-year history major; goal: teach history and math; one semester of calculus as first-year student
Jesús	Saw description in the catalog Entered at start of Session 1	Fourth-year applied math major 13 math courses
Sasha	Saw description in the catalog Entered at start of Session 1	First-year student, intending computer science major; Calculus, discrete math, Putnam course, Math camps & 3 high school competitions
Stephen	Looking for some "easy units" Entered at start of Session 1	Physics major
Diane	Looking for a "fun class" Attended Sessions 1 and 2	Genetics major, calculus sequence Liked problem solving
Richard	Attended Sessions 1 and 2	Computer science major part-time student Calculus sequence, 1.5 years before Worried about "rusty background"
Mitch	Read about the course Entered at start of Session 1, auditing	Graduate student in computer science Calculus sequence, discrete math, linear and abstract algebra
Sharon	Heard about Schoenfeld via family member Attended Session 1 only, auditing	Varied academic background; intending math major; Calculus, logic, and statistics

*The William Lowell Putnam Mathematical Competition is administered annually in December by the Mathematical Association of America to students who have not yet received a college degree (Reznick, 1994, p. 19). Neither of the students who attended the Putnam course (H90, Honors Undergraduate Seminar in Mathematical Problem Solving, also offered in the fall of 1990) mentioned taking the Putnam exam though they were interviewed early in 1991.

Session #2. Schoenfeld began by emphasizing the importance of working as a community and presenting results to one's peers. Upon request, one student volunteered to present his constructive proof that a square can be inscribed in an arbitrary triangle. His argument was fundamentally sound, but directed almost entirely to Schoenfeld who was standing at the side of the room. Schoenfeld noted this deference and explained that the class must become the judge of mathematical validity of proposed solutions. The student then addressed the class more directly, repeating his solution with slightly more detail. This discussion lasted twenty-five minutes. Smith analyzes in detail the way in which Schoenfeld directed the discussion on this problem.

Schoenfeld then drew students' attention to the third problem of the set, placing the integers from 1 to 9 to make a 3 by 3 magic square. Another student volunteered to present his solution, and its correctness was immediately apparent. The next forty minutes were spent in discussion of different solution paths that could produce the same result. Schoenfeld led this discussion, involving students in substantive ways and introducing many new heuristics. Kessel analyzes this discussion in detail.

The final fifteen minutes of the session were devoted to quick solutions of the next problems in the set, which will not be discussed in this paper. In sum, the next three sections of this paper cover most of the whole-class instructional episodes of the first two two-hour class periods.

PRESENTING AND DOING MATHEMATICS:
AN INTRODUCTION TO HEURISTICS
Luciano Meira

Solving problems is a considerable part of what mathematicians do, and learning to solve problems is part of learning to think mathematically. Shaping the culture of the classroom so that his students learn to think mathematically is the heart of Schoenfeld's teaching enterprise. Therefore his central goal is to create a classroom community which embodies selected values, beliefs, and activities of the professional mathematical community.

But within this parallel, Schoenfeld has also acknowledged the individual and collective differences between professional mathematicians and the students taking his course.

> The class itself is a mathematical community (better, a micro-community in which certain mathematical values are highly prized) in which the students interact with each other in ways very much like the ways that mathematicians interact—but at a level appropriate to their knowledge and abilities. At their own level the students *are* mathematicians, engaged in the practice of mathematical sense-making. They *do* mathematics, with the same sense of engagement and involvement. The difference is that boundaries of understanding that they challenge are the boundaries of their own (commu-

nity's) understanding, rather than those of the mathematical community at large. (Schoenfeld, 1988, author's emphasis)

His characterization of the relevant differences centers on issues of mathematical background. Students' views of problems and significant results reflect their own understanding, which is substantially more limited than professional mathematicians'. But are the differences between these two communities only a matter of what constitutes shared knowledge and problems at the edge of collective understanding? We think not, especially in the first sessions of the class when much "shaping" of the community is being done. We propose that there are other important (and sometimes subtle) differences that follow directly from a second and equally obvious difference, that the classroom community is deliberately shaped and "engineered" by Schoenfeld, whereas the professional mathematical community has no recognized single authority or leader.

To explore the subtleties of these differences, we introduce the distinction between "presenting" and "doing" mathematics. "Doing mathematics" means engaging in reasoning that reflects the thinking of mathematicians: resourcefully tackling and making progress on hard mathematical problems. In order to bring students to the point where they can approximate mathematical doing, some "presenting" must take place, in both traditional and less traditional forms. As will become evident below, we use "presenting" to characterize different acts of teaching, though all forms involve the display of some mathematical concept or part of mathematical practice for students.

The contrast between doing and presenting mathematics is enacted by Schoenfeld during work on the first problem, summing the telescoping series. We analyze this contrast in three consecutive segments of class activity: (1) his mock lecture on the standard solution to the problem, where Schoenfeld critiques a traditional form of teacher presentation in college mathematics classrooms; (2) his presentation of a heuristic-based solution as an important part of the practice (the "doing") of professional mathematicians; and (3) his lecture on and subsequent use of mathematical induction to prove that the solution found is general.

Caricaturing mathematics teaching as presenting: The mock lecture

Finding the sum of the telescoping series is a well-known problem, appearing in most first-year calculus courses. It asks for the sum of the following terms,

$$\frac{1}{1 \times 2} + \frac{1}{2 \times 3} + \frac{1}{3 \times 4} + \frac{1}{4 \times 5} + \cdots + \frac{1}{n(n+1)}.$$

In placing this problem first, Schoenfeld's apparent goal was to demonstrate the value of heuristics as tools to unpack results which are either unknown or recalled but not understood.

After some twenty minutes of group work, where students worked on the telescoping series and other problems in the set, Schoenfeld called the class together to present a "lecture" on the textbook solution. This was not just any lecture, but a play that caricatured the "typical" calculus professor presenting the standard solution to the problem. We quote the transcript at length so that the content and tone of the play are clear. Note that the goal of differentiating between presenting and doing mathematics was explicit from the start.

> Let me show you what you were shown, by metamorphosing into the typical calculus professor for three minutes, and lecturing on the solution to that problem as it's typically presented in a calculus class and then talk about the way it gets *done* rather than the way that the solution actually gets *presented*. Well, I won't quite be the typical mathematics professor, 'cause I won't mumble at the board [giggles from class] but ... it goes something like this. [Schoenfeld walks toward the door, turns, and starts back toward the board as if he were another person.]

> All right. Well, the problem I asked you to look at was find the sum: [writes rapidly, banging the chalk, on the board and states the formula simultaneously]

$$\sum_{i=1}^{n} \frac{1}{i \times (i+1)} = \frac{1}{1 \times 2} + \frac{1}{2 \times 3} + \frac{1}{3 \times 4} + \cdots + \frac{1}{n(n+1)}.$$

> Now, all you need to know is the obvious algebraic observation that [he writes and speaks simultaneously]

$$\forall i \quad \frac{1}{i \times (i+1)} = \frac{1}{i} - \frac{1}{i+1}.$$

> That's trivial. You can check it algebraically, OK; I don't waste my time with such things at the board.

> [Writes as he speaks; the italicized text below is what also is written.]

> Now that says that 1 over 1 times 2 [he points to $\frac{1}{1 \times 2}$ in the first formula] is equal to

$$\frac{1}{1} - \frac{1}{2},$$

> [A student, perhaps recognizing this, says, "Ah ... yeah."]

$$\frac{1}{2 \times 3} \quad \text{is} \quad \frac{1}{2} - \frac{1}{3},$$

$$\frac{1}{3 \times 4} \quad \text{is} \quad \frac{1}{3} - \frac{1}{4}.$$

> [He writes "$+ \cdots +$".] The next to the last term is $\frac{1}{n-1} - \frac{1}{n}$ and the last term is $\frac{1}{n} - \frac{1}{n+1}$. [The following formula (*) is now on the board:]

$$(*) \qquad \left(\frac{1}{1} - \frac{1}{2}\right) + \left(\frac{1}{2} - \frac{1}{3}\right) + \left(\frac{1}{3} - \frac{1}{4}\right) + \cdots + \left(\frac{1}{n-1} - \frac{1}{n}\right) + \left(\frac{1}{n} - \frac{1}{n+1}\right).$$

> Got that? [no pause] All right [giggles from class].

Well, now all we need to do is make the observation that [he pushes board[3] upon which he has been writing under top board so all but (*) is covered] I've got minus a half and plus a half next to each other, and they cancel [he strikes through canceled terms], I've got minus a third and plus a third next to each other and they cancel, minus a fourth and plus a fourth and they cancel, this [pointing to the term one nth] cancels with the previous term—minus an nth plus an nth and they cancel—so the only terms left are the first one, and the last one, namely 1 over $n + 1$. [Formula (*) now looks like:]

$$(\tfrac{1}{1} - \tfrac{1}{2}) + (\tfrac{1}{2} - \tfrac{1}{3}) + (\tfrac{1}{3} - \tfrac{1}{4}) + \cdots + (\tfrac{1}{n-1} - \tfrac{1}{n}) + (\tfrac{1}{n} - \tfrac{1}{n+1}).$$

[He pushes the board upon which he has been writing up so it is completely covered by the board above.] The first one was 1 over 1, minus the last one: 1 over $n + 1$; or ... n over $n + 1$ ... [writes formula (†)]

(†) $$= 1 - \tfrac{1}{n+1} = \tfrac{n}{n+1} \qquad \text{Q. E. D.}$$

Q. E. D. You all know what Q. E. D. stands for, don't you?

Student: Quod Erat Demonstrandum.

Yeah, the Latin is Quod Erat Demonstrandum, "that which was to be shown"; the English ... "Quite Easily Done." OK.

Now, I can do things like that, that's why I'm a mathematician. We don't expect you to do things like that but you can memorize them. That's why I'm up in front at the board and you're down there. OK. End of lecture, see you next time. [He pauses; returns to normal demeanor.]

We take the overall purpose of the play to be straightforward. In acting out an objectionable teaching practice, Schoenfeld sets the stage for presenting himself and his course as a new and more positive mathematical experience for students. We identify the following negative elements in this caricature of "traditional" teaching:

- The caricatured professor stated the problem exactly as it is printed in the problem set and began his lecture without any preliminary discussion of the problem that might engage students in the task. In traditional mathematics classrooms, the curriculum (problems and solutions) is seen as uniquely defining the activity.
- He spoke and wrote on the board very rapidly. Such high speed deliveries have additional inhibitory effects on student contributions, over and above the standard expectations, among both faculty and students, implying that interruptions to lectures should be minimized.

---

[3]The classroom has a blackboard with three sections. The central section has two panels which slide vertically over a third fixed panel. Schoenfeld writes the first three formulas on the lower of the two sliding panels, and the remaining formula (†) on the fixed panel.

- He assumed that the key algebraic reformulation was obvious and never addressed the source of the insight, suggesting only that students could undertake the remedial task of "checking" its validity.

- He maintained a haughty and arrogant attitude throughout, but especially in his implication that his students had seen the solution in calculus but apparently forgotten it and in his emphasized difference between professors who know and students who memorize.

- He asked no real questions during the lecture. The two queries posed to the class were not serious invitations to discussion, since he did not wait for a student response. These "questions" were merely rhetorical ornaments in the lecture.

- It was evident from the videotape record that he wrote the key algebraic steps on panels of the moveable chalkboard but then quickly removed them from the students' view behind the fresh panels he was sliding into place. On one occasion, he covered a long computation just as he began to summarize it.

The mock lecture was clearly a set-up, a worst-case scenario of traditional mathematics teaching practices where teachers "tell" students the facts and procedures they think are important and students memorize them. Schoenfeld's enactment of this caricature communicates at least two related messages to his class: "I know about your experience with the mathematics teachers, particularly college professors" and "I will make your experience with me different." As is evident from the start, the mock lecture serves as counterpoint between students' impoverished past experience and the yet-to-be seen, but allegedly real mathematical practice. What properties of real mathematical practice are effectively modeled by Schoenfeld in these first sessions of his class? How does he say that mathematics "gets done"?

Presenting professional mathematical doing

Immediately after the mock lecture, Schoenfeld presented a heuristic-based solution that "serves as a window into the practice of mathematicians." He began by declaring that mathematicians do not solve problems by recalling algebraic identities, but by applying well-known problem solving strategies:

> Now, if I called up any member of the math department at four in the morning and said, "Hey, your house is on fire but before you leave, what's the sum of this series?" they could tell me because it's part of the mathematicians' collective unconscious. If I gave them a slightly more complicated problem, being mathematicians, they'd probably stop to solve it before they ran out of their house anyway—they're a little weird that way—and what they'd do is *not* pull a rabbit out of their hat, the way I just did to solve this one, but rather to use a reasonably, (well, a very) well-known and quite comfortable strategy to all of them, which is [begins writing] long-winded, but it's worth writing down.

[Writes as he speaks; the italicized text below is what also is written.]

If you've got a problem you need to make sense of and it has an—jargon coming up!—integer parameter n, that is something that takes on values . . . (whole number values, and I'll be explicit about what that is in a minute) . . . *try values of n = 1, 2, 3, 4, 5, . . . and see if you can find a pattern.* That pattern may suggest what the answer is and may even suggest how you can verify it—if that's the answer.

This is the strategy. It's our first official strategy of the course (put it in a box to make it pretty) [he draws a box around what he's just written] and introduces the first serious piece of jargon for the course. It's called a *heuristic strategy.*

[The following is on the board:]

> If you've got a problem you need to make sense of and it has
> an integer parameter n, try values of $n = 1, 2, 3, 4, 5, \ldots$ and
> see if you can find a pattern.

HEURISTIC STRATEGY

In our analyses, we will refer to this heuristic as "if a problem has an integer parameter, try specific values and look for a pattern," or Try Specific Values for short. Schoenfeld was quite explicit about how Try Specific Values could be applied to this problem. "This [problem] asks for the sum of n terms, and you can ask: What's the sum of the first one, the first two, the first three etc." He wrote the first four partial sums and retrieved their results from the class,

$$\frac{1}{2} = \frac{1}{2}$$
$$\frac{1}{2} + \frac{1}{6} = \frac{2}{3}$$
$$\frac{1}{2} + \frac{1}{6} + \frac{1}{12} = \frac{3}{4}$$
$$\frac{1}{2} + \frac{1}{6} + \frac{1}{12} + \frac{1}{20} = \frac{4}{5}$$

and suggested that the next sum would be $5/6$. With the emergent pattern in hand, he queried the class about verification.

AS: So at this point, I've seen the pattern, convinced myself on the basis of a number of examples that it's probably right. Am I done?

Sasha: Can you prove your result?

AS: Probably. [He pauses, someone, perhaps Sasha, laughs.] Patterns *can* be deceiving, I mean this is pretty compelling evidence. But we'll see some examples later this semester where they're not, where a compelling pattern doesn't necessarily come true. Since this is a math class, I feel a moral obligation to actually confirm that the pattern holds. How do I do that?

Sasha: Math induction.

Two features of this segment are worth comment. Schoenfeld's query to the class, "Am I done?" was his first real question, a serious request for students' contributions to the solution.[4] He invited students to collaborate, modeled a standard move in mathematical thinking where solved problems are beginnings, not ends, and drew a sharp contrast with the haughty, one-sided nature of his mock lecture. This question signaled that his own teaching, not the traditional calculus instructor's, was beginning. But with this overture to students, he also explicitly indicated that he had sure command of the course content (some patterns would deceive) and a ready proof of the pattern of partial sums. In short, he presented the use of heuristics, a key component of real mathematical activity, and began to engage the students as thinkers in the real practice of mathematics, without straying off the path to a complete solution.

Presenting some mathematics

Following Sasha's suggestion, Schoenfeld asked:

How many of you guys feel comfortable with induction? [pause, students are not visible or audible on the videotape at this point] OK, let me ask it the other way: How many of you feel uncomfortable with induction? [pause] OK, good. [erases blackboard panel, pushes it up] I'm not going to spend too much time on it in the course but it will occasionally be a useful tool. So I'll give you an example of how it works here and if it turns out to be an issue, then come talk to me in my office hours and we'll worry about it then. OK?

He presented the principle of mathematical induction and used it to show that the emergent pattern in the partial sums holds for all positive integers n. This exposition was straightforward, except for two important features: his use of a staircase metaphor to help the students make intuitive sense of induction and his increasing requests for students' contributions to the evolving proof by induction.

The general idea of mathematical induction was stated in the standard manner but also characterized as "the mystical algebraic formulation." "If you'd like to show something is true for, in the simplest case, all whole numbers, 1, 2, 3, 4, ... prove the statement is true for $n = 1$ [first inductive hypothesis]; and prove that if it's true for $n = k$, then it must also be true for $n = k + 1$ [second inductive hypothesis]." To illustrate induction, he drew a staircase on the board and said that, if one were on any given step of the staircase, the second inductive hypothesis allowed jumping to the next step, while the first inductive hypothesis allowed one to get on the staircase.

---

[4]Schoenfeld's requests to students to calculate the partial sums, $1/2 + 1/6$ and $1/2 + 1/6 + 1/12$, were not questions in the same sense. Because students' knowledge of the addition algorithm for fractions could be assumed, only the speed of their response—not the content—was an issue.

This [second] part, if it's true for $n = k$, then it's true for $n = k + 1$, where k can be anything, is a funny inductive assumption ... so that's an assumption that allows you to jump from the third floor to the fourth floor .... Now in and of itself, that statement may or may not do you any good. It simply says, if you've managed to show that it's true for some value, then it's true for the next value as well .... The problem is getting on the staircase in the first place .... That's why you need the first part .... You show that if the statement is true for $n = 1$, I can get on the staircase .... So, that's the two parts to an inductive argument: first there's the place where you get on the staircase; second, you can climb one step at a time.

The sum of the telescoping series was then solved for the third time. Schoenfeld rewrote the problem statement, proved it for the trivial $n = 1$ case, assumed the statement true for $n = k$, and proved it for $n = k + 1$ by adding the $k + 1$st term $(k + 1)$ to both sides of the $n = k$ equation and simplifying the resulting algebra. He requested student contributions many times in building the inductive assumption:[5]

AS: Then what do I want to show?

A student: [Inaudible] prove it's true for $k + 1$.

AS: OK, so I assume this is true, what I want to show is: And now the question is: How do I write this statement for n equals $k + 1$?

[No response.]

AS: What does the left-hand side of it look like?

A student: The same as [inaudible] but with one more term.

AS: Yeah, it's going to look the same except the last term is going to be $k + 1$, 'cause I'm doing it for $n = k + 1$, $(k + 1)(k + 2)$. OK. So what I want to show is: 1 over 1 times 2, plus—and I'll write the next to last term—to make life easy for myself. The last term is 1 over $k + 1$ [times] $k + 2$. The next to last term is going to be what? ... What's the right-hand side going to be if n is equal to $k + 1$?

A student: $k + 1$ over ....

The solution of the telescoping series came to an end with Schoenfeld's transition back to the more general application context for Try Specific Values:

When you see an n, sometimes it'll be explicit as it is here, sometimes it'll be implicit, you just look at it and say to yourself, "Hey, it's *really* a problem that has different values for n equals 1, 2, 3, 4, 5, even though there's no n in the problem formulation." Then, if you need to make progress on it, it often helps to look for systematic patterns.

---

[5]These student(s) could not be identified from the videotape.

Discussion

Our characterization of the telescoping series problem has interwoven two levels of analysis of Schoenfeld's teaching. First, we have emphasized the many introductions he makes in this first session: to his own teaching as different from other, content-oriented, classes; to heuristic strategies as a crucial component of problem solving; and to his mastery and expertise both as a teacher and as a mathematician. But none of these features is surprising, since they are described in Schoenfeld's own written accounts of the course (1983; 1985; 1991; 1994). We believe our contribution consists in providing another level of analysis. We have used the distinction between "doing" and "presenting" to capture the more fundamental connection between his teaching and the practice of mathematicians that underlies those introductions. Figure 1 presents a model of Schoenfeld's teaching with the telescoping series as relationships between doing and presenting mathematics.

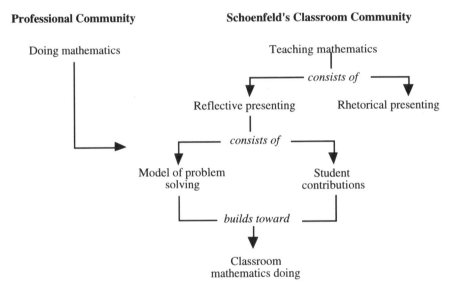

FIGURE 1.   Schoenfeld's pedagogy as doing and presenting mathematics

At the top level, the model distinguishes the practice of mathematicians (professional "doing") from teaching. Despite Schoenfeld's intentions to construct a classroom community to parallel professional mathematical practice, he was a "messenger" who modeled professional practice for his students, probably because he thinks that at the beginning, modeling is a way to help that community to emerge. In contrast to that professional "doing," Schoenfeld's teaching in this segment of the class involved two forms of "presenting": *reflective* and *rhetorical*. We characterize his mock lecture as a rhetorical presentation because it was a skillful performance that he enacted alone to encourage students to follow his lead in developing contrasting forms of classroom dialogue and practice. His reflective presentations, as exemplified in his discussions of Try Specific Values and mathematical induction, were more frequent and characteristic of his teaching throughout the course. They involved his modeling of significant parts of skilled problem solving including both knowledge and decision-making and his solicitation of student contributions within these goal-directed activities.

We consider them as "reflective" for different reasons. Some presentations introduced new knowledge (e.g., Try Specific Values) in particular problem contexts and highlighted for students the importance of thinking when and where that knowledge can be used again (recall Schoenfeld's closing comments on Try Specific Values). The reflection here involved the relationship between knowledge and the (problem) contexts where that knowledge is applied. In other cases, he modeled specific actions of a skilled problem solver, e.g., control questions such as "Am I done?" Reflection there involved an awareness of the relation between the state of a person's evolving solution and the problem context. All such presentations contained (1) an introduction to a necessary "tool of the trade" in one context, and (2) pointers to how knowledge and skill relate to a wider range of contexts. The intent of these presentations was to help students carry away from the course a different form of classroom mathematical practice.

Because they were the places where Schoenfeld presents new knowledge and skill to students, it is important to contrast reflective presentations with simpler forms of "transmission" teaching common to college and precollege instruction in mathematics. Both involve teachers' display of mathematics knowledge and skill for students who are understood to lack that knowledge and need it to make further progress. We see elements of transmission in the introduction and use of Try Specific Values and in the review of mathematical induction. Moreover, the context and content of Schoenfeld's reflective presentations differed from traditional "teaching by telling" as well as "socratic teaching" in significant ways. In emphasizing process in problem solving, he shifted the focus from mathematical *content* to issues of how mathematics is *done*. His solicitation of student contributions was a step toward fulfilling the expectation, stated during the first twenty minutes of the course, that students would soon take over and use the tools he presented without his assistance. In our view, it is the complex interweaving of transmission and student participation in Schoenfeld's reflective teaching combined with his explicit statements and illustrations of the goals of his actions that makes his course a good example of teaching towards sense-making.

Finally, it is worth emphasizing that our analysis has not centered on the practice of the mathematical community (professional "doing"), but on "presenting" in the classroom context. Indeed schools are unique and specialized contexts for mathematical thinking. We think the analysis shows that the differences between his classroom community and that of professional mathematicians lies not only in shared knowledge and skills, as Schoenfeld has suggested, but also in the *nature and goals* of the practices in these two contexts. His presentations of mathematical content and heuristics had clear instructional goals and employed rather tightly controlled mechanisms for student participation. His intent was that students construct appropriate models of and beliefs about mathematical activity in the professional community. But this teaching practice did not make his classroom part of the professional mathematical community. Rather it helped to close the gap between the two, creating in students the sense of belonging and contributing to a more authentic mathematical practice.

MAKING THE CASE FOR HEURISTICS:
AUTHORITY AND DIRECTION IN THE INSCRIBED SQUARE
John P. Smith III

To teach his students to solve challenging problems, Schoenfeld must himself solve a difficult instructional problem: how to introduce Pólya-type heuristics so that students quickly appreciate their power and slowly learn to apply them productively across a wide range of problems.

As his own past teaching and research has shown, this problem does not submit to easy solutions (Schoenfeld, 1985; 1992a). Students can struggle to see how and where to apply particular heuristic strategies because of their general character as "rules of thumb." Schoenfeld could address this part of the problem by presenting more specific versions of each strategy with clearer conditions of application. But if he did, the list of useful heuristics would become too long and cumbersome to teach and learn (the "specificity" problem). So the generality of strategies (and their attendant vagueness) must be retained. Given the generality of these strategies, students must be thoughtful in selecting, applying, and evaluating them, but such thoughtfulness is difficult to teach. How, for example, should students evaluate their work so that they avoid committing too much time to unproductive approaches? Even if students select productive heuristics, applying those strategies usually involves many steps, and mistakes at any one point can undermine the entire effort (the "implementation" problem). Finally, the skillful use of heuristics is not neutral with respect to content knowledge. If students do not know or cannot recall the necessary mathematical concepts or procedures, even workable solution plans can fail (the "resource" problem).

Many curricular approaches to problem solving fail to take these problems seriously. It is common, especially at the pre-college level, either to cast problem solving as recreation—a separate activity from the "real" task of learning procedures (e.g., Cooney, 1985)—or to teach students to practice and master each strategy separately. These efforts, as Schoenfeld (1992a) has argued, fundamentally miss the mark.

Problem solving in the spirit of Pólya is learning to grapple with new and unfamiliar tasks when the relevant solution methods (even if only partially mastered) are not known. When students are drilled in solution procedures ..., they are not developing the broad set of skills Pólya and other mathematicians who cherish mathematical thinking have in mind. (p. 354)

One central element in teaching problem solving is identified here: Students must regularly work on real problems, not "exercises" that are clearly tied to standard procedures or methods. But even with such problems in hand, how then can you teach problem solving, introduce and highlight heuristics as important "content," and avoid the pitfalls identified above?

In this section we analyze one important step Schoenfeld made toward solving this problem, using the solution and discussion of the challenging inscribed square problem as data. Our main claim is that Schoenfeld's approach involved leading the class through the solution in a carefully planned and directive manner. In so doing, he acted in accord with traditional classroom norms (e.g., the teacher is the mathematical authority) that he aimed to undermine and change. Though his students eventually chose their own approaches to problems and evaluated their attempts and solutions (and those of their peers), they were shown their way through these issues on this particular problem. Schoenfeld's choice to play the strong leader and director indicates that his actions and local goals early in the course did not map onto his long-term intentions and achievements in any simple way. Getting the problem solving class "off the ground" was a quite different task than teaching it in its mature, stable form—the stage emphasized in his written accounts (Schoenfeld, 1988; 1989; 1991; 1994).

The problem and two relevant heuristics

The task of inscribing a square in an arbitrary triangle was second on the problem sheet after the telescoping series. Its wording and accompanying diagrams are reproduced below (Figure 2).

The questions posed in the problem statement raise the issues of existence and construction. First, there is the problem of showing that a square can be inscribed in the given triangle. But an existence proof may not necessarily lead to the construction of the square, so the question of whether the inscribed square can be constructed using Euclidean ruler and compass techniques remains. The existence/construction distinction influenced the class's work in two ways. Students struggled at first to understand the problem statement, and a major part of their confusion was their difficulty in separating these two issues. Schoenfeld also used the distinction to structure the discussion. He drew on his knowledge that some existence arguments generate constructions more easily than others to support the students' progress toward a solution (see Schoenfeld, 1985, pp. 84–91 for his analysis of the problem).

In contrast to the preceding problem (summing the telescoping series) and the subsequent one (the 3 by 3 magic square), the class found both parts of the inscribed square challenging. Much of the students' work prior to specific suggestions from their teacher was devoted simply to understanding the problem.

You are given the triangle on the left in the figure below. A friend of mine claims that he can inscribe a square in the triangle—that is, that he can find a construction that results in a square, all four of whose corners lie on the sides of the triangle. Is there such a construction—or might it be impossible? Do you know for certain that there's an inscribed square? Do you know for certain there's a construction that will produce it?

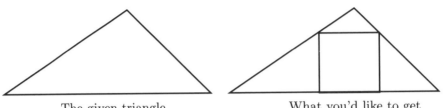

The given triangle   What you'd like to get

Is there anything special about the triangle you were given? That is, suppose you did find a construction. Will it work for all triangles, or only some?

FIGURE 2

Statement of Problem 2:

Inscribing a Square in an Arbitrary Triangle

The difficulty they experienced in getting started provided Schoenfeld with an early context for demonstrating the power of heuristics in solving problems.

Two related heuristics, both attributed to Pólya, were introduced in solving this problem. The very general strategy, *Look for a related problem that is easier to solve and try to exploit its solution to solve the original problem*, was the first. Schoenfeld's presentation of it was cautionary, if not somewhat negative. A number of "easier, related" problems were generated and found to be either hard to solve or difficult to exploit to solve the original problem. These cautions set up the second heuristic, *If there is a special condition in the problem, relax that condition and look for the desired solution in the resulting family of solutions*. Two "special conditions" are embedded in this problem: (1) that the inscribed figure must be a square (a rectangle is easier) and (2) that it must have all four vertices on the triangle (three vertices are easier). Relaxation of either condition can (and did) produce an existence proof.

The classroom solution

Overview. Schoenfeld's work with this problem can be divided into four phases, spanning some 70 minutes of class time. Some students worked on the problem during the first 20 minutes of group work prior to the discussion of the telescoping series solution. Immediately following that discussion, Schoenfeld directed the class, again in groups, toward the inscribed square problem with the strong "hint" to Solve An Easier Related Problem (Phase 1). When he called the groups back together to discuss their progress (Phase 2), three different related problems were suggested, two by students, one by Schoenfeld. They were considered and ultimately rejected. The second heuristic, Relax a Condition, was then introduced and applied in Phase 3. The two conditions were identified, and Schoenfeld used each to produce an existence proof. At the end of the first session, he sent the class away with some general directions to investigate one of the existence proofs more closely. The second class session opened with Devon's constructive proof (Phase 4). Schoenfeld used his solution as context to state some features of the mathematical community he desired.

Clarifying the problem and presenting Solve an Easier Related Problem (Phase 1). When the discussion of the telescoping series problem ended, Schoenfeld directed the class to the inscribed square.

> This [telescoping series] is a fairly straightforward example. We'll encounter a lot more later in the class that are not so straightforward. What I want to do to nudge you in the direction of a solution to problem 2, but not get you far enough yet most likely, is mention a second strategy and have you think about problem 2 a little bit. Which is: [writes and speaks] *If you can't solve the given problem, try to solve an easier related problem and then exploit your solution.* That's a statement that's almost verbatim what it comes out of—from Pólya. See if you can use that to solve problem 2.

The arrangement of the class at this point—still in small groups—is reproduced below (Figure 3).

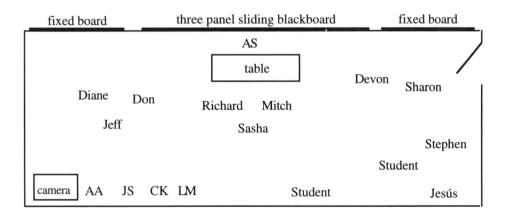

FIGURE 3

Arrangement of the Class in Small Groups

Session 1: Inscribed Square

The class did not immediately move to this task. Snippets of conversation from the four groups indicate that each returned to discuss the telescoping series solution, solve the series problem that was given just after the telescoping series problem,[6] or discuss the principle of mathematical induction. About halfway into these 20 minutes, one group after another turned to the inscribed square problem. Schoenfeld worked his way around the room, discussing the problem statement with each of the four groups. Members of two groups questioned him about what exactly the problem was asking. His responses emphasized the distinction between existence and construction. These quick "check-ins" not only assisted students in understanding the problem but allowed Schoenfeld to observe the work of each group and see which particular "easier related" problems they generated.

In opening the whole group discussion, Schoenfeld declared his expectation that students would come to the board in the next class session and present their work on problems. He then focused their attention on the inscribed square problem with a question, "What does problem 2 tell you to do?" When there was no immediate response from the class, he explained the two parts of the problem and used the example of an angle bisector to distinguish existence from construction. The existence of the angle bisector was established by considering all rays interior to the angle whose endpoints are the vertex and using a continuity argument. He then drew students' attention back to Solve an Easier Related Problem, reminded them that they would be reading Pólya's discussion of it in *How to Solve It* (a supplemental reading for the course). But his stance was cautionary, "... remember I said lots of people thought Pólya didn't quite work and this is an example of why. We need to push him a little bit further." Even as he promoted heuristics, he hinted at difficulties in using them, in this case the specificity problem.

Evaluating Solve an Easier Related Problem (Phase 2). When Schoenfeld asked a more specific question, "What easier related problems did people try? I'm curious," three students responded. For each suggestion, Schoenfeld gave a quick verbal restatement and wrote the suggested approach on the left-hand blackboard (leaving the center board empty and available). We reproduce the major elements of this dialogue below because it is crucial to understanding and interpreting his approach.

Mitch: Relax the constraint on the square and try a rectangle.

AS: OK, let me get to that in a minute [chuckles]. OK, um. So the problem says, stick a square inside the triangle and each corner is on the triangle, one easier related problem is: Don't go for the square, go for a rectangle. [Writes "1. Try a rectangle instead" under the list heading "Related Prob-

---

[6]The second part of problem 1 was, "For those of you who've seen this series, how about $1/2! + 2/3! + 3/4! + \cdots + n/(n + 1)!?$"

lems."] What else did people try? I saw people doing different things, so I know that you tried.

Devon: I tried to disprove it for an arbitrary triangle.

AS: OK. Try to find a counterexample. So, this is if you don't believe it's true, that's not part of the strategy but, [Writes as he speaks, "Look for a specific counterexample," well below suggestion #1] And that's a generally useful thing to do. [Some of AS's short commentary on the benefits of looking for specific examples and counterexamples is omitted here.] Other things that people tried? Yup? [responding to student]

Student: A circle. [This student was not visible on the videotape.]

AS: OK. The problem was, stick in a square inside a triangle. An easier related problem might be, [writes as he speaks, "Try a circle," just below suggestion #1]. Other things that people tried? Yeah? [responding to Sasha]

Sasha: Is that a square in a circle or a circle in a triangle?

[AS appeals to the student who made the suggestion and clarifies that suggestion #2 was to inscribe a circle in a triangle. He outlines the construction of the square in the circle but states it is not useful for solving the problem.]

AS: Other things people might have tried?

[no response for approximately 5 seconds]

I can mention at least one more that I thought I saw people doing, and that I've certainly seen before. Instead of making an arbitrary triangle, make a special kind of triangle, try either the isosceles or equilateral triangles. [He writes, "3. Instead of an arbitrary triangle, try special triangles—isosceles, equilateral."] Let me leave number 1 alone for a short while. I'll get back to that and a couple of others, and talk about the general process and illustrate it with numbers 2 and 3. 'Cause this is a general discussion of, what happens when you try to use the suggestions.

The final written list of suggested approaches to problem 2 is reproduced in Figure 4 below.

Two important teaching decisions are notable in this exchange; both are related to the task of structuring the discussion of Solve an Easier Related Problem and the problems it generated. First, Schoenfeld did not list the suggestions in the order in which they were given. The suggestion to look for a counterexample was listed below the others and separated from them by a squiggly line. The message seemed to be: this is a different sort of suggestion, and we should treat it differently. Second, he chose not to consider the suggestions in the order in which they were given. At the end of the interchange, he declared his intention

<u>Related Problems</u>
1. Try a rectangle instead.
2. Try a circle in a triangle.
3. Instead of an arbitrary triangle, try special triangles—isosceles, equilateral.

Look for a specific counterexample.

FIGURE 4

Schoenfeld's Restatements of Students'
Easier Related Problems for the Inscribed Square

to "discuss" suggestions 2 and 3 before suggestion 1, though the latter was certainly a straightforward example of an "easier related" problem. These choices suggest that Schoenfeld had lessons he wanted to draw from this problem, that some student suggestions fit more easily with his plan than others, and that to draw out these lessons he needed to consider the students' suggestions in a particular order.

To frame the discussion of the "general process" of using related problems (and the attendant pitfalls) he drew an application scheme for the second heuristic on the board and identified a question relevant to each step. For the first step, if you can identify what seems to be an easier related problem, can you solve it? For the second and perhaps more important step, does that solution help to solve the original problem? This scheme is reproduced in Figure 5 as he drew it on the board.

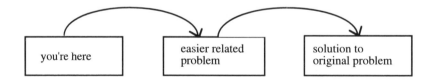

FIGURE 5

Schoenfeld's Application Scheme
for Solve an Easier Related Problem

With this general frame before the class, he sketched a circle inscribed in a triangle, stated that the construction could be done (referring again to work in high school geometry), but declared that it could not be used to solve the original problem.

So for that particular problem, this part is easy [tracing the arrow between the "you're here" and the "easier related problem" box] at least at the level of yes, you can take that step ... but *I've never found anyone* who was actually able to take that particular thing, go from having a circle inscribed in a triangle and be able to use that to inscribe a square in a triangle. So the problem is that you can spend a fair amount of effort getting here [pointing to the "easier related problem" box] and then *I know of no way to get there* [pointing to the "solution to original problem" box]. So that's an example of a stepping stone that only doesn't do you too much good because it only gets you halfway there. [emphasis added]

His treatment of the two special triangles which followed was similarly brief. Instead of drawing either an isosceles or equilateral triangle on the board, he simply stated that both possibilities fail by both criteria, easier and related.

It looks like it should be easier to inscribe a, square in something nice and regular like an isosceles triangle instead of a random triangle, or maybe even equilateral, but it turns out *I don't know of anyone who has actually managed to do that in an easy way, and I don't know of anyone who's been able to show how you can go from a solution of that to the general solution.* [emphasis added]

From these illustrations of the problematic nature of Solve an Easier Related Problem, Schoenfeld stated his general point, "When you're working on a complicated problem that involves using a stepping stone, you want to think both about getting to the stepping stone and whether or not you can get from there on." The stage was now set for reformulating this heuristic in a more specific and deterministic form.

Presenting Relax a Condition (Phase 3). Declaring his intention to help students be more specific about how they might generate easier related problems, Schoenfeld introduced the third heuristic of the day, "a more elaborate version of Pólya's strategy," alternately speaking and writing on the board.

Suppose the problem asks for something, that's what I mean by a specific condition in the problem you want, Pólya says relax the condition, ask for something, ask for less. Since you're less demanding, there ought to be more solutions. There could be a whole family of them. So if you get a whole family of them, maybe you'll find the one you want in that family. [His written statement reads, "If there is a special condition in the problem you want, relax the condition—ask for less. Since you're less demanding, there should be a whole *family* of solutions. Look for the one you want among them."] [his emphasis]

Turning then to the issue of specific conditions, he asked, "What does the problem ask you for?" A combination of student suggestions and Schoenfeld's interpretation produced two conditions which were also written on the board: (1) the desired figure was a square and (2) all four of its vertices must lie on the square.

He chose to tackle the first condition, asking the class what was easier than a square. A student (invisible to the camera) responded quickly, "A rectangle."

When Schoenfeld asked how a rectangle could be inscribed in the triangle he had drawn on the board, Devon began to outline a construction using three perpendicular segments. Schoenfeld accepted and completed his procedure, quickly producing three different rectangles, including a "short and fat" and a "tall and skinny" example, as reproduced below in Figure 6.

FIGURE 6
Three Inscribed Rectangles

From these three examples, Schoenfeld completed the continuity argument for the existence of the inscribed square: if the short, fat rectangle were transformed continuously into the tall, skinny one, that process must generate a rectangle with equal base and height (i.e., a square) somewhere along the way. He added that this was "actually the same continuity argument that I used before for the angle bisector." But with this existence proof in hand, he then denied the possibility of elaborating it into a constructive proof.

> Now that's a nice existence proof. *I don't know how to turn that into a constructive proof.* So that's actually argument number one, that's part of the problem but not the whole problem and to this day, I don't know how to take that nice, little existence proof and say, "Yeah, you can use that and, out of that here is a sequence of things you can do with straightedge and compass." [emphasis added]

He then turned to the second condition and asked for volunteers to generate squares with three vertices on the triangle that he'd drawn on the board. Three students, Sasha, Devon, and Stephen, came to the board, each producing an "inscribed" square of different size and orientation (Figure 7).

Stephen's construction assumed the top angle of the triangle was a right angle. After noting this flaw, Schoenfeld erased that square, leaving two. He asked once more for other examples and, hearing no volunteers, noted his surprise that no one drew a square in the opposite corner to Devon's, because that "normally happens." He then drew increasingly larger squares with the same orientation as Devon's (see Figure 8) and asked, "What you can tell me about that family, what happens to the fourth corners?" Sharon responded, "They're given any range of sizes and then when you finally meet a distance where the, where the fourth one, where the fourth vertice meets the triangle, you have four equal sides." Schoenfeld drew a squiggly locus connecting the fourth vertices of the

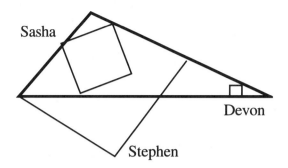

FIGURE 7
Three Students' Partially Inscribed Squares

squares (Figure 8) and restated Sharon's response in terms of the intersection of the locus and the triangle, thus completing the second existence argument.

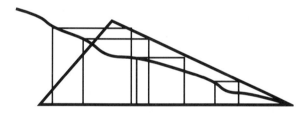

FIGURE 8
The Squiggly Locus Connecting the Fourth Vertices of "Inscribed" Squares

With the end of class approaching, he directed the class to "play with this example for Wednesday and see what you discover." This "assignment" seemed a clear indication that the second existence argument was more likely to generate the missing construction than the first.

The constructive argument (Phase 4). At the start of the next class two days later Schoenfeld pointed the class back to the problem, "We left with problem 2 partly solved and partly up in the air. Does anyone have anything to say about problem 2?" When Devon volunteered and came to the board to show his solution, Schoenfeld turned to the class and described some of his longer-term goals for the class.

> One of things that I want to do during the course of the semester is get us talking like a mathematical community and ultimately using the standards of the mathematical community which means not like mumbling on the board, but instead being fairly clear, lucid, really making arguments clear so that all of us can understand precisely what's going on. So I'm

going to push for those kind of standards in explanation, which means not just beautiful finished products, but also explanations of how and why it's reasonable that you did what you did and things like that. OK?

Figure 9 gives the location of the participants in the classroom at that point in Session 2.

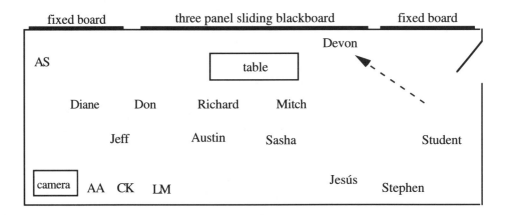

FIGURE 9

Arrangement of the Class: Start of Session 2
Devon's Construction of the Inscribed Square

Devon's argument was based on his insight that the inscribed square could be produced by simply scaling another square up or down and therefore that the problem could be solved using similarity. He first explained how to construct a square with three vertices on the square and the fourth lying outside the triangle (Figure 10, frame 1).

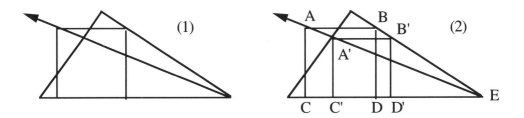

FIGURE 10

Devon's Drawings Illustrating the Inscribed Square Construction

Then he drew the line from the far vertex of the triangle (point E, in frame 2) through the outside vertex of the square. (This line is the accurate representation of Schoenfeld's "squiggly locus.") The point of intersection of that line with the triangle (point A' in frame 2) is one vertex of the inscribed square, and the rest of the square $A'B'D'C'$ can be constructed from that point by dropping perpendiculars to the other two sides of the triangle. Devon went to show how, via similar triangles (e.g., $\triangle ABE \sim \triangle A'B'E'$), the fact that $ABDC$ was a square guaranteed that $A'B'D'C'$ was also.

Throughout his presentation, Devon faced and addressed himself primarily to Schoenfeld, not the class. Schoenfeld, still seated in the front corner of the room, called students' attention to this phenomenon and suggested different standards for their presentations in class.

A comment and a question: The comment is that what just happened in terms of [Devon's] behavior is exactly what happens on the second day of class every time I teach this course, which is that: I ask someone to do something at the board and he spends 90 percent of his time looking at me for approval. I'm actually pretty good at playing poker and not revealing whether something is correct or not. I'm going to do that a lot, because ultimately I don't want to be the judge of what's right or wrong. The judge of what's right or wrong in some sense is the mathematics and in another sense, it's the class. And what I want this to be is a community that develops its own standards about mathematical correctness and it argues about when it buys an argument or not. So that's my comment. The question then is, did you guys buy what you've seen? Is that sufficiently compelling that you all believe the construction that [Devon] suggested? [pause during which Mitch says, "I'm not really convinced it's a proof."] I saw three heads nodding [Jeff's was one], I saw a bunch that didn't react.

Perhaps in response to Mitch's skepticism, Devon said that he "could argue for it." His restatement added more detail, e.g., $\triangle ABE \sim \triangle A'B'E'$ and $\triangle ACE \sim \triangle A'C'E'$ guaranteed that $A'C' = A'B'$, but included no major changes. When he finished, Schoenfeld again asked the class if they were convinced, and this time no one spoke up. Devon went back to his seat, and Schoenfeld returned to the center board and explained how he would generally evaluate students' presentations. His evaluation of Devon's argument was different and explicitly positive, though with qualifications.

One of the things that I'm going to do throughout the period of the course is ask nasty questions. Some of the times when I ask a nasty question that will indeed be true that it turns out that will be the case and that will knock your argument apart. Some of the times it turns out that your argument's right and I'm just being nasty [murmur of amusement from class]. That's because again the idea is what we're trying to do is make sure that the arguments are right. I buy this argument, and it needs a little bit of cleaning up maybe to be comprehensible to anyone who hasn't had

[Devon] explaining it to them. But the structure of it, I think, is pretty nice and straightforward. It's still a little bit, looks like a rabbit pulled out of a hat, in that you have a nice explanation for something that's sort of presented there full-blown.

Then to connect Devon's proof to the previous day's line of development—and in particular to Relax a Condition—he showed how the proof could be interpreted in terms of relaxing conditions. Next came the standard "final" query, "Are we done?" A student (possibly one of the two students who entered the room during Devon's presentation) responded, "Think so." Schoenfeld replied,

> You'll learn within two weeks that's almost always a rhetorical question. The answer is "No" because there's still more we can do with that. Let me [erases board], let me return to a point where we left off on Monday and that actually will wind up with the same construction but might give a different idea of how it actually works. He reconstructed a series of partially inscribed squares in a triangle, highlighted the fourth vertices, and asked what might be true about this locus. A student (not visible on the videotape) responded that it might be linear. Schoenfeld then left it for the class to verify that the locus was indeed a straight line.

Discussion

Of the many instructional issues Schoenfeld addressed early in the course, none was more important than the task of introducing heuristics so that students quickly appreciate their importance and gradually begin to use them intelligently. What does Schoenfeld's management of the solution of the inscribed square reveal about his approach to this teaching problem?

Before turning to the solution itself, it is important to consider the place of the inscribed square in the course as a whole. Two major components of Schoenfeld's curriculum are his problems and the heuristics that he introduces with them. If students are ever to see heuristic strategies as problem solving tools worth learning, they must face problems that do not easily submit to techniques they already know. In contrast to the two other problems discussed in detail in the first week, most students found it difficult to make progress on the inscribed square. Because that problem stumped most of the class, Relax a Condition could then demonstrate the power of heuristics. Likewise, Try an Easier Related Problem illustrated that one needs experience, skill and even patience in order to use heuristics—that they can't be applied in rote fashion. The discussion of the pitfalls of easier related problems helped to clarify their non-deterministic, "rule of thumb" character and show the importance of how you apply them. So Schoenfeld's solution of the instructional problem required demonstrably hard problems and quickly useful, if non-deterministic, heuristics.

But difficult problems and potentially useful strategies are only part of the story. Schoenfeld's extensive experience with the inscribed square problem provided well-grounded expectations about what students' likely responses would be (e.g., which easier related problems they would generate). These expectations complemented his knowledge of which solution paths would be more accessible to students than others (e.g., which existence proofs led toward constructions). This knowledge made it easier to recognize and interpret his students' suggestions and guide their efforts toward a successful conclusion.

These three top-level features (problems, heuristics, and prior experience with the problems) are all consistent with Schoenfeld's stated goals for the class. Solving problems (as opposed to exercises) supports his claim that the activity in and around the class reflects important aspects of professional mathematical practice. Learning to judge when, if, and how to apply particular heuristics is an important part of that practice. And the fact that extensive teaching experience with particular problems was central to using those problems productively reflects the complex relationship between problems and heuristics. But his management of the solution itself, particularly his appropriation (or not) of students' suggestions, bears a more complex relationship to his goals for the class.

It is important to recognize that the students played an active and substantive role in solving the inscribed square. Nearly half of the class contributed some piece of the evolving solution, and Devon's work, especially his construction, was more than simply "a contribution." Schoenfeld deliberately solicited their participation, but he also carefully organized and controlled it. Student input was solicited at certain points in the solution (e.g., when a range of possible approaches was needed) and not others, and their suggestions were assimilated into his instructional plan. His role as instructional leader and, at crucial junctures, mathematical authority was central to the pace and process of the solution. He orchestrated student participation within a relatively traditional model of roles for teachers and students, where teachers decide what choices to offer to students and when it is best to do so. These traditional elements of teaching appear—at first blush—to run counter to his stated long-term goal of creating a mathematical community where authority rests with the mathematics and community as a whole.

Before attempting to resolve this apparent contradiction, we review the evidence that undergirds these interpretative claims. First, what indicates that Schoenfeld came in with a pre-existing plan for solving the inscribed square? Though we did not question him at the time about his plans, he has written about his purposes for using the problem (to demonstrate the difficulties of applying heuristics), the easier related problems he expects to see (try a rectangle, try a circle, try a special triangle), the two existence proofs, and the difficulty of obtaining a construction from one of them (Schoenfeld, 1985, pp. 84–91). Most of the major elements of the solution that he orchestrated with the class are present in this written account. Given the strong similarities between the two, it is difficult to doubt the existence of a detailed instructional plan. Schoenfeld chose the inscribed square as the second problem of the course for particular reasons, and the main elements of the discussion were in place for him before the problem sheet was given to students.

This plan then became the framework for guiding the class through the solution and underscoring major points along the way. To achieve these goals in a reasonable time frame, he directed the class down certain pathways (and not others) and used his own mathematical experience and authority to justify these choices. As warrant for this interpretation, we summarize in chronological order the instances where Schoenfeld used his personal authority to direct the course of the solution.

- He wrote Devon's suggestion to seek a counterexample below the other suggestions and did not seriously consider it in the subsequent discussion.
- He delayed dealing with Mitch's suggestion to relax the condition on the square and try a rectangle (suggestion 1) until he discussed suggestions 2 and 3.
- He asserted that inscribing a circle in the triangle could not be adapted to inscribing a square in a triangle.
- He asserted that the solutions for isosceles and equilateral triangles were neither easy to produce nor to adapt to the arbitrary triangle.
- He asserted that the first existence proof could not be adapted into a constructive proof.

What can we learn about his teaching from these choices? First, given the match with his plan for the solution, each move is an example of how teachers appropriate students' ideas and suggestions to their own plans (Newman, Griffin, & Cole, 1989). Appropriation is a tool for balancing the dual goals of engaging students' interest and participation and sustaining progress toward important instructional goals. Second, while these instructional decisions were all explicit in the data, they were not all identical in character. The first two were management choices; they were decisions about what to take up for discussion and what to set aside, more than direct evaluations of what could be done mathematically. The first decision was sensible since the search for counterexamples would have been very difficult to assimilate into his plan. So Schoenfeld honored the suggestion in general terms and set it aside. The second decision was equally sensible since developing this suggestion first would have removed the possibility of teaching the lesson about the pitfalls of easier related problems. In that sense, Mitch's suggestion to relax a condition on the square was too good.

The last four, however, all involved Schoenfeld's explicit judgment of what is possible and productive mathematically and were justified by appeal to his own mathematical experience. Essentially they communicated the message, "Trust me. I have explored this problem extensively, and I know its 'ins' and 'outs'." Like the management of Easier Related Problems, these declarations sped the solution along, by curtailing potential solution paths that Schoenfeld knew to be unproductive. But to do so, he implicitly asked students to accept his role as the mathematical leader and decision-maker.

How then do these teaching moves fit with the overall goal of creating a mathematical community in the classroom? More generally, how do mathematics educators deal with mathematical authority, balance their informed authority against emerging student autonomy, and support students' growth toward a powerful and independent mathematical competence?

The first step toward a resolution is to acknowledge the mismatch: the solution of the inscribed square was inconsistent with some of the overarching goals of the course. Schoenfeld's directed solution does not easily square with the ideas of a classroom mathematical community pursuing its own solutions, and his statements about what was possible mathematically are not consistent with the methods of public justification employed by the professional community. On the other hand, the Overview points to evidence that Schoenfeld's teaching has moved students substantively toward his declared long-term goals, and our observations suggest this was the case for the 1990 class as well. Students became more proficient problem solvers; they learned to use heuristics productively; they interacted as a community of problem solvers; and they accepted the task of judging and nudging each other's ideas and arguments. So the question must be restated as, "Why was the direction not counterproductive to the long-term goals?" Our view is that there were more important goals for Schoenfeld early in the course and that these may have required his exercising a leadership role in deciding some issues for the class. He must convince students that they have important things to learn in the course and that he will support them in that effort. If he did not strongly guide students' problem solving in the early days, they could easily flounder, pursue too many deadends, and come to question the entire enterprise. Instead, Schoenfeld made sure that they struggled enough to realize that they could not solve the problem easily but could be successful with his direction and the proper tools. These experiences were part of the transition toward more independent problem finding, problem solving, and justification. In short, his directive instruction gave priority to some goals over others.[7]

Our goal in emphasizing the complex relationship between instructional goals and teaching practice in this segment has not been to question or endorse the optimality of Schoenfeld's decisions. Rather, we have shaped the analysis to illustrate the interaction of ambitious educational goals, detailed instructional plans, teaching moves, and students' contributions. One main lesson is that innovative teaching oriented toward ambitious, non-traditional goals can embrace both traditional and non-traditional elements. The achievement of such goals may depend as much on the traditional elements as the non-traditional and on skillful balancing of short-term objectives and quite different long-term goals. This conclusion, we believe, undermines simple descriptions and explanations of

---

[7]We acknowledge that Schoenfeld did take some explicit actions toward building the classroom community and shifting the locus of authority in the first week, e.g., his statement to the class about standards for written and oral arguments before Devon presented his constructive argument and his statement about asking nasty questions to the class afterward. Our argument is that this was not his primary goal in the first week.

successful non-traditional mathematics teaching. We need to look more closely to understand what works in these settings and why.

PRACTICING MATHEMATICAL COMMUNICATION: USING HEURISTICS WITH THE MAGIC SQUARE[8]
Cathy Kessel

> *The language is not alive except to those who use it.*
> (Thurston, 1994, p. 167)

Schoenfeld (1991) gives an account of a classroom discussion of the magic square problem. Here is the version of the third problem he gave to his students in the class.

Can you place the numbers 1, 2, 3, 4, 5, 6, 7, 8, and 9 in the box below, so that when you are all done, the sum of each row, each column, and each diagonal is the same? This is called a magic square.

In his account of the discussion of this problem Schoenfeld describes briefly how the problem, though trivial, can be used to illustrate many heuristics and other important aspects of mathematical thinking: Establishing Subgoals, Working Backwards, Exploiting Symmetry, Working Forwards, using systematic generating procedures, focusing on key points for leverage, exploiting extreme cases, solving a problem in more than one way, and using a problem as a springboard for further mathematics. At the end of his account he says that an important aspect of the discussion, the classroom dynamics which "reflected the dynamics of real mathematical exploration" was not described. One might wonder how a classroom discussion could reflect the dynamics of mathematical exploration and how such a discussion could happen on the second day of a course. The goal of this section is to examine the classroom dynamics of another magic square discussion, led by Schoenfeld in the fall of 1990, and to consider some of the features of mathematical practice it reflected.

Several aspects of this discussion are striking. Very little was written on the blackboard. What did appear were heuristics, diagrams, an equation, and a

---

[8]I would like to thank Alan Schoenfeld for the many ways in which he helped to make this article possible. His support, and that of the Functions Group and the School of Education at the University of California have helped me to learn about and do research in education. For comments, criticisms, and encouragement as this article slowly evolved, my thanks go to: Margaret Carlock, Marisa Castellano, Judith Epstein, and Jean Lave; the *RCME* editors: Ed Dubinsky and Jim Kaput; the *RCME* reviewers: Barbara Pence, Beth Warren, and one anonymous reviewer; Mary Barnes, Sue Helme, and Derek Holton; and my co-authors: Abraham Arcavi, Luciano Meira, and Jack Smith.

question, rather than the line by line theorems and proofs of traditional upper division courses or the line by line theorems, examples, and solutions of lower division courses.

The kind of speaking in Schoenfeld's classroom also differed from that of a traditional class. For example, in one seventeen-minute segment of the whole-class discussion of the magic square, though the teacher was at the front of the class and the students were not working in groups or presenting solutions, there were fourteen utterances—questions, comments, suggestions about the mathematics at hand—made by students. One would expect only questions in a traditional class and very few at that.

These differences suggest that communication is an important feature of this class and that research on language and communication might illuminate some of the reasons why Schoenfeld has chosen to conduct his class in this manner. In this section I use some analytic frameworks from sociolinguistics to describe classroom communication and to compare it with that of research mathematicians. I have been an undergraduate, graduate student, and faculty member at various mathematics departments across the U.S., and I draw on this experience as well as on written accounts to describe the teaching and research practices of mathematicians.

Differences in speaking and writing

At the beginning of the first day of a typical upper division undergraduate mathematics class, the professor writes her or his name, office location, and office hours on the board. After a brief statement about determination of course grades, she or he begins to lecture, starting with definitions and notational conventions and perhaps reaching some new material midway through the first class. There are few, perhaps no, questions from the students, which will be true for the rest of the term. The professor writes almost everything on the blackboard and almost everything has one of the following labels: theorem, lemma, corollary, proof, example, axiom, conjecture, definition, notation. One exception is pictures or diagrams, another (in applied mathematics classes) is applications. With such a lot of writing to do, blackboards, chalk, and erasers become extremely important. Professors become skilled at arranging their writing on the board, not erasing theorems or diagrams until they won't need to refer to them again. (An inattentive professor may also cover one sliding board with another so quickly that students can't finish copying the writing on the board. Schoenfeld did this on the first day of class in his enactment of the typical calculus professor, as described in Meira's section.)

The main focus of the typical mathematics class is the blackboard and students' main activity is taking notes, and following the lecture. As in written mathematics the statement of results tends to be impersonal. Names occur mainly in important theorems, definitions or axioms, e.g, Stokes' Theorem, Green's Theorem, Gödel's Incompleteness Theorem, the Zermelo-Frankel axioms of set theory, the Peano Postulates, Noetherian ring, Abelian group. The time at which the object was constructed isn't often mentioned. (Later, as students reach the edges of mathematical knowledge in graduate school, names and dates appear with much greater frequency.[9])

The classroom language of the typical mathematics professor reflects the way mathematics is presented in writing. "Assume the following holds . . . ," "it follows easily that . . . ," "it is not the case that . . . " are frequent phrases (for more examples see Pimm, 1987). Rotman (1993, p. 7) describes written mathematics as "riddled with *imperatives*, with commands and exhortations such as 'multiply items in w,' 'integrate x,' 'prove y,' 'enumerate z' " and "completely without *indexical* expressions, those fundamental and universal elements of natural languages whereby such terms as 'I,' 'you,' 'here,' 'this,' as well as tensed verbs, tie the meaning of messages to the physical context of their utterance." For example, the magic square problem could have been stated in the following way: "Place the numbers 1 through 9 in the boxes to the right so that the sum of each row, column, and diagonal is the same. Such an arrangement is called a magic square." This imperative statement doesn't mention where and when the action of placing numbers in boxes is occurring, nor who is acting.

Chafe and Danielewizc (1987) characterize a style with few indexical expressions as "detached," "show[ing] an interest in ideas that are not tied to specific people, times, and places, but which are abstract and timeless" and which avoids mentioning concrete doers. They note that this style predominates in writing and suggest a reason for it—"for writers, the audience is usually unseen, and often unknown" (p. 19). This detached style of speaking and writing about mathematics suggests to listeners and readers that mathematics is independent of time and place. This is consistent with the epistemology (a mixture of formalism and Platonism) held by many mathematicians (Davis, 1986; Davis & Hersch, 1986; Ernest, 1991; Fauvel, 1988). It is also consistent with the epistemology held by many high school students that learning mathematics is mostly memorizing facts (National Center for Educational Statistics, 1993) and that the ideas of mathematics have always been true and will always be true and were discovered (not invented) by mathematicians (Clarke, Wallbridge, & Fraser, 1992). And it is also consistent with the mathematics classroom experiences of undergraduates (Mura, 1995).

In contrast, note Schoenfeld's wording of the magic square problem which begins, "Can you place" rather than "Place the numbers." We shall see many indexicals —"I," "we," "you," "Devon's question," "what Jeff guessed last time"—in Schoenfeld's speech. Chafe and Danielewizc call a style with many indexicals "involved" and note that it is characteristic of, though not limited to, spoken language. They also note, "In most spoken language an audience is not only

---

[9]This description is not meant as a condemnation. Some of my happiest and most instructive hours have been spent in such courses. I appreciate well-tended blackboards and good chalk and my spoken language reflects written mathematics. At the end of this section I suggest some reasons why not all students are so fortunate.

physically present, but has the ability to respond with language of its own" (pp. 18–19). This suggests that, in addition to acknowledging their presence, an involved style may invite listeners to respond.

And Schoenfeld does want his listeners to respond. Because a main goal of his course is the creation of a "mathematical community," one of his goals for the first days of the course is to get the students to talk: "Clearly what I need to do is begin pulling things from [the students] because part of what the course is supposed to do is turn things over to them" (audio taped discussion, May 22, 1991).

Schoenfeld's language is not only involved, but informal and non-technical with occasional shifts in style to language that reflects written mathematics. Such shifts are known as code-variation. Saville-Troike (1989) defines codes as "different languages, or quite different varieties of the same language" and code-variation as a change in code within a speech event. She notes that code-variation may serve many different purposes, depending on context. Here, Schoenfeld's shift to language reflecting written mathematics serves to display his group affiliation as well as to help the students to become familiar with mathematical language. Just as patients don't have faith in a doctor who "doesn't talk like one" despite the miscommunication that can occur when doctors use technical language (Saville-Troike, 1989), students may not have faith in a professor who doesn't talk like one. Schoenfeld must talk a fine line between being understandable, approachable, and interested in students' contributions, and maintaining his status as the knowledgeable member of the mathematics community depicted in his monologue at the beginning of the first class session. His informal language may suggest to students that it is acceptable if they reply in the same manner. It also contrasts with and emphasizes the few technical words he does use: names of heuristics (which he sometimes labels "jargon") and mathematical terms.

As with spoken language, there are differences in how much Schoenfeld writes, what he writes, and the way he uses writing. This difference suggests a different emphasis, and a different view of what is important in this classroom. Not only does Schoenfeld write considerably less than a traditional mathematics professor, but when and what he writes are different. Both mathematics and heuristics appear on the blackboard as one would expect in a class on heuristics and their use. The diagrams in this class would not be seen in a textbook or an article, they are used to work with, rather than to illustrate. They are altered throughout the course of the discussion and erased only when the discussion is over. This use of diagrams allows Schoenfeld to avoid technical language as well as to make the problem more immediate and his descriptions more direct. The other blackboard writings are names and brief descriptions of heuristics. The connection between mathematics and heuristics is not recorded on the blackboard, it is made through questioning, and interaction with the class. Formal proofs aren't given, instead, their genesis is enacted in the classroom discussion. Later in the term, students will present their own conjectures and proofs.

Not only are there differences between the informal, involved style of his language and the detached style of a traditional professor of mathematics, there are also differences in the content of Schoenfeld's language and its mode of use. Its content includes what is traditionally thought of as the subject matter of mathematics classes, but is also *about* math, about how math gets done, about revealing "the tools of the trade," and about learning that trade. This suggests a different emphasis—not only is mathematical content important, but how one does mathematics is a legitimate topic of classroom discussion.

As Arcavi points out in the overview, Schoenfeld has two different modes of communicating with the class as a whole: presenting and involving the class in discussion. As we have seen in the previous sections and shall see in this section, Schoenfeld uses these different modes of communication for different purposes. In general, Schoenfeld presents heuristics, either as an explanation of a mathematical suggestion given by a student, a name for a process that's just been illustrated, or to give direction to the solution of a mathematics problem. In the latter case, the heuristic is frequently instantiated in the mathematical context at hand by the students.

Schoenfeld gets the students to instantiate heuristics by a method of questioning similar to that described by Pólya (1973) in *How to Solve It*.

> The teacher's method of questioning ... is essentially this: Begin with a general question or suggestion on our list [of heuristics], and, if necessary, come down gradually to more specific and concrete questions or suggestions till you reach one which elicits a response in the student's mind .... It is important, however, that the suggestions from which we start should be simple, natural, and general, and that their list be short .... The suggestions must be general, applicable not only to the present problem but to problems of all sorts .... The list must be short in order that the questions may be often repeated, unartificially, and under varying circumstances .... It is necessary to come down gradually to specific suggestions, in order that the student may have as great a *share of the work* as possible .... Our method admits a certain elasticity and variation, it admits various approaches ... it can and should be applied so that questions asked by the teacher *could have occurred to the student himself*. (pp. 20–21)

Schoenfeld has taught his class many times before. Though he does not know his students well at the beginning of the course, as in the cases of the telescoping series and the inscribed square, he knows most of the responses students will make to his questions about the magic square. Students are not completely predictable though and Schoenfeld's management of the discussion also had opportunistic elements (Hayes-Roth & Hayes-Roth, 1979; Schoenfeld et al., 1992). Students' questions and suggestions, both predictable and unexpected, were used to serve goals of the discussion and of the course.

The nature of the problem

Both the magic square problem and the way in which it is used are important elements of this discussion. The magic square was the third problem on the sheet given to the students and the third to be discussed. One difference between the magic square problem and those preceding it is that its solution is indubitable (it can be checked by a simple calculation), and easy to reach. Unlike the problem of inscribing a square in a triangle, it is easy to solve, and couldn't be used to convince the students that they needed to learn heuristics. It may even suggest to students that they have been using "raw" heuristics—heuristic tendencies that need refinement before they are likely to be consistently useful (Silver, 1985).

However, the magic square serves as an excellent vehicle for the introduction and illustration of heuristics. Because the mathematics involved is elementary, students can discuss it without the fear of displaying ignorance—it's easy to talk about (Schoenfeld, audio taped discussion, May 22, 1991). Because there is no need to focus on getting a solution, students can focus on the process of arriving at a solution. What follows is an account of the discussion of the magic square. Annotations and interpretations in brackets are interspersed. Italics is used in two different ways in the transcript: Italicized phrases were both spoken and written on the blackboard; single words in italics indicate words emphasized by the speaker.

The discussion of the magic square

Schoenfeld asks for volunteers to present the magic square problem. Jeff volunteers and presents his group's solution. After Jeff sits down, Schoenfeld goes back to the board, acknowledges the solution ("the answer speaks for itself") and indicates a transition to another activity "What I want to do is play with this a little bit. First of all it's not a problem you want to do by *pure* trial and error." He then gives a standard combinatorial argument to show how many different ways there are of filling a 3 by 3 grid if one places the digits from 1 through 9 randomly in its cells. He notes, "There are 9 ways that you can stick any number, say [points to top left square of grid], in this square, 8 in that one [points to top middle square] after you've used one, 7 in the next one" and so on. This yields 9! ways to fill in the 3 by 3 grid—but, he observes, the magic square has eight-fold symmetry, so there are

$$\frac{9!}{8} = 9 \times 7 \times 6 \times 5 \times 4 \times 3 \times 2 \times 1$$

non-equivalent ways one might fill it. Then, saying intermediate products aloud, he quickly calculates the result.

[Professors teaching undergraduate courses don't often do computations involving large numbers in front of their classes. One reason for doing it here might be to emphasize the improbability of obtaining a solution by random search. This will contrast with the solutions obtained by the use of heuristics that will follow. Another might be to display mathematical expertise to those who consider quick calculation a sign of expertise. A more subtle message which this calculation may convey is that none of the students used pure trial and error. They all solved the problem.]

During his calculation Schoenfeld mentioned the eight-fold symmetry of the square. Devon asks if there were any solutions to the magic square not equivalent using symmetry. Schoenfeld replies "That's a good question, let's leave that as something to look at" and writes the question on the sideboard where it remains for the rest of the discussion.

[Schoenfeld's knowledge of the magic square and its different solutions allows him to make this response, knowing that the question will be answered before the class ends. His action serves several purposes: It legitimizes the student's question without immediately changing the flow of the activity, begins a community history and gives an example of mathematical practice—questions are important, they may not be immediately answered, but one may later note as Schoenfeld will do, that a particular question has been answered by a proof or construction.]

Schoenfeld says "So if you don't want to do it by trial and error then what you really want to do is look for ways to reduce the number of things you've got to consider" and summarizes Jeff's presentation of group's work as a strong appeal to symmetry "... if you make those two guesses, 5 is in the center and 15 is the sum then you don't have too much trial and error to do before you get there. And that's a good sane way to go about doing the problem." [Here the students may be reassured, they all solved the problem, and their solutions weren't gotten by pure trial and error. The "two guesses" will reappear as instantiations of heuristics, again suggesting that the students may be using "raw heuristics" which can be refined.]

First (re)solution: By establishing subgoals and working backwards

First subgoal: What is the sum? So far heuristics haven't been mentioned. Schoenfeld shifts the focus to heuristics, says "What I want to do is ask a couple of questions that illustrate some of Pólya's strategies and use the answers to make progress on this problem again so we're going to revisit the problem a little bit." He erases the board and states "We're back to the beginning, we want to place the digits from 1 to 9 into this [the empty grid he has just drawn] so that the sum of each row, column, and diagonal is the same." Now he introduces a heuristic. [Note the shift in the meaning of "you" in Schoenfeld's first utterance. At the beginning "you" is an unspecified person, perhaps one of the listeners. At the end it is Richard.]

AHS: The first question is generic: *What piece of information would make the problem easier to solve?* [He turns to face the class.] That's a really broad generic question. But you're facing a problem, it's posed in a particular way. Now you can ask yourself is there some piece of information, some bit of knowledge, so that if you just had that, the problem would be significantly easier to solve? [To Richard] And you're nodding your head yes, what would it be? [Schoenfeld moves closer to Richard.]

Richard: Just to look around for the sum of the triples ... and add the three smallest numbers for the minimum, the three largest for the [inaudible].

AHS: OK. So the key piece of information is, or certainly a key piece of information is: this says that the sum of each row, column, and diagonal should be the same, it would be awfully nice to know what that number is, so what is the sum? [He writes "What is the sum?" on the board.] And we had a suggestion about how to think about this that I'll mention in a second. Let me throw some more jargon at you. This is called, as simple as it seems, in other contexts it's a little bit more complicated, and worth having a name, *Establishing Subgoals*.

Now Schoenfeld starts on the work of answering the question What is the sum? by noting easy upper and lower bounds on the magic number—it must be less than the sum of the largest three numbers in the magic square, 9, 8, and 7; and larger than the smallest three 3, 2, and 1. He invites a response from the class by saying "Is there anything else I can say about that sum?" Gary[10] responds. He seems to assume that Schoenfeld is considering a magic square with 1, 2, and 3 in a row, column, or diagonal because he says "You can narrow it even closer because if you used 1, 2, 3 in a single column, row, or diagonal then you know that you're going to be building something even larger, because 2 and 3 for instance are already gone so you have to use 4, 5, and 6." [Here Gary responds to Schoenfeld's use of "I" by using "you" both of which suggest that Schoenfeld is engaged in doing mathematics, rather than presenting a finished product. Gary's use of "you" also suggests a collegial relationship with Schoenfeld.]

Rather than clarifying his earlier statements, Schoenfeld rephrases Gary's response: "OK, so in some sense the very least I can get for a sum if somewhere I've used 1, 2, and 3 in a row, that might try this row, that row, or something like that, the 3's going to be involved in another sum, and that's going to use at least 4 and 5." He writes in the empty grid

1		
2		
3	4	5

saying, "And if that uses 4 and 5 ... [his voice trails off and he pauses] What

---

[10]This student did not stay long in the course. He does not appear in our overview of students.

else can I say? [pause] This says that there's going to be one sum that's at least 12. [pause] Can you say anything else?" During the next utterances the square on the blackboard undergoes the following changes (an arrow indicates that the square to its left has been altered to yield the square on its right):

1		
2		
3	4	5

→

1		7
2	6	
3	4	5

→

1	6	7
2	8	
3	4	5

Gary: If you actually wanted to build it this way then you'd go up on the right with 6, and 7 next.

AHS: Well, that's good, you go 3, 6, and 7. Is the argument now that every sum has to be at least 16? That's what it looks like we just proved, right? No matter what magic square you draw, you're going to get one sum that's going to add up to 16? [pause]

Diane: No, because you could put the 3, 6, and 7 after the 1 [inaudible].

AHS: So the claim is, well I could put the 6 and 7 after the 1, that gives me a 14, but then I've got to use an 8 and that says now I've got a proof that I get at least a 16—a 17. [pause] What's happening here? [pause] We already saw that there's a magic square with a 15, but it looks like we just proved that you've got to get an 18. [pause] What's happening?

Gary: Well, we know that we can't have 1, 2, and 3 in the same line anyway because we can't construct a magic square from it.

AHS: [confidently and quickly in contrast to his previous utterances] OK. What we just showed is if you start with a 1, 2, and 3 in a row then you're going to get some fairly large sums, that doesn't mean that every sum has to be that way. OK. [Erases square.] So the sums are going to be larger than 6.

[Gary's line of inquiry, trying 1, 2, and 3 in the same column to begin a solution to the magic square, was not quickly curtailed as in the inscribed square discussion, though it also does not lead to a solution. In fact Schoenfeld encourages Gary by writing his suggestions on the board and asking "What else can I say?" (though in a rather uncertain tone of voice). This path is curtailed in an obvious sense by Schoenfeld, he erases the magic square and changes the subject. However, in contrast to the dead-ends in the inscribed square discussion, a student is involved as a collaborator in this action; Gary has noted that the assumption that 1, 2, and 3 are in the same column of a magic square can't be true.]

He asks "Is there any other way we can get a handle [on this] besides good guessing? And I don't at all, want to put good guessing down, a symmetry guess is an excellent way to go. Is there any other way we might get a handle on what this might be?" Devon responds that the sum of the three rows of the magic square must be equal to the sum of the numbers from 1 to 9. He then shows, using the grid, how its use might give rise to Devon's answer, and continues to show how the observation yields a proof that the magic number is 15. The subgoal has been achieved.

[Devon's suggestion has provided a "natural" way to introduce Working Backwards and to give an example of illuminating the source of a mathematical idea—showing that Devon's suggestion is not a "rabbit pulled out of a hat." Schoenfeld's use of this suggestion to introduce Working Backwards, a heuristic which he would bring up during the magic square discussion in any case, is an example of the opportunism described by Hayes-Roth and Hayes-Roth (1979).]

Second subgoal: What goes in the center? This is a natural moment to again invoke Establishing Subgoals since finding the center of the magic square is a useful next step. Schoenfeld pulls down the board with Establishing Subgoals and erases all but Establishing Subgoals. [Here is an example of traditional blackboard expertise and evidence of Schoenfeld's plan for this discussion.] He says,

> Since I have this statement, Establishing Subgoals, in a nice box on the board, why don't I take advantage of it again. We now know that the sum of each row, column, and diagonal is supposed to be 15. What's the next major piece of information that would help me make significant progress on this problem?

He again uses Pólya's method of questioning. Student 1[11] responds "What goes in the center." Schoenfeld answers "Yeah. What goes in the center" and presents another heuristic, Consider Extreme Cases. He then gives its mathematical instantiation in this context.

AHS: So let's ask an extreme case, can 9 go in the center of the square? That's as extreme as you can get. [He writes 9 in the center of the square.]

Student 1: No.

AHS: Why not?

---

[11]This student was invisible to the camera and can't be identified with certainty. His voice appeared to be coming from the right side of the room.

Student 1:   You run out of numbers that you can add pairs of to 9.

AHS: If the magic number is 15, that raises a serious problem, where's 8 going to go? If I put an 8 there [he writes 8 in upper left corner] I need a −2 over there and I ain't got none. If I put an 8 there [the upper middle square], I need a −2 over here and so on. OK? So 9 can't go in the center. [He erases 9.]

[Here the code-shift from "that raises a serious problem" to the attention-getting "I ain't got none" emphasizes the reason why 9 can't go in the center of the square and mirrors the student's rather awkward sentence. Writing and erasing serve to dramatize what Schoenfeld is saying and to display his reasoning.] He continues more and more quickly through the cases of 8, 7, 6, gets to 5, says "Maybe. How about the other extreme?," writing 1 in the center of the square. He continues and eliminates the remaining possibilities. The subgoal of finding the center has been achieved. Schoenfeld doesn't point this out explicitly but makes the transition to the next activity by saying,

> Having gotten that far we could consider some trial and error. But we ought to at least take advantage of symmetry to see how much trial and error we really have to do. So let me ask the question, how many different places are there that we might stick a 1? There are really only two different places . . . [corner and side pocket].

He then explicitly shows the symmetry he has mentioned several times, using hand gestures accompanied by his verbal description of rotating the board. [The gesture of rotating the board is an example of a deictic (McNeill, 1992). It is a visual analogue of Schoenfeld's involved language: he, not some undescribed mechanism, is the rotater of the square. His gestures also allow him to give a definition of symmetry without using technical language.]

> There are really only two different places. If I had a solution with a 1 over here [writes 1 in the upper left corner] then—and all the rest of these were filled in, I could take that solution [puts his right hand, crooked left, over the center of the grid and straightens his wrist], take the board, and rotate it 90 degrees [he puts his right hand above the grid, his left below, and rotates them about the center of the grid so that the left hand ends above the grid], that gives me a solution with 1 over here [points to upper right corner]. Or equivalently, if I had a solution with 1 in the corner over here [points with his left hand to upper right corner], rotating it that way [his left hand moves up and to the right as he reverses his previous rotation gesture] gives me a solution with the 1 over here [points to the 1 in upper left corner]. Same for the other corners [points to the two lower corners]. So a solution with a 1 in the corner is equivalent to, or generates a solution with a 1 in any other corner. Similarly for 1 in a side pocket. That generates any of these [pointing to each side pocket in turn].

Another heuristic is quickly noted (it's just been illustrated); Schoenfeld writes Exploit Symmetry, saying "That's another strategy that comes in handy" and returns to the work at hand. He writes 1 in the corner of the square, notes that 9 must go in the corner diagonally opposite, and discusses the placement of 2. Using symmetry one need only check three places. Schoenfeld indicates each and shows that no matter where 2 is placed some row, column, or diagonal will not add up to 15. He concludes "So what I've just showed is there's no solution with a 1 in the corner. That leaves us a 1 in the side." He erases 1 and writes 1 in the side pocket, discusses the placing of 2 and finishes the solution. [Looking at the case where 1 is in the corner first makes the discussion smoother since this case doesn't hold. Such a choice is usual in both classroom and professional mathematical presentations.]

Now he summarizes, "What we've proved along the way that the 1 has to go in the side pocket, the 2 has to go in one of the two bottom positions opposite, and the rest is forced, so the answer is that's the only solution modulo symmetry, which answers Devon's question." [A mathematician who solves a problem posed by person X will, especially if X is famous, frequently say in an account of the solution "This answers a question of X." The episode of Devon's posing of a problem to its solution outlines in miniature the way a problem is posed and solved amongst professional mathematicians.]

Second (re)solution: By working forward

Schoenfeld asks the ritual question "Are we done?" and Jeff replies "We're never done." (The students are beginning to internalize the new classroom rituals.) Schoenfeld replies "You're learning" and makes the transition to a new activity "What I want to do is to go back to this problem in an entirely different way," summarizing the approach used before, erasing the board, then giving a description of the new approach which he's termed (1991) Working Forward. Here he doesn't label it, just describes and gives an instantiation of this approach—listing triples whose sum is 15.

Now he initiates the students' participation by asking for triples. Different students call out responses hastened by Schoenfeld's "Any more?" or "Another one?" which follows quickly after he writes each triple on the board. He lists 159, 294, 258, 168, 357, and 195, says "Oops, we got that already" and crosses it out. They continue 456, 762, and stop. Schoenfeld says "Are we done, is that all of them?" A student[12] produces 834 and Schoenfeld asks "Are there any more?" No one replies.

Schoenfeld tells the class, "This is now something like the 142nd time I've used this particular problem, 142nd time I've asked this particular question, "Are there any more?," and I get to ask the same next question for the 142nd time: How the hell would you know? You've sort of generated them randomly,

---

[12]It was difficult to identify the students who participated in this segment, but possible to tell that different students were calling out triples.

so you got a whole bunch of them, but you might of caught them all and you might not."

[Here again code-shifting serves several goals: "hell" emphasizes the seriousness of the students' dilemma, and "generated" and "random" suggest mathematical affiliation. As he says to the students, Schoenfeld has seen classes implement his suggestion of listing triples of numbers unsystematically before. Here again, in contrast to the inscribed square discussion he's allowed, in fact encouraged, the class to follow a path which will not easily lead to a solution. The nature of the magic square makes this dead-end more quickly reached and more obvious than those occurring in the inscribed square discussion. One reason for doing this is to show the students that they're in need of his teaching as well as the heuristic, Be Systematic. Another is to illustrate the issue of control, the students don't know how to implement his suggestion in such a way that they know when they've achieved it.]

He mentions the strategy whose omission led the class into its predicament, writing "IT HELPS TO BE SYSTEMATIC!" on the side board. He summarizes the difficulty, pointing to the crossed out triple 195 which serves as a record of the students' activity and suggests a way to instantiate the strategy—listing the triples in increasing order and beginning the list with all the triples that start with 1.

To start this new path he erases the unsystematic list of triples from the board and starts the new list with 1 5 9. The class calls out the rest of the triples. Schoenfeld points out the connection between the triples and the magic square,

> So we've got a total of eight triples, ..., that's nice, because there are eight rows, columns and diagonals. Now what was the most important square? In the magic square? The middle. How many sums was that square involved in? [Here he uses the empty magic square to calculate, drawing horizontal, vertical, and diagonal lines through the middle square to show that it is involved in four sums.] How many digits appear four times? Only the 5, that's the only digit that appears four times. So if there's a solution: Guess what, this is a completely independent proof, 5 has to go in the center square. [He writes 5 in the center.]

He uses this idea to show where the other numbers in the magic square must be placed—numbers which appear in only two of the listed triples must go in "side pockets" and numbers which appear in three of the listed triples must go in corners.

The finding of two solutions has been enacted.

> Now we've beat it to death. Are we done? [He pauses and looks at the class.] Of course not, because so far we've only solved the problem I gave you. If that's how mathematics progressed, mathematics wouldn't progress. Solving known problems is not what mathematicians get paid for nor is it anything they have fun doing.

Schoenfeld's closing statement illustrates some themes of the course, that problems may have multiple solutions and that solving a given problem is only the beginning (problems can be generalized, extended, etc.). This is one of the aspects of the course that reflects mathematical practice (Kitcher, 1984). After Schoenfeld's statement, students suggested extensions and generalizations of the magic square. In session 3, the class discussed ways of generating 3 by 3 magic squares with entries other than the numbers from 1 to 9. In session 4, after finding there are no non-trivial 2 by 2 magic squares, the students conjectured that there is no even-dimensional magic square, Mitch discussed a procedure for generating a 5 by 5 magic square, Christina[13] described a procedure for generating one of odd dimension, and Devon showed that the magic number of a 3 by 3 magic square is always divisible by 3 and that the number in the center is always one third of the magic number. This was followed by a discussion of what a magic cube might be. In session 9 Schoenfeld provided a counterexample to the conjecture that no non-trivial magic squares of even dimension exist by showing the students an engraving of Dürer's *Melancholia* which depicts a 4 by 4 magic square.

Why teach a class this way?

Implicit in the preceding description is the question of why Schoenfeld chooses to conduct his class in the manner he does. A proof that the magic square has a solution that is unique modulo symmetry could have been given in far less time. Why do it this way?

I'll begin with the issue of blackboard writing. The writing that appeared on the blackboard was devoted to names of heuristics, diagrams, an equation, and a question. One might consider Schoenfeld's blackboard writing to be in conflict with traditional mathematical practice, since it differs greatly from the kind of writing seen in textbooks and articles and in other mathematics classrooms. It was, as Schoenfeld says, "sparse and sloppy" (audio taped discussion, March 8, 1991) while that of textbooks, articles, and traditional mathematics classes is profuse and precise.

Certainly writing is an important part of mathematical discourse. However, its relationship with the way mathematics is done is not obvious to those who aren't mathematicians. Mathematicians' descriptions of mathematics show that writing is but one way of communicating mathematically. Davis and Hersh's (1986) Ideal Mathematician communicates results to fellow experts "in a casual shorthand" but in published writings "follows an unbreakable convention: to conceal any sign that the author or the intended reader is a human being." Stewart (1993) points out that,

> Much of mathematics is communicated by informal discussions over coffee, seminars, lectures, and other media that do not produce permanent records. When important mathematical ideas are "in the air," other mathematicians

---

[13]Christina was a computer science major who entered the class in the third session.

get to hear of them by these informal routes, long before anything appears in a technical journal. (p. 121)

Thurston's description of mathematical communication gives a sense of the differences between spoken informal mathematics and formal written mathematics.

> One-on-one, people use wide channels of communication that go far beyond formal mathematical language. They use gestures, they draw pictures and diagrams, they make sound effects and use body language. Communication is more likely to be two-way, so that people can concentrate on what needs the most attention .... In talks, people are more inhibited and more formal .... In papers, people are still more formal. Writers translate their ideas into symbols and logic, and readers try to translate back. (1994, p. 166)

The description of the genesis of a proof by De Millo et al. (1986) suggests that written mathematics is the end of a long process which begins with informal communication.

> In its first incarnation, a proof is a spoken message, or at most a sketch on a chalkboard or a paper napkin. That spoken stage is the first filter for a proof. If it generates no excitement or belief among his friends, the wise mathematician reconsiders it. But if they find it tolerably interesting and believable, he writes it up. After it has circulated in draft for a while, if it still seems plausible, he does a polished version and submits it for publication. If the referees also find it attractive and convincing, it gets published so it can be read by a wider audience. (p. 272)

This aspect of mathematics is generally hidden from students (Rogers, 1992). One doesn't often see the genesis of a proof in a classroom, instead one sees the end-product of the process described above, presented in detached language that erases its author and origins. Such classroom experiences help to explain why students' ideas about the nature of mathematics are sometimes so very different from those of mathematicians. Some students may not even believe that mathematics is done by human beings (Belenky et al., 1986) just as some city children used to believe that milk grows in bottles. Work in cognitive science has shown that students' beliefs about the nature of a subject may have profound effects on their learning of it (McLeod, 1992). De-emphasizing writing and formal mathematics, not only reflects mathematical practice, but may also change students' beliefs about the nature and the doing of mathematics.

De-emphasizing writing and formal mathematics may have other consequences for students' learning. Thurston suggests that familiarity with the ideas of a subfield of mathematics may need to precede the ability to recognize the same ideas in written form.

> People familiar with ways of doing things in a subfield recognize various patterns of statements or formulas as idioms or circumlocutions for certain concepts or mental images. But to people not already familiar with what's

going on the same patterns are not very illuminating; they are often even misleading. The language is not alive except to those who use it. (p. 167)

In general, students of mathematics, like those new to a subfield of mathematics, are not already familiar with what's going on. Mathematicians who want to learn about a subfield usually ask what the ideas, questions, and objects of that subfield are. Unlike mathematicians, students may not know to ask those questions and to look for idioms and circumlocutions in written mathematics. When they encounter written mathematics they may be focused on its form rather than its meaning; reading each line of a proof, rather than trying to understand the ideas behind it. More importantly, they may not have any sense that such ideas exist.

This suggests that an emphasis on formal written mathematics causes difficulty for students, both from a cognitive and a metacognitive perspective. Students don't appear to perceive and interpret formal mathematics as mathematicians do.[14] Their beliefs about the way mathematics is done and hence how they should learn mathematics are derived from presentations of finished products. It seems unlikely that their beliefs could be changed by seeing even more formal mathematics, particularly since the students' means of interpreting that formal mathematics would have to be addressed at the same time. Biographies of many mathematicians suggest that informal mathematical experiences, often occurring outside of the classroom, were an important factor in their mathematical development (see for instance, Albers & Alexanderson, 1985; Albers, Alexanderson, & Reid, 1990; Hersh & John-Steiner, 1993; Ulam, 1976; Weil, 1992).

Thurston's statement, "The language is not alive except to those who use it" and Schoenfeld's (1994) statement, "When mathematics is taught as dry, disembodied, knowledge to be received, it is learned (and forgotten or not used) in that way" outline extreme cases which might illuminate the problem of how to teach students mathematics. What I have tried to suggest in analyzing the language of Schoenfeld's classroom discussion, is that the discussion is an example of embodying mathematics—presenting it as a particular kind of communication to be used by all the people in that classroom, rather than as knowledge to be learned. The complexity inherent in the word "communication" is suggested by listing some of its components (Saville-Troike, 1989): linguistic knowledge; interaction skills (this includes perception of salient features and norms of interpretation); cultural knowledge (this includes values, attitudes, and schemata). In this view, transmission of knowledge and skills is just one aspect of communication. Similarly, communication among mathematicians is not restricted to formal writing, it includes other methods: informal writing, as well as talking, gesturing. Moreover, values, attitudes, and schemata are an important part of mathematical communication. The work of Schoenfeld and others suggests that these other aspects of mathematical communication play an important role in

---

[14]In cognitive science terms, students don't appear to have schemata for formal mathematics similar to those of mathematicians.

students' learning of mathematics. Schoenfeld's classroom suggests that such aspects of mathematical communication may be taught inside as well as outside the classroom and thus, unlike me and many other mathematicians, students need not wait until they begin doing research to start communicating mathematically.

CONCLUDING DISCUSSION

In this section we synthesize our analyses of the early stages of Schoenfeld's problem solving course and offer some implications. We began this article with an illustration of some long-term goals of Schoenfeld's problem solving course: That the class become a "mathematical community" advancing and defending conjectures and proofs on mathematical grounds; and that the locus of authority be the "mathematical community," not the teacher. Because students' experiences in mathematics classrooms are, in general, very different from those of the community he wishes to create, achieving these goals is not easy and the path from the beginning of the course to a microcosm "of selected aspects of mathematical practice and culture" (Schoenfeld, 1994, p. 66) is not obvious. Rather than examining its later stages when its beginnings were likely to be invisible, we focused on the course at its inception. Our initial question was: How does Schoenfeld create a community of problem solvers where undergraduates learn to think and do mathematics, when their past experience in mathematics has mainly involved listening, writing notes, and learning procedures?

Short-term goals

After twelve or more years of schooling, undergraduates usually have well-developed expectations about how mathematics classes will run and how mathematics teachers will behave. Instructors of courses that differ from these expectations often find that students question their competence, the value of the course, or what they are expected to do in the class. Because Schoenfeld's course is an elective, if students decide he is not competent, that the course is not of value, or they don't understand what they will be asked to do, they may well leave the course. The students who stay in the course will need to understand what they are expected to do. Schoenfeld's path to achieving a "classroom mathematical community" includes the short-term goals of:

- establishing his "credentials";
- showing the students that heuristics are an important part of mathematics;
- giving the students a sense of what the course is about;
- communicating his expectations for classroom behavior.[15]

The first two goals are related to an ancient pedagogical problem (cf. Plato's *Protagoras*): How can a student ignorant of a subject judge whether or not some-

---

[15]Or as Schoenfeld put it (audiotaped discussion, May 22, 1991) "letting them know what they're in for."

one is capable of teaching it? The last two goals address a similar problem: How can students be asked to do mathematics (in some ways) like mathematicians if they have no idea how mathematicians do mathematics?

Schoenfeld's solution includes illustration and enactment. Here we use "enactment" in a somewhat theatrical sense. His introduction to the course and his treatment of the telescoping series portrayed him, though by different means, as both a member and critic of the mathematical community. The introduction was a monologue not involving the students. In contrast the caricature of the "typical calculus professor" enacted the distinction between how mathematics is presented in classrooms and how it is done by mathematicians using heuristics. Rather than telling the students about the drawbacks of traditional mathematics teaching, Schoenfeld depicted them in his caricature, then modeled the solution of a mathematician. During the discussion of the next two problems the students responded with traditional behaviors and then, with Schoenfeld's prompting, enacted some of the mathematical behaviors that he was trying to establish.

The discussion of the inscribed square illustrated the power of heuristics and the skill required to use them successfully. Students will, on average, not succeed in showing that a square can be inscribed in an arbitrary triangle, whether or not the heuristic Try an Easier Related Problem is suggested, so they will consider it a difficult problem. Because that difficult problem will yield, when an appropriate heuristic is suggested and its use scaffolded (Collins, Brown, & Newman, 1989), the inscribed square problem serves to show the power of heuristics in obtaining a solution—as well as the skill required to use them successfully. Allowing students to struggle may be an essential part of this process, both in showing the power of heuristics and Schoenfeld's ability to teach them. Students often aren't conscious of the important role that non-traditional teachers' suggestions and questions play in their progress toward a solution and sometimes conclude that such teachers don't know very much mathematics—otherwise they would tell them the answer. The first student presentation gave Schoenfeld an opportunity to mention a traditional student behavior, looking to the teacher for approval, and to have one of his expectations for classroom behavior enacted, that students not look to him for approval. This was a step toward the long-term goal of shifting the locus of authority away from the teacher and having the class, aided by Schoenfeld's "nasty questions," develop its own standards of correctness. The presentation also allowed the enactment of another expectation, that of "not just beautiful finished solutions but also explanations of how and why."

The discussion of the magic square served different goals: illustrating uses of heuristics and the theme of multiple solutions, and as a vehicle to engage students in discussion. It showed that different heuristics can be used singly or in combination to solve the same problem. (In contrast, the inscribed square showed that the same heuristic can be used in different ways on the same problem, a different illustration of the theme of multiple solutions.) Because it is easy to solve, the magic square could not be used to illustrate the power of heuristics in obtaining a solution. Instead it allowed students to focus on the use of heuristics. Students find generalizations of the magic square easy,[16] hence Schoenfeld could and did use it to have students enact another long-term goal of the course: That students take problems and make them their own by extension or generalization.

Pedagogy

Planning, direction, and authority

The sequence of problems and associated activities (Schoenfeld's introduction to the course, lectures, reflective presentations, student presentations, small-group work, and whole-class discussions) give an overall structure for the first days of the course. The problems are not chosen to cover content in the traditional sense, but to make certain points about heuristics and the course. Schoenfeld has used the telescoping series, inscribed square, and magic square for years. He was thus familiar with probable student responses to each in the contexts that he provides. For example, he knew what students are likely to do with the inscribed square without heuristics, and with the heuristics Try an Easier Related Problem and Relax a Condition. In this sense he controlled the class in the same way someone who digs a ditch controls the water flowing through it: The overall structure for the course channeled students' "natural" responses in directions that served many of Schoenfeld's goals. At some points (for example in the discussion of "easier related problems" for the inscribed square) without additional direction students might have become entangled in a fruitless exploration—an authentic mathematical experience, but one which was not likely to encourage students to stay in the course or have confidence in its teacher. At such points Schoenfeld used his authority as a teacher and mathematician to guide the flow of the discussion. However, a goal of the course is that the teacher not remain the sole authority. Schoenfeld's delegation of authority to the students during Devon's presentation of his solution for the inscribed square problem was a step toward satisfying this long-term goal.

Opportunism

Within the structure imposed by the sequence of problems, the heuristics illustrated by the problems, and the activities surrounding them there is room for opportunism (Hayes-Roth & Hayes-Roth, 1979; Schoenfeld et al., 1992). Schoenfeld's knowledge of the problems (and of mathematics) allowed him to take advantage of student remarks such as Devon's suggestion about a solution for the magic square. Here the analogy might be to a navigator who knows how to get to a particular location in any event, but is able to take advantage of an unexpected wind not only to arrive, but arrive sooner. In this case, Devon's suggestion provided a context not only for discussing Working Backwards which Schoenfeld

---

[16] "Easy" like "difficult" has an operational definition in this context—if, on average, students readily suggest generalizations of this problem, then generalizations of the problem can be said to be easy.

would do in any case (Schoenfeld, 1991), but showing it as a possible source for Devon's suggestion. This satisfied the goal of discussing Working Backwards and additional goals: incorporating student suggestions and again illustrating the notion of "not just beautiful finished solutions but also explanations of how and why."

Discourse and communication

Schoenfeld also used Pólya's method of questioning to involve the students in using heuristics. This method of questioning has social and cognitive aspects. On the one hand, Schoenfeld was asking for a response from the students which got them talking, helping to begin the community he wished to establish. On the other, the method of questioning scaffolded the students' applications of heuristics to particular cases. Other features of classroom communication (involved language, involved gestures, informal blackboard writings) suggested that the class was doing mathematics rather than being presented with mathematics.

In summary, we suggest that important elements in achieving the short-term goals for the first days of the course were:

- the sequence of problems Schoenfeld used;
- his knowledge of probable student responses to the problems;
- his knowledge of possible solutions to the problems and the heuristics that generate them;[17]
- his use and delegation of authority;
- his patterns of written and oral communication, and classroom discourse.

Implications

We will not venture to draw universal implications from a study of two days in one classroom. Nor is our intent to prescribe a teaching method. Instead, we hope this example will help to illuminate the difficult task of teaching mathematics.

Teaching is sometimes dichotomized as either transmission or discovery.[18] In the language of calculus reform (e.g., *UME Trends*, 1995) a teacher is either a "sage on the stage" or "guide on the side." Because it contains elements of both, Schoenfeld's teaching provides a counterexample to this notion. The form (though not always the content) of his presentations to the class contains traditional elements such as lecturing and blackboard expertise, but he combines these with non-traditional elements such as questioning and student work in groups. Furthermore, our analyses show that characterizing teaching in terms

---

[17]What we have labeled here "knowledge of probable student responses to the problems" and "knowledge of possible solutions and the heuristics that generate them" is related to Shulman's notions of pedagogical content knowledge and subject matter knowledge (Fennema & Franke, 1992; Shulman, 1987).

[18]We thank Barbara Pence for reminding us of this.

of use and frequency of methods such as lecture, small-group work, and whole-class discussion is inadequate because such characterizations omit the complex interaction between curriculum and pedagogy.

The problem solving course also counters the notion that a curriculum must be composed of individual strategies which are learned and practiced separately. Traditional algebra and calculus courses do just that—and instructors find to their dismay that students know the strategies, but may not know when to apply them. However, instructors who simply change course curricula without addressing student beliefs and expectations often find their students bewildered or resistant (see e.g., Cipra, 1995; Culotta, 1992). In turn, instructors often react by returning to traditional practices, and thus the status quo is maintained.

The curriculum and pedagogy of Schoenfeld's problem solving course suggests a way to alter unmathematical student habits—that they be enacted, mentioned, and revised. For example, the unsystematic listing of the triples in the magic square or the student looking to the teacher for approval were situations in which typical student behavior occurred (and was expected to occur), was commented upon, and an alternative enacted. Such situations can be engineered in other courses as they are in the problem solving course. Here is a brief sketch of an example: Students can be asked to work a problem that can be solved by a strategy that has just been taught, then asked to work a problem that is superficially similar but which can't be solved using the same strategy. Students' usual response is to try the most recently taught strategy. The instructor is then provided with an opportunity to mention that an important part of knowing a strategy is the recognition of the situations in which it can and can not be used—and to comment on the expectation that problems given in class are to be solved using the material that has been most recently taught. As with all curricular and pedagogical changes, this one would probably require several cycles of trial and refinement.

Final commentary

Pólya wrote in 1963:

> Everybody demands that the high school should impart to the students not only information in mathematics but know-how, independence, originality, creativity. Yet almost nobody asks these beautiful things for the mathematics teacher—is it not remarkable? . . . Here, in my opinion, is the worst gap in the subject matter knowledge of the high school teacher: he [or she] has no experience of active mathematical work. . . . (Pólya, 1981, p. 113)

Current reforms in precollege education make the experience of active mathematical work even more necessary for teachers now than in 1963. Moreover, studies suggest that prospective mathematicians, as well as prospective teachers, benefit from such an experience (Tucker, 1995). But it is still the case that few undergraduate courses offer students the opportunity to do, rather than ingest, mathematics (Tucker, 1995). Instructors have little opportunity to observe such courses and those who do may have little time in which to make sense of their curriculum and pedagogy. We hope in this article to have provided a useful substitute for a visit to one such course.

REFERENCES

1. Albers, Donald J. & Alexanderson, Gerald. L. (Eds.) (1985). *Mathematical people: Profiles and interviews*. Boston: Birkhauser.
2. Albers, Donald. J., Alexanderson, Gerald. L., & Reid, Constance. (Eds.) (1990). *More mathematical people: Contemporary conversations*. Boston: Harcourt Brace Jovanovich.
3. Ball, Deborah L. & Chazan, Dan. (1994 April). An examination of teacher telling in constructivist mathematics pedagogy: Not just excusable but essential. Paper presented at the 1994 Annual Meeting of the American Educational Research Association, New Orleans, April.
4. Belenky, Mary F., Clinchy, Blythe M., Goldberger, Nancy R., & Tarule, J. M. (1986). *Women's ways of knowing: The development of self, voice, and mind*. New York: Basic Books.
5. Brousseau, Guy. (1986). Fondements et méthodes de la didactique des mathématiques. *Recherches en didactique des mathématiques* 7(2) 33–115.
6. Chafe, Wallace & Danielewizc, Jane. (1987). *Properties of spoken and written language*, Technical report no. 7. Berkeley, CA: Center for the Study of Writing: University of California.
7. Cipra, Barry (1995). The bumpy road to reform. *UME Trends* 6(6) 16, 19.
8. Clarke, David. (1995 April). Using assessment to renegotiate the didactic contract. Paper presented at the 1995 Annual Meeting of the American Educational Research Association, San Francisco, April 18–22.
9. Clarke, David, Wallbridge, Margarita, & Fraser, Sherry. (1992). *The other consequences of a problem-based mathematics curriculum*. Research Report No. 3. Victoria, Australia: Mathematics Teaching and Learning Centre, Australian Catholic University, Christ Campus.
10. Collins, Allan, Brown, John Seeley, & Newman, Susan. (1989). Cognitive apprenticeship: Teaching the crafts of reading, writing, and mathematics. In Lauren B. Resnick (Ed.), *Knowing, learning, and instruction: Essays in honor of Robert Glaser* (pp. 453–494). Hillsdale, NJ: Lawrence Erlbaum Associates.
11. Cooney, Thomas J. (1985). A beginning teacher's view of problem solving. *Journal for Research in Mathematics Education, 16*, 324–336.
12. Culotta, Elizabeth (1992). The calculus of education reform. *Science* 255 (1060–1062).
13. Davis, Philip J. (1986). Fidelity in mathematical discourse. In Thomas Tymoczko (Ed.), *New directions in the philosophy of mathematics* (pp. 163–175). Boston: Birkhauser.
14. Davis, Philip J. & Hersh, Reuben (1986). The ideal mathematician. In Thomas Tymoczko (Ed.), *New directions in the philosophy of mathematics* (pp. 177–184). Boston: Birkhauser.
15. De Millo, Richard A., Lipton, Richard J., & Perlis, Alan J. (1986). Social processes and proofs of theorems and programs. In Thomas Tymoczko (Ed.), *New directions in the philosophy of mathematics* (pp. 267–285). Boston: Birkhauser.
16. Ernest, Paul. (1991). *The philosophy of mathematics education*. Basingstoke, England: Falmer Press.
17. Fauvel, John. (1988). Cartesian and Euclidean rhetoric. *For the Learning of Mathematics* 8(1), 25–29.
18. Fennema, Elizabeth & Franke, Megan L. (1992). Teachers' knowledge and its impact. In Douglas A. Grouws (Ed.), *Handbook of research on mathematics teaching and learning* (pp. 147–164). New York: Macmillan.
19. Hayes-Roth, Barbara & Hayes-Roth, Frederick. (1979). A cognitive model of planning. *Cognitive Science 3*, 275–310.

20. Hersh, Reuben & John-Steiner, Vera. (1993). A visit to Hungarian mathematics. *The Mathematical Intelligencer 15*(2) 13–26.

21. Kitcher, Philip. (1984). *The nature of mathematical knowledge*. New York: Oxford.

22. Lester, Frank K., Garofalo, Joe, & Kroll, Diana L. (1989). *The role of metacognition in mathematical problem solving: A study of two grade seven classes*. Final report to the National Science Foundation of NSF project MDR 85-50346.

23. McLeod, Douglas B. (1992). Research on affect in mathematics education: A reconceptualization. In Douglas A. Grouws (Ed.), *Handbook of research on mathematics teaching and learning* (pp. 575–596). New York: Macmillan.

24. McNeill, David. (1992). *Hand and mind: What gestures reveal about thought*. Chicago: University of Chicago Press.

25. Mason, John, Burton, Leone, & Stacey, Kaye. (1982). *Thinking mathematically*. New York: Addison Wesley.

26. Mura, Roberta (1995). Images of mathematics held by university teachers of mathematics education. *Educational Studies in Mathematics 28*, 385–399.

27. National Center for Educational Statistics. (1993). *Data compendium for the NAEP 1992 mathematics assessment of the nation and the states*. Washington, DC: National Center for Educational Statistics.

28. Newman, Denis, Griffin, Peg, & Cole, Michael. (1989). *The construction zone: Working for cognitive change in schools*. Cambridge: Cambridge University Press.

29. Pimm, David. (1987). *Speaking mathematically: Communication in mathematics classrooms*. London: Routledge & Kegan Paul.

30. Pólya, George. (1973). *How to solve it: A new aspect of mathematical method*. Princeton NJ: Princeton University Press (Second printing).

31. Pólya, George (1981). *Mathematical discovery*. New York: Wiley.

32. Reznick, Bruce (1994). Some thoughts on writing for the Putnam. In Alan H. Schoenfeld, Ed., *Mathematical thinking and problem solving* (pp. 19–29). Hillsdale, NJ: Erlbaum.

33. Rogers, Pat (1992). Thoughts on power and pedagogy. In Leone Burton (Ed.), *Gender and mathematics: An international perspective* (pp. 38–45). London: Cassell.

34. Rotman, Brian (1993). *Ad infinitum: The ghost in Turing's machine*. Stanford: Stanford University Press.

35. Saville-Troike, Muriel (1989). *The ethnography of communication*. Oxford: Basil Blackwell, Ltd.

36. Schoenfeld, Alan H. (1982). Measures of problem solving performance and of problem solving instruction. *Journal for Research in Mathematics Education 13*(1), 31–49.

37. Schoenfeld, Alan H. (1983). *Problem solving in the mathematics curriculum: A report, recommendations, and an annotated bibliography*. Washington, DC: Mathematics Association of America.

38. Schoenfeld, Alan H. (1985). *Mathematical problem solving*. New York: Academic Press.

39. Schoenfeld, Alan H. (1987). What's all the fuss about metacognition? In Alan H. Schoenfeld (Ed.), *Cognitive science and mathematics education* (pp. 189–215). Hillsdale, NJ: Lawrence Erlbaum Associates.

40. Schoenfeld, Alan H. (1988). Ideas in the air: Speculations on small-group learning, environment and cultural influences on cognition, and epistemology. *International Journal of Educational Research, 13*, 71–88.

41. Schoenfeld, Alan H. (1989a). Teaching mathematical thinking and problem solving. In Lauren B. Resnick and Leopold E. Klopfer (Eds.), *Toward the thinking curriculum: Current cognitive research* (pp. 83–103). Alexandria, VA: Association for Supervision and Curriculum Development.

42. Schoenfeld, Alan H. (1989b). The curious fate of an applied problem. *College Mathematics Journal, 20*(2), 115–123.

43. Schoenfeld, Alan H. (1991). On mathematics as sense-making: An informal attack on the unfortunate divorce of formal and informal mathematics. In James Voss, David Perkins and Judith Segal (Eds.), *Informal reasoning and education* (pp. 311–343). Hillsdale, NJ: Erlbaum.

44. Schoenfeld, Alan H. (1992a). Learning to think mathematically: Problem solving, metacognition, and sense making in mathematics. In Douglas Grouws (Ed.), *Handbook of research on mathematics teaching and learning* (pp. 334–370). New York: Macmillan.

45. Schoenfeld, Alan H. (1992b). On paradigms and methods: What do you do when the ones you know don't do what you want them to? *Journal of the Learning Sciences 2*(2) 179–214.

46. Schoenfeld, Alan H. (1994). Reflections on doing and teaching mathematics. In Alan H. Schoenfeld (Ed.), *Mathematical thinking and problem solving* (pp. 53–70). Hillsdale, NJ: Lawrence Erlbaum Associates.

47. Schoenfeld, Alan H., Gamoran, Miriam, Kessel, Cathy, Leonard, Michael, Orbach, Rachel, & Arcavi, Abraham. (1992). Toward a comprehensive model of human tutoring in complex subject matter domains. *Journal of Mathematical Behavior, 11*(4), 293–320.

48. Schoenfeld, Alan H., Minstrell, Jim, & van Zee, Emily. (1996 April). The detailed analysis of an established teacher carrying out a non-traditional lesson. Paper presented at the 1996 Annual Meeting of the American Education Research Association, New York, April 8–12.

49. Schoenfeld, Alan H., Smith, John P., & Arcavi, Abraham. (1993). Learning: The microgenetic analysis of one student's understanding of a complex subject matter domain. In Robert Glaser (Ed.), *Advances in Instructional Psychology (Volume 4)* (pp. 55–175). Hillsdale, NJ: Erlbaum.

50. Shulman, Lee. (1987). Knowledge and teaching: Foundations of the new reform. *Harvard Educational Review 57*(1) 1–22.

51. Silver, Edward A. (1985). Research on teaching mathematical problem solving: Some underrepresented themes and needed directions. In Edward A. Silver (Ed.), *Teaching and learning mathematical problem solving: Multiple research perspectives* (pp. 247–266). Hillsdale, NJ: Erlbaum.

52. Stewart, Ian (1993). Möbius's modern legacy. In John Fauvel, Raymond Flood, and Robin Wilson (Eds.), *Möbius and his band: Mathematics and astronomy in nineteenth-century Germany* (pp. 121–160). New York: Oxford University Press.

53. Thurston, William P. (1994). On proof and progress in mathematics. *Bulletin of the American Mathematical Society 30*(2) 161–177.

54. Tucker, Alan C. (ed.) (1995). *Models that work: Case studies in effective undergraduate mathematics programs*, MAA Notes no. 38. Washington, DC: The Mathematical Association of America.

55. Ulam, Stanislaw M. (1976). *Adventures of a mathematician*. New York: Scribner.

56. *UME Trends* (1995). [Issue on calculus reform] *6*(6).

57. University of Michigan (1993). *The new calculus at the University of Michigan progress report*. Ann Arbor, MI: University of Michigan.

58. Weil, Andre (1992). *The apprenticeship of a mathematician* (Jennifer Gage, Trans.). Boston: Birkhauser. (Original work published 1991).

Appendix A: Schoenfeld's introduction to the course

OK ... Let me give you a little sense of what the course is about—a little bit of history. My name is Alan Schoenfeld. This is Math 67. It's a course in problem solving. It's a hands-on course. You'll spend most of the time in class solving problems, talking about them, doing mathematics. This is one of the rare courses in the department—in the country—where you actually *do* mathematics from the very beginning. The idea is to give you a chance to do some explorations, learn some neat stuff about problem solving.

Here's some of the history ...

Way back in what seems like the dark ages—early 1970's—I was a young mathematician, had finished my degree, was a topologist and measure theorist happily proving theorems as beginning assistant professor, when I tripped across a book called *How to Solve It* written by George Pólya in 1947. Pólya is— was one of the eminent mathematicians of this century—probably one of the ten, fifteen greatest mathematicians of the 20th century. When he was about sixty, he decided—that was in the late 1940's—he decided: "You know, I've led a long and productive life. It's time for me to sit down and maybe think about start writing some things that would help other people to do and learn about mathematics." So he wrote this little thing called *How to Solve It*, in which he did a lot of introspection, said basically: "You know, there are some things that seem to be productive ways to solve problems, for me, for other mathematicians—ways of thinking that we've picked up, tricks of the trade that enable us to be really successful at solving problems. And they help us a lot. Maybe if I wrote them down—shared them—it would make life a little bit easier for other people as well." He went on, stayed in that business for another thirty or so years, productively until his mid-nineties.

I read the book in 1974 when I was a very young mathematician, and had a very funny reaction to it. I started out, read a few pages ... and he said, "Mathematicians do this." I read a few more ... he said, "Mathematicians do this." And I started to smile. "Hot damn, I must be a real mathematician—I do all the things Pólya says they do!" Then got pissed off, and said, "Hey, wait a sec. You know, here I am. I finished an undergraduate career. I went through an entire career as a graduate student. I'm a young professional. *Now* for the first time I'm reading about these tricks of the trade. Why didn't they tell me when I was a freshman, and save me the trouble of discovering all of them for myself? Maybe it's a version of the medieval trial by gauntlet: the only people we want are the ones who succeed without knowing the rules." I don't know ...

So I asked around, and I asked some of the people who prepared people for problem solving competitions. There is a thing called the Putnam exam that a lot of people study for—if you do well on it you're guaranteed admission to the graduate school of your choice. I asked people who were in mathematics education. And the uniform response I got was:

Every mathematician I talked to said, "Yup, Pólya is absolutely right. My guts tell me he is right. I do the things he writes about." And every problem solving coach, and everyone I talked to who was involved in getting students to solve problems better, said, "You know, it's a strange thing. I've never been able to use Pólya's ideas in such a way that my students actually wound up being better at it. So I don't use them very much anymore."

That was the intellectual dilemma that in the mid-1970's got me to turn to problem solving and got me to focus on it, as the main thing that I would do for the next 15 years. 'Cause on the one hand, I believe in the ideas that Pólya had. And on the other hand I believe the people who said, "As constituted, Pólya's ideas don't work." So what I've been involved in largely for the past 15 years is figuring out how to make those ideas work—figuring out what it is that it takes to use the kind of problem solving strategies that he talks about, effectively; and through the years building and changing and modifying this course so that it works. And the one thing that I can guarantee you is: It does work. By the end of this course you will have an arsenal of problem solving tools and techniques that will enable you to be much more successful, not only in solving problems that you've been shown how to solve, but also at encountering new things and making sense of them—which is something that your math courses don't normally train you how to do.

I'll tell you about the ideal goals for a course like this and then, what I actually did as evidence of what you can expect to be in for; and then I'll tell what the structure of the course will be; and then I'll stop talking and we'll do what we should do, which is get on to solving problems.

The goal of this course is to give you enough experience and exposure to solving problems and learning about the tools and techniques of the trade so that you walk out of this course a far more resourceful and better problem solver, ... again, at not only at dealing with the kinds of things I've shown you to deal with in the course, but also when you encounter something new—having at your disposal a set of techniques that will enable you to make progress on and make sense of a problem that you haven't been shown how to solve.

Here's the ideal test for the course. I've been in problem solving for fifteen, twenty years. There are other people who have massive reputations for such things. There's a guy named Paul Halmos who used to be editor of the *American Mathematical Monthly*, who's been writing about problem solving forever. The kind of thing you might want to do is say to Halmos, "Hey, look. Schoenfeld's gonna teach his problem solving course. Here are the backgrounds of his students. Here are the kind of people you can expect to see in the course. What we'd like you to do is make up two tests. Make up a matched pretest and posttest, which in some sense are identical in content. And, he won't know what's in your tests; you won't know what's in his course. If he really does what he says he does, then his students should do far better on the posttest than they did on the pretest. And other kids taking, say math H50A, or analysis, or Riemann surfaces, shouldn't really show any performance difference." *That* would be the sort of iron-clad test that I did something in this course.

I never had the nerve to do that [giggles from the class, Schoenfeld smiles]. But I'll tell you what I did—which was worse—some two or three versions of the course ago. I gave an in-class final exam. (Now I actually prefer, although rules require in-class exams ... what you'll be doing is a couple of take-homes, for the mid-term and final, just a *pro forma* simple in-class written exam.) I gave an in-class final, and there were three parts to the final exam. The first part was problems like the problems we solved in class. No surprise, you expect people to do well on those. The second part was problems that could be solved by the methods that we used in class—but ones for which if you looked at them you couldn't recognize that they had obvious features similar to the ones that we'd studied in class. So yes, you had the tools and techniques, but you had to be pretty clever about recognizing that they were appropriate. And, the class did pretty well on those too. Part three of the final exam . . . There's a collection of books called the *Hungarian Problem Books* which have some of the nastiest mathematical problems known to man and woman. I went through those, and as soon as I found a problem I couldn't make any sense of, whatsoever, I put it on the final. (I know that makes you feel good.) [Laughter from class, Schoenfeld smiles.] The class did spectacularly well, and actually wound up solving some problems I didn't, OK—which is pretty good proof that amazing things happen in the class. And they happen, I think, because we're serious about really doing mathematics— which is the name of the game. So let me tell you a bit about what's gonna happen.

Most days I'm going to walk in (today being only a slight exception in the sequence), and hand out a bunch of problems. I've got enough here to probably keep us busy for two days or so. And what you're seeing here is unusual, because you won't be seated in rows watching me talk. Instead you're going to break into groups of three or four or five, and work on problems together. As you're working on them, I'll circulate through the room, occasionally make comments about the kinds of things you're doing, respond to questions from you. But, by and large, I'll just nudge you to keep working on the problems.

Then at some point I'll call us to order as a group, and we'll start discussing the things that you've done, and talk about the things that you've pushed and why; what's been successful, what hasn't. I'll mention a variety of specific mathematical techniques as we go through the problems. Many of the problems are chosen so that they illustrate useful techniques. So you'll work on one for a while; may or may not make some progress; and then we'll talk about it. And as we talk about it what I'll do is indicate some of the problem solving strategies that I know, and that are in the literature, that might help you make progress on this problem, and progress on other problems. And we'll use those strategies as a means of bootstrapping our way into the problems.

The course is pretty wide-open. I've taught it now seven or eight times, every other year, thereabouts. And every year the course is different, because it turns out to be a creature of the people in it. Everything mathematical is fair game in here, which means that you'll find if we get turned on by a problem, we'll push it. If we see interesting things, we'll pursue that particular domain of mathematics for a while. The bottom line is: I'm happy when we're doing real mathematics. What that means may not be clear to you now but it will become increasingly clear during the semester ... and this for me is the course I most love teaching 'cause it's the greatest fun and the one that is most involving for both me and my students.

As I said, what's going to happen is: Most days I'll hand out problems. We'll work on them in class. Some of the problems can be solved fairly fast and some of them merely serve as introductions to more conjectures and more problems. Other problems may be things that we visit for two or three days—of classes—maybe even a week or two as we do something, find something interesting in it, but don't make enough progress as a group; so I'll say, "Fine, let's get back to it next time" and we'll keep working on the problem over a period of days. So what we do the vast majority of times in here is just do and talk mathematics. And learn some mathematics.

The grading for the course. Well, a week or two into the class I'll give you the opportunity to write out a problem or two for me so that I can get a sense of the kind of writing you do, and give you some feedback on the kind of writing I expect. The first main thing we do is: about half-way through the course I'll give you a two-week take-home. It'll consist of about ten problems and they will occupy you for a long time. But you'll make progress on them and you'll do reasonably well on them. And then, the final. Again, the department formally requires me to give an in-class final, so I usually wind up giving a one-problem in-class final to meet the rules and regulations. That's about ten percent of the final exam grade. The rest of it is another take-home that you'll have two weeks to work on. There are some funny rules, which are that:

What counts is not simply the answer, what counts is doing mathematics. And that means, among other things, if you can find two different ways to solve a problem, you'll get twice as much credit for it. If you can extend the problem and generalize it and make it your own, you'll get even more. The bottom line is, I'd like to have you doing some mathematics and I will do everything I can—including using grading—as a device for having you do that. Grades turn out to be pretty much of a non-issue in the course. What usually happens is, people get sucked into it. You get out of the course what you put into it, basically—that becomes clear. If you haven't done much through the semester, you'll find you're not ready to do terribly well on the midterm and final; if you have, you'll find that you'll do fairly well. Anyone who kicks in and just participates actively during the semester (it's obvious) and no one who's done that has ever gotten less than C+. Typically, the grades have been mostly A's and B's because people have done very well on what's demonstrably good mathematics. So we can say more about grading when the time comes, but it really will turn out to be a non-issue. Today what I'm going to do, is just now, stop talking—that will make us all feel better—and then hand out a bunch of problems. They're especially chosen for the first day, to make a couple of points—rhetorical points about problem solving strategies. I will make those points clearer after you've worked on the problems for a while. But I think designed to give you a sense of what the rest of the semester is going to be like. OK. Anybody got any questions? [Pauses, no questions.]

OK. Then what you ought to do is break into groups of three or four or thereabouts; and you should be prepared to work together ...

[Refers to the fact that someone is videotaping the class.] Oh, the man with the camera. As I said, this is—this has been part of my own enterprise now for about 15 years. And over the years the course has developed and grown in interesting ways. And one of the things that I like to do is make sense of what happens in the course myself. I often write about it as part of my research, as well as part of my teaching. (They go hand in hand because my research is about understanding the nature of mathematical thinking and using that understanding to help build courses like this.) So that camera is a record for me of what's happened in the course, so that I can reflect on it, in the hope of making sense of it and making it better for the next round of students.

WEIZMANN INSTITUTE OF SCIENCE, ISRAEL

UNIVERSITY OF CALIFORNIA, BERKELEY, U.S.A.

UNIVERSIDADE FEDERAL DE PERNAMBUCO, BRAZIL

MICHIGAN STATE UNIVERSITY, U.S.A.

CBMS Issues in Mathematics Education
Volume **7**, 1998

On the Implementation of Mathematical Problem Solving Instruction: Qualities of Some Learning Activities

MANUEL SANTOS-TRIGO

Introduction

What type of learning activities tend to promote mathematical values during the implementation of problem solving instruction? What kind of tasks help students to engage in mathematical discussion in the classroom? What type of evaluation could be used to assess students' progress in mathematical problem solving? These are issues that need to be addressed in order to evaluate the potential use of mathematical problem-solving instruction. Valuable information about these questions comes from research programs that have focused on the importance of analyzing what students do while working with problems as a result of instruction based on mathematical problem solving. This independently produced paper expands on the content of Arcavi et al. by dealing with Schoenfeld's course taken as a whole. I will first set the context for the course by relating it to two other widely recognized approaches to teaching mathematics through problem solving.

Background

Problem solving has been part of the K-12 mathematics education program since the 1980 National Council of Teachers of Mathematics agenda for problem solving. Stanic and Kilpatrick (1988) stated that "the term problem solving has become a slogan encompassing different views of what education is, of what schooling is, of what mathematics is and of why we should teach mathematics in general and problem solving in particular." Indeed, problem solving curricula, instructional methods, and research programs differ in their principles, general goals, and instructional foci. Moreover, although there are general principles associated with problem solving instruction such as the importance of relating the practice of doing mathematics to the process of learning it, and the active participation of the students during class activities, more than one instructional approach is consistent with these principles. In consequence, it is important to document the different effects in students' learning of mathematics associated with different approaches.

Different approaches to problem solving instruction

In the early 80's several instructional approaches relied on Pólya's four-phase model as the main structure of the class (Krulik & Reys, 1980). Later, an important line of research identified fundamental differences between the behaviors of mathematicians and students as they worked on mathematical problems (expert-novice studies), and more attention was given in instruction to the role of nonroutine problems and the presence of metacognitive strategies (Schoenfeld, 1987). Recently interest has focused on the role of social factors during the learning of mathematics. "Learning occurs as people engage in activities and the meaning and significance of objects and information derive from their roles in the activities that people are engaged in" (Greeno, Smith, & Moore, 1993, p. 100). Indeed, one important feature of Schoenfeld's problem solving approach is that the students act as a mathematical community.

Three different instructional approaches are listed below. The first focuses on the importance of studying a specific mathematical idea through the discussion of particular problems; these problems often are recognized as nonroutine tasks. The second is an example in which the students directly reconstruct the main theorems associated with the course. The third focuses on the development of both cognitive and metacognitive strategies that could help students solve diverse types of problems. Schoenfeld's course falls into the third category. However, few studies have analyzed the implementation of these types of instruction in detail (Lester, 1994). Hence, we discuss not only the general principles but also the specific problems and actions taken during the course. We supplement the Arcavi et al. analysis by including further concrete problem-based examples.

Problem situations. Schroeder and Lester (1989) identify what they call teaching mathematics via problem solving as an approach to learning mathematics. The fundamental idea here is that a problem is used as a means to learn mathematical content.

> ... problems are valued not only as a purpose for learning mathematics but also as a primary means of doing so. The teaching of a mathematical topic begins with a problem situation that embodies key aspects of the topic, and mathematical techniques are developed as reasonable responses to reasonable problems. (p. 33)

Schroeder and Lester suggest that this approach could be used to study the formal content studied at school by selecting specific problems. During the discussion of such problems the students will have the opportunity to develop the mathematical content needed to solve the problems. In practice, given the rigidness and extent of the content to be covered in a regular course, difficulties might arise in selecting appropriate problems. A common variant of this approach is to use problems as a motivation to introduce specific content to the class. Another interpretation of this approach might be that the content itself is treated as a problematic situation to be discussed under the consideration of its representations, connections, and applications. Lester (1994) mentions that teaching mathematics via problem solving has not been subjected to enough research scrutiny to make any claims about its potential (footnote, p. 666). However, most of the new middle and secondary school curriculum projects currently being published employ this strategy, confronting directly the challenge of organizing large amounts of mathematical content through rich and engaging problems.

Moore method. Halmos used another instructional approach to teach a linear algebra class. The material to be studied during the development of the course consisted of the main theorems that appear in a first linear algebra course. "The first day of class, I handed each student a set of 19 pages, ..., there were ... nothing but fifty theorems stated correctly but brutally, with no expository niceties" (Halmos, 1994, p. 853). Thus, the theorems were the initial departure for discussion of various strategies, representation of information and relationships, to look for means to prove them, and then to examine and extend possible connections. Regarding his role as an instructor during the class, Halmos stated:

> I must not only be the moderator of what can easily turn into an unruly debate, but I must understand what is being presented, and when something fishy goes on I must interrupt with a firm but gentle "would you explain that please—I don't understand." (p. 853)

It may be clear that Halmos' students require a certain level of mathematical maturity to be engaged in the class discussion. Indeed, this course was offered to honors students who had shown some interest in pursuing mathematics in their careers. In relation to the success of the course, Halmos stated:

> It worked. At the second meeting of class I said "O.K., Mr. Jones, let's see you prove theorem 1," and I had to push and drag them along before they got off the ground. After a couple of weeks they were flying. They liked it, they learned from it, and they entered into the spirit of research—competition—..., glory, and all. (p. 853)

Halmos' instructional approach is a variant of the famous "Moore Method." Here, the main goal of the students is to determine whether various mathematical statements are true. The students' responses are based on providing mathematical proofs or counterexamples on their own. The Moore Method has produced well known mathematicians (Mary Ellen Rudin and Ralph Phillips to mention two); however, at the undergraduate level, students come with different mathematical backgrounds and little experience of doing proofs. As a consequence, this approach may not engage some students (Schoenfeld, 1990).

Schoenfeld's approach. Schoenfeld, in the course being studied in this volume, does not address specific content directly in the sense that choice of content follows from other goals and objectives. However, throughout the course, his students deal with specific mathematical content. For example, the basic concepts of geometry (constructions), number theory, combinatorics, and calculus are topics that frequently appear as a context in the problem solving class. It may be that the course helps students to reconceptualize their ideas about mathematics and deal with problems without focusing on specific content. However, the fact that basic mathematical ideas are addressed consistently during the course suggests an alternative organization of curriculum around problem solving and the underlying processes of mathematical practice. This idea is consistent with some curriculum proposals in which emphasis is given to the study of the essential or key mathematical concepts (Steen, 1990).

This paper focuses on documenting some events that appear consistently when using this third approach. The features of the problem solving course discussed in this paper were identified from videotapes of the 1990 course, and observations and field notes of the 1994 course. We do not intend to analyze what happened during every class, but document features of the sessions that appeared consistently throughout the course. The examples used to illustrate this approach were taken from the 1994 version of the course.

Instructional problems: The presence of mathematical morals

A basic property of the problems chosen for the course is that they offer opportunities for the students to become engaged in mathematical discussions. Another important feature of the problems discussed in the class is that there is always a mathematical moral to be derived. For example, we have seen from Kessel's discussion of the magic square problem (Can you place the numbers 1, 2, ..., 9 in a three by three box, so that the sum of each row, each column, and each diagonal is the same?) how students see and discuss the great power of the heuristic strategies. During the solution process, students discuss strategies that include establishing subgoals, working backwards, trying special cases, exploiting symmetry, making a systematic list, and exploring extreme cases. An important moral derived from the magic square problem is that what initially seems to be a trivial problem can produce interesting and even "new" mathematical knowledge for the students. This problem was, later in the course, presented to the students in a different context. There, students were challenged to recognize and apply their knowledge to other situations. The statement of the problem isomorphic to the magic square is:

> Nine counters with the digits from 1 through 9 are placed on a table. Two players with the imaginative names of A and B take turns selecting counters from the table. The winner is the first player who has a set of counters including three counters whose sum is 15. (For example: If on the 9th pick you just picked up the 7 to give yourself the set 2, 3, 6, 7, 9, then

you've won. Your opponent has 1, 4, 5, 8 and no three of those add up to 15—but your {2, 6, 7} do.) The question: Does either player have a winning strategy?

Schoenfeld did not identify explicitly that the problem was a transfer situation. However, when the problem was discussed with the whole class, some students recognized the same features as the magic square and its connection to the tic-tac-toe game. This problem was given to the students a month after they had worked the magic square problem.

Magic square seen as a tic-tac-toe game

It is important to mention that it is common for the students to work on problems involving different mathematical structures during a single two-hour class period. For example, the above counters problem was addressed by the students after they had worked on a problem that involved the use of expected value to analyze the fairness of a game. An instructional principle here is that students should develop mathematical tools and abilities to identify problem structure, and then be able to access a set of strategies and resources to attack the problem. Thus, students are aware that the ideas being discussed during the class or a previous problem are not guaranteed to work for the next one as they do in most textbooks. In this context, to access proper mathematical resources in order to attack the problems becomes an important goal for the students.

Many of the problems that students work during the course offer opportunities to explore the information of the problem, analyze different representations, and evaluate particular cases. During this process, students might re-state the problem, establish a specific connection, find a pattern, or develop a generalization. An important moral drawn from several problems is that conjectures emerging from the students' exploration must be supported with mathematical arguments. For example, the following problem was discussed during class:

Suppose you pick n points on the boundary of a circle. You then draw all of the line segments that connect pairs of those points. If the points have been chosen so that no three of the segments intersect at the same point (that is, the circle is divided into the maximum possible number of regions), into how many regions is the circle divided?

An attractive and common way to approach this well known problem is to try special cases in order to find a pattern or general expression. This strategy had been used in previous sessions to approach problems that included: What is the sum of the coefficients of $(x + 1)^n$? or How many subsets does a set of n elements have? Indeed, the moral of working those problems was that the students need to provide a mathematical argument (proof) to support their conjectures. Thus, with this background, the students worked on the "region problem" and computed the following cases:

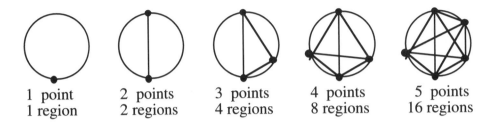

| 1 point | 2 points | 3 points | 4 points | 5 points |
| 1 region | 2 regions | 4 regions | 8 regions | 16 regions |

HEURISTIC: TRYING TO FIND A PATTERN

Based on this work some students were ready to conjecture that the total number of regions for n points could be expressed as 2^{n-1}. However, the search for a mathematical argument to support the conjecture led students to examine other approaches to find the conjecture. One student drew the case for $n = 6$ and showed that the number of regions did not follow the suggested conjecture (you never stop short). The class discussion focused on analyzing relationships among lines, points of intersection, and number of regions. It was observed that the maximum number of regions when connecting two points is obtained by placing the n points on the circle in such a way that at most two connecting lines intersect at the same point. Then the number of regions will be given by the expression:

$$1 + C(n, 2) + C(n, 4); \text{ where } C(n, r) = \frac{n!}{r!(n-r)!}.$$

(Note that this expression yields the same value as 2^{n-1} for $n = 1, 2, 3, 4,$ and 5.) During the class discussion, students had the opportunity to analyze particular cases and observe what happens to the number of regions when a point is added on the boundary.

Several morals were drawn from the whole-group discussion of this problem, principally that, in one student's words, "the only way that [an expression] is going to be true is that you have to prove it." Empirical work is a powerful tool to explore mathematical ideas, but assertions must be supported with a mathematical proof. Making connections between empirical and formal work plays an important role in the development of mathematics in this course.

Homework assignments and the importance of solution processes

Students are consistently engaged in discussion analyzing and comparing methods of solutions, looking for applications and extensions of problems.

For example, students often show approaches that include the use of particular and general methods. When the students were dealing with the problem "prove $|\tan x + \cot x| \geq 2$," a first approach was to use trigonometric identities to transform the left side of the inequality. That is, expressing the left side as

$$\left| \frac{\sin x}{\cos x} + \frac{\cos x}{\sin x} \right| = \left| \frac{1}{\cos x \sin x} \right| = \left| \frac{2}{\sin 2x} \right|$$

which is always greater or equal than 2.

A more general approach was also used. That is, representing the left side as:

$$\left| \tan x + \frac{1}{\tan x} \right| \geq 2 \quad \text{or} \quad \left| z + \frac{1}{z} \right| \geq 2.$$

Then, the inequality could be represented as

$$z^2 + 1 \geq 2z \quad \text{or} \quad (z - 1)^2 \geq 0.$$

This approach appeals more to an abstract form to represent the original expression rather than the specific content of the problem. This general approach is what Pólya calls "the inventor's paradox" in which a more general problem may, on occasion, be easier to solve than a given problem.

Similarly, homework assignments include problems in which students have the opportunity to discuss differences and qualities of each approach used to solve them. A typical written assignment not only requests that students search for multiple solutions, but that they write their ideas clearly and support their methods with mathematical arguments. Here, the students get to see that mathematics is not a finished product but a growing discipline in which there are always new developments. In fact, students' verbal and written communication play an important role in the discussion of limitations and extensions of mathematical ideas. An example of a problem given to the students for homework was:

How many rectangles are there on an 8×8 chess board? Be careful to count them all—any rectangle with its sides as grid lines in the chess board "counts." As an example, note that the 2×2 chess board,

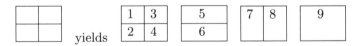

for a total of nine rectangles.

As was mentioned above, an important part of the problem solving instruction is that students are encouraged to communicate their ideas not just orally but also in writing. While working on the homework problems, the students are asked to approach the problems in different ways and to write about the qualities of the approaches. The solution methods reported here came from a whole-class discussion in which students described their approaches to the homework problems.

The use of special cases. An initial approach might involve trying to find a pattern by looking at special cases. So the problem is broken into a manageable steps that allow to count the number of rectangles for some particular cases. For example, focusing on how many rectangles there are in a $1 \times n$ board leads to the expression

$$1 + 2 + 3 + 4 + \ldots + n = \frac{n(n+1)}{2}.$$

Similarly, counting the number of rectangles in a $1 \times m$ board and combining both results leads to the solution of the problem

$$\frac{n(n+1)}{2} \cdot \frac{m(m+1)}{2}.$$

The use of coordinates. Another approach involves the use of a coordinate system to determine the number of rectangles. In the table below, the total number of rectangles is the sum as i goes from 1 to 8 of

$$i(1 + 2 + 3 + \cdots + 8).$$

That is, the sum of all the columns is $(1 + 2 + \ldots + 8)2$. For the general case of an $n \times m$ grid, the same reasoning can be applied to arrive at

$$\frac{n(n+1)}{2} \cdot \frac{m(m+1)}{2}.$$

8×1	7×1	6×1	5×1	4×1	3×1	2×1	1×1
8×2	7×2	6×2	5×2	4×2	3×2	2×2	1×2
8×3	7×3	6×3	5×3	4×3	3×3	2×3	1×3
8×4	7×4	6×4	5×4	4×4	3×4	2×4	1×4
8×5	7×5	6×5	5×5	4×5	3×5	2×5	1×5
8×6	7×6	6×6	5×6	4×6	3×6	2×6	1×6
8×7	7×7	6×7	5×7	4×7	3×7	2×7	1×7
8×8	7×8	6×8	5×8	4×8	3×8	2×8	1×8

THE USE OF A TABLE TO COUNT THE NUMBER OF RECTANGLES

The use of combinations. Yet another approach involves combinations of vertical and horizontal grid lines. That is, a rectangle can be chosen by identifying two horizontal grid lines (top and bottom) and two vertical grid lines (left and right sides). Thus, when considering the $n \times m$ case, there are $n+1$ vertical and $m+1$ horizontal lines, so the total number of choices of two horizontal and two vertical lines is:

$$\frac{n(n+1)}{2} \cdot \frac{m(m+1)}{2}.$$

The approaches shown above are a sample of how a homework task is expected to be done by the students. It is clear that they are asked to do more than just finding the solution of a problem. Brown (1994) points out that extending problems to other domains is an important step in helping students to think of their own problems. It seems that the work done by the students outside of the classroom is an extension of what they normally do inside the classroom. It is important to mention that the written assignments presented by the students are carefully reviewed by the instructor. In addition, the solutions proposed by students are discussed with the whole class and students' work is part of the evaluation they will receive at the end of the course.

It is clear that Schoenfeld has spent a great amount of time selecting, formulating, and redesigning the problems to be used during instruction. The problems illustrate the use of different mathematical ideas and in general are intended to engender mathematical morals and dispositions. However, the problems themselves are not enough to guarantee substantial discussion on the part of the students, but are an important ingredient of a class environment in which the students participate actively. Creation of a community that values and respects students' ideas is perhaps another ingredient that makes Schoenfeld's course successful.

Concluding remarks

The problem solving course discussed in this paper includes several instructional activities that are identified as crucial in the learning of mathematics. It appears that in order to develop the students' mathematical disposition to learn mathematics it is important to provide an environment in which students are consistently asked to:

- work on tasks that offer diverse challenges;
- use and discuss the importance of using different strategies including metacognitive strategies;
- participate in small-group and whole-class discussions;
- reflect on feedback and challenges that emerge from interactions with the instructor and other students;
- communicate their ideas orally and in writing;
- search for connections and extensions of problems.

These learning activities play a crucial role in helping students see mathematics as a dynamic discipline in which they can authentically participate.

REFERENCES

1. Brown, Stephen I. (1994). The problem of the problem and curriculum fallacies. In Paul Ernest (Ed.), *Constructing mathematical knowledge: Epistemology and mathematics education* (pp. 175–189). London: The Falmer Press.
2. Greeno, James G., Smith, David R., & Moore, Joyce L. (1993). Transfer of situated learning. In Douglas K. Detterman & Robert J. Sternberg (Eds.), *Transfer on trial: Intelligence, cognition, and instruction* (pp. 99–167). Norwood, NJ: Ablex Publishing Corporation.
3. Halmos, Paul R. (1994). What is teaching. *The American Mathematical Monthly 101*(9), 848–854.
4. Krulik, Stephen & Reys, R. (Eds.). (1980). *Problem solving in school mathematics. 1980 Yearbook.* Reston, VA: National Council of Teachers of Mathematics.
5. Lester, Frank. K. (1994). Musing about mathematical problem-solving research: 1970-1994. *Journal for Research in Mathematics Education, 25*(6) 660–675.
6. National Council of Teachers of Mathematics. (1980). *An agenda for action: Recommendation for school mathematics of the 1980s.* Reston, VA: National Council of Teachers of Mathematics.
7. Schoenfeld, Alan H. (1987). Confessions of an accidental theorist. *For the Learning of Mathematics, 7*(1), 30–38.
8. Schoenfeld, Alan H. (Ed.). (1990). *A source book for college mathematics teaching.* Washington, DC: Mathematical Association of America.
9. Schoenfeld, Alan H. (1992). Learning to think mathematically: Problem solving, metacognition, and sense making in mathematics. In Douglas A. Grouws (Ed.), *Handbook of research on mathematics teaching and learning* (pp. 334–370). New York: Macmillan.
10. Schroeder, Thomas L. & Lester, Frank K. (1989). Developing understanding in mathematics via problem solving. In Paul R. Trafton & Albert P. Shulte (Eds.), *New directions for elementary school mathematics* (pp. 31–56). Reston, VA: National Council of Teachers of Mathematics.
11. Stanic, George, M. & Kilpatrick, Jeremy. (1988). Historical perspectives on problem solving in the mathematics curriculum. Randall I. Charles & Edward. A. Silver (Eds.), *The teaching and assessing of mathematical problem solving* (pp. 1–22). Reston VA: National Council of Teachers of Mathematics.
12. Steen, Lynn. A. (Ed). (1990). *On the shoulders of giants: New approaches to numeracy.* Washington, DC: National Academy Press.

CENTER FOR RESEARCH AND ADVANCED STUDIES, MEXICO

CBMS Issues in Mathematics Education
Volume **7**, 1998

Reflections on a Course in
Mathematical Problem Solving

ALAN H. SCHOENFELD

1. Introduction and Overview

This paper must begin with a sincere note of thanks to my friends and colleagues Abraham Arcavi, Cathy Kessel, Luciano Meira, Manuel Santos, and Jack Smith for their interesting and thoughtful analyses of my problem solving course. Their analyses have revealed and highlighted some important issues related to the course. Some are issues that I have not written about; indeed, some are issues I had not actively thought about. My colleagues' papers serve as a welcome stimulus for reflection. Moreover, they provide an opportunity for me to re-think some aspects of the course in the light of my current research on the nature of teaching.

For some years the Teacher Model Group at Berkeley has been developing a model of the teaching process. Simply put, our goal is to develop a theory of teaching-in-context—a complete and coherent explanation of how and why teachers do what they do in the midst of classroom interactions. This overview provides an explanation of what we mean by a model. The paper proceeds with a description of some of the main elements of our model of teaching. It then illustrates how the model can be used to characterize how and why I do what I do when teaching the problem solving course. It concludes with a discussion of the modeling process in general.

My purpose here is to provide some context for what follows, for the phrase "model" is used in very different ways in different fields. Roughly speaking, the

---

I would like to thank the members of the Teacher Model Group at Berkeley for the pleasures of collaboration that led to this paper, and for their contributions to it. Special thanks go to Cathy Kessel for help with all aspects of the manuscript.

enterprise in which we are engaged is that of modeling a system. The system represents the teacher's "on line" decision-making, which takes place in a particular context or environment (a classroom). The model consists of objects representing the teacher's goals, knowledge, and beliefs, and relations among them. Those relationships determine how the system behaves.

Perhaps a useful analogy to describe the enterprise in which we are engaged is the modeling of human physiology. In thinking about a model of physiology, one asks: what physical systems and subsystems does one need to describe, and how does one characterize the ways in which they interact? In general terms, one provides descriptions of the circulatory system, the respiratory system, the digestive system, the skeletal system, and so on; one describes the ways these function as (nearly) closed systems, and the ways they function interactively. If the right systems are described in the right ways, what results is a general model of physiological functioning. Then, this general structural description can be used to produce a model of a particular person's physiological state and the ways in which that person is likely to react to various circumstances. For example, if you take the structure of a general physiological model and specify within it the particulars of my circulatory system, my respiratory system, my digestive system, and so on, what results is a model of my physiological state. Note that this capacity to model individuals is what allows one to evaluate how well the model works, in terms of structure, accuracy, and scope. In terms of structure, there are issues of completeness: does the model seem to have the right pieces and to account for the right things? In terms of accuracy: if you describe the individual being modeled in some detail, how well does the model capture or "predict" the behavior of the individual?[1] In terms of scope: does the model provide good descriptions of a wide range of people, or only a small set?

Our goal is to create something analogous for the teaching process. As explained below, our model of teaching focuses on the teacher's beliefs, goals, and knowledge (the last of which includes the teacher's established classroom behavior patterns). It also focuses on the ways those categories interact. If the structure represented in the model is right, then we should be able to fill in the particulars to build models of a particular teacher's instruction. That is, for a particular teacher in a particular instructional context,[2] we can put into the

---

[1]There are a host of fascinating issues related to the use of models in the physical sciences and in medical and educational research—e.g., what do we mean by "prediction"? Note, for example, that models of atomic structure allowed for predictions of the existence of as-yet undiscovered elements, given "gaps" in the periodic table. Physiological models do not typically provide such precise predictions, but they do provide probabilities. So do the kinds of models to be discussed here. I shall, elsewhere, deal with such issues head on (see Schoenfeld, 1997). For the discussion that follows, the common-sense analogy to models of physiology will suffice.

[2]Obviously, the context matters. For the same teacher, things will be very different in a large introductory lecture and in a small advanced seminar, or in the same course at different points of the year.

general structure of the model detailed representations of that teacher's beliefs, goals, knowledge, established classroom behavior patterns, etc. We can then "run" the model, and see if it produces a reasonably good simulation of the teacher's classroom actions.

We have been engaged in this kind of endeavor for the past few years. As it happens, while my colleagues Arcavi, Kessel, Meira, Santos, and Smith have been analyzing my course, I have been engaged in a similar activity with regard to some introductory lessons taught by Jim Minstrell. Minstrell is a teacher-scholar who has received the Presidential Award for Secondary Science Teaching in recognition of his innovative instruction in physics. The Teacher Model Group recently completed the analysis of one of Minstrell's introductory lessons, as an analytic case-in-point for the model (Schoenfeld, Minstrell, & van Zee, 1996). Having turned our analytic lens on Minstrell, it only seems fair to turn it back in my direction—to subject my teaching to similar scrutiny and see if the model will provide an adequate characterization of it as well. In the process, I shall say much that is compatible with the claims made by my colleagues in their analysis of my problem solving course—indeed, I will lean on their analyses for detail. The main differences, and the advances represented by the modeling approach in general, are that (a) it is synthetic, dealing simultaneously with the various aspects of (my) teaching such as my beliefs, goals, and the ways in which I draw upon my knowledge base to achieve them; and (b) it provides explanations of what I (or more generally, any teacher) do, at a level of mechanism. With the specification of my beliefs, my goals for the lessons analyzed, and the knowledge base I draw upon, you can run the model and predict the ways in which I will react to various circumstances that arise in the classroom. The full analysis will not be given here—it would run the length of the paper by Arcavi et al.—but I will at least suggest its main dimensions.

This paper proceeds as follows. Section 2 provides a description of the main features of our model of teaching. Goals for the problem solving course as a whole are outlined in Section 3, with more specific goals for the first few days of the course elaborated in Section 4. Section 5 provides the first handout for the course, which describes what the students are in for and contains the set of problems that we work on for the first few days. This problem set provides the grist for the discussion, in Section 6, of my goals and "lesson image" for the first few days of the course—specifically, what I hope to achieve with each of the problems, and how I expect to achieve it. The analysis by Arcavi et al. provides many of the details of what actually took place. In Section 7 I shall provide some supplementary analysis, discussing the opening few days of the course from the perspective of the model. That section, and the paper, conclude with a brief discussion of the prospects and implications of the kind of modeling approach described here.

2. Aspects of a Model of Teaching

There is a huge literature on the study of teaching. The literature ranges from fine-grained studies of what happens in classrooms to broad policy studies regarding the "context effects" that shape what is possible (or, at least, perceived to be possible) within classrooms. Rather than summarize that literature, I shall simply provide pointers to it. Though it is now better than a decade old (and the field has changed rapidly), the once-definitive volume and the starting place for bootstrapping one's way into the general literature on teaching is the third edition of the *Handbook of Research on Teaching* (Wittrock, 1986). Of specific interest are the introduction by Lee Shulman, which describes the state of the art as of the mid-1980s, the chapter "Teachers' thought processes" (Clark & Peterson, 1986), which provides an overview of then-contemporary research on teachers' thinking, and the chapter by Romberg and Carpenter, which describes the disjunction between then-contemporary research on what it means to learn mathematics and what it means to teach it. A more current introduction to topical issues regarding teaching is volume 20 of the *Review of Research in Education* (Darling-Hammond, 1994), which has a section of articles devoted to teaching knowledge and practice. Finally, two recent handbooks contain syntheses of the current literature on teaching. The *Handbook of Research on the Teaching and Learning of Mathematics* (Grouws, 1992) contains a section of articles on mathematics teaching that includes reviews of classroom culture, the effects of teaching practices, teachers' beliefs, and teacher knowledge; see especially the reviews by Thompson (1992) and Fennema and Franke (1992). The more recent *Handbook of Educational Psychology* (Berliner & Calfee, 1996) contains a series of current summaries of the literature on teaching and instruction; see especially the chapters by Borko and Putnam (1996) and Calderhead (1996). These works provide a general context for our work—a context that is, in fact, significantly more general than the scope of our model. The broad literature inquires into all the factors (sociological, economic, historical, etc.) that shape what happens in the classroom. The task the Teacher Model Group has set for itself is more constrained (and thus doable). Our work focuses on building a theory of teaching-in-context. We ask why the teacher—who enters the classroom with a particular set of beliefs, knowledge, and intentions for instruction—winds up doing precisely what he or she does, in response to what takes place in the classroom.

At its core, the model of teaching we are working on is grounded in some very simple notions. The main components of the model, which have already been suggested in prose, are outlined in Figure 1.

Figure 1 can be read metaphorically as follows. The "action"—what the teacher decides to do, and why—is a function of the teacher's beliefs, knowledge, and goals. What the teacher is doing *now* is a function of those, in response to what happens in the current context (this classroom, these students). That

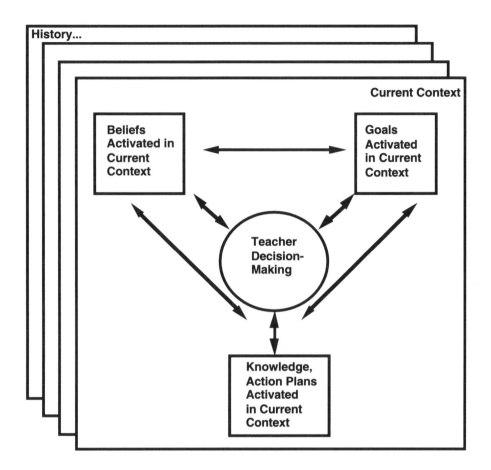

FIGURE 1. Main components of the model of teaching. (reprinted from Schoenfeld, 1996, with permission)

is what we model. At the same time, we recognize that what takes place now is a function of history: e.g., of the teacher's prior experiences with these students, of trying to teach this topic with varied success in the past, and so on. The background layers in Figure 1 serve as a metaphorical reminder that a full account of teaching would have to take those into account as well.

Of course, the key questions regarding the model are "What's in the boxes and in the oval?" and "What goes along the arrows (that is, how are the entities represented in Figure 1 related, and how do decisions actually get made)?" In the next few pages I shall suggest the answers in brief. Much more extensive detail is provided in the Teacher Model Group's technical papers (see, e.g., Aguirre & Speer, 1996; Schoenfeld, 1996; Schoenfeld, 1997; Schoenfeld, Minstrell, & van Zee, 1996; Sherin, Sherin, & Madanes, 1996; Zimmerlin & Nelson, 1996). Here the intention is to provide an overview of the big ideas.

• **Knowledge.** It goes without saying that what a teacher knows is a major factor shaping what the teacher can do in the classroom. Hence, delineating the teacher's knowledge, and how that knowledge is organized and accessed, is a major part of the modeling process. Since this discussion is non-technical, I shall for the most part bypass discussions of knowledge organization and access.[3] However, it is worth noting that there are various kinds of knowledge that come into play in teaching—one of which may be unfamiliar to the mathematical community. Familiar notions are *content knowledge* (the mathematics the teacher knows) and *pedagogical knowledge* (the general knowledge of teaching possessed by the teacher). In terms of classroom actions, however, there is a very important third type, first labeled by Lee Shulman (1987). Shulman refers to *pedagogical content knowledge*—knowledge of student learning of specific topics. Such knowledge includes knowing typical student learning pathways (including mistakes), and of ways to deal with them—for example, knowing the various ways calculus students are likely to have difficulties with the chain rule (or limits, or . . .) and having various "tricks of the trade" designed to address those difficulties. Whereas novice teachers (or even experienced teachers who are teaching new material) might be surprised by particular student behaviors or misunderstandings, experienced teachers often know what to expect, and have contingency plans for dealing with them. Indeed (see "lesson image" below), they may envision extended sequences of interactions to deal with misconceptions or to get particular ideas across.

Of central interest in modeling any teacher's performance, then, is the teacher's "tool kit"—the set of resources in memory that the teacher can draw upon. Teaching, like any acquired skill, rests on a foundation of skills and knowledge. Perhaps the two most important relevant findings from the psychological literature are that (a) human memory is associative, in that thinking of particular topics or ideas tends to "bring to mind" related thoughts or ideas; and (b) the contents of memory are organized in chunks or clusters that can be accessed or generated in "ready-to-modify-slightly-and-use" form. (The technical term for a chunk of knowledge ready to be accessed and used is "schema.") To make the point in an obvious way: virtually any faculty member can, without preparation, give an impromptu lesson on the definition of the derivative or on mathematical induction. When the mathematician does so, what is brought to mind is not a memorized lesson, verbatim. Rather, key information related to the topic (e.g., definitions and examples) is retrieved from memory and tailored to the circumstances at hand. Modeling a particular teacher teaching a particular lesson thus calls for delineating the relevant knowledge accessible to the teacher, and how that knowledge is likely to be accessed. It calls for delineating a range of peda-

---

[3]A central issue for the model is "How is knowledge organized, and how does particular knowledge get accessed?" There is an extensive psychological literature on the topic, which focuses on the notion of schema and its analogues (script, frame, routine, etc.). For accessible introductions to this topic, see Silver (1987) and chapter 2 of Schoenfeld (1985).

gogical skills. At the university level, one obvious class of such skills is related to lecturing: faculty have ways of organizing and laying out mathematical content for students. But there are various other resources, at various levels of grain size, as well. For example, there are techniques for involving students in discussion (whether via collaborative groups, or asking questions in lecture or recitation). There are ways to do classroom management, to motivate students to break up tedium, and so on. All of this is part of the knowledge base, the box at the bottom of Figure 1.

In what follows we will need some terminology for distinguishing among what the teacher expects to do in the classroom, what the teacher decides to do in response to classroom contingencies, and for what actually takes place in the classroom. (They can be the same, of course, but they often are not!) As elaborated below, the teacher's *lesson image* is her or his envisioning, before instruction, of what is likely to take place. The lesson image (related to but more elaborate than a written plan; see below) shapes what the teacher expects to happen. I shall use the term *action plan* to describe what the teacher intends to do. Action plans exist at various levels of grain size and they are often nested. For example, one can have a large-scale action plan to review homework for 15 minutes, a smaller-scale plan to review a particular topic covered in the assignment, and an even smaller-scale one to conduct a discussion elaborating on that topic. Some action plans are pre-determined as part of the teacher's lesson image—for example, the teacher may walk into the classroom expecting the lesson to begin with a brief recap of the content that had been discussed the previous day, or expecting to launch the introduction to a new topic with a carefully chosen example. Other action plans emerge spontaneously. For example the teacher might, without any prior planning, decide to review induction because students didn't appear to be adequately comfortable with the topic. In that case, the decision to conduct such a review (relying on information brought from memory to carry it off), is the on-the-spot creation of an action plan.

In short, lesson images and action plans are anticipatory thoughts and decisions made by the teacher. Part of our work includes inferring these mental structures and decisions—they are among the tools the teacher brings to bear. Another part of our work involves comparing the teacher's intentions with the reality of what actually took place in the classroom. When we analyze a lesson, we will use the term *action sequences* to describe what actually took place. A representation for delineating the action sequences that took place in a lesson segment is presented later in this section.

• **Goals.** Simply put, we assume that people do things for good reason: the actions in which they engage are undertaken to satisfy some goals. The core structure of the model links goals and actions. Given an action sequence in which the teacher is engaged, we want to be able to delineate the set of goals the action sequence is intended to achieve (e.g., the teacher is reviewing induction because the students need to be comfortable with it, and it appeared from classroom discussion that they were not). Conversely, with the knowledge of which goals are currently highest priority for the teacher, and the delineation of the teacher's knowledge base, we want to be able to specify the action plans that the teacher is most likely to use to meet those goals.

The simplest goal, but too vague to be useful for modeling, is that we teach so that "the students will understand the subject matter." But there's much more. What do we mean by "understand"? Do we want students to be able to use procedures, answer certain kinds of conceptual questions, develop a feel for the discipline, etc.? The same general goal may mean different things to different teachers when elaborated, and may result in different actions being taken in the classroom. Teachers have goals related to content, as described above. They also have social goals. For example, some faculty want a class to function as a "community of inquiry" and try to structure lessons to encourage conjecture and discussion. Others want an environment where material will be presented lucidly so that students have a clear sense of what they are supposed to learn, and so on. Goals range from very large-scale ("focus on conceptual understanding" or "establish a community of inquiry") to very small-scale ("make sure the statement of the fundamental theorem is clear" or "reassure John, he looks uncomfortable"). Goals may be established before the teacher enters the classroom door ("I want to cover X") or may be established in the midst of a lesson ("They really don't understand Y. I'd better do a review").

Of course, the goals with which the teacher enters the classroom are shaped in fundamental ways by the planning process. One might think of a teacher's plan for instruction as a linkage of action plans and goals—the sequence of intended actions is intended to help achieve the teacher's high priority goals. In this context, we need to say a bit about planning and the term lesson image.

The term that is familiar to most people is "lesson plan." This has a slightly negative connotation. A lesson plan is usually considered to be the set of notes the teacher uses to structure what is intended to take place in the classroom. Lesson plans—formal, structured ones at least—are typically thought of as the obligatory preparatory notes that student teachers have to create before going into the classroom. Of course, those of us (mea culpa!) who have, at times, looked at the book just briefly before class to prepare for it are well aware that in practice the written trace of a plan can be negligible, if it exists at all. This does not mean, however, that there has not been planning or that the teacher does not have a very rich sense of what will unfold in the classroom. Rather, experienced teachers carry a lot of that information in their heads. Typically, scratch notes saying "Discuss X" can be unpacked to reveal that the teacher expects to provide a context for discussion with a particular example, and to have students respond with suggestions; that on the basis of previous experience, the teacher expects that three or four "standard" suggestions will be made; that the teacher will follow up on them in particular ways; and so on. This rich set of "envisionings" of what is likely to take place is part of the teacher's lesson image. Depending on the context, of course (how familiar is the material, how many times has the teacher taught it?), the teacher's lesson image may range from relatively vague to very detailed. It may include an essentially linear plan ("We'll go through these problems in order, then . . ."), or a plan that is constraint-based ("I'll field whatever they throw at me in response to my question, but I'll make sure that X, Y, and Z are covered before we're done"). Either way, this image of what will take place is a strong factor in determining what actually does take place.

● **Beliefs.** It may seem strange at first to consider beliefs as a fundamental factor shaping what takes place in the classroom—but the fact is that they do. The teacher's beliefs about what is important (about the subject matter, about learning, about the students, and so on) play a critical role in shaping what the teacher does, both in terms of planning and in terms of what happens "on the fly" as instruction takes place.

To first make the point via caricature, consider your image of a teacher who is committed to "mastering the basics" versus that of one committed to "learning by discovery." Even if the two teachers are working from the same text, you can imagine that they will structure their lessons (and classroom environments) very differently, and will respond very differently to the same questions posed by students.

Teachers' beliefs—which may not be articulated—play a major and continuous role in shaping what takes place in the classroom. This is the case at all levels of grain size, from large-scale decisions about what the class will engage in to small-scale decisions about what to do next. Beliefs about what is important will shape the choice of material and what is done with it. Beliefs about classroom behavior will shape the nature of the learning environment. (Does the teacher believe a noisy classroom is a bad classroom? If so, you're not likely to find students working in groups, or if you are, the nature of the group interactions will be constrained by the level of noise it generates.) At a more fine-grained level, instructional decisions are continuously grounded in the teacher's beliefs about what is important. Suppose a student raises an issue that is related to the topic at hand, but that will probably take a substantial amount of time to explore. How important does the teacher believe it is to "honor student inquiry"? How important does the teacher believe it is to cover the planned material? Depending on the answers to these questions, the teacher might decide to (a) pursue the question, despite the disruption to the planned lesson; (b) note the question and return to it at a later time, (c) discuss it after class with the student, or (d) deflect the issue and continue. Such decisions are made all the time, and they are made on the basis of what the teacher believes.

● **Putting the pieces together.** What happens in the classroom? Here is a cursory description, enough to make sense of what follows. Details are in our more technical papers. As suggested above, the teacher has a lesson image, a general sense of how the class will go. The lesson image should be (one hopes!) consistent with the teacher's beliefs and goals; it draws upon the various kinds of knowledge described above. The lesson image includes action plans for getting things started, for major transitions, for ways that chunks of the lesson will be approached, and so on.

So, the teacher starts off the class. At this point what happens takes on a life of its own, in interaction between the teacher and the class. (Or at least, it can. The degree to which what the teacher does will depend on student reactions varies widely.) The teacher begins to implement some action plan, which is tied to some major goals—that is, the teacher does X, to achieve Y. What happens then depends on the class response. If things go smoothly and Y is achieved the teacher moves to the next part of the lesson. Since some goals have been achieved, there is a new constellation of high priority goals; the teacher then to implements an action plan that corresponds to those goals. If things do not go as planned (e.g., the students have unexpected difficulties, or perhaps a student raises an interesting issue that warrants exploration) some high priority goals may get deferred or removed altogether, and a new goal or set of goals may be given highest priority. Given this constellation of goals, the teacher searches for an appropriate action plan—that is, an action plan that can be used or modified to address many of the goals that now have highest priority. (An example of this kind is the on-the-spot decision by a teacher to give a quick review of induction that was mentioned above.) If this adaptation to contingencies works (that is, the new action plan achieves many of the goals it was intended to achieve), deferred goals might once again be given high priority, in which case the lesson will pick up at the point where it was before the interruption. Or, deferred goals might be reassigned lower priority (perhaps they are not as relevant as they was before, or other things may have to be dealt with), and the goals corresponding to the next part of the lesson image might then have highest priority. So it goes, until the end of the class.

In sum, the idea is this. Teachers have particular things they want to achieve (goals), and various ways of achieving them (action plans). As a lesson evolves, various goals are achieved. As a result new goals attain high priority status (in a manner consistent with the teacher's beliefs and lesson image), and new action plans are implemented to achieve those goals.

Before getting to the specifics of my course, I want to introduce the representation that we use to demarcate the instructional chunks of a lesson and the goals that correspond to them. The idea behind the representation is to provide an explicit linkage between action sequences (the implemented versions of action plans) and goals. By way of introduction, Figure 2 provides a generic version of such a representation. We shall return this form of representation in Section 7, where (see Figure 3) this notational device is used to capture some aspects of what happened during the first of the two lessons analyzed by Arcavi et al.

The basic idea behind the representation is simple. In the leftmost column you can imagine the full transcript of the segment of instruction that is being analyzed. That large chunk is represented iconically in the second column as

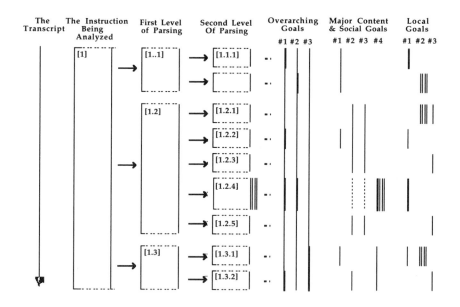

FIGURE 2. An abstract representation of the parsing of a body of instruction, including the transcript, the iterative decomposition of the instruction into chunks, and goal traces corresponding to those chunks. (reprinted from Schoenfeld, 1996, with permission)

one box, labeled [1]. At the first level of parsing (decomposition into coherent sub-units), the box [1] is decomposed into a series of lesson segments that have a phenomenological integrity of their own. In Figure 2 there are three chunks, [1.1], [1.2], and [1.3]; one might imagine that they correspond to some introductory comments, the main substance of the lesson, and closing comments. (If the lesson happened to deal with two main topics, then the first-order parsing might have four boxes.) Each of these chunks is further decomposed at the second level of parsing, and so on.

In each of the boxes on the left-hand side of Figure 2 is a series of annotations regarding the nature of that chunk of instruction. Those annotations address issues such as the following: What triggered that action sequence? Was it planned? What resources in the knowledge base did it depend on? What goals were satisfied when the action sequence was ended?

On the right-hand side of Figure 2 is a representation of the goals that had high priority during various chunks of instruction—each goal trace corresponding to (that is, represented as the horizontal projection of) some chunk of instruction at some level of parsing. To continue the hypothetical decomposition above, one might imagine that the main substance of the lesson, [1.2], was intended by the teacher to have four segments—say, working through four problems. The second level of parsing (which captures what happened, not what was intended) might then represent something like the following. Instruction started as planned in [1.2]. The discussion of the first three problems went as planned, with the relevant (local) content goals for each problem being initiated and achieved. Then, at the end of [1.2.3], a student said something that raised a new issue— perhaps indicating to the teacher that there might be the need for a review of some prerequisite material, which was undertaken in [1.2.4]. During [1.2.4], the high priority goals instantiated at the beginning of [1.2] were put on hold. They were reinstated, however, when the review in [1.2.4] was completed. The fourth example was successfully worked in [1.2.5], at which point the local goal for chunk [1.2.5] and the larger goal for [1.2] had both been achieved. At that point, the goals for [1.3] came to have highest priority.

This, of course, is a top-level gloss. A complete analysis of the instructional segment would identify the goals, beliefs, and knowledge with which the teacher began the instruction. At each point in the interaction between teacher and students, each of those categories would be updated. Are things going according to plan? If so, then when an action sequence is brought to a close, one or more of the current high priority goals has been achieved. The termination of one action sequence (which corresponds to an action plan in the teacher's lesson image) serves as a trigger to move on to the next action sequence, and a new set of high priority goals corresponding to that part of the lesson is put in place. If, however, things do not go according to plan, a different set of high priority goals is established in response to this situation, and action plans consistent with this new set of goals are implemented. These on-the-spot choices of goals and action plans are made in accord with the teacher's beliefs, given the teacher's perception of available resources and constraints.

Note that the kind of parsing represented in Figure 2, when fleshed out with descriptions of knowledge and belief structures, can be used for both descriptive and predictive purposes. At the descriptive level, it provides a fine-grained description of why the teacher did what he or she did, and what resources he or she depended on in the process. But, you can imagine (for purposes of testing the accuracy of the model) having a fine-grained characterization of the knowledge, beliefs, goals, and lesson image of a teacher, and being shown the transcript or videotape of a lesson up to a certain point. Something happens at that point. What will the teacher do? Of course, no-one can say for certain. But, one can run the model. In the model, is the event likely to trigger some strong beliefs held by the teacher (and thus result in some new goals being given high priority), or reinforce some potential high priority goals? If so, is there an action plan accessible that might achieve those goals? Are the goals strong enough to warrant implementing the action plan? If so, the model sets out to implement the action plan. That, in effect, is a prediction that the teacher would do the same. Running the model and observing how well the model's predictions correspond to what really happened serves as one major way of assessing its accuracy.

We now turn to the discussion of my course. As might be expected, the discussion will be framed in terms of the issues considered thus far.

3. Goals for My Problem Solving Course as a Whole

As described by Arcavi and Santos and as elaborated in a series of books and articles (Schoenfeld, 1983; 1985; 1988; 1991a; 1991b; 1992; 1994; 1996), I have a series of long-term goals for my problem solving course—goals for the way it will function, and for the kinds of understandings that students emerge with from it. In this section I briefly recapitulate some top-level goals for the students and for the way the course must run in order for it to achieve what I want.

In broadest terms, my goals are that the students will learn to *think mathematically*. This means far more than their merely "knowing" a particular body of mathematics, or even problem solving skills. It means having a predilection to see the world through a kind of mathematical lens (a specifically mathematical perspective), and having the tools to act mathematically when it seems appropriate. Let me introduce the idea via anecdote.

Years ago I attended a talk given by Henry Pollak, who was at that time Vice President of Bell Labs. Henry mentioned having gone into two local supermarkets, which served pretty much the same clientele and had the same kind of general "no frills" ethos. In one market, shoppers in the express lane were allowed to purchase no more than six items. In the other, express lane shoppers were allowed to purchase as many as fifteen items. "This didn't seem right," said Henry. "This is clearly an optimization problem, and the range of solutions can't possibly be so large as to encompass six and fifteen." So, Henry made some assumptions about the nature of the problem, and solved it.

Now, what does the story indicate? First, Henry saw a mathematics problem where others wouldn't. For him, a relatively innocuous context—two supermarkets allowing different numbers of purchases in their express lanes—begged to be formulated as a mathematics problem. Of course, mathematics problems need not have applied origins; just about anything can be the seed for mathematical inquiry. (Erdös's passion for formulating mathematical questions is another case in point.) The observation here is that part of thinking mathematically includes *having a predisposition to look for mathematical structure and to explore it*. Along with this predilection go a number of others: the predilection to explore (you're not done with a problem when you've solved it—there might be other solutions, generalizations, connections to other mathematics, etc.), a sense of ownership and authority (Henry makes the problems his own, and he knows when he's solved them—he doesn't need an external authority to certify that he's gotten the right answer), and more. Second, Henry had the tools to get the job done. The tools, it should be stressed, include much more than knowing a wide range of mathematical facts and procedures. They include knowing a large number of problem solving strategies, knowing how to use what you know efficiently and effectively (the technical term for reflecting and acting on what you know is "metacognition"), and having a set of beliefs about yourself and mathematics that foster productive behavior. There is a large literature indicating that those who are mathematically effective differ widely on these dimensions from those who are ineffective. See Schoenfeld (1992) for a general review, and De Franco (1996) for a discussion of the knowledge and perspectives of world-class mathematicians versus more or less ordinary Ph.D.s.

In sum, my goals for the students are that they develop appropriately mathematical predilections, knowledge, and skills. I want them to be aggressively mathematical—to see mathematics where it can be seen, to pursue mathematical connections, extensions, generalizations; to know how to make good conjectures, and know how to prove them; to have a sense of what it means to understand mathematics and good judgment about when they do. And, I want them to have the tools that will enable them to do so. That means having a rich knowledge base, a wide range of problem solving strategies, and good metacognitive behavior.

My goals for the course follow from these. Simply put, I believe a large part of learning to think mathematically comes from participating in a community in which mathematical sense-making is the norm. Hence I work hard to create a classroom context where the things I care about are part of the environment. If the class is to function as a(n obviously constrained) mathematical community, students must learn to value some of the things mathematicians value: explorations, connections, conjecture, proof, multiple solutions, extensions, and so on.[4] If students are to feel comfortable making conjectures, the climate must support conjecturing—it must be the ideas that are at stake, and not the people who propose them. Hence I must work to create an atmosphere where there is enough trust (between the students and me, and among the students) so that students are not afraid to float ideas. At the same time, I must also work to develop in the classroom community (and ultimately in each of the students) an appropriate standard of mathematical precision and correctness—namely the standard held by the community of professional mathematicians.

It is worth noting that the success or failure of the effort also depends heavily on the curriculum for the course—i.e., the problems and what we (can) do with them. Prior to teaching the first version of my course in the mid-1970s, I spent a year in the library looking for problems that had the "right" properties. Those properties include the following (see Schoenfeld, 1991b, for more detail):

- The problems are (relatively) accessible. I like problems that are easily understood and that do not require a lot of vocabulary or machinery in order for students to make progress on them.

---

[4] As Arcavi et al. note, there are some interesting tensions in the creation and maintenance of such a community. On the one hand, I work actively to demote my status as "authority" or "certifier of mathematical correctness": ultimately it is the mathematics that judges, not I. At the same time, I do not hesitate to use my leverage as teacher to nudge things in desired directions: the reward structure for the course gives multiple credit for multiple solutions to a problem, additional credit for extensions and generalizations, etc.

- The problems can be solved, or at least approached, in a number of ways. This leads to discussions of mathematical richness, of connections, and of strategy choice.

- The problems should serve as introductions to important mathematical ideas. The topics and mathematical techniques involved in the problem solutions should be of agreed importance, or the solutions to the problems should illustrate important problem solving strategies.

- The problems should, if possible, serve as starting points for honest-to-goodness mathematical explorations. Good problems lead to more problems. If the domain from which a problem comes is rich enough, students can start with the problem that has been posed to them and proceed to make the domain their own.

4. And in the Beginning . . .

The preceding section described my goals for the course as a whole. This section, in response to the focus of the paper by Arcavi et al., describes my goals for the first few class sessions. Needless to say, goals and the means to achieve them are not homogeneous throughout the course. Some goals have highest priority early on, and others emerge or take on greater importance once various aspects of the classroom culture have been established.

The first few days of the course are simultaneously typical and atypical with regard to both content and pedagogy. They are in many ways representative of the ways the students and I will work for the whole of the semester; any less would be false advertising. Yet they are also special in that the first few days will make the course or break it—the success of the entire course depends on having the students understand and buy into the "rules of the game" by the end of the first week. Thus I have some high priority goals for the two sessions that comprise the first week, above and beyond my goals for the course as a whole and for the particular problems we explore. Among those goals are to:

- convince the students I have something to teach them. I will be asking them to do a number of non-standard things, some of which require a lot of work and some of which will cause a fair amount of discomfort. If they don't think it's worth it, they won't stay engaged.

- have the students understand that the standard "rules of the game" do not apply in this course. There is extensive class participation. The emphasis on thinking, as well as content, is unusual. Forms of assessment are different (there are two-week long take-home midterm and final exams). The students need to understand and feel comfortable with these.

- establish a climate of trust, both with regard to me and with regard to the kinds of conversations we will have in the class.

- begin shaping the kind of interactive environment I want to emerge, in which the students will be making major contributions.

- introduce some of the main themes of the course:
  - heuristics
  - metacognitive aspects of decision-making
  - the idea that the goal is not just to get "the answer," but to explore mathematically—to obtain multiple solutions, generalizations, etc.
  - the idea that the role of certifying mathematical correctness should not reside solely in my hands—that the students can come to internalize appropriate standards of mathematical justification, and know for themselves when an argument is correct.

The first course handout, which covers the first week or so of class, is (of course) designed to provide me with the opportunities to achieve these goals. The handout is reproduced immediately below. I will use it as a springboard for a discussion of my goals and lesson image. This discussion will set the stage for my concluding comments about the nature of teaching and the model discussed in the first part of this paper.

5. The First Day's Handout

The following provides the content of the handout I used for the version of the course studied by Arcavi, Kessel, Meira, and Smith.

AN INTRODUCTION TO
"MATHEMATICAL PROBLEM SOLVING"

This is a "hands on" course where we spend most of our time working problems and discussing their solutions. We'll study a number of techniques that will make you better problem solvers, and we'll get a lot of practice along the way. The problems will come from all branches of mathematics, and are chosen to give you a sense of the range of "mathematical thinking." You will not need the calculus to solve them. You will need some patience, but you'll also have help from your friends; a lot of our work in class is in small groups.

Our primary text is the most recent edition of:

Mason, John, Burton, Leone, & Stacey, Kaye. *Thinking Mathematically*. London: Addison-Wesley.

Supplemental readings are:

Polya, George. *Mathematical Discovery* (paperback edition). New York: Wiley, 1981.

Polya, George. *How to Solve It* (paperback edition). Princeton, 1957.

My office is 4653 Tolman, and I'll be there after class Wednesdays until 6:00.

The problems on the attached sheets will give you some sense of the kinds of things we'll worry about this term. There's a lot here; don't be concerned if we don't come close to finishing them. (We've got the whole term.)

SOME PROBLEMS FOR FUN
(Believe it or not)

1. What is the sum of the numbers

$$\frac{1}{1 \times 2} + \frac{1}{2 \times 3} + \frac{1}{3 \times 4} + \frac{1}{4 \times 5} + \cdots + \frac{1}{n \times (n+1)}?$$

For those of you who've seen this series, how about

$$\frac{1}{2!} + \frac{2}{3!} + \frac{3}{4!} + \frac{4}{5!} + \cdots + \frac{n}{(n+1)!}?$$

2. You are given the triangle on the left in the figure below.

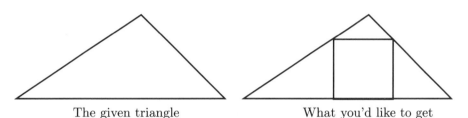

| The given triangle | What you'd like to get |

A friend of mine claims that he can inscribe a square in the triangle—that is, that he can find a construction that results in a square, all four of whose corners lie on the sides of the triangle. Is there such a construction—or might it be impossible? Do you know for certain that there's an inscribed square? Do you know for certain there's a construction that will produce it?

Is there anything special about the triangle you were given? That is, suppose you did find a construction. Will it work for all triangles, or only some?

3. Can you place the numbers 1, 2, 3, 4, 5, 6, 7, 8, and 9 in the box below, so that when you are all done, the sum of each row, each column, and each diagonal is the same? This is called a magic square.

If you think that the 3×3 magic square is too easy, here are two alternatives.
   (1) Do the "4 × 4" instead of the "3 × 3".
   (2) Try to find something interesting to ask about the 3 × 3.
      (This alternative is better. There are lots of things you can ask.)

4. Take any three-digit number and write it down twice, to make a six-digit number. (For example, the three-digit number 789 gives us the six-digit number 789,789.) I'll bet you $1.00 that the six-digit number you've just written down can be divided by 7, without leaving a remainder.

OK, so I was lucky. Here's a chance to make your money back, and then some. Take the quotient that resulted from the division you just performed. I'll bet you $5.00 that quotient can be divided by 11, without leaving a remainder.

OK, OK, so I was very lucky. Now you can clean up. I'll bet you $25.00 that the quotient of the division by 11 can be divided by 13, without leaving a remainder?

Well, you can't win 'em all. But, you don't have to pay me if you can explain why this works.

5. What is the sum of the first 137 odd numbers?

6. For what values of "a" does the pair of equations

$$x^2 - y^2 = 0$$

$$(x - a)^2 + y^2 = 1$$

have either 0, 1, 2, 3, 4, 5, 6, 7, or 8 solutions?

7. Here's a magic trick. Take any odd number, square it, and subtract 1. Take a few others and do the same thing. Notice anything? Does it always happen? Must it? Can you say why?

8. Since $3^2 + 4^2 = 5^2$, we know that there are three consecutive positive whole numbers with the property that the sum of the squares of the first two equals the square of the third. Can you find three consecutive positive whole numbers with the property that the sum of the cubes of the first two equals the cube of the third?

9. The figure below was found in an old cemetery in the midwest. Can you decipher the message?

6. Goals, Lesson Images, and Reality: A Discussion of My Opening Commentary and the First Problem Set

My introduction to the course, given in full as the Appendix of Arcavi et al., is designed to set the stage for what follows. In the Appendix the reader will find a number of comments deliberately aimed at the goals for the first week of the course. The opening commentary provides assurances that the students will learn a great deal (see, e.g., the story about my putting nearly impossible problems from the *Hungarian Problem Books* (Kurchak, 1963) on the final exam, and the fact that my students solved them), specifics about the rules of the game (how the class will be conducted and graded, including multiple credit for multiple solutions), and the idea that problem solving strategies *can* be learned. With that context established, the class begins work on the problems.

In this section I begin by making some comments about the collection as a whole, and how it is aimed at the top-level goals described in Section 4. Then I proceed with a problem-by-problem discussion. My focus will be on the first three problems, since what happened in the classroom discussion of those problems was the main object of Arcavi, Kessel, Meira, and Smith's analysis. The remainder of the problems will be given a more cursory discussion, aimed at fleshing out my intentions for the first week.

General Comments.

The problems have been chosen, collectively, to help make and reinforce the main points highlighted in Section 4. First, the students need to be convinced that I have something to teach them. In some sense all of the problems have this property. But, some, such as problems 1 and 6, are chosen to make the point dramatically. Most of the students will have forgotten the "telescoping series" solution to problem 1, and they will be stymied by the problem. The students are almost certain to approach problem 6 algebraically, and to find it intractable. When they work together in small groups, they will make little progress on those problems, finding them frustrating and difficult. I know from long experience that when I make some simple suggestions such as "try a few simple cases and look for a pattern" for problem 1 and "draw a diagram" for problem 6, the students will then be able to solve the problems without difficulty. They will be impressed—I *do* know some tricks of the trade, and they really make a difference! (In fact, I tell them later that they were set up. Problem solving isn't that easy, but the strategies they used to solve these problems are indeed useful and important.) Second, my experience is that these problems tend to invite student participation, allow for multiple approaches and generalizations, and provide the grist for rich interactions. As discussed below, problems 2, 3, and 4 have been carefully chosen for these properties. Whole-class discussions of the problems, following small-group work, provide a context for demonstrating very clearly the rules of the game for doing mathematics and for classroom interactions. Likewise, these problems provide ample opportunities for laying out the tools of the trade.

Details are given in the problem-by-problem commentaries, which follow.

Problem 1: The telescoping series.

As indicated by Meira, this problem is intended to satisfy multiple goals. One major goal is to introduce a simple but powerful heuristic strategy: *Given a problem that contains an (implicit or explicit) integer parameter* **n**, *try the values* **n** = *1, 2, 3, 4, . . . , and see if a pattern emerges.* A second goal, noted immediately above, is to have the experience be powerful for students—to have them feel "I couldn't get this problem, and he showed me how simple it really is. I'll learn a lot in this class." (The second part of the problem is a fail-safe, designed to achieve that goal for the students who happen to remember the solution to the first part.) A third is to introduce the idea that proof is a serious component of the course. Although we have seen a rather compelling pattern in the analysis of the first few cases (and some students are content with the pattern), I insist that we follow through with an inductive proof. (This discussion also gives me a chance to see how comfortable the class is with proof by induction, and to do a quick review if necessary.) Other major goals, enacted through the mock lecture, are more social in orientation. As Meira points out, I need to indicate that I *know* what their experience in typical mathematics classrooms has been like. Their knowing that I know puts me in a better position to change the rules of the game. My explicit attention to such issues also makes it clear that there is a thought-out justification (rather than random caprice) for the non-standard things I do in the classroom. Finally, it doesn't hurt to be entertaining—I do want the students to want to come back.

[A note on lesson image and the role of the knowledge base: My expectation, based on long experience, is that the problem solution will typically unfold almost exactly as it did that year (see the transcript in Arcavi et al.). There are some contingencies in my lesson image: I may or may not decide to review induction, for example. But the structure is in place, and decisions about how deeply to pursue any direction can be made easily on line. It may sound odd, but the fact is that for these problems, which I've taught dozens of times with varied groups of students, it is easy to predict most of what the students will say before they say it. With this knowledge, I am prepared to deal with the things they are likely to bring up. It is also worth noting that because I am working on such familiar terrain, I am not "stretched" mentally; I have the mental energy left to focus on other things, such as attending to the reactions of individual students or dealing with somewhat unexpected events. This illustrates the critical role of the knowledge base, with regard to pedagogy as well as content. There is only so much the teacher can attend to. The more the teacher is on familiar territory, the freer he or she can be to adapt to what students do. We have seen parallels in our analysis of Jim Minstrell's instruction. He too is on familiar (though non-standard) ground in a lesson we have analyzed, and is thus able to respond flexibly when something new comes up. We have also seen a sharp contrast in the case of a beginning teacher, who finds himself juggling so many things at once (classroom management, content he has not taught before, etc.) that he is stretched very thin when students respond in an unexpected way to a question he poses. See Section 7 for a discussion.]

Problem 2: Inscribing a square in a triangle.

This problem provides an introduction to some of the more complex themes of the course. Unlike problem 1 it does not yield easily to a heuristic strategy, although ultimately it does. Hence this problem serves as a potential corrective mechanism for an impression the students might get from the first problem—that heuristics are cute tricks that unlock problems in the way that a key unlocks a door. Our work on problem 2 makes it clear that we have to work at problem solving, even if we have the tricks of the trade at our disposal. The problem also raises the metacognitive issue of strategy choice: Given that there are a number of "easier related problems" that one might pursue, how does one decide which ones might be worth pursuing, which ones not? The solution to this problem is not "show and tell" like the solution to problem 1. Rather, the class as a whole gets deeply engaged in the solution. Moreover, the subject of the conversation is the set of strategies we use to solve the problem—how strategies like "exploit an easier related problem" or "relax a condition of the problem and then re-impose it" actually work. In short, this problem begins to introduce the students to the intellectual substance of the course.

The discussions of the problem are also intended to introduce students to some of the metamathematical issues dealt with in the course. When Devon volunteers to present a solution to the problem, I remind the students that

> one of the things that I want to do during the course of the semester is get us talking like a mathematical community and ultimately using the standards of the mathematical community, which means . . . making arguments clear so that all of us can understand precisely what's going on. So I'm going to push for those kind of standards in explanation, which means not just beautiful finished products, but also explanations of how and why it's reasonable that you did what you did and things like that. OK?

And, when Devon presents his solution to me (not the class), looking for certification of its correctness, I refuse the role of "certifier":

> What just happened . . . is exactly what happens on the second day of class every time I teach this course, which is that: I ask someone to do something at the board and he spends 90 percent of his time looking at me for approval. . . . I don't want to be the judge of what's right or wrong. The judge of what's right or wrong in some sense is the mathematics and in another sense, it's the class. And what I want this to be is a community that develops its own standards about mathematical correctness and it argues about when it buys an argument or not . . .

> Did you guys buy what you've seen? Is that sufficiently compelling that you all believe the construction that Devon suggested?

By the time the class has finished this problem the students and I have covered some interesting mathematical territory, begun our engagement with some complex strategies, discussed issues of metacognition and strategy use, and begun to deal with metamathematical issues such as standards of proof and mathematical authority. In short, the students now have a real sense of what the course is going to be about. (As Smith observes, we spent about 70 minutes total, over a two day period, working through various aspects of this problem.)

It is worth noting that Smith's analysis provides the grist for a discussion of the constraint-based nature of my lesson image and the way it plays out in practice. In general, the claim is that teachers' plans for instruction in classes other than straightforward lecture or recitation are often not linear. (For documentation see Schoenfeld, Minstrell, and van Zee, 1996.) Even in classes where there is a substantial amount of interaction, a plan that is constraint-based in nature can, at some level of detail, anticipate everything that will take place.

Consider the following informal description of the way a teacher might carry out the open-ended solicitation and elaboration of ideas from a class. The teacher asks the students for suggestions. Typically the suggestions are listed and then pursued in the order that they were generated. However, if a student makes a suggestion that would derail the intended conversation, the discussion of that suggestion will be deferred. And, the teacher may toss into the mix a suggestion that the students should have made but didn't.

In effect, this kind of solicitation-and-decision strategy can be modeled[5] with a relatively simple set of rules:

1. Ask for a suggested approach.
2. When a student makes a suggestion . . .
    a. and a discussion of it would be unproblematic, add the suggested approach to the list. Ask if there are more suggestions.
    b. and a discussion of it would be problematic (e.g., the lesson flow would be disrupted seriously), put the suggested approach on hold, to be discussed after the other suggestions have been dealt with. Ask if there are more suggestions.
3. If the students fail to make a suggestion . . .
    a. but the list of ideas is relatively complete, then begin a discussion of the ideas in order.
    b. but at least one important suggestion is not in the list, mention it as one that students have generated in the past, add it to the list, and then begin a discussion of the ideas in order.

---

[5]Note that I say *modeled*—there is no claim that I or others follow such rules when we teach, consciously or otherwise. The point is that there is often a large degree of consistency in what some experienced teachers do, even in classes that appear as free-form as this one does. (Indeed, the students are completely unaware that there is this kind of structure to what takes place. When some students in my research group who had taken my problem solving course read in Schoenfeld (1994) about my knowing, in advance, what they were going to do, they said they were astonished "It just seemed like you were reacting to what we did on the fly!")

That, indeed, is how the discussion of the inscribed square problem played out in the lessons analyzed by Smith. This segment of the lesson was simultaneously free-form and responsive to what the students generated while proceeding precisely according to plan. It is, as is the lesson taught by Minstrell, an example of a contextually-driven response to a constraint-based plan. (To put this more precisely, a model of my teaching this class would contain the constraint-based plan. If you ran the model up to any point in the lesson and asked what I would do next, the model should make a prediction that corresponds very closely to what happened in the classroom. The same is the case for our model of Minstrell teaching his introductory lesson.)

It should be noted, again, that the implementation of such a plan in the classroom need not be, or seem to be, like the implementation of a step-by-step algorithm. Here is an analogy. When one watches an accomplished cook preparing a number of complex dishes simultaneously for dinner, it may not look like there is a straightforward plan, or that recipes are being followed. What you see is fluid and flexible performance. But that flexibility and fluidity may well depend on a well-internalized set of constraints and understandings. Core aspects of recipes may be held in memory—they're there, you just don't see them. In preparing any of the dishes, it may be that some things can be done whenever the opportunity allows, while some must be done at particular times. These constraints are taken into account "on line," without there being "rule following" in a conscious sense. But, the systematicity is there. It is the support structure that enables the competent performance, and it can be simulated in a constraint-based model.

Problem 3: The magic square.

This problem is designed to satisfy a set of goals that complement those of problem 2. While problem 2 is difficult for the students, problem 3 is easy. It is safe to assume that all of the student groups will obtain solutions by trial and error within a few minutes. Since the mathematics of the problem as posed is trivial, I am free to focus on a variety of metamathematical issues. As Kessel notes, those include identifying and elaborating on the following heuristic strategies: establishing subgoals, working backwards, exploiting symmetry, working forwards, using systematic generating procedures, focusing on key points for leverage, and exploiting extreme cases.

Equally important, the problem serves as a vehicle for highlighting the fact that multiple solutions, extensions, and generalizations are valued in the course. Typically, the first few times the class solves a problem and I ask the (soon to become) ritual question "Are we done?" the students say "Yes." They are somewhat surprised when I say we are not: "We've only solved it one way, and we haven't looked for other solutions." (To hammer the point home, I mention that there is a book in our mathematics library that gives more than 100 proofs of the Pythagorean theorem, and that any member of our mathematics department would be delighted to discover yet another proof. The joy is in making connections.) The students catch on fast. As Kessel observes, the following takes place after we have solved the magic square problem two different ways: "Schoenfeld asks the ritual question 'Are we done?' and Jeff replies 'We're never done.'" And, after we have obtained yet another solution to the problem, the ritual is repeated:

> Now we've beat it to death. Are we done? [pause] Of course not, because so far we've only solved the problem I gave you. If that's how mathematics progressed, mathematics wouldn't progress. Solving known problems is not what mathematicians get paid for, nor is it anything they have fun doing.

This approach is somewhat heavy-handed, but it works: the students come to anticipate the questions, and I no longer need to hammer at them. In fact, about a month into the course, one of the students asked "How come you're not asking us 'Are we done?' any more?" The question was easy to answer: "I don't need to at this point."

As with problem 2, both my lesson image and the discussion of the problem as it evolved are constraint-based. While it is impossible to know what individual students might say or do, the group of students as a whole is quite predictable. It's a pretty safe bet, for example, that if I urge the students to generate triples that add up to 15, they will do so randomly—and that I will then have the opportunity to chastise them for being unsystematic, as I did in the lesson Kessel analyzed.

Problem 4: Factors of abc, abc.

This problem, too, has multiple solutions. Working through it allows me to reinforce the points made in problems 1, 2, and 3. Among the solutions:

Working backwards. I ask, and we work through, what the problem "really asks you to show"—that is, that the 6-digit number you create is divisible by 7, then by 11, and then by 13. What does this mean? When the students see that this is the same as dividing by $7 \times 11 \times 13$, the problem is essentially solved.

Working forwards. I ask the class to explore carefully what the problem gives us to work with. In its general formulation, the problem says we should create a number of the form abc, abc, and then say something about its factors. So, what are the factors of abc, abc? (Determining the answer involves unpacking base 10 notation, which is useful.)

Induction. A completely unexpected solution was found some years ago by a senior English major who was "giving math one last chance." Working on this problem between the first and second days of the class, she tried the integer parameter strategy that we had discussed when working on problem 1. She took the three-digit numbers 001, 002, and 003, and did what the problem suggested. The number 001,001 was precisely equal to $7 \times 11 \times 13$; the number 002,002 was twice that product; and the number 003,003 was three times that product. The pattern was obvious! (Telling this story to my students when we discuss the problem allows me to make another important point: students in the course can make mathematical discoveries that are new to me, even though I've been teaching the course for many years.)

Problem 5: Sums of odd numbers.

In simplest terms, this problem is reinforcement for the "patterns" strategy and for doing proof by induction that were introduced in the solution to Problem 1. But, again, there are multiple solutions, which also lead to some amusing anecdotes and pieces of history. If one writes $S = 1 + 3 + 5 + \ldots + 2n - 1$ forward and backwards, and adds them up, one gets:

$$
\begin{array}{ccccccccc}
S & = & 1 & + & 3 & + & 5 & + & \cdots & +2n - 1 \\
S & = & 2n - 1 & +2n - 3 & +2n - 5 & + & & \cdots & + & 1 \\
\hline
2S & = & 2n & + & 2n & + & 2n & + & \cdots & + & 2n \quad (n \text{ times})
\end{array}
$$

so $\quad 2S = 2n^2.$

This proof can lead to a discussion of Gauss's summing up the numbers from 1 to 100.

Depending on how far afield one wants to get, this kind of argument can lead to the informal proof for the sum of a geometric series,

$$
\begin{array}{cccccccc}
S & = & 1 & + & \dfrac{1}{2} & + & \left(\dfrac{1}{2}\right)^2 + & \left(\dfrac{1}{2}\right)^3 + & \cdots \\
-\dfrac{S}{2} & = & -[& & \dfrac{1}{2} & + & \left(\dfrac{1}{2}\right)^2 + & \left(\dfrac{1}{2}\right)^3 + & \cdots] \\
\hline
\dfrac{S}{2} & = & 1
\end{array}
$$

from which it follows that $S = 2$, and a discussion of its correctness, which is exploded by the analogous proof for a geometric series where the multiplier is larger than 1:

$$
\begin{array}{ccccccccc}
T & = & 1 & + & 2 & + & 2^2 & + & 2^3 & + & \cdots \\
-2T & = & -[& & 2 & + & 2^2 & + & 2^3 & + & \cdots] \\
\hline
-T & = & 1
\end{array}
$$

from which it follows that $T = -1$. (!!!)

Excursions of this type are partly for entertainment value (remember, I need to have the students come back!), but they also serve to raise interesting issues about mathematical rigor and the need for proof. Those are themes to which we return consistently during the course.

Finally, there is a lovely "picture proof" of the result,

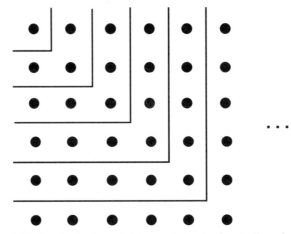

Readers and their students might want to look at *Proofs Without Words* (Nelsen, 1993) for more such examples.

Problem 6: Solving simultaneous equations.

As noted above, this is a set-up. It makes the point powerfully that certain heuristic strategies, such as draw a diagram, really can make a difference.

Problem 7: Exploring $(2n + 1)^2 - 1$.

This problem picks up on the themes raised in preceding problems, for example:

- patterns can be seen by looking at simple examples (there is an inductive proof that the given expression is divisible by 8); and
- representation is important ("What do we mean by an odd number?"). This reiterates and reinforces the theme introduced in the "working forwards" solution to problem 4.

In addition the problem is our first excursion into number theory. Both the answer itself and (more importantly) the method used to solve it will be used to deal with other problems later in the course.

Problem 8: Pythagorean cubes.

This problem, like problem 7, exploits the power of mathematical representation. (Simple as it seems, some students will not think immediately to express the problem statement in algebraic terms.) It provides the context for a review of methods of determining rational roots of polynomials, and reminds students that graphing an algebraic expression can help determine its roots. It also, of course, provides a context for a discussion of Fermat's last theorem.

Problem 9: The cemetery picture.

For your amusement, and the students'. This problem is also a set-up. I make sure to be on my way out the door at the end of class when I reveal the solution to those who haven't yet found it . . .

7. Discussion

I want to end this paper as it began, with a note of thanks to my friends and colleagues for shedding light on my problem solving course and causing me to reflect on it once more. Abraham Arcavi and Manuel Santos provided readers with the big picture, in effect providing the context for this paper as well. Luciano Meira explored and explained a potentially contradictory claim I make about the course, that a classroom—an obviously artificial environment—can serve as the home for a community that possesses some of the most important properties of the mathematical community at large. Jack Smith explored two potential contradictions (or at least, two common misunderstandings), his analysis showing that a highly interactive classroom need not be unstructured and that a teacher can scaffold students into taking on mathematical authority without simply abdicating it himself.[6] Cathy Kessel brought all of these themes together, showing how a particular discourse style that violates the traditional rules of the game can serve as a tool for building the "microcosm of selected aspects of mathematical practice and culture" into which the class is supposed to evolve. The analyses are subtle, the results provocative.

At this point, by way of synthesis, I would like to return to the idea of modeling the teaching process that was introduced in Sections 1 and 2. As noted, our model of teaching-in-context is intended to explain how and why teachers do what they do, in the midst of classroom interactions. While a full analysis of my opening lessons is out of the question given the space available here, I would like to at least suggest what that analysis would look like. Following that brief discussion, I shall reflect on the modeling enterprise itself.

A major part of the analysis includes the delineation of my beliefs and goals, the relevant parts of my knowledge base, and my lesson image—what I carry with me when I enter the classroom. In my case (and in Jim Minstrell's, which is analogous in many ways), these are also deeply tied to the curriculum for the course: I have spent a great deal of time searching out problems that support the kinds of classroom discussions I would like to see take place.

Much has been written about my general goals for the course (cf. Section 3 and the sources it cites) and the beliefs that support them. In addition to content goals, there are a wide range of social goals. In the most general terms, I need for the class to function well as a community of a particular type. There needs to be an atmosphere of trust and support: students need to feel free to float ideas without the fear that they will be scorned if the ideas turn out wrong. (Indeed, students need to feel that it's a good thing to float ideas. Sometimes seemingly

---

[6]Here I should make the same caveat regarding my own instruction that I made when analyzing an early lesson of Jim Minstrell's (Schoenfeld, Minstrell, & van Zee, 1996). The lessons examined here are at the very beginning of the course, where the authority and direction provided by the teacher have to be substantial. Sessions later in the course are more free-form and less constrained. As the norms of our classroom community get established, there is decreased need for structuring and scaffolding from me.

oddball suggestions pay off.) But at the same time, the intellectual standards we maintain have to be those of the mathematical community: assertions have to be clear and justifiable, and everything anyone including myself says must be open for scrutiny and possible rejection. Beyond this balancing act, I have the concerns of any teacher. I have to worry about the students who seem to demand too much "air time" and those who are reluctant to speak. As I get to know the class, I develop goals specific to individual students, so that my response to a comment from one student may not be the same as my response to the identical comment from another student would be. Ultimately, to provide a line-by-line analysis of (some segment of) the course, all of this detail would have to go into the model.[7]

In a similar way, a full analysis would call for a much more extensive delineation of my lesson image and the knowledge base that supports it. How many levels of give-and-take do I imagine? Where do I expect the dialogue to go? How do I expect to pose the problems, lead the discussion? What do I expect the students to say in response to my questions? How am I likely to respond? Where does the lesson image stop and leave me to my own devices—my content knowledge, pedagogical knowledge, etc.? What is that knowledge, and how do I tend to use it? Note that I am of course one informant on these issues, but also that answers to these kinds of questions may emerge only from intensive analyses of videotapes of my lessons. For example, until reading Arcavi et al.'s analysis and reviewing the videotape I was not consciously aware of using a strategy like the one described in the discussion of problem 2, above. Similarly, the Teacher Model Group's research suggests that some of the very complex question-and-answer interactions in Minstrell's lessons can be modeled with a rather simple set of decision rules.

Armed with information of this type, one can then analyze a lesson (or lesson segment) in very fine-grained detail. The question, at every point of the interaction, is: do we have good reason to claim we understand why the teacher is doing what he or she is doing, and what he or she might do next?

I assert that in the three cases that we have analyzed in substantial detail— a relatively new teacher conducting a rather traditional lesson (Zimmerlin & Nelson, 1996), an experienced and highly regarded teacher conducting an innovative but very familiar lesson of his own design (Schoenfeld, Minstrell, & van Zee, 1996), and my own teaching—there is reason to believe that the analyses are accurate, informative, and predictive. Details of the other two studies are found in the papers referenced, and in Schoenfeld (1997). Here I offer just a bit more detail about the modeling of my own instruction. The papers by Santos and Arcavi et al. provide a good deal of the background for our analyses, with the model itself providing some of the "glue" that binds things together—the key issue being how and why I do what I do. Some of that detail is at least

---

[7]Such detail is bypassed here, since the discussion only goes a few levels "deep" into the parsing of the lesson.

foreshadowed by Figure 3, which represents the first few levels of the parsing of the opening day of my problem solving course. There, at least, one sees that at a global level the lesson unfolded in a way that is consistent with my lesson image. A more fine-grained analysis (the core of which is found in Arcavi et al.) would, for example, look in detail at chunk [1.5.2] and would document that my interactions with the students did indeed conform to the decision rule suggested above.

Extending the analysis suggested in Figure 3 is a straightforward matter. As noted above, capturing my knowledge and behavior in that form provides a fine-grained explanation of what I did and why. In a slightly odd way, this kind of description allows for "predictions" that provide a check on the accuracy of the model: one can watch the tape of the class up to a point where a student makes a suggestion, run the model, and then see if my response is the one predicted by the model. Of course, in this case, the "prediction" is post hoc; you are merely seeing whether the description captures my behavior. (It is anything but a trivial test, however: the details of the model, which include my beliefs, goals, and action plans, all have to play out in the right ways to suggest what I will do "next.") Beyond that kind of test, however, it is also the case that I have taught the course at other times (including this year). In those instances the model, after being updated to take into account my lesson image for the instruction being analyzed, can actually be used to make legitimate a priori predictions of what I am likely to do.[8] While we have not done any formal analyses, informal analyses of this year's instruction suggest that the model holds up pretty well. For example, the discussions of the first few problems were in some ways quite different—comments and suggestions from students came in a different order than in the course analyzed by Arcavi et al., and (of course) there were some new wrinkles. But such differences are handled easily by the model, so that, for example, the discussion of problem 2, although in a different order than the one discussed in Arcavi et al., was still captured by the constraint-based decision strategy delineated above. I wouldn't want to make too much of this finding. But, triangulation of any sort is the kind of thing we look for in testing out potential explanatory frames.

We have reached the end of this paper, and it is time for the conclusions. The main question one has to ask about this kind of enterprise is the following. Besides the fact that doing such analyses is fun (for those with a particular analytical bent), what is the value of engaging in them? I think there is both pragmatic and theoretical value. Here, in brief, is why.

---

[8] Again I must stress that teachers are not robots and that their behavior is not predictable in any simple or reductive sense. The use of the model to make predictions as discussed above is one test of its accuracy. If we think it captures someone's teaching fairly well, then there should be times when we feel (and the model predicts) that we have a pretty good handle on the way the teacher will respond to a particular situation. If this turns out to be the case, then we feel increasingly confident about the accuracy of the model. If it is not, then we have to be concerned about our misplaced confidence.

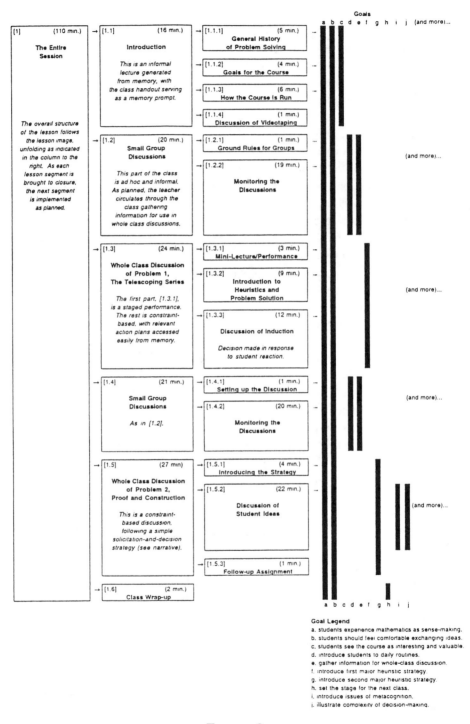

FIGURE 3

A Top-Level Parse of the First Lesson in the Problem Solving Course

On the pragmatic side, our analyses of beginning and accomplished teachers have begun to explain some of the underpinnings of the skilled classroom performance demonstrated by accomplished professionals, and some of the pitfalls that new teachers can fall prey to. In the case of the lesson analyzed in Zimmerlin and Nelson (1996), we see much more than the fact that a new teacher has difficulty dealing with an unexpected set of responses from his students. We see how his lesson image left him unprepared for what the students said; we see how, given his knowledge base (specifically, the pedagogical strategies he had available), he would quickly find himself in a bind. In the case of Minstrell's lesson (Schoenfeld, Minstrell, & van Zee, 1996), we see how the teacher's extensive knowledge base (especially certain kinds of pedagogical content knowledge) allow him to deal with the unexpected. This is important in two ways. First, an understanding of the nature and complexity of the knowledge bases possessed by accomplished teachers can help us to develop an understanding of the terrain that new teachers must traverse as they evolve into skilled professionals. (In a much simpler domain, chess playing, analyses of the foundations of expertise demonstrated why, no matter how smart you are, you will have to play thousands of hours of chess before building up a "vocabulary" of positions that will enable you to play at a high level.) The more realistic our views of teaching competence and the knowledge that supports it, the wiser we can be about professional development. Second, these analyses sometimes enable us to see potential simplicity in acts of substantial complexity. For example, no-one is about to claim that Minstrell or I follow simple rules when engaging in extended interactions with students. But, if straightforward decision procedures such as the ones described in Section 6 come close to capturing some important aspects of what we do, then explicit decision procedures such as these might be useful as scaffolding to help other teachers to develop similar skills.

Next, theory. Simply put, the goal of our modeling work is to create a theory of teaching-in-context. Our intention is to be able to say how and why teachers do what they do, on the fly, in the midst of classroom interactions. Of course, the pieces of the puzzle that form the components of our model of teaching are not new. As discussed in Section 2, there is a large literature on teacher beliefs; there is an equally large literature on teacher planning; and there is a much larger general literature on knowledge organization and access to it. However, what has been lacking to this point is a picture of how those pieces fit together, at a level of mechanism. That is what the model offers. It says: suppose a particular event happens at a particular point in the classroom. Given this teacher's beliefs, he or she is likely to give certain goals high priority. Given this teacher's knowledge base, certain action plans are most consistent with this new constellation of goals and beliefs, and are thus most likely to be implemented. In short, this kind of approach seeks to explain how things work; it say what will happen, and why. This kind of approach takes us from mere descriptions of which components are important to careful descriptions of how they actually function. That's not only fun, it's what doing science is all about.

References

1. Aguirre, Julia, & Speer, Natasha. (1996). Examining the relationship between beliefs and goals in teacher practice. Paper presented at the annual meeting of the American Educational Research Association, New York, April 8–12, 1996.

2. Berliner, David C., & Calfee, Robert C. (Eds.). (1996). *Handbook of educational psychology*. New York: Macmillan.

3. Borko, Hilda, & Putnam, Ralph. (1996). Learning to teach. In David C. Berliner & Robert C. Calfee (Eds.), *Handbook of educational psychology* (pp. 673–708). New York: Macmillan.

4. Calderhead, James. (1996). Teachers: Beliefs and knowledge. In David C. Berliner & Robert C. Calfee, *Handbook of educational psychology* (pp. 709–725). New York: Macmillan.

5. Clark, Christopher, & Peterson, Penelope. (1986). Teachers' thought processes. In M. C. Wittrock (Ed.), *Handbook of research on teaching* (Third edition, pp. 255–314). New York: Macmillan.

6. De Franco, Thomas C. (1996). A perspective on mathematical problem-solving expertise based on the performances of male Ph.D. mathematicians. In James J. Kaput, Alan H. Schoenfeld, & Ed Dubinsky (Eds.), *Research in Collegiate Mathematics Education II* (pp. 195–214). Washington, DC: Conference Board of the Mathematical Sciences.

7. Fennema, Elizabeth, & Franke, Megan. (1992). Teachers' knowledge and its impact. In Douglas A. Grouws (Ed.), *Handbook of research on mathematics teaching and learning* (pp. 147–164). New York: Macmillan.

8. Grouws, Douglas A. (Ed.). (1992). *The handbook of research on the teaching and learning of mathematics*. New York: MacMillan.

9. Kurchak, J. (1963). *Hungarian problem books, Vols. 1 and 2* (Elvira Rapaport, Trans.). Washington, DC: Mathematical Association of America.

10. Nelsen, Roger B. (1993). *Proofs without words*. Washington, DC: Mathematical Association of America.

11. Romberg, Thomas A., & Carpenter, Thomas P. (1986). Research on teaching and learning mathematics: Two disciplines of scientific inquiry. In M. C. Wittrock (Ed.), *Handbook of research on teaching* (Third edition, pp. 850–873). New York: Macmillan.

12. Schoenfeld, Alan H. (1983). *Problem solving in the mathematics curriculum: A report, recommendations, and an annotated bibliography*. Washington, DC: Mathematics Association of America.

13. Schoenfeld, Alan H. (1985). *Mathematical problem solving*. New York: Academic Press.

14. Schoenfeld, Alan H. (1988). Ideas in the air: Speculations on small-group learning, environment and cultural influences on cognition, and epistemology. *International Journal of Educational Research, 13*, 71–88.

15. Schoenfeld, Alan H. (1991a). On mathematics as sense-making: An informal attack on the unfortunate divorce of formal and informal mathematics. In James Voss, David Perkins, & Judith Segal (Eds.), *Informal reasoning and education* (pp. 311–343). Hillsdale, NJ: Erlbaum.

16. Schoenfeld, Alan H. (1991b). What's all the fuss about problem solving? *Zentrallblatt fur didaktik der mathematik, 91*(1), 4–8.

17. Schoenfeld, Alan H. (1992). Learning to think mathematically: Problem solving, metacognition, and sense making in mathematics. In Douglas Grouws (Ed.), *The handbook of research on the teaching and learning of mathematics* (pp. 334–370). New York: MacMillan.

18. Schoenfeld, Alan H. (1994). Reflections on doing and teaching mathematics. In Alan H. Schoenfeld (Ed.), *Mathematical thinking and problem solving* (pp. 53–70). Hillsdale, NJ: Lawrence Erlbaum Associates.

19. Schoenfeld, Alan H. (1996). Elements of a model of teaching. Paper presented at the annual meeting of the American Educational Research Association, New York, April 8–12, 1996.

20. Schoenfeld, Alan H., Minstrell, Jim, & van Zee, Emily. (1996). The detailed analysis of an established teacher carrying out a non-traditional lesson. Paper presented at the annual meeting of the American Educational Research Association, New York, April 8–12, 1996.

21. Schoenfeld, Alan H. (1997). Can we build a comprehensive model of what teachers do in the classroom? And if so, why should we care? *Issues in Education*.

22. Sherin, Miriam G., Sherin, Bruce, & Madanes, Rodrigo. (1996). Where terms collide: Clarifying diverse accounts of teacher knowledge. Paper presented at the annual meeting of the American Educational Research Association, New York, April 8–12, 1996.

23. Shulman, Lee S. (1987). Knowledge and teaching: Foundations of the new reform. *Harvard Educational Review 57*(1) 1–22.

24. Shulman, Lee S. (1986). Paradigms and research programs in the study of teaching: A contemporary perspective. In M. C. Wittrock (Ed.), *Handbook of research on teaching* (Third edition, pp. 3–36). New York: Macmillan.

25. Silver, Edward A. (1987). Foundations of cognitive theory and research for mathematics problem-solving instruction. In Alan H. Schoenfeld (Ed.), *Cognitive science and mathematics education* (pp. 33–60). Hillsdale, NJ: Erlbaum.

26. Thompson, Alba. (1992). Teachers' beliefs and conceptions: A synthesis of the research. In Douglas Grouws (Ed.), *Handbook of research on mathematics teaching and learning* (pp. 127–146). New York: Macmillan.

27. Wittrock, Merlin C. (Ed.). (1986). *Handbook of research on teaching* (Third edition). New York: Macmillan.

28. Zimmerlin, Daniel, & Nelson, Mark. (1996). The detailed analysis of a beginning teacher carrying out a traditional lesson. Paper presented at the annual meeting of the American Educational Research Association, New York, April 8–12, 1996.

UNIVERSITY OF CALIFORNIA AT BERKELEY

CBMS Issues in Mathematics Education
Volume **7**, 1998

A Cross-Sectional Investigation
of the Development of the
Function Concept

MARILYN P. CARLSON

ABSTRACT. This study investigates students' development of the function concept as they progress through undergraduate mathematics. An exam measuring students' understandings of major aspects of the function concept was developed and administered to students who had just received A's in college algebra, second-semester honors calculus, or first-year graduate mathematics courses. Follow-up interviews were conducted with five students from each of the three groups. Analyses of the exam results and interview transcripts reveal that even our best students do not completely understand concepts taught in a course, and when confronted with an unfamiliar problem, have difficulty accessing recently taught information.

Acknowledgments. I am grateful to Uri Treisman and Josef Dorfmeister for guiding each phase of this research. Thanks to Josef Dorfmeister, Uri Treisman and Dick Stanley for their careful reviews, insights and recommendations. Thanks to my children, Tim and Joni, for their love, support and encouragement.

The college algebra students had a narrow view of functions and believed that all functions were definable by a single algebraic formula. They did not understand the function language, were unable to interpret dynamic graphical information, and did not know how to use function notation to represent "real world" relationships. Their inability to speak and think about functions as processes which accept input and produce output suggests they conceptualized functions as actions. Second-semester calculus students had a much more general view of functions and much greater ability to speak and use the language of functions. Although they were able to interpret dynamic graphical information, they were unable to use information taught in early calculus and had difficulty interpreting and representing covariant aspects of a function situation. The beginning graduate students understood most aspects of the function concept and had a greater tendency to access concepts of beginning calculus and the ability to represent covariant aspects of a function situation.

These high performing students believed that their mathematical abilities were acquired during high school and were developed as a result of confronting difficult problems in an environment where they were encouraged to reflect, persist, and engage in constructive activities. They wanted to understand newly presented concepts and were frustrated that the rapid pace of particular classes had led them to abandon understanding and retreat to memorization. These results indicate that an individual's view of the function concept evolves over a period of many years and requires an effort of "sense making" to understand and orchestrate individual function components to work in concert.

Introduction

The function concept is an important and unifying concept in modern mathematics [9, 5, 18], central to many different branches of mathematics [8], and essential to related areas of the sciences [18]. A strong understanding of the concept of function is a vital part of the background of any student hoping to comprehend calculus [2]. Beyond their use in calculus and analysis, functions are widely used in the comparison of abstract mathematical structures. For example, functions are used to determine whether two sets have the same cardinality and whether two topologies are homeomorphic. Functions can also be used as elements of abstract mathematical structures such as vector spaces, rings, and groups. Further, functions are used extensively in the sciences for modeling such phenomena as brain activity, population density, and electrical fields. Despite the fact that functions are currently recognized as a unifying mathematical concept and an important mathematical construct, Cooney and Wilson's [4] historical investigation of the function curriculum demonstrates that textbook authors have not made the function concept a unifying principle of early algebra curriculum.

As early as 1921, the National Committee on Mathematical Requirements of the Mathematical Association of America recommended that the study of functions be given central focus in secondary school mathematics [4]. The NCTM *Curriculum and Evaluation Standards* [15] calls for the inclusion of function-related activities as early as fourth grade (p. 60), continuing through the high school mathematics curriculum where the concept of function is a unifying idea (p. 154). In *Everybody Counts* [16], the authors state, "if undergraduate mathematics does nothing else, it should help students develop function sense" (p. 51). Although curriculum reform efforts are beginning to respond to calls for change, and researchers have begun to identify many of the difficulties students experience with understanding aspects of the function concept [6], ongoing analysis of student understanding of the function concept is necessary for guiding future curriculum decisions. Without such analysis, curriculum decisions stand little chance of being guided by informed judgments of how students acquire understanding of essential function components.

This study investigates how high-performing undergraduate students acquire an understanding of major aspects of the function concept. A 25-item exam was developed and administered to students who have just received A's in college algebra, second-semester calculus, or beginning graduate mathematics courses. The written exam was designed to investigate the following research questions:

- What differences exist among the three groups relative to their understanding of major aspects of the function concept?

- When are students' understandings of major aspects of the function concept acquired?

Following the administration of the written exam, follow-up interviews were conducted with five students from each of the three groups. The follow-up interviews were designed to investigate the following research questions:

- What factors in students' backgrounds contribute to existing differences among the three groups relative to their understandings of major aspects of the function concept?

- What factors in high-performing students' backgrounds have influenced their mathematical development and continued study of mathematics?

Although researchers have investigated many different aspects of students' understandings of the concept of function, such as: students' ability to interpret various types of graphs [24]; students' conceptual view of functions [2]; and students' ability to translate between various function representations [5, 21, 19], a comprehensive study aimed at guiding educational reformers has not yet been devised. To make this study more inclusive, research investigating many aspects of the function concept which previously had been considered separately [2, 14, 5] was brought together. This research investigates students' abilities to:

- Characterize "real world" functional relationships using function notation;

- Operate with a particular type of function representation, such as a formula, a table, or a graph;

- Move between different representations of the same function;

- Represent and interpret covariant aspects of the function situation (i.e. recognize and characterize how change in one variable affects change in another);

- Interpret "static" and "dynamic" functional information (i.e. interpret graphs representing position and rate of change);

- Interpret and describe local and global function properties: slope, continuity, and differentiability;

- Construct functions using formulas and other functions;

- Recognize functions, non-functions and function types;

- Conceptualize a function both as a process and as an object;

- Interpret and understand the language of functions; and

- Characterize the relationship between a function and an equation.

This list of abilities provides a framework for investigating changes in students' function conceptions. It takes into account Breidenbach et al.'s [2] and Monk's [13] classifications of students' conceptual views and additional aspects of a mature function understanding which were identified by this study. As students gain a more complete understanding of functions they acquire more of these abilities. This list of function abilities was developed and refined over a four-year period, each one measurable on multiple levels and frequently separated by fine distinctions. This framework provides flexibility in the investigation of relationships among students' function abilities and conceptual views. For example, a student's function conception can be related to her or his ability to represent covariant aspects of a function situation and/or ability to interpret graphs representing rates of change.

Background

Research results show that acquisition of essential aspects of the function concept is extremely complex [18]. Students have difficulty translating between different representations [19] and applying basic concepts at different levels of abstraction [9]. Ayers et al. [1] and Vinner and Dreyfus [21] report that many students think a function must only be represented by a single algebraic rule describing a continuous, one-to-one function. Selden and Selden [18] also report that students think the graphs of functions should be "nice," and all functions must be one-to-one.

Monk [11, 12, 13] has done extensive research investigating students' interpretations of graphs. His recent research [13] has shown that students often experience problems interpreting dynamic graphical relationships over subintervals of the domain of a function. Monk [13] and Kaput [7] both report that students expect the shape of a graph to reflect visual aspects of the situation described by the graph, rather than a representation of the relationship between two variables.

Educational researchers have classified students' understandings of functions according to their conceptual views. Breidenbach et al. [2] have categorized students' function conceptions as prefunction, action, process, and object. They suggest that early function curricula should aim toward moving students from the action conceptualization, a view of the function as a repeatable mental or physical manipulation of objects, to that of a process conceptualization, the interiorization of actions so that all actions can take place entirely in the mind of the subject. Students attaining this level of understanding will view an expression as "what you get" when you evaluate it says Thompson [20], and will have no difficulty understanding function composition or the relationship between a function and its inverse [2]. Once the student attains a high degree of awareness of a process in its totality, this process can be encapsulated to obtain an object conception [2].

Subjects, Procedures and Data Analysis

The student subjects for the study were selected from three different levels of mathematical preparation: college algebra, second semester calculus, and beginning graduate study in mathematics. Group 1, comprising 30 students just completing college algebra with a high A (greater than 95% class average), was the lowest level group participating in the study. Group 2 consisted of 16 students just completing second semester calculus with a grade of A, and group 3 contained 14 graduate students who had just completed their first semester of graduate level mathematics with a grade of A in either complex analysis or abstract algebra. The college algebra curriculum involved an early introduction of functions in small lecture sections, and the calculus curriculum was taught using a traditional text with lecture also as the primary mode of instruction. The graduate students were products of undergraduate and graduate traditional mathematics curricula. The written exam was administered to each group upon completion of their respective courses. Prior to distributing the written exam, the author announced a monetary incentive for completing the exam with diligence, dedicating at least one and one half hours to the task and showing a serious effort in responding to each item. Exams were scored using a carefully developed and tested five-point rubric for each exam question. After scoring each exam, group means and standard deviations for each group on all exam items were computed. Group differences relative to each question were determined using an F-test, with follow-up pairwise comparisons using the Tukey test at an overall α level of .05.

Follow-up interviews were conducted with fifteen students, five from each of the three groups. Interview subjects were selected by identifying students within each group who performed at various levels on the written exam. Invitations to participate in the interview were given to a broad group with diverse performance in order to have the best representative sampling available. Although the interviews for this study were primarily unstructured, with the interviewer spontaneously reacting to students' descriptions of their solutions, some structure was imposed by preparing interview questions in advance. During the interview, the researcher initially read each exam question aloud and made general reference to the response the student had given. The student was given a few minutes to review the response, then prompted to describe her or his solution and asked to provide justification and clarification to the solution offered. After the student's summary, the researcher made general inquiries, such as, "explain" or "clarify," and continued to ask more specific questions, if necessary, until a response was elicited or it appeared that all knowledge had been elaborated. If one of the main components of the question was correctly answered, the student was queried to recall when and how the concept was acquired. This process was repeated for each question on the written exam.

Interview length varied from 90 to 150 minutes. Group 1 students expended the least amount of time due to their limited ability to articulate responses to some of the more difficult exam items. During the interview, correct responses were acknowledged and students were encouraged to communicate their ideas both verbally and symbolically. The interview tone was amiable and nonthreatening, and efforts were made to make students comfortable with providing candid responses.

Analysis of the interview results involved a careful reading of each interview transcript, while attempting to identify common student responses and misconceptions. The percentage of students providing each response type was then determined for the collection of interviews for each group.

During interviews, students were also asked to describe what they believed had affected the development of their mathematical abilities, as well as their interest in continuing to study mathematics. These sections of the interview transcripts were analyzed separately to provide information regarding the factors that influence successful students' mathematical maturation and motivation. Common responses were identified and the percentages of students providing each response type, for each group, were determined.

Final results were obtained by analyzing both the quantitative and qualitative results relative to each group, as well as the individual.

Development of the Research Instruments

The written exam was designed to measure major aspects of acquiring an understanding of the function concept. The exam development paralleled the identification of these attributes. Different exam problems sometimes measure different levels of understanding of the same function attribute, and one problem frequently provides information about more than one function ability. Many of the exam items were constructed in collaboration with experts in the field; and others were borrowed from the literature. For example, Monk's "speed vs. time for two cars" problem [14] was used to measure students' abilities to interpret static and dynamic graphical information, and selected items from Breidenbach et al.'s [2] exam measured students' function conceptualizations.

Five-point rubrics were written for each exam question. Each rubric was developed to measure the accuracy, strength of justification and degree of conceptual understanding shown by responses. Prior to developing the individual rubrics, a general rubric guideline combining aspects of both the Kansas and California rubrics used in state mathematics testing, was devised to define criteria for determining individual points for specific rubrics.

Development and verification of the 25 rubrics involved a lengthy process of refinement. Following the development and refinement of individual rubrics, four experts were solicited to review all rubrics, noting inconsistencies between their opinions and the developed rubrics. There were few such inconsistencies, though minor refinements were made using the experts' feedback. After scoring each exam twice, resolving all inconsistencies between the two scorings, and again making minor refinements to individual rubrics, the reliability of the rubrics was verified by asking each expert to score one exam from each group. The average variation between scores was 3.5% and the greatest variation between two scores was 4.8%. No score on an individual test item varied more than one point out of five. Since the experts were familiar with the problems and had been working closely with the researcher during the development of the exam, six additional individuals, three mathematicians and three mathematics educators, were solicited to score three exams, again one from each group. With this scoring, the average variation between scores was 5.5% and the greatest variation was 7.2%.

The research interview was designed to determine the knowledge motivating written responses and gain additional information concerning how and when particular constructs were acquired. Its development was guided by careful examination of each written exam response. During an initial reading of all exams, common responses for individual items for each group were identified. The exams were read once again, while tallying the number of students within each group who provided each of the response types. Prior to conducting each interview, the interviewee's exam was re-read, and notes were made concerning evidence of incomplete understanding. This information and the tallied common responses provided guidance for developing interview questions and focus for conducting individual interviews.

Results

Because of the large amount of data collected, details are presented only for selected exam items. Rubric scores for all items are in Appendix B. For a complete description of results for the 25-item exam for all groups, see Carlson [3].

The presentation of results includes a statement of the question, a brief discussion of the results, and a table presenting exam scores and common written responses for each of the three groups. This is followed by a discussion of the interview results of the group which provided the most interesting interview results for that item, followed by excerpts of individual interview transcripts for each interview subject within the group.

Item 5. (Instructions for items 5–7: Give an example to confirm the existence of such a function. If one does not exist, explain why.)

Does there exist a function all of whose values are equal to each other?

Groups 2 and 3 performed relatively well on this item (Table 1), with group 1 having a mean score of 1.07 (out of 5.0). Both groups 2 and 3 performed significantly higher than group 1, while group 3 did not perform significantly higher than group 2. A correct example was constructed by only 7% of group 1 students, while 69% of group 2 and 92% of group 3 students provided a correct example. Twenty-five percent of group 2 students constructed the example $y = x$ and 8% of group 3 students constructed an example containing minor errors.

TABLE 1. Quantitative Results for Item 5

| | Group | | |
	1	2	3
Mean score[a]	1.07	4.00	4.67
Standard deviation	1.76	1.87	1.15
Common responses (%)			
No answer	60	0	0
$y = x$	23	25	0
Minor error in example	10	6	8
Correct example	7	69	92

[a] The differences between the means of groups 1 and 2, and groups 1 and 3 were significant at $\alpha = .05$.

Four of the five students interviewed from group 1 persisted with "$y = x$" as the answer, when asked to construct a function all of whose values are equal to each other. The interviews for this question suggest that group 1 students do not understand that the function values represent the y-values (assuming traditional labeling). When prompted to explain what is meant by the phrase, "all of whose values are equal to each other," two students gave a response indicating that all the x-values are equal (students B and E), and two students indicated that all x-values must equal all y-values (students A and C). The interview transcripts for group 1 students revealed that high-performing college algebra students are not able to translate verbal function language to algebraic function notation for a basic, but essential, aspect of functions.

Interview Transcripts—Group 1.

Student A.

Int: Can you define a function all of whose values are equal to each other?

A: I really cannot compute anything on that. Its values are equal? I really do not know. Is that a function?

Int: Would $y = 5$ work?

A: I guess it is equal, but I do not know.

Int: Do you think it meets the criteria, a function all of whose values are equal to each other?

A: I guess, not really, because $y =$ anything that is not $y = 5$.

Int: So when you hear, "all of whose values are equal to each other," what do you think of?

A: I was just thinking when x equals to y, or two different variables equal to each other.

Student B.

Int: You said yes, but did not give an example. Can you think of one?

B: I just thought about the one at $\{(0,0), (1,1), (2,2)\}$. I don't know if that is right.

Int: How would you write that function?

B: Like $x = 1$, $y = 1$. So at $(0,0)$, $(1,1)$. Is that what you were thinking of?

Int: What am I referring to when I ask, "whose values are equal to each other"?

B: Like as if x values are always equal. Then it would be a vertical line.

Student C.

Int: You said yes, and you constructed the function $y = x$. Explain to me why you think this function works.

C: I was thinking all x values are equal to all y values, like if you got one side of the equation, a number is the same number on the other side of the equation. That would fill in the whole chalk board. No, it would not fill in everything, it would be a line.

Int: Does this meet the criteria that all values are equal to each other?

C: A function all whose values are equal. No, because what you want is something where y equals and all of the x would be equal, so you want x

to be the same. That will be a straight line, a vertical line. But it would not be a function, because you cannot have a vertical line as a function, because it would not pass the vertical line test.

Int: How did you determine that you wanted all of the x values equal to each other?

C: y is just arbitrary. I mean, not arbitrary but a solution. If you want all values equal to each other, then the x values that you plug in the formula are equal to each other. So all x need to be the same.

Int: It looks like you are still thinking.

C: Well, there is something that I am not quite grasping.

Student D.

Int: You left this blank. Can you think of a function all of whose values are equal to each other. What do you think I'm asking you to find?

D: I would just think that no matter what value you put in there, you have to get the same thing. I guess, if you have a function $f(x) = x^0$, that would work.

Int: Excellent! How about $f(x) = 7$, would that work?

D: Yes. In that one, there is no variable there, so there will be no change. I was thinking you had to have a variable.

Student E.

Int: You said yes, and wrote absolute value and negative absolute value. Can you explain your answer?

E: I just think of the graph when $x = y$. I mean absolute value. I was thinking of this graph of a straight line. They are all equal to each other. When $x = 2$, $y = 2$.

Int: So, how do you interpret, "whose values are equal to each other"?

E: All x's equal all y's.

Item 12. Imagine this bottle filling with water. Sketch a graph of the height as a function of the amount of water that's in the bottle.

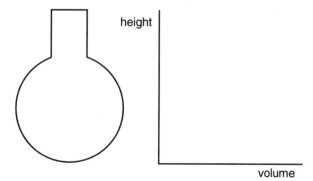

The mean scores for the three groups were significantly different for item 12 (Table 2), with group 3 performing higher than both groups 2 and 1, and group 2 performing significantly higher than group 1. Group 2's scores are more variable than those for group 1 and 3, with group 2 receiving a mean score of 2.41. Analysis of the written exam revealed that 74% of the group 2 subjects constructed a strictly concave down or concave up graph for the portion of the graph corresponding to the spherical portion of the bottle.

TABLE 2. Quantitative Results for Item 12

| | Group | | |
	1	2	3
Mean score[a]	1.47	2.41	4.33
Standard deviation	1.31	1.46	0.89
Common responses (%)			
Constructed an increasing straight line	47		
Another incorrect graph	26		
Constructed a strictly concave up graph	27	56	14
Constructed a strictly concave down graph		18	14
Correct graph, except for slope of line		13	21
All aspects of graph were correct		13	51

[a] The differences between the means of groups 1 and 2, and groups 1 and 3, and groups 2 and 3, were significant at $\alpha = .05$.

Given a bottle filling with water and asked to express height of water in the bottle as a function of volume, group 2 interview results reveal very different levels of understanding of covariant aspects (i.e. how change in height affects change in volume) of this real world situation. One of the five students (L) provided a strong justification, which clearly demonstrated understanding of the physical situation in terms of calculus. He provided a clear description of the concavity change in terms of the rate of change, and fluently discussed the changing sign of the second derivative. Two students (J and N) provided a clear analysis of the situation, using algebraic reasoning. Student M demonstrated no ability to attend to the covariant aspects of the situation. He simply argued that the height would always be increasing, so its graph would be a straight line. Student K provided a strictly concave down graph. Although this student demonstrated some awareness of the changing rate of height with respect to volume, he concluded the interview supporting the incorrect graph.

Interview transcripts—Group 2.

Student J.
Int: Describe how you sketched the graph (graph is correct).

J: I knew it changed different for the bottom part because it's circular and the top part has straight walls. If you look at it as putting the same amount of water in each time and look at how much the height would change, that's basically what I was trying to do. So for the first part, the height would be changing more quickly, and in the middle if you add the same amount of water, the height would not change as much as it would at the bottom. It's symmetric.

Int: How does that affect the graph?

J: Higher slope in the beginning, then it levels out, then a higher slope again. Then for the neck part it's basically a straight line because you're filling the same area with each amount.

Int: Nice explanation. What is the slope of the straight line?

J: About like the curve right here (pointing to the junction of the curve and line).

Student K.

Int: Explain your solution (graph is concave down).

K: This is my least favorite problem. I tried to solve for height in terms of volume and it was a mess.

Int: Can you analyze the situation without explicitly solving for h?

K: OK, the more water, the higher the height would be. In terms of height of the water, that is what we are talking about. If you are talking about the height left over, that is basically decreasing. Right here the height will be zero and the volume is zero. As you go up a little more, height increases and the volume increases quite a bit. Once you get there, the height increases slower. I guess from here to there height increases the same as the volume increases, and once you get here it increases slower. I guess from here to there height increases the same as the volume increases. No, I am wrong again. So, every time you have to put more and more volume in to get a greater height towards the middle of the bottle. Then once you cross the middle point of the bottle you have to put less and less in to get a greater height. Once you get here, it would be linear, probably. So, it's always going up (he traces his finger along the concave down graph), then it would be a line.

Int: So, what does the graph look like?

K: Like this (pointing to the concave down graph he has constructed), but it has a straight line at the end.

Student L.

Int: Explain how you obtained your graph (correct graph).

L: Well, looking at the volume of the sphere, if you take that, I remember my units have to be cubic, so I know it's some sort of cubic equation. For this cylinder part, I know it's going to be linear, since for the cylinder it's related by volume which equals area times height. And so we have area as a constant. So what we have is a linear equation for height as it's related to volume. Getting to that point, I knew it was filling at a cubic rate somehow, so it would have something like a cubic equation. When you take the inverse of that equation it whips it like that. But I was also able to see here that when you start out, it's going to be filling rapidly, so you are going to have a great slope. (Some confusion and continues.) But as you increase the volume, you're going to get less of a height change until you get up to here. As you get past the half-way point, it's going to go from concave down to concave up and you're going to have an inflection point.

Int: Can you tell me why it changes concavity there (pointing at the inflection point)?

L: Because if you take the second derivative of this volume in terms of height, you'll get a zero. On this side you have a negative acceleration. But once you reach the half-way point, then you start becoming a positive second derivative.

Int: Good.

Student M.

Int: Can you explain your solution (graph is concave up)?

M: I tried to solve for h. But I think I need to define it as a piecewise defined function. Maybe then I can figure it out.

Int: Did you try to get an idea of the general shape of the graph by imagining the bottle filling with water?

M: As the volume comes up, the height would go up at a steady rate.

Int: How would you represent this graphically?

M: It would be a straight line.

Int: So, the entire graph is a straight line.

M: Yes.

Student N.

Int: Can you explain how you determined your graph (graph is correct, except for the slope of the linear portion)?

N: When you're given a flask like this, the way I thought of it was, you have to start the coordinates at $(0,0)$ with volume equal to 0, and the height equal to 0. When you start filling something that has such a wide base like this, the height is going to not increase as fast as the volume, so that's why I have more of a line which is sloped more, like a little less than 1. Then when it gets past the circle, the largest diameter, here is when it is going to switch to the height increasing faster than the volume and thus the slope is going to be greater than 1 and increase that much quicker.

Int: What happens when it gets back to the neck?

N: The height will increase unit-wise compared to the volume, so it should be a straight line, I guess.

Int: How does the slope of the straight line correspond to the slope of the graph where the linear portion begins?

N: The slope would be just a little bit greater. It would be more like it was right where it went into that neck.

Item 4a. (Part B) Tom sees a ladder against a wall (in an almost vertical position). He pulls the base of the ladder away from the wall by a certain amount and then again by the same amount and then again by the same amount, and so forth. Each time he does this he records the distances by which the top of the ladder drops down. Do the amounts by which the top of the ladder drop down remain constant as Tom repeats this step; or do they get bigger, or do they get smaller? EXPLAIN.

The mean scores for the three groups are significantly different for item 4a, part B of the written exam (Table 3), with group 3 performing significantly higher than both groups 1 and 2, and group 2 performing significantly higher than group 1. Both quantitative and qualitative results indicate that group 2 and 3 students had very different levels of understanding and employed many different approaches to solving this problem. Group 1 responses were weak, with 67% of the written exam responses indicating that the ladder either remains constant or gets smaller. Twenty-three percent of group 2 students provided the correct solution, with an algebraic justification, and 29% provided the correct answer, but did not provide any explanation for their answers. Ninety-one percent of group 3 students provided the correct response, with 58% providing an algebraic justification and 33% using calculus to justify their answers.

TABLE 3. Quantitative Results for Item 4a (Part B)

| | Group | | |
	1	2	3
Mean score[a]	0.63	2.41	4.33
Standard deviation	1.03	1.46	1.61

[a] The differences between the means of groups 1 and 2, and groups 1 and 3, and groups 2 and 3, were significant at $\alpha = .05$.

Group 1 students were unable to represent the position of the ladder on the wall using algebraic techniques, though two of the five interview subjects attempted to reason through a solution by constructing their own physical models with their pencils. Group 2 students' responses varied dramatically on this item, with each interview subject providing a different approach. Individual responses for group 2 students ranged from totally correct with a clear justification using calculus to a response that the ladder drops down by a constant amount, followed by an incorrect algebraic argument. Analysis of group 2 interview results reveals that when analyzing real-world relationships second-semester calculus students do not demonstrate the tendency to access the formal mathematics that they know. However, four of the five interview subjects for group 3, without hesitation, set up the Pythagorean relationship representing the position of the ladder on the wall. Three of these students finished their solutions by computing the derivative, followed by a correct justification using the language of calculus. The other student provided a correct algebraic justification. The only group 3 student unable to provide a correct solution had just returned to graduate school and had not interacted with early calculus for over 8 years. The students who accessed tools of calculus when justifying their responses had recently taught a course in introductory calculus.

Item 2d. Compute $f(x + a)$ given $f(x) = 3x^2 + 2x - 4$.

Group 2 and 3 students demonstrated little difficulty (Table 4) with this item. However, group 1 students' mean score of 2.07 is surprising, since their college algebra course had provided explicit instruction in algebraically computing $f(x + a)$ for both linear and quadratic functions. The most common incorrect written exam response (43% of group 1 students) was to simply add an a to the expression on the right side of the equal sign. Group 2 and 3 students had no difficulty with this item, although one group 2 student failed to complete the question.

TABLE 4. Quantitative Results for Item 2d

| | Group | | |
	1	2	3
Mean score[a]	2.07	4.76	5.00
Standard deviation	2.32	0.97	0.00

[a] The differences between the means of groups 1 and 2, and groups 1 and 3, were significant at $\alpha = .05$.

Although four of the five group 1 interview subjects provided correct justifications for their correct responses, their justifications provided insights into how group 1 students think about the evaluation of $f(x + a)$. Group 1 students described their solutions either as a substitution of $x + a$ for x, or a procedure of adding a to every x. When prompted for a more in depth explanation, none of the interview subjects referred to the fact that they were evaluating f at another point, or the input to f was now $x + a$, rather than x. The student who simply added a to the expression on the right of the equal sign indicated that he had arrived at this solution by substituting $3x^2 + 2x - 4$ into the x in $f(x + a)$. Additionally, students C and E stated that they once had difficulty with this type of problem because they did not know "which one to plug into which one." Although no interview subject viewed the problem as simply adding a to both sides of the equal sign, this justification did occur when piloting the interview procedures. These responses suggest that group 1 students view function evaluations as collections of actions to be carried out, and do not yet view a function as a process which accepts input and produces output.

In their interviews, group 2 and 3 students either discussed their correct solutions by describing $x+a$ as the input of the function, or indicated that they were evaluating the function f at $x+a$, and that the solution after the evaluation was the output to the function. These responses suggest that group 2 and 3 students have a process view of functions (i.e. they think of a function as a process which accepts input and produces output).

Item 8a. The given graph represents speed vs. time for two cars.

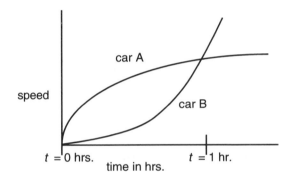

State the relationship between the position of car A and car B at $t = 1$ hr. (assume the two cars start from the same position and are traveling in the same direction). Explain.

Item 8d. What is the relative position of the two cars during the time interval between $t = .75$ hr. and $t = 1$ hr.? (i.e. is one car pulling away from the other?)

Results—8a.

On item 8a, group 3 with a mean score of 5.0, performed significantly higher than groups 2 and 1. Group 2, with variable scores (Table 5), performed significantly higher than group 1. Forty-seven percent of group 1 students stated that the cars were in the same position and 34% responded that car B was passing car A. These responses suggest that 88% of group 1 students interpreted the graphs literally as the paths of the cars, rather than interpreting the functional information displayed by the graphs. Somewhat surprisingly, 29% of group 2 students also demonstrated this misconception. However, all group 3 students provided the correct response with 42% justifying their answer by comparing the relative areas under the curves.

Two group 1 interview subjects indicated that the cars are colliding at $t = 1$ hr., since their paths are intersecting, and another student stated that the cars are moving away from one another at $t = 1$ hr. The remaining two subjects pro-

TABLE 5. Quantitative Results for Item 8a

| | Group | | |
	1	2	3
Mean score[a]	0.83	2.82	5.00
Standard deviation	1.74	2.48	0.00
Common responses (%)			
The two cars are at the same position	47	29	0
Car B is passing car A	34	0	0
Correct solution, algebraic justification	19	53	58
Correct solution, used calculus to justify	0	18	42

[a] The differences between the means of groups 1 and 2, groups 1 and 3, and groups 2 and 3 were significant at $\alpha = .05$.

vided a correct explanation, justifying that car A was ahead of car B since it had been traveling faster for the entire time. Although attempts were made during the interviews to redirect the students' attention to the information displayed by the graphs, none of the students who provided incorrect responses attempted to rethink the problem. They all continued to provide responses suggesting they were interpreting the graphs as the paths of the cars. Group 2 interview subjects all provided the correct response, stating that car A is ahead of car B, with two subjects comparing the relative areas under the curves, and three subjects comparing the relative speeds of the two cars. Four of the group 3 interview subjects justified their correct responses by comparing the relative areas under the curves. The remaining student provided an algebraic justification comparing the relative speeds of the two cars.

Results—8d.

Group 3 performed significantly higher than group 2, but group 2 with a mean score of 1.18, did not perform significantly higher than group 1. The majority of group 1 students provided an incorrect response to this item (Table 6). In fact, 43% of the written exams for group 1 indicated that car B is catching up to car A, and 33% indicated that the cars are "moving toward" or "crashing in" to each other. Groups 2 and 3 also had difficulty with this item, with 63% of group 2 and 42% of group 3 students stating that car B is catching up to car A.

Each group 2 interview subject justified the incorrect response (car B is catching up to car A), by stating that greater acceleration means "catching up." These students all demonstrated heavy reliance on this incorrect information, rather than relying on the information displayed by the graph. In addition, only three of the five group 3 interview subjects gave the correct response, providing the justification that car A is traveling faster the entire time. The remaining two group 3 interviewees persisted with incorrect arguments, one stating, like group 2 interview subjects, that acceleration equates with "catching up," and the other

TABLE 6. Quantitative Results for Item 8d

| | Group | | |
	1	2	3
Mean score[a]	0.43	1.18	3.83
Standard deviation	1.17	1.38	1.27
Common responses (%)			
Cars are moving in to each other/crashing	33	12	
Car B is catching up to car A	43	63	42
Another incorrect response or no response	14		
Car A is pulling away from car B	10	25	58

[a] The differences between the means of groups 1 and 3, and groups 2 and 3, were significant at $\alpha = .05$.

indicating car B is getting closer since the difference in the areas under the curves is getting smaller.

Interview transcripts—Group 2.

Student J.

Int: Why do you say car B is catching up to A?

J: A is ahead of B, but B is accelerating more quickly than A, so even if they stay at the same velocity, B is eventually going to catch up and pass A.

Int: Where does B pass A?

J: A good guess would be at one hour I guess.

Int: So, if one car is accelerating more than another, that car will be catching up?

J: Yes.

Int: Look at their relative speeds again. Which car is going faster for the time interval between $t = .75$ hr. and $t = 1$ hr.?

J: Car A.

Int: Does this give you any additional information for answering this question?

J: It will be ahead of car B, but while it's going faster it's not going to keep up with car B.

Student K.

Int: You said car B will be catching up. Can you explain your answer?

K: Car B is going to be catching up because car A is slowing down. Car A's acceleration is not as great as car B's acceleration and so the distance is becoming less and less between the two.

Int: Because car B is accelerating more?

K: Because if you pick a time, say $t = .5$ hr., then car A is still going quite a bit faster than car B, and average speed of A is still greater, and so there is going to be a certain distance between them. And if you pick $t = .75$

hr., car A's speed, even though it is greater than car B's; still it is not as much greater because of the acceleration. So that means distance must be decreasing. So car B is catching up to car A.

Student L.

Int: You said car B is gaining on car A. Can you explain this?

 L: Car B is behind car A at that point. But car B is rapidly gaining on Car A because car A is pretty much done gaining speed and is just moving along. Car B is still going faster. At the start, car A had more start off power.

Int: Your response is that car B is gaining on car A?

 L: I guess if you wanted to you could say that car B is still dropping behind, but not as fast as it used to be. It's not being left behind. Car A is still pulling ahead though, but not in each time increment as much as it did in the previous. So in that sense car B is gaining on car A.

Student M.

Int: You said car B is gaining on car A. Can you explain this?

 M: Car B is gaining on car A because its acceleration was greater.

Int: So, you say car B is gaining?

 M: I think the tangent line is the secret here.

Int: Why?

 M: It compares the accelerations.

Int: Why did you choose to compare the accelerations rather than the speeds?

 M: I guess acceleration simply describes the system better.

Student N.

Int: You said car B makes up ground on car A because it starts to accelerate. Can you explain this?

 N: It's gaining because it's accelerating more. Car B increased more than car A right before one hour, Since its accelerating quicker, you know that car B is making up ground on car A. If its accelerating quicker, you know that its changing speed faster, thus its going to make up more distance in that interval.

Int: What do you mean by make up more distance?

 N: Well, Car A is ahead of car B at $t = .75$ hr. by so much, and car B decreases that amount in that last interval because it's accelerating.

Int: Because it's accelerating it's closing the gap?

 N: Yes, it's closing the gap.

Int: Why don't you consider the relative speeds in that hour?

 N: Well, car A is moving faster than car B is, car B's curve, I don't know what you....(trailing off, mumbling).

Int: So you say?

 N: Car B is moving faster relative to car A based on what I told you about the acceleration closing the gap.

Int: So you say car A is going faster than car B. Try to use that information to answer this question, keeping in mind that car A is going faster than car B.

N: The relative position would be that car A is always ahead.

Int: If it's going faster, would it be pulling ahead or would car B be catching up?

N: Well just because it's going faster, I would still say that car B is catching up because it's accelerating at a rate where its change in speed is quicker than the change in speed of car A and this is why car A will still be ahead, but car B is still closing the gap.

Item 1. Express the diameter of a circle as a function of its area and sketch its graph.

On item 1, the mean score for group 1 is 1.00, with group 2 scoring significantly higher than group 1 (Table 7). Group 3, with a nearly perfect score, also scored significantly higher than both groups 2 and 1. On this item, group 2 and 3 students had no difficulty providing the algebraic representation of the function. However, students in both groups either neglected to construct the graph, or provided an incorrect graph.

TABLE 7. Quantitative Results for Item 1

| | Group | | |
	1	2	3
Mean score[a]	1.00	3.29	4.83
Standard deviation	1.08	1.10	0.39

[a] The differences between the means of groups 1 and 2, and groups 1 and 3, and groups 2 and 3, were significant at $\alpha = .05$.

When asked to express the diameter of a circle as a function of its area, the interview responses for students in group 1 varied, with only one student providing a correct algebraic response, supported by a well-formulated verbal justification. Interview transcripts indicate that two of the interview subjects did not know the formula for the area of a circle, and when provided with the formula made no attempt to solve for the diameter d. The other two students knew the area formula and successfully substituted $d/2$ for r, but did not attempt to isolate d. During the interviews, each student who provided incorrect responses was asked as a follow-up question to explain what is meant by the statement, "express s as a function of t." One student responded that this statement means that you are trying to find where s and t are equal. Another student responded, "find the zeros," and another said, "kind of how it related to." These responses suggest that group 1 students are unable to translate a verbal function description into algebraic function representation (i.e. they do not know what it means to express one quantity as a function of another). During the interviews, group 2 and 3 students had no difficulty providing a correct response and justification for this item.

Students' Backgrounds and Beliefs

In addition to investigating students' understanding of the function concept, at the beginning of each interview, students were asked to describe their mathematical backgrounds, including any factors which contributed to their mathematical development. Since the group 3 interview results were most revealing and provided interesting insights regarding the background and beliefs of mathematically successful students, a discussion of group 3 interview data is presented and contrasted with those of groups 1 and 2. This discussion is followed by a representative group 3 interview transcript.

Group 3 Interview Subjects.

Group 3 interview transcripts reveal that group 3 interview subjects all possess attitudes, habits and beliefs which equip them to approach mathematics with maturity not found in most members of the other two groups. In addition, the author observed that, while each group 3 subject struggled with a complex task during the interview, he or she exhibited exceptional persistence and confidence. As reported by the students in the interview, their persistence was motivated by different factors: student T, his competitive personality; student U, her curiosity and joy of doing mathematics; student S, her trained discipline instilled by a high school math teacher; student R, her desire to do well and gain control of the many things she had forgotten; student Q, his genuine interest in mathematics and solving difficult problems. In contrast, with the exception of one group 2 interview subject, all group 1 and 2 interview subjects were reluctant to persist, demonstrating little or no confidence in their abilities.

During the interviews, each group 3 interviewee also reported a willingness to dedicate remarkably large amounts of time when attempting to solve challenging problems. Student R, when asked what had contributed most to her mathematical success responded, "I do above and beyond anything that is required. I do the assigned problems and then try some of the harder problems on my own." Student T, when asked if he works hard in his math classes responded, "Yes, I do now, I always try to figure things out if they don't make sense. I put in whatever amount of time that it takes to understand things."

Group 3 interview subjects also indicated that they were influenced by an individual who guided them in learning how to approach mathematics. For student U, it was a high school teacher who made math interesting and taught her how to think mathematically, study for exams, and read mathematical texts (see interview below); for student Q, it was his big brother who stimulated his interest in thinking about challenging problems; and for student R, it was her father who exposed her to thought-provoking and challenging problems as she was growing up. Like the exceptional group 1 and group 2 students, all group 3 interview subjects report that they value teachers who ask challenging questions and encourage independent thinking. Several also indicated that they appreciated teachers who made them feel comfortable in asking questions. Four of the five subjects indicated that their problem-solving skills and mathematical habits were acquired prior to entering the university, and their math instruction at the university level had not noticeably changed their approaches to doing mathematics. Three interview subjects had cautiously re-enrolled in a course they had already taken, in order to recall information or gain better understanding. This created an opportunity to genuinely understand the concepts rather than superficially learn what was necessary to acquire a grade. For student T, retaking first-semester calculus provided the first high grade he had ever received in a math course. Subsequently, he expected mathematics to make sense. Several group 3 interview subjects also indicated that, on at least one occasion, they had received an undeserved A, as they believed they had little understanding of the material taught in the course. This statement was in tandem with a description of this course and an admission that, during this course, memorization had been frequently substituted for the pursuit of understanding. All group 3 interview subjects appeared to possess excellent study habits and exceptional persistence when attempting to find solutions to challenging problems. This last trait appears to be the most important and distinguishing quality of these subjects. Since this is a cross-sectional investigation, it cannot be assumed that these beliefs and habits were acquired between the completion of second semester calculus and the completion of first-year graduate mathematics.

Mathematical background of Student U—Group 3.

Int: Tell me about your mathematical background, classes and teachers.

U: I went to a good high school in Northern Virginia, and I had one really excellent math teacher during my last year of high school and the others before that were pretty good, mostly.

Int: What class did you take your senior year?

U: It was called Math Analysis. It was a combination of algebra and trigonometry.

Int: Why did you think your teacher for that class was so outstanding?

U: She inspired us to think and made me feel like I could come up with solutions on my own. So it was more of an adventure than just memorization of information like my other math classes.

Int: Did she give you problems that stretched your abilities?

U: I don't know if it was so much the problems, but the way she taught it was she would allow us to think and offer our opinions by asking questions like, what do you think about this? It was one class in which I stayed awake. The whole class was very competitive and that's when I really became interested in math. Actually I didn't even think I could do well in math until I had this class. I had very bad math experiences before that class.

Int: Why were your earlier experiences so bad?

U: Early math was really hard like arithmetic, can you believe it? I don't know, it wasn't obvious that it had to work that way. We just did a lot of computational things and it just didn't make much sense. I always fell behind and wasn't really motivated to work. It wasn't until my senior math class that I realized math is pretty interesting.

Int: Where did you build your problem solving skills?

U: I think it was that class. I never knew how to read a math text before that class and I never knew how to study for a test until then. She taught us how to sort things out and told us to try to work the problem and then go back and figure out what things went wrong if we didn't totally get it. Never before that class did I go back and read my own work. I think now I could pick up a math text and teach myself just because of that class.

Int: What class did you take as a freshman in college?

U: I started in business calculus, because I didn't think I wanted to do five hours of math a day. I've always had a lot of interests and at that point really didn't think I wanted to go into math.

Int: What did you take after business calculus?

U: I guess I liked calculus enough that I went on and took the math calculus sequence, but they weren't required since I was a Spanish major. I had a great 122 (second-semester calculus) teacher (a TA).

Int: When did you decide to be a math major?

U: About a year and a half ago.

Int: You've had a lot of math in a very short amount of time.

U: Yes, after I came back from Costa Rica, I decided I really wanted to be a math major. Math is all I really want to do, but I really didn't think I could do it.

Int: So what changed your mind?

U: After I took set theory then I decided I really wanted to continue and I took several more courses after that.

Int: So how many classes are you taking this semester?

U: Both 791 (abstract algebra) and 765 (complex analysis).

Int: Have you had any post-secondary experiences that affected your mathematical habits?

U: I can't say that any professor has helped me to be a better problem solver, and I think that most of my mathematical habits were developed by my high school teacher. My high school math teacher made you feel every question is valid in class and she didn't put you down. Just the fact that a question is valid creates a whole attitude that every question should be valid and that's how it should be. It allowed you to search until you really understand. I've never had professors inspire me in the same way as my high school math teacher did.

Discussion

Gaining an understanding of the many components of the function
complex. It requires acquisition of a language for talking about its many
and the ability to translate that language into several different representations.
Once students possess the skills for translating between these representations,
they must learn to interpret features of each representation for many different
types of functions. Then we ask that they recognize the usefulness of each representation for many different types of functions. Concurrently they are expected,
on demand, to demonstrate the ability to construct each representation for a
variety of real world situations. To further complicate matters, we ask that they
learn a formal definition, somewhat inconsistent with the ways in which they
use functions, and expect them to precisely apply this definition in arbitrary
situations. At the same time, a process view of functions must emerge for understanding to become complete. Even this daunting scenario is no doubt an
over-simplification of what really takes place as an individual struggles to make
sense of functions. However, it suggests that understanding and assimilating the
many aspects of functions requires a great deal of "sense making" on the part of
the student.

Results indicate that as students progress through the undergraduate mathematics curriculum, function constructs develop slowly. Although students are
eventually able to use concepts taught previously, even for our best students,
complex concepts are slow to develop and new information is not immediately accessible. This was evident by identifying the collection of questions for which each
group performed well and the collection of items for which each group performed
poorly (see Appendix A and Appendix B). College algebra and second-semester
calculus students had difficulty with the items assessing aspects of the function
concept which were central to their respective courses. Despite these difficulties,
second-semester calculus students performed very well on items measuring aspects of functions taught in early algebra, and graduate students demonstrated
little difficulty with items measuring aspects of functions taught in beginning calculus. These results show that even the highest performing college algebra and
second-semester calculus students demonstrate difficulties with much of the information explicitly taught during their courses. Interview results suggest that
only after repeated access of a concept, in ways which require one to explore
extreme cases and continue learning more about the various uses of the concept, does that knowledge become immediately accessible when confronted with
a problem.

The successful college algebra students in this study had limited understanding of many of the components of the function concept. Their narrow view of
functions was demonstrated by the fact that they thought any function could
be defined by a single formula and that all functions must be continuous. They
did not understand the function notation and had difficulty understanding the
role of the independent and dependent variable given a functional relationship.

They could not explain what is meant when asked to express one quantity as a function of another, and were unable to verbalize the meaning of $f(x + a)$ given a quadratic function f. They were unable to speak the language of functions and during the interviews had difficulty referencing algebraic symbols. Although group 1 students were able to interpret points on a graph, they had difficulty interpreting graphical function information over intervals. They were able to construct the graphs of simple algebraic functions and algebraically evaluate functions for specific input values. According to Monk's [14] classification, group 1 students appeared to possess a pointwise view of functions.

Furthermore, the analysis of group 1 interview results reveals that college algebra students view the evaluation of a function as nothing more than an algebraic substitution. They speak of the function input as an item to be substituted and, as revealed in the interviews, have memorized the process. Group 1 students did not appear to distinguish between solutions of an equation and zeros of a function. Their immersion in an equation-oriented curriculum appeared to compromise their understanding of functions. They did not yet view functions more generally as a process which accepts input and produces output. In the Breidenbach et al. [3] classification, group 1 students appeared to possess an action level conceptualization of functions.

The high performing second-semester calculus students possessed a much broader view of functions. They demonstrated modest understanding of the language of functions, and had no difficulty when prompted to describe a physical situation using functions. They clearly understood what it means for one item to be a function of another and in most situations viewed functions more generally as processes. Although they had no difficulty interpreting static graphical information and very little difficulty interpreting dynamic graphical information, in certain situations they interpreted the graphical information literally rather than relying on their ability to interpret functional information displayed by the graph. Their understanding of function notation was accurate for simple algebraic function representations. However, when confronted with a more complex function expression they demonstrated some difficulties. When asked during the interview to determine graphically what was represented by the expression $F(\frac{x+y}{2})$, given a quadratic function F, most group 2 students had difficulty. In addition, they were unable to speak about $\frac{x+y}{2}$ as the input to this function. As well, the high-performing second-semester calculus students demonstrated surprising difficulties when attempting to solve problems requiring the use of beginning calculus. They also believed that functions are defined by a relationship between the items of two sets which is, in principle at least, predictable. Like group 1 students, some group 2 students still had difficulty distinguishing between an equation and a function and sometimes used the term "zero" synonymously with "solution." As a group they did not demonstrate confidence in their problem-solving abilities, nor did they access recently acquired calculus tools when solving unfamiliar problems. Most group 2 subjects were unable to interpret and graph covariant aspects of a real world situation. When attempting to graph height as a function of the volume of a spherical bottle filling with water, 74% of group 2 interview subjects constructed a graph which was either strictly concave down or concave up for the portion of the graph corresponding to the entire spherical part of the bottle. Even though they performed much better than group 1 students when asked to construct discontinuous functions, as a group they continued to demonstrate some difficulties defining piecewise functions. Although second-semester calculus students had begun to demonstrate a more general view of functions, when confronted with more demanding problems, they had a tendency to regress to lower level skills and, at times, demonstrate weak understanding. According to the Breidenbach et al. model [2], group 2 students appeared to be in transition from an action view to a process view of functions.

The beginning graduate students possessed a very general view of functions and had acquired attitudes, beliefs, and approaches of a maturity not possessed by members of the lower two groups. Although their motivations for studying mathematics were diverse, they all possessed perseverance, confidence and a willingness to work extremely hard in solving challenging and unfamiliar problems. They believed they were responsible for making sense of new information and indicated that at various points in their lives they assumed this responsibility personally.

The graduate students had no difficulty using the language of functions. Like the second-semester calculus students, they spoke about functions in terms of independent-dependent relationships, and viewed functions more generally as processes which accept different input values. Additionally, their general view is reflected by the fact that they accept the function definition, and unlike group 2 interview subjects, had no difficulty recognizing how an arbitrary mapping between two sets could determine a function. When required to determine a piecewise function, group 3 interview subjects all provided a correct response, indicating no difficulty describing different rules for different parts of the domain. When asked to interpret graphical information for ranges of the domain, group 3 students, like group 2, had no difficulty providing a correct response and valid justification. On items which could more easily be solved using tools of calculus (e.g. analyzing the relative areas under the curve, examining the slope of the tangent line, analyzing how changing rate affects concavity, etc.), group 3 students more frequently accessed their knowledge of calculus to justify their response. In addition, group 3 students demonstrated a much greater tendency to interpret covariant aspects of a situation as demonstrated by their analysis of the "bottle filling with water" problem, and the "rate of change of temperature" problem [3]. When required to analyze and compare complicated expressions for a quadratic function, group 3 students demonstrated very little difficulty. All group 3 interview subjects discussed $F(\frac{x+y}{2})$ as a process of averaging the input values, followed by an evaluation of the function for that value;

and $\frac{F(x)+F(y)}{2}$ as evaluating the function for two different inputs, followed by averaging the two functional values. Group 3 subjects gave graphical representations for each of these expressions with very little difficulty and were able to compare the expressions for different quadratics. In general when group 3 students demonstrated difficulty they were able to correctly analyze the situation with very little prompting and provide a correct response.

Collectively, the interview results suggest that students acquire concepts at very different rates. Though each group consisted of A students, dramatic differences were noticed among the interview subjects of each of the two lower groups. In fact, two of the second-semester calculus interview subjects frequently demonstrated understanding at the same level as the graduate students, as illustrated by their high scores on the written exam, and their exceptional ability to reason through difficult problems during their interviews. College algebra interview subjects' understandings of major function components had a range from very weak to exceptional.

A continual effort of sense making occurs as students progress through undergraduate mathematics. However, the rapid pace at which new information is presented eliminates needed time for reflection and appears to encourage students to settle for superficial understanding. It is likely that many capable students prematurely discontinue their study of mathematics due to their unwillingness to substitute understanding with memorization. In fact, the student who demonstrated the greatest understanding among the group 1 interview subjects indicated that this was the reason she had decided to pursue a Ph.D. in English, versus continuing her study of mathematics.

As students struggle to understand new information presented at a rapid pace, it is difficult to predict what will be retained by a particular student, since individuals appear to be willing to devote varying amounts of effort to sort out information. Additionally, I suspect that different levels of intelligence and memory capabilities also affect their ability to understand newly presented information at a fast rate. However, this research suggests that even the very best students frequently abandon efforts to understand new concepts when those concepts are presented at a rate which does not allow time for reflection and exploration of special cases. This raises questions concerning the level of understanding that occurs in average and below-average mathematics students.

Despite these difficulties, some students do survive undergraduate curricula and eventually acquire excellent mathematical habits and abilities. Group 3 subjects, students who successfully completed undergraduate mathematics degrees, demonstrated understanding of major aspects of functions and possessed exceptional problem-solving strategies. They reported specific experiences which fostered the development of their mathematical habits (see Backgrounds and Beliefs of Group 3 Interview Subjects), and indicated that concept development was facilitated by a variety of factors: solving challenging problems, repeated exposure to essential concepts, repeating a course which was already taken, accessing

the same information when taking a higher-level course, or teaching a cou
a later point in their development. Further, results suggest that concept
opment appears to be facilitated by engaging in experiences that encourage the
acquisition and assimilation of many sub-concepts. Group 3 students also exhibited exceptional persistence and confidence when responding to complex tasks
during the interview. In contrast, group 1 and 2 interview subjects were reluctant to persist and demonstrated little or no confidence in their mathematical
abilities. Consequently, good mathematical habits (e.g., persistence, problem-
solving strategies, etc.) and confidence, in addition to concept development,
appear to be essential for students to continue their study of mathematics.

Conclusions and Implications

The following are general conclusions reached as a result of this research.

1. Function constructs develop slowly and their development appears to be facilitated by reflection and constructive activities. Interview results suggest
that when students are confronted with engaging activities and provided time
for reflection, student understanding is promoted. These results agree with
those of Breidenbach et al. [2]. Their study found that understanding of functions was noticeably improved as a result of engaging students in constructive
activities.

2. Even the most talented students at the completion of college algebra still
have many misconceptions. Analysis of the exam responses and interview
transcripts for group 1 indicates that these students:

   - Do not understand the language of functions, in particular:
       What it means for one quantity to be a function of another.
       The role of the parentheses in the function representation.
       That the "functional value" is referring to the y-value
       (assuming conventional labeling of the axes).

   - Do not know how to represent real world functional relationships using
     algebraic or graphic function representations.

   - Do not make a distinction between zeros of functions and solutions of equa-
     tions.

   - Do not effectively interpret dynamic graphical information.

   - Do not understand the general nature of a function. They think any func-
     tion must be definable by a single algebraic formula and all functions must
     be continuous. This result is consistent with the results of Ayers et al. [1]
     and Vinner and Dreyfus [21].

   - Do not understand the role of the independent and dependent variables in
     an algebraic function representation.

- Do not represent graphically, covariant aspects of a real world situation.

- Do not possess helpful mathematical habits. They do not view their mathematics as useful for solving problems, do not expect mathematics problems to "make sense," and have little confidence in their abilities to solve unfamiliar problems.

3. The most talented second-semester calculus students, at the completion of the course, demonstrate some difficulty:

- Interpreting rate of change information from a dynamic situation.

- Demonstrating an awareness of the impact change in one variable has on the other; interpreting and graphically representing covariant aspects of a real-world situation.

- Accessing beginning calculus to analyze a real world situation.
- Defining a discontinuous function using a different rule for different parts of the domain. Group 2 students still think that any function must be definable by a single algebraic formula.

- Interpreting dynamic graphical information over intervals.

- Understanding function notation for function representations.

- Translating from complicated algebraic to graphic representations.

- Using tools of calculus to analyze a dynamic situation.

4. High-performing students do not appear to access recently acquired function information to solve unfamiliar problems (see Appendix B), and do not demonstrate belief in their mathematical knowledge as useful when they are required to solve an unfamiliar problem, even when it is solvable using the mathematics they know. This result is consistent with the findings of Schoenfeld [17]. When investigating students' abilities to apply known geometric information to geometric construction problems, Schoenfeld [17] found that successful mathematics students gave evidence of knowing certain mathematics but then proceeded to ignore the information when attempting the constructions.

5. It appears that curriculum developers underestimate the complexity of acquiring an understanding of many of the essential components of the function concept. Many of the weaknesses identified in group 1 and group 2 students are not specifically addressed in current curricula. For example, current curricula provide little opportunity for developing the ability to: interpret and represent covariant aspects of functions, understand and interpret the language of functions, interpret information from dynamic functional events, etc.

6. Students report that they replace understanding with memorization in the absence of time for reflection, questioning, and exploration of extreme cases

and special situations. All group 3 (graduate level) interview subjects and most group 2 (second-semester calculus) interview subjects indicated that the rapid pace of a particular class had led to frustration and the abandonment of understanding for memorization.

7. In order to develop good mathematical habits, good students believe they need to be challenged by working more difficult problems. All interview subjects in group 3 and most of the interview subjects in group 2 indicated that their approach to doing mathematics had been acquired when they were encouraged, challenged, and given guidance regarding different strategies for solving what seemed like a difficult problem (see Backgrounds and Beliefs section).

8. Good students report that they want mathematics to "make sense," prefer mathematics to be taught in context, and like being challenged by difficult problems. They report that they do not like monotonous, repetitious activities, rather they enjoy engaging in rich mathematics that is interesting and purposeful. They praise their teachers for providing challenging problems while guiding their solution attempts and creating a non-threatening classroom environment.

9. Full concept development appears to evolve over a period of years and appears to require an effort of "sense making" to understand and orchestrate individual function components to work in concert [3].

This investigation provides empirical evidence for the importance of constructive activities in the development of one concept. Further, this study has identified essential aspects of the function concept which need increased attention, while providing insights concerning the types of experiences and curricula which may foster their development. The pace at which content is presented, the context in which it is presented, as well as the types of activities in which we engage students appear to have an enormous impact on what students know and what they can do when they exit a course. Consequently, curriculum developers have a tremendous responsibility to gain as much information as is currently available describing how students acquire the concepts specific to a course, as well as mathematical concepts in general.

REFERENCES

1. Ayers, T., Davis, G., Dubinsky, E., and Lewin, P., *Computer experiences in learning composition of functions*, Journal for Research in Mathematics Education **19 (3)** (1989).
2. Breidenbach, D., Dubinsky, E., Hawks, J. and Nichols, D., *Development of the process conception of function*, Educational Studies in Mathematics (1992), 247–285.
3. Carlson, M.P., *A Cross-sectional investigation of the development of the function concept*, unpublished Ph.D Dissertation, Department of Mathematics, University of Kansas, 1995.
4. Cooney, T. and Wilson, M., *Teachers' thinking about functions: historical and research perspectives*, Integrating research on the graphical representation of functions, Lawrence Erlbaum Associates, Hillsdale, NJ, 1993, pp. 131–138.
5. Dreyfus, T. and Eisenberg, T., *Intuitions on functions*, Journal of Experimental Education **52** (1984), 77–85.

6. Dubinsky, E. and Harel G., *The concept of function, aspects of epistemology and pedagogy*, Mathematical Association of America, Washington D.C., 1992.

7. Kaput, J., *Patterns in students' formalization of quantitative patterns, The concept of function aspects of epistemology and pedagogy*, MAA Notes **25** (1992), 290–318.

8. Kleiner, I., *Evolution of the function concept: a brief survey*, The College Mathematics Journal **20** (1989), 282–300.

9. Leinhardt, G., Zaslavsky, O., and Stein, M. K., *Functions, graphs and graphing: tasks, learning and teaching*, Review of Educational Research **60(1)** (1990), 11–64.

10. Moschkovich, J., Schoenfeld, A. and Arcavi, A., *Aspects of understanding: on multiple perspectives and representations of linear relations and connections among them*, Integrating research on the graphical representation of functions, Lawrence Erlbaum Associates, Hillsdale, NJ, 1993.

11. Monk, Steve, *Students' understanding of functions in calculus courses*, Unpublished manuscript, University of Washington, Seattle (1987).

12. Monk, Steve, *A framework for describing student understanding of functions*, paper presented at the American Educational Research Association, San Francisco (1989).

13. Monk, Steve, *A study of calculus students' constructions of functional situations: the case of the shadow problem*, paper presented at the American Educational Research Association, San Francisco, CA (1992).

14. Monk, Steve, *Students' understanding of a function given by a physical model, The concept of function, aspects of epistemology and pedagogy*, MAA Notes **25** (1992), 175–194.

15. National Council of Teachers of Mathematics, *Curriculum and evaluation standards for school mathematics* (1989), Reston, VA.

16. National Research Council, *Everybody counts* (1989), National Academy Press, Washington, DC.

17. Schoenfeld, A. H., *On mathematics as sense-making: an informal attack on the unfortunate divorce of formal and informal mathematics*, Informal reasoning and education, Erlbaum, Hillsdale, NJ, 1989.

18. Selden, A. and Selden, J., *Research perspectives on conceptions of functions: summary and overview, The concept of function, aspects of epistemology and pedagogy*, MAA Notes **25** (1992), 1–16.

19. Sierpinska, A., *On understanding the notion of function, The concept of function, aspects of epistemology and pedagogy*, MAA Notes **25** (1992), 25–58.

20. Thompson, P. W. *To experience is to conceptualize: a discussion of epistemology and mathematical experience*, Epistemological foundations of mathematical experience, Springer-Verlag, New York, 1991.

21. Vinner, S. and Dreyfus, T., *Images and definitions for the concept of function*, Journal for Research in Mathematics Education **20(4)** (1989), 356–366.

APPENDIX A
The Written Exam

Student Background Information

On Parts A and B of the Functionality Test, students were asked to supply the following background information:

Name (optional)

Level in School

Last math course completed

Semester last math course was completed

Math courses completed

Grade expected in current math course (Part A only)

Functionality Test—Part A

1. Express the diameter of a circle as a function of its area and *sketch its graph.*

2. a) Given $f(x) = 2x + 3$, what is the relationship between $f(x+1)$ and $f(x)+2$ for the given function?
   Explain.

   b) Find k so that $g(x + 1) = g(x) + k$, given that $g(x) = 3x + 5$.
   Explain.

   c) Compute $h(x + a)$ given $h(x) = 2x + 3$.

   d) Compute $f(x + a)$ given $f(x) = 3x^2 + 2x - 4$

3. If possible, describe the following situations using a function. If not, explain why.

   a) The string, "ABCDEFG"

   b) $\{2n + n^3 : n$ in $[1..100]\}$

   c) $y^4 = x^2$

   d) The club members' dues status.

Name	Owed
Sue	$17
John	$6
Sam	$27
Bill	$0
Iris	$6
Eve	$12
Henry	$14
Louis	$6
Jane	$12

4. This graph shows the speed in meters per second of a cyclist over a 10 minute period.

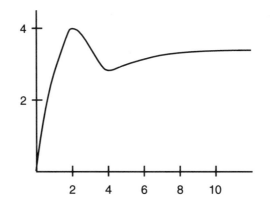

a) When is the speed greatest?

b) When is the speed changing most rapidly?

c) Does the cyclist travel further during the first five minutes or during the last five minutes?

In questions 5 through 7, give an example to confirm the existence of such a function. If one does not exist, explain why.

5. Does there exist a function all of whose values are equal to each other?

6. Does there exist a function whose values for integer numbers are non-integer and whose value for non-integer numbers are integer?

7. Does there exist a function which assigns to every number different from 0 its square and to 0 it assigns 1?

8. The given graph represents speed vs. time for two cars. (Assume the cars start from the same position and are traveling in the same direction.)

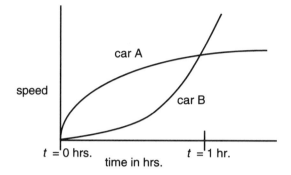

a) State the relationship between the position of car A and car B at $t = 1$ hr.: Explain.

b) State the relationship between the speed of car A and car B at $t = 1$ hr.: Explain.

c) State the relationship between the acceleration of car A and car B at $t = 1$ hr.: Explain.

d) What is the relative position of the two cars during the time interval between $t = .75$ hr. and $t = 1$ hr.? (i.e. is one car pulling away from the other?) Explain.

9. The table on the left represents specific values of the function $f(x) = x^3 - 3x^2 + 2x$. Fill in the table on the right, which represents the function $g(x) = x^3 - 3x^2 + 2x + 1$.

x	y	x	y
0	0	0	
1	0	1	
2	0	2	
3	6	3	
4	24	4	

10. Sketch rough graphs of $f(x) = x^2 - 4$ and $g(x) = 3x$, and discuss the solution to the equation $f(x) = g(x)$ in terms of these graphs.

11. Sketch a rough graph of $h(x) = (x-4)(x+1)$ and discuss the relationship of the solution of the equation $h(x) = 0$ to the solution of the equation $f(x) = g(x)$ from 10 above.

12. Imagine this bottle filling with water. Sketch a graph of the height as a function of the amount of water that's in the bottle.

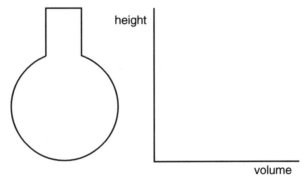

13. Suppose this is the graph of height as a function of volume as a bottle is filling with water. Sketch the shape of the bottle.

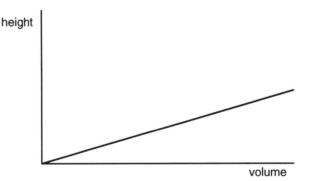

14. Given the graph of the rate of change of the temperature over an eight hour time period. Draw a rough sketch of the graph of the temperature over the same eight hour time period. Assume the temperature at time, $t = 0$, is 0 degrees Celsius.

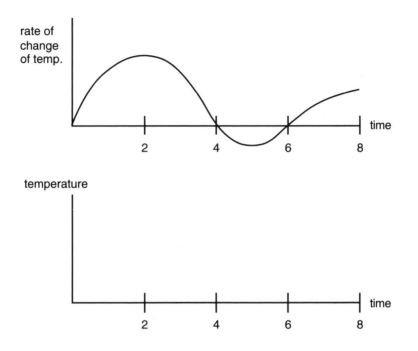

Functionality Test—Part B

1. a) What is a function?

   b) Describe the different ways a function can be represented.

   c) What is the value of studying functions?

2. Assume $F(x)$ is any quadratic function.

   a) True or False: $F(\frac{x+y}{2}) < \frac{F(x)+F(y)}{2}$

   b) Justify your answer.

3. a) Find the equation of the line(s) through the point (a, a^2) that intersects the graph of $y = x^2$ exactly once.

   b) Explain your solution.

4. a) Tom sees a ladder against a wall (in an almost vertical position). He pulls the base of the ladder away from the wall by a certain amount and then again by the same amount and then again by the same amount, and so forth. Each time he does this he records the distances by which the top of the ladder drops down. Do the amounts by which the top of the ladder drops down remain constant as Tom repeats this step; or do they get bigger, or do they get smaller? EXPLAIN.

   b) Newt, the science nerd, then comes along and puts wheels on the bottom of the ladder. He connects them to a motor so that the bottom rolls away at a constant, but very slow, speed. Does the top of the ladder move down at a constant speed, or does it speed up or does it slow down? EXPLAIN.

   c) Draw a graph which represents the relationship between the horizontal and vertical positions of a ladder as it slides down a wall, starting at a vertical position and finally resting on the ground. EXPLAIN.

APPENDIX B
Quantitative Results
Part A—Written Exam

Question No.		Group 1 mean	Group 2 mean	Group 3 mean	2 > 1 $\alpha = .05$	3 > 2 $\alpha = .05$	3 > 1 $\alpha = .05$
**	1	1.00	3.29	4.83	yes	no	yes
**	2a	1.67	4.18	4.75	yes	no	yes
*	2b	1.53	3.71	4.75	yes	yes	yes
**	2c	2.43	4.94	5.00	yes	no	yes
**	2d	2.07	4.76	5.00	yes	no	yes
	3a	.80	1.71	4.58	no	yes	yes
*	3b	.47	3.35	4.67	yes	yes	yes
*	3c	1.07	2.71	4.50	yes	yes	yes
	3d	.70	.53	5.00	no	yes	yes
	4a	4.30	4.71	5.00	no	no	no
**	4b	2.60	4.12	5.00	yes	no	yes
*	4c	3.93	4.88	5.00	no	no	no
**	5	1.07	4.00	4.67	yes	no	yes
*	6	.17	1.00	5.00	yes	yes	yes
*	7	.50	3.18	4.75	yes	yes	yes
*	8a	.83	2.82	5.00	yes	yes	yes
**	8b	2.80	4.80	5.00	yes	no	yes
*	8c	2.10	3.35	5.00	yes	yes	yes
	8d	.43	1.18	3.83	no	yes	yes
	9	4.60	4.94	5.00	no	no	no
**	10	3.30	4.47	4.50	yes	no	yes
**	11	1.63	4.35	4.67	yes	no	yes
*	12	1.47	2.41	4.33	yes	yes	yes
	13	1.27	5.00	4.92	yes	no	yes
*	14	.33	2.59	4.92	yes	yes	yes

* Group 2 performed significantly higher than group 1 and group 3 performed significantly higher than group 2.

** Group 2 performed significantly higher than group 1 and group 3 did not perform significantly higher than group 2.

Quantitative Results
Part B—Written Exam

	Question No.	Group 1 mean	Group 2 mean	Group 3 mean	2 > 1 $\alpha = .05$	3 > 2 $\alpha = .05$	3 > 1 $\alpha = .05$
	1a	2.07	2.71	5.00	no	yes	yes
	1b	2.63	3.18	5.00	no	yes	yes
*	1c	1.67	3.53	5.00	yes	yes	yes
*	2	.10	1.35	4.33	yes	yes	yes
*	3	.50	2.06	3.33	yes	yes	yes
*	4a	.63	2.41	4.33	yes	yes	yes
*	4b	.43	2.24	4.08	yes	yes	yes
	4c	.63	2.06	4.33	yes	yes	yes

* Group 2 performed significantly higher than group 1 and group 3 performed significantly higher than group 2.

** Group 2 performed significantly higher than group 1 and group 3 did not perform significantly higher than group 2.

APPENDIX C
Scoring Rubric Guidelines

The following general guidelines were used for constructing a rubric for each exam question.

General Evaluation

Question
Scoring

5   Superior response:
- -Complete in responding to all aspects of the question.
- -Shows complete mathematical understanding of the problem's ideas and requirements.
- -Includes only minor computational errors, if any.

4   Assign to those responses falling between 5 and 3.

3   Adequate response:
- -Demonstrates understanding of the main idea of the problem.
- -Is not totally complete in responding to all aspects of the problem.
- -Shows some deficiencies in understanding aspects of the problem.
- -Exhibits a moderate amount of reasoning but reasoning is incomplete.

2   Assign to those responses falling between 3 and 1.

1   An inadequate response:
- -Attempts, but fails to answer or complete the question.
- -Shows very limited or no understanding of the problem.
- -Contains words, examples, or diagrams that do not reflect the problem.

0   No response:
- -The question was left blank.
- -The written information made no attempt to respond to the problem.
- -The written information was insufficient to allow any judgment.

Rubrics for Specific Problems

Part A

Question 1

(3 pts. for algebraic solution and 2 pts. for graph.)

1 pt.   Writes formula for the area of a circle.

2 pts.   Substitutes $(d/2)$ for r.

3 pts.   Solves for d, $d = 2\sqrt{A/\pi}$, and recognizes that the range is restricted, diam. is always positive. (Deduct 1 pt. for including "+" and "−".)

1 pt.   Constructs graph, but graph has errors, i.e. both the positive and negative square root are graphed.

2 pts.   Correctly sketches the graph. (Note: A picture of a circle receives 0 pts. for graph.)

Question 2a

1 pt.   Evaluates $f(x + 1)$ or $f(x) + 2$.

or

States that $f(x + 1)$ is a left shift and $f(x) + 2$ is an upward shift of $f(x)$.

2 pts.   Evaluates $f(x + 1)$ and $f(x) + 2$.

3 pts.   Sets $f(x + 1)$ equal to $f(x) + 2$.

4 pts.   States that $f(x + 1)$ is equal to $f(x) + 2$.

5 pts.   Valid explanation is provided.

States that $f(x + 1)$ and $f(x) + 2$ represent the same line and provides justification of their equality, i.e. discusses why adding 1 to the input results in adding 2 to the output.

Question 2b

1 pt.   Evaluates $g(x + 1)$ or $g(x) + k$.

2 pts.   Evaluates $g(x + 1)$ and $g(x) + k$.

3 pts.   Sets $g(x + 1)$ equal to $g(x) + k$ and determines that k is equal to 3.

4 pts.   Weak explanation is provided.

An algebraic explanation is provided.

5 pts.   Strong explanation is provided.

Provides a discussion concerning the relationship of k and the slope of g. Discusses how adding one to the input affects the output.

Question 2c

0 pts.   Adds "a" to the output, $h(x + a) = (2x + 3) + a$.

5 pts.   Correctly evaluates $h(x + a)$.

$h(x + a) = 2(x + a) + 3$

or

$h(x + a) = 2x + 2a + 3$.

Question 2d

1 pt.   Partial attempt to replace x with $(x + a)$.
$$f(x + a) = 3(x + a)^2 + 2x - 4$$
or
$$f(x + a) = 3x^2 + 2(x + a) - 4.$$

4 pts.   Error in simplifying 5 pt. answer.

5 pts.   Correct evaluation of $f(x + a)$
$$f(x + a) = 3(x + a)^2 + 2(x + a) - 4$$
or
$$f(x + a) = 3x^2 + 6xa + 3a^2 + 2x + 2a - 4$$

Question 3a

4 pts.   Minor errors in 5 pt. answer.

5 pts.   Not possible because there is only one set and two sets are needed to define a function.

5 pts.   A valid association of a selected input with each letter of the string.

5 pts.   A valid association of the selected input with the entire string.
$f(1) = A$, $f(2) = B$, $f(3) = C$, $f(4) = D \ldots f(7) = G$
or $f(a) = A$, $f(b) = B$, $f(c) = C$, $f(d) = D \ldots f(g) = G$
or $f(5) = $ABCDEFG
or defines the string as a point, which maps the string to itself, $f(\text{ABCDEFG}) = \text{ABCDEFG}$.

Question 3b

2 pts.   Statement that the given representation is a function.

3 pts.   A valid explanation which represents understanding of the functional nature of the situation, but no function is defined.

4 pts. $f(n) = 2n + n^3$, error in domain or no domain is stated.

5 pts. $f(n) = 2n + n^3$, n is an element of the integers and $1 \leq n \leq 100$.

Question 3c

2 pts.   A valid function representation which restricts the domain and range of the function $y = \sqrt{x}$.

3 pts.   A valid function representation which restricts the domain or the range: $y = (+ \text{ or } -)\sqrt{x}$
or
$y = \sqrt[4]{x^2}$.

4 pts.   All points are represented by the equation, but no indication that the student recognizes that this is not a function. $y = (+ \text{ or } -) \sqrt{|x|}$.

5 pts.   Above answer with qualification that the equation is not a function.

5 pts.   Not possible to describe the set of points with a function, since any attempt will violate the function restriction.

Question 3d
  1 pts. Statement that a pairing is possible, but no pairing is constructed.
  2 pts. Pairing which associates the two sets. However, the pairing is not a
          function, i.e. $f(17) = $ Sue, $f(6) = $ John, $f(6) = $ Iris.
          or
          Not possible since the function is not one-to-one.
          (Student recognizes a pairing exists, but thinks all functions must be
          one-to-one.)
  5 pts. Pairing the two sets in such a way that a function is defined.
          Use of arrows to make association
          or (Sue, 17), (John, 6),...
          or $f($Sue$) = 17$, $f($John$) = 6$, ...

Question 4a
  1 pt.   Student writes a "4."
  2 pts. Student writes "4 meters/second."
  5 pts. Any answer indicating the speed is the greatest when $t = 2$ minutes.
          At $t = 2$ minutes or at $t = 2$ minutes when speed $= 4$ mph or (2,4).

Question 4b
  1 pt. $t = 2$ min. to $t = 4$ min.
          or
          $t = 3$ min. to $t = 4$ min.
  2 pts. $t = 2.5$ minutes
          or
          Any subset of the interval from $t = 1$ to $t = 2$ minutes.
  3 pts. $t \sim .5$ minutes.
  5 pts. $t = 0$ to $t = 2$ minutes.
          or
          $t = 0$ to $t = 1$ minutes.

Question 4c
  0 pts. First 5 minutes.
  5 pts. Last 5 minutes.

Question 5
  1 pt. $f(x) = x$.
  3 pts. Writes a point, not in set notation (i.e. (3,5)).
  5 pts. A function meeting the condition that all function values are
          equal to each other (i.e. $f(x) = c$ or $\{(3,5)\}$).

Question 6

1 pt. Responds with "yes." Provides no explanation or example.

2 pts. Function satisfies one of the criteria- "value for integer values are non-integer" or "value for non-integer values are integer," i.e., $f(x) = \frac{1}{x}$ or $f(x) = [x]$.

4 pts. Minor errors in 5 pt. answer.

5 pts. Valid function definition using a split domain.

$f(x) = 5$ if x is not an integer.

$f(x) = \frac{1}{x}$ if x is an integer.

Question 7

1 pt. Responds with "yes." Provides no explanation or example.

or

Constructs a function such that $f(0) = 1$ (i.e. $f(x) = c^x$).

2 pts. A valid graph, but responds with "no" and states as a reason that the graph is not continuous. (Student thinks all functions must be continuous.)

4 pts. Minor errors in 5 pt. answer.

5 pts. $f(x) = x^2$ if x is not equal to 0

$f(x) = 1$ if $x = 0$.

Question 8a

0 pts. States that the cars have traveled the same distance.

1 pt. States that car A or car B is accelerating.

2 pts. States that car A and car B are both accelerating.

3 pts. Correct statement of position with no explanation.

Car A is ahead of car B.

4 pts. Correct statement of position with weak justification.

The graph of car A is higher.

5 pts. Correct statement of position with valid explanation.

Car A is ahead of car B, since car A has been going faster the entire time.

or

Car A is ahead of car B, since the area under the graph of car A is greater than the area under the graph of car B.

Question 8b

3 pts. Correct statement of the speed of the two cars at $t = 1$ hr.

The cars are going the same speed at $t = 1$ hr.

4 pts. Correct statement of the speed with weak justification.

The graphs intersect.

5 pts. Correct statement of speed with strong justification.

The cars are going the same speed since their graphs intersect at $t = 1$.

or

The cars are going the same speed since at $t = 1$, the speeds are the same.

Question 8c

3 pts. Correct statement of the relative accelerations at $t = 1$ hr.

The acceleration of car B is greater than the acceleration of car A at $t = 1$ hr.

4 pts. Correct statement with weak justification.

Car B's speed appears to be increasing faster.

5 pts. Correct statement of relative accelerations and valid explanation.

Acceleration of car B is greater than the acceleration of car A, since the graph of car B is steeper than the graph of car A at $t = 1$ hr.

or

Acceleration of car B is greater than the acceleration of car A, since the slope of the tangent line of the graph of car B is greater than the slope of the tangent line of the graph of car A at $t = 1$ hr.

Question 8d

0 pts. Car B is catching up with car A. No explanation.

1 pt.   Car B is gaining on car A, because car B's acceleration is greater than Car A's acceleration.

3 pts. Correct statement of the cars' relative positions between $t = .75$ hr. and $t = 1$ hr. Car A is pulling away from car B.

5 pts. Correct statement of the cars' relative positions with a valid explanation.

Car A is traveling faster than car B during the entire time interval from $t = .75$ to $t = 1$ hr., so car A is pulling away.

Question 9

1 pt. awarded for each ordered pair.

(Method used to obtain the table entries is noted.)

Question 10

1 pt.   Correct graph of f or g.

2 pts. Correct graph of f and g.

3 pts. Statement that the solutions are the pts. where the graphs intersect.

4 pts. Identification of the two points as the solution of the equation.

5 pts. Identification of the x values of the points of intersection as the solution to the equation (i.e. $x = 4$ and $x = -1$).

Question 11

   1 pt.   Correct sketch of the graph of h.

   2 pts.   States the solution is the points where h crosses the x-axis.

          or

          Identifies the two points, $(-1,0)$ and $(4,0)$, as the solutions to $h(x) = 0$.

   3 pts.   Identifies the x-values where h crosses the x-axis as the solution to $h(x) = 0$, $x = -1$, $x = 4$.

   4 pts.   States that the solutions of $h(x) = 0$ are also the pts. of intersection of $f(x)$ and $g(x)$.

   5 pts.   States that the solutions of $h(x) = 0$ are the same as the solutions to $f(x) = g(x)$ from 10 above, $x = -1$, $x = 4$.

          or

          States that the observed relationship is that $h(x) = f(x) - g(x)$.

Question 12

          Award 1 pt. for correct display of each of the following graphical features.

   1 pt.   The graph of the function is always increasing.

   1 pt.   Graph shows a change in concavity and nonlinear portion is symmetric about the concavity change.

   1 pt.   Graph changes from concave down to concave up.

   1 pt.   Graph becomes linear.

   1 pt.   Slope of the linear portion of the graph is the same as the slope of the tangent line of the last point of the curve before becoming linear.

Question 13

   0 pts.   Any figure other than the two described below.

   2 pts.   Draws a cylindrical shaped figure with neck.

   5 pts.   Draws a cylinder.

Question 14

   0 pts.   Draws the same graph which is given.

          Award 1 pt. for correct display of each of the following graphical features.

   1 pt.   The graph is increasing from $t = 0$ to $t = 4$.

   1 pt.   The graph is decreasing from $t = 4$ to $t = 6$.

   1 pt.   The graph is increasing from $t = 6$ to $t = 8$.

   1 pt.   The graph changes from concave up to concave down at $t = 2$.

   1 pt.   The graph changes from concave down to concave up at $t = 5$.

Part B
Question 1a

1 pt.   An example of one function representation, equation, graph, correspondence or an equation with an independent and dependent variable.

2 pts.   A graph which passes the vertical line test.

3 pts.   Provides a general description without reference to the function restriction, i.e. a relation between two sets.

4 pts.   Minor error in 5 pt. answer.

5 pts.   A relation which maps each element of one set to exactly one element of another set or another correct definition.

Question 1b

1 pt.   Provides example(s) of function(s).

2 pts.   Describes one way of representing a function, i.e. an equation or a graph.

3 pts.   States two forms of algebraic function representations.
        Explicitly defined in terms of y and implicitly defined in terms of y.

4 pts.   An equation and a graph.

5 pts.   Includes another valid function representation, i.e. table, verbal, Venn diagram, written description, set of pts.

Question 1c

3 pts.   To learn more math.

5 pts.   Answer demonstrates that studying functions has some personal value to the student, i.e. to describe real world relationships mathematically.

Question 2

0 pts.   Student responds with "true" or "false" with no explanation.

1 pt. $F(\frac{x+y}{2})$ or $\frac{F(x) + F(y)}{2}$ is represented algebraically or geometrically.

2 pts.   Both $F(\frac{x+y}{2})$ and $\frac{F(x) + F(y)}{2}$ are represented algebraically or geometrically.

3 pts.   Weak attempt to compare $F(\frac{x+y}{2})$ and $\frac{F(x) + F(y)}{2}$ algebraically or geometrically.

4 pts.   Same as 5 pt. solution with minor errors.

5 pts.   Algebraic solution demonstrating that $F(\frac{x+y}{2}) < \frac{F(x) + F(y)}{2}$ when $\alpha < 0$.
        or
        Geometric argument demonstrating that $F(\frac{x+y}{2}) < \frac{F(x) + F(y)}{2}$ when the parabola opens downward.

or

Answer of "False" with a valid counterexample.

False when $x = y = 0$, since $F(\frac{x+y}{2}) = \dfrac{F(x) + F(y)}{2}$ when $x = y = 0$.

Question 3

(3 pts. awarded to tangent line and 2 pts. awarded to vertical line.)

1 pt.   Computes $y' = 2x$.

or

Determines a specific tangent and/or vertical line at a point (i.e. $x = 0$ at $(0,0)$ or $y = 0$ at $(0,0)$).

2 pts.   Determines that the slope of the line is 2a

or

Draws the graph of a quadratic, labels the pt. (a, a^2) and draws a tangent line through the pt.

3 pts.   Writes the equation of the tangent line.
$$y - a^2 = 2a(x - a)$$

2 pts.   Writes the equation of the vertical line through a, $x = a$.

Question 4a

1 pt.   Larger, no justification.

2 pts.   Larger, weak justification (i.e. the angle between the ladder and the wall increases, because of Pythagorean theorem, etc.).

or

Writes Pythagorean relationship, but states that the change remains constant.

3 pts.   Larger, argues by use of a physical model.

Draws successive pictures of the base of the ladder being pulled away from the wall.

4 pts.   Minor errors or incomplete 5 pt. answer.

5 pts.   Larger, strong mathematical justification.

A complete algebraic solution is provided with discussion of why $\dfrac{dy}{dx}$ must be getting larger.

or

A strong numerical argument is provided by substituting values into the Pythagorean relationship.

or

A graph of ht. as a function of distance from the wall is provided along with the argument that the slope of the tangent line becomes steeper (larger) as the ladder gets closer to the floor (ht. gets closer to 0), so $\dfrac{dy}{dx}$ gets bigger.

or

A valid trigonometric solution is provided.

Question 4b

   1 pt.   Speeds up with no justification.

   2 pts.   Speeds up with weak justification.

           or

           Pythagorean relationship is provided, but response is incorrect, i.e. slows down or stays the same.

   3 pts.   Speeds up with informal practical argument.

   4 pts.   Speeds up and minor errors in 5 pt. argument or uses results from 4a to make an informal argument.

   5 pts.   Speeds up with strong mathematical justification.

           Computes $\dfrac{dy}{dt}$ and argues that the speed gets larger as x, the distance from the wall, increases and $\dfrac{dx}{dt}$ is held constant.

Question 4c

   1 pt.   Provides Pythagorean relationship, $x^2 + y^2 = z^2$.

           or

           Provides picture of ladder sliding down the wall.

   2 pts.   Solves Pythagorean relationship for one of the variables and no graph is provided or

           Graph is incorrect (i.e. $y = \sqrt{z^2 - x^2}$).

   4 pts.   Same as 5 pt. answer w/o correct labeling of the x and y-intercepts.

   5 pts.   Provides complete graph of functional relationship with correct labeling of the x and y-intercepts.

           (Graph is upper rt. quarter of a circle with radius = length of ladder.) Note: 0 pts. are to be awarded for a function which looks like the graph of $f(x) = \dfrac{1}{x}$ in the first quadrant.

DEPARTMENT OF MATHEMATICS, ARIZONA STATE UNIVERSITY, TEMPE, AZ 85287–1804

CBMS Issues in Mathematics Education
Volume **7**, 1998

Honors Students' Calculus Understandings: Comparing Calculus&Mathematica and Traditional Calculus Students

DAVID E. MEEL

ABSTRACT. This study compared the understandings of third semester honors calculus students from the *Calculus&Mathematica* (*C&M*) curriculum (n=16) and a traditional calculus (*TRAD*) curriculum (n=10). Three instruments examined students' understandings of limit, differentiation, and integration: a) a technology-restricted, written test, b) a problem-solving interview permitting technology, and c) an understanding interview. Analysis of test performances revealed significant differences, favoring *TRAD* students, on the limit tasks, on conceptually-oriented items, and on tasks presented without figures. Detailed analysis uncovered few between-group differences but many similarities, e.g., a dynamic view of the limit, conceptual difficulties with differentiation, and understanding of integration's properties. Problem-solving interviews found the *C&M* students to be more successful and flexible in solving real-world problems than their *TRAD* counterparts. In the understanding interviews, *C&M* and *TRAD* students had difficulties explaining limits and differentiation; however, they displayed formalized understanding of integration. Additionally, the study discussed curricular advantages and disadvantages mentioned by students and focused on the technological differences. The *TRAD* students pointed to the *TRAD* curriculum's restriction of technology as an undue hardship whereas the *C&M* students felt technology aided them in developing understandings but perceived it did not strengthen by-hand skills especially when the skills were needed entering upper level undergraduate mathematics courses.

During the last couple of decades, a number of researchers conducted studies examining the similarities and differences between students involved in a

This article is based upon dissertation research directed by Edward A. Silver and supported by a grant from the University of Pittsburgh's School of Education; University of Pittsburgh; Pittsburgh, Pennsylvania. My thanks to John Hayes, Terrilyn Meel, Fred Reif, Bruce Sherwood, Edward Silver, and Herb Simon for their very helpful comments on earlier versions of this paper.

technology-enhanced calculus course and those involved in a traditional calculus course. Most of the studies have been large-scale, quantitative attempts to model the effects of attitudinal and experiential variables on overall performance [17, 18, 19]. However, as Ratay [43] stated "Calculus grades of course do not tell the whole story. The interesting feedback is yet to come: did these students . . . Learn more concepts . . . ?" (p. 111). Schoenfeld et al. [48] called for investigations which develop "a broad and coherent way of examining student understanding in calculus—to clarify goals of instruction, and to develop and refine ways of examining student behavior to help the mathematical community understand whether and how new forms of instruction are helping students attain those goals" (p. 4). This study, continuing in a larger frame of recent studies addressing Schoenfeld's call, conducted a detailed examination of honor students' understandings of calculus concepts and their application using a variety of instruments undergirded by a theoretical framework and previous research.

In particular, this study conducted a comparative analysis of the calculus understandings and the problem-solving proficiencies developed by honors students completing their third semester under two different calculus curricula. The first calculus sequence utilized the *Calculus&Mathematica* (*C&M*) curriculum [7] which integrates the computer algebra system *Mathematica*^{TM}. The second curriculum employed the Stewart textbook [51] in traditionally taught calculus courses (*TRAD*) based on paper-and-pencil techniques. Through the use of a paper-and-pencil instrument composed of ten open-ended items, this study provided a blunt assessment of student understandings of several historically central concepts of calculus. Problem-solving and understanding interviews obtained deeper and broader insight into student understandings and their usages. Specifically, this study answered the following research questions:

1. What are the between-group similarities and differences with regard to performance on the items of the paper-and-pencil instrument?

2. What is the nature of the between-group cognitive similarities and differences with regard to performance on the items of the paper-and-pencil instrument?

3. What are the between-group differences in global schema, strategies, modes of representation, quality of mathematical justification, and errors with regard to performance in solving, with technological support, four text-only application questions?

4. What are the between-group differences in understanding of the historically central calculus concepts of limit, differentiation, and integration as evidenced in responses to the questions of the understanding interview?

Along with answering these four questions, this study examined the aspects of the two curricula that were seen as either advantageous or disadvantageous to the students.

Related Research

Beyond being influenced by previous studies of student performance where students were involved in calculus curricula incorporating Computer-Algebra Systems (CAS), this study's theoretical framework was influenced by Pirie and Kieren's model of mathematical understanding. Additional guidance was drawn from prior research focused on student understanding of the historically central topics of calculus of limit, differentiation, and integration. The discussion below will briefly characterize the bodies of research supporting this study.

CAS-integrated Calculus Curricula

Four major computer-algebra systems have been integrated into calculus curricula: *Maple*, *Derive*, *Theorist*, and *Mathematica*. As mentioned previously, many of the early studies focused on comparing final grades and attitudes between students involved in a traditional calculus class and students of a innovative calculus class. Over the past ten years, movement occurred which changed the focus away from studying responses to common finals and attitude surveys toward examining conceptual, procedural, and problem-solving differences between students of CAS-integrated calculus curricula with respect to students of traditional calculus curricula.

A variety of researchers, including Judson [24], Schrock [49], Keller [25], Melin-Conejeros [31], Bookman and Friedman [5] and Park [37], examined differences between students of a CAS-integrated calculus curricula with respect to comparative students of traditional calculus curricula. Judson [24] examined the impact of resequencing skills and applications with elementary business calculus students using a *Maple*-enhanced calculus curriculum. She found skill acquisition not to be prerequisite to developing conceptual understanding since no significant achievement difference, with respect to skills, concepts, and applications, between the experimental and control groups was detected. Schrock [49] examined students' comprehension and computational skills and found that the group of calculus 1 students using a *Maple*-enhanced calculus curriculum displayed a significantly higher level of conceptual understanding but no significant difference was displayed in terms of computational capabilities when compared to the control group of students receiving traditional instruction emphasizing computation. In addition, Schrock [49] noted that the attitudes of the students of the *Maple*-enhanced curriculum were positively effected by the use of *Maple*. Keller [25] examined the impact of two innovative calculus curricula, one integrating *Maple* and the other *Theorist*, with respect to the development of symbol sense and student achievement against information gathered from a control group. The control group, unconstrained by the technological restrictions associated with most traditional curricula, was allowed graphics calculator use. The results from a comprehensive final examination pointed to no difference in achievement between the control and the *Maple* group; however, a difference between the control and the *Theorist* group was found favoring the control. In addition, Keller's study indicated that the type of symbol manipulator may not factor into the development of symbol sense and that the form of exploration/instruction may play a larger role than the type of CAS.

The study by Melin-Conejeros [31] examined the effects of doing calculus homework assignments in a mathematics laboratory equipped with the CAS *Derive* on student achievement. The study found no significant difference between the experimental group and the control group in terms of overall performance, skills achievement, or conceptual achievement. However, when interviewing the students, Melin-Conejeros [31] detected that the students who used the CAS *Derive* had a better understanding of increasing and decreasing functions, asymptotes, concavity, limits of functions, and continuity compared to control group students. Bookman and Friedman [5] focused on the problem-solving performance of students using the Project CALC curriculum with *MathCAD* and *Derive* in comparison to students of a traditional calculus curriculum. A problem solving test comprised of five questions was administered to the two groups of students and found that in general the Project CALC students performed significantly better than the traditional students on the problem solving test and in particular significantly better on three of the five questions. According to Bookman and Friedman [5], the results should not be startling since the tests as a whole were skewed toward the Project CALC program due to the nature and complexity of the questions. However, they did provide some evidence that the Project CALC program appeared to be accomplishing its goal of developing student problem solving skills. Park [37] examined the achievement of students of a *Calculus&Mathematica* course and those of a traditional calculus curriculum. The study found that *C&M* students did not significantly lose computational proficiency and were significantly better at conceptual understanding than their counterparts of a traditional calculus curriculum as evidenced by performance on an achievement test. Additionally, Park [37] found that the *C&M* students developed favorable conceptual understandings of calculus concepts as manifested by the analysis of concept maps, were more likely to try multiple approaches to a problem, were indistinguishable with respect to by-hand computation, and demonstrated richer ability to identify relations between calculus concepts than the students matriculating under a traditional calculus curriculum.

These comparative studies indicated that CAS-integrated calculus curricula either minimally or significantly impacted student achievement on conceptually-oriented items in comparison to the achievement evidenced from performances by traditional calculus students on instruments designed specifically to gather this information. These studies also confirmed that computational proficiency was not compromised by the incorporation of computer algebra systems into innovative calculus curricula. The differences which were evident focused on students of CAS-integrated calculus curricula having richer webs for discussing elementary calculus concepts than students of traditional calculus curricula. In addition, studies [5, 37] indicated that the use of a CAS-enhanced calculus curriculum improved students achievement and flexibility in using multiple problem-solving approaches when investigating application problems.

In addition to the aforementioned comparative studies, several non-comparative studies conducted by Crocker [11], Bennett [3], and Ellison [16] examined the impact of CAS-integrated curricula on students' understandings. Crocker [11] used classroom observations, student interviews, and student questionnaires to examine the interactions, conceptual development, and problem solving skills of students enrolled in a calculus curriculum which incorporated the CAS *Mathematica*[TM]. She found that students improved their understanding of the derivative over the course of the study and this improvement took the form of a strong connection between the concept of derivative and that of slope. When examining the developed problem solving skills, Crocker [11] noticed four different response types being displayed (a) No response and failure to engage in the problem solving activity, (b) single-strategy applied, no alternate methods applied, (c) multiple strategies utilized although no partial or complete solutions are achieved, and (d) multiple strategies utilized with either a partial or complete solution achieved. The examination of student problem-solving abilities led to the conclusions that low to medium ability students tended to be more exploratory and open to the use of multiple approaches to solving problems whereas the high ability students tended to have more difficulty and more often failed to use multiple strategies to solve the problems. The research by Bennett [3] examined the effects on student concept images of the function concept when transformations of functions were presented in a computer environment that animated the transformations. She found that the concept image of the function changed from an equation/numerical relationship to the consideration of functions as independent variables and graphs of functions as dependent variables as a result of the computer interactions. The study by Ellison [16] investigated, using a qualitative case study method, the evolution of students' concept images of the derivative as they matriculated under a calculus curriculum augmented by the TI-81 and the computer software *A Graphic Approach to the Calculus* [53, 55]. She found that the students who received computer-enhanced instruction were positively affected since they could mentally construct an appropriate concept image of the derivative. However, a few of the students had difficulty with some components necessary for making this construction. The particular identified difficulties included: (a) identification of the graph of the derivative with its parent function, (b) identification of the characteristics of the parent function when given a graph of the derivative, and (c) identification of the linkage of the formal definition with that of a visual image of the limiting slope of the secant lines [16].

In general, both these comparative and non-comparative studies point to the conclusion that recent incarnations of integrating computer algebra systems with innovative calculus curricula had positive effects on achievement and the development of understanding. These more recent research studies indicated that the incorporation of CAS into innovative calculus curricula does not hurt the students and can be beneficial when utilized to emphasize their strengths. This study continues the examination of CAS-integrated innovative calculus curricula with a focus on honors students and examines if the results appear to correlate with previous conclusions.

Model of understanding

Pirie and Kieren [**38**] defined mathematical understanding as the following:

> Mathematical understanding can be characterized as leveled but non-linear. It is a recursive phenomenon and recursion is seen to occur when thinking moves between levels of sophistication. Indeed each level of understanding is contained within succeeding levels. Any particular level is dependent on the forms and processes within and, further, is constrained by those without. (p. 8)

Using this definition, Pirie and Kieren conceptualized their model of mathematical understanding as containing eight potential levels which has been shown graphically in figure 1.

FIGURE 1.
A diagrammatic representation of Pirie and Kieren's model of understanding

The process of coming to understand begins at the core of the model called the *primitive knowing* (PK) level. Primitive connotes a starting place rather than low level mathematics. The core's contents is the information brought to the learning situation by the student. These contents have been discussed under various names: "intuitive knowledge" [**28**], "situated" knowledge [**8**], and "prior" or "informal" knowledge [**45**]. This primitive knowing level for any particular concept can include a host of information or very little information. The amount contained in the core of the model is concept dependent. For example, Resnick and Omanson's research [**44**] on arithmetic understanding indicated that students entering their mapping instruction held a mental representation of block subtraction attached to a rich knowledge base associated with subtraction. In contrast, Hiebert and Wearne [**23**], examining decimal learning, found students to perceive decimal symbols as part of a new symbol system accompanied by a new set of rules thereby minimizing the linkage to previously learned material. The discrepancy between the core's information and its organization can impact the process of understanding.

At the second level, called *image making* (IM), the learner is able to make distinctions based on previous abilities and knowledge. These images are not thought to be necessarily a "pictorial representation" but rather are to convey the meaning of any kind of mental image. The actions at this level concern the development of connections between referents and symbols as described by Hiebert and Wearne [**23**], Greeno [**20**] and Brownell [**9**]. At the next level, called *image having* (IH), single-activity associated images are replaced by a mental picture. The development of these mental pictures, or more precisely, mental objects, frees the learner's mathematics from the need to perform particular actions [**41**]. These mental objects have been discussed under the guise of several names: "concept image" [**13**], "frames" and "knowledge representation structures" [**12**], and "students' alternative frameworks" [**14**]. The freedom to conceptualize a mathematical object without the constraints of associated processes required to form the image is useful in mathematical knowing. The learner can begin to use these images to recognize the global properties of the mathematical objects.

At the fourth level, the learner can examine a mental object (image) and determine the various attributes associated with the image. This level is referred to as *property noticing* (PN) and is the outermost level of unselfconscious knowing [**38**]. Besides noticing the properties internal to a specific object, the learner is capable of noticing the distinctions, combinations or connections between multiple mental objects. These properties can then be combined to construct "case-restricted" definitions which identify particular characteristics but ignore other elements of the concept. According Pirie and Kieren [**40**], the difference between image having and property noticing is the ability to notice a connection between images and explain the method of establishing a verification of the connection. It may be at this property noticing level that the learner notices commonalties of various images and develops a concept definition [**56**] which incorporates multiple images.

At the fifth level of understanding, called *formalising* (F), the learner is able to cognize about the properties to abstract common qualities from classes of images. At this level the learner has class-like mental objects built from the noticed properties, the abstraction of common qualities, and abandonment of the origins of one's mental action [**38**]. Description of these class-like mental objects results in the production of full mathematical definitions. The language used to describe a concept does not have to be formal mathematical language;

however, the general descriptions provided by students must be equivalent to the appropriate mathematical definition. The following level of understanding, *observing* (O), entails the ability to consider and reference one's own formal thinking. Beyond the learner engaging in metacognition, the learner is also able to observe, structure and organize personal thought processes as well as recognize the ramifications of thought processes. At this level, the learner has progressed to the production of verbalizations concerning cognitions about the formalized concept.

Once one is capable in organizing one's formal observations, the natural expectation is to determine if the formal observations are true. This requires the awareness of one's assumptions and the associations and sequencing intrinsic to the observations. When the learner becomes aware of such assumptions and associations, the interrelationships of observations can be explained by an axiomatic system [38]. This level is called *structuring* (S). At this level, the learner is no longer concerned with a particular topic, but rather has placed the understanding into a larger structure. Therefore at this level, the learner's conceptualizations reach beyond the physical entities associated with the image making level, the action-oriented equivalencies associated with the property noticing level, and the resultant of formal algorithms associated with the formalizing level. The learner would now be able to conceive proofs of properties associated with a concept and view actions taken on the concept as following from other logical properties [40, 41]. The outermost ring of the Pirie and Kieren's model of mathematical understanding is called *inventising* (I). This does not imply that one cannot invent at other inner levels, but rather is used to indicate the ability to break free of a structured knowledge which represents complete understanding and create totally new questions which will result in the development of a new concept. At this level, the learner's mathematical understanding is seen as unbounded, imaginative and reaching beyond the current structure to contemplate the question of "what if?" This questioning results in the learner's use of structured knowledge as primitive knowing to investigate questions beyond the initial domain of investigation. These activities have resulted in the development of new types of mathematics such as Hamilton taking a structured understanding of complex numbers and extending it to form the quaternions [40].

There are many interesting characteristics of Pirie and Kieren's model of understanding. The model is dynamic for it can be used to capture the changing essence of understanding over time. There is a *fractal quality* to the model, for the inner core of *primitive knowing* is comprised of many topics each understood at its own level. The most critical feature of the model is the process of *folding back*. Folding back occurs when one experiences a quandary for which present understanding does not satisfy the problem's cognitive demands. The learner reexamines lower levels of understanding in light of this disconfirming piece of information and then reorganizes the lower level understanding to accommodate the new information. Another quality of the model is called the don't need boundaries which are denoted by the heavy black lines shown in figure 1. Transcending these boundaries signifies the movement of the learner to a more elaborate and stable understanding which does not necessarily require lower level elements [41]. The last quality of the model is called the *complementarity of a process and a form oriented action*. For each level of their model, Pirie and Kieren believe that one must display certain actions and verbalizations in order to be considered operating at the particular level [26, 39]. The above description has characterized these; although for any particular concept, specific actions and verbalizations would be delineated in light of the general model. These form-oriented actions and verbalizations act as evidence of the student's inner conceptualizations to an external agent. Without such evidence, the external agent might think that the level of understanding has not been achieved. Therefore, if the learner does not demonstrate such complementarity in process and form-oriented action, the learner is not considered to have achieved the level of understanding.

Limits

Even though the concepts of differentiation and integration are built upon the concept of limit; the concept of infinity's connection to the limit concept obstructs student understandings of these concepts [29, 50]. Beyond students' misconceptions associated with infinity, other misconceptions can affect students' conception of the limit such as the common language used to describe the limit process [10, 52]. Other misconceptions can develop from the definitions posed for the concept of limit. A variety of case-restricted definitions have been found to be held, sometimes simultaneously, which are valid in certain situations but not in others [30]. Additionally, students have been found to implicitly require a monotonicity for the sequence examined by the limit. Other common misconceptions include: (a) the belief that a last term of the sequence (a_∞) could be obtained, (b) the assumption that sequences have an obvious consistent pattern, and (c) the confusion between the fact that n does not reach infinity and the question of whether the sequence may reach the limit L [13].

Differentiation

Three main interpretations of the derivative have been presented in discussions of differential calculus: the tangent line at a, the instantaneous rate of change at a, and the slope of a highly magnified portion of the graph of f. Each interpretation has its own set of common misunderstandings. For the tangent line interpretation, some students tend to incorrectly associate lines of tangency at cusps and disallow the existence of a tangent at a point of inflection [4]. In addition, they have difficulty with the relationship between secants and tangents [34, 54]; and they describe derivatives as approximations for slopes of tangent lines [22]. The instantaneous rate of change interpretation contains a few obstacles to developing a comprehensive understanding: the linkage with the limit concept, the difference between average rate of change and instantaneous rate of change, and the linkage of the slope of the tangent line to instantaneous rate of change [**34, 46**]. The slope of a highly magnified portion of a graph characterization was developed by Tall [**54**] to overcome the conceptual obstacles associated with the limit process's impact on understanding of the concept of differentiation. However, this interpretation can elicit a misconception, i.e., students considered a tangent as a straight line passing through two very close points on the curve [**15**].

Integration

According to Bressoud [**6**], integration can be interpreted in several different ways: mensuration of area; limit of the sum of vanishing quantities; inverse operation of differentiation; and actions upon a step function in looking forward to the Lebesgue integral. The first three are of importance in the study of undergraduate calculus. Orton [**35**] found students to be facile in the application of basic integration techniques in determining the area under a curve. However, students showed little understanding of the procedure of dissecting an area or volume into narrow sections, obtaining an exact answer for the area by narrowing the width of sections and increasing the number of sections utilizing the limit process. In addition, students exhibited difficulties understanding the procedure of integrating over an interval which contains a discontinuity or cusp of a piecewise-defined function. When investigating understanding of integration as the inverse operation of differentiation, researchers found many students had difficulty in separating the attributes of an original graph from those of its integral or utilizing the information of the derivative to construct the basic nature of the integral [**1, 33**].

Methodology of This Study

Sample

The data collection was conducted in two phases thereby necessitating the use of two sets of participants. The participants involved in the second phase of the study formed a subset of the participants involved in the initial phase of data collection. The participants in the initial phase were 26 third-semester honors calculus students drawn from two classes sanctioned by a large, urban university's Honors College. Sixteen of the students matriculated under a sequence of calculus courses based upon the *Calculus&Mathematica* curriculum (*C&M*) and ten students participated in a traditional calculus sequence based upon Stewart's [**51**] *Calculus* text (*TRAD*). Since the study sought to examine the mathematical understandings developed by students from the two curricula over the three semesters of calculus, the honors students' SAT-M scores and intended majors were used as measures of prior mathematical experience and career focus. These two measures were chosen in order to determine if the two groups were comparable when they entered the sequences even though self-selection into the two curricula occurred. Statistical analysis indicated that the two groups were not statistically different on both SAT-M ($H = 0.04$, $p > 0.05$) and intended major

$(\chi^2(6, 26) = 10.005, p > 0.05)$ with most students being either engineering or pure science majors.

The second phase of the data collection required only five participants of the *C&M* group who were match paired with five participants of the *TRAD* group forming five distinct pairings. These pairings were designed to equate the two members of each pairing based on performance on the limit, differentiation, and integration subsections of the paper-and-pencil instrument administered in the initial phase of data collection. In addition, the set of pairings were chosen to reflect the span of performances exhibited by the participants on that instrument.

Curricula

The *C&M* curriculum completely integrated the powerful computer algebra system, *Mathematica*^{TM}, and its full symbolic, numeric, graphic, and text capabilities. The implementation of the *C&M* curriculum was a lab course based on the model developed at the University of Illinois by H. Porta and J. Uhl and at Ohio State University by W. Davis [**32**]. Instead of attaching technology at the end of the learning process, *C&M* used the technology as a front-end, exploratory tool to initiate the learning process where students experimented with abstract concepts prior to their discussion [**7**]. In order to accomplish this, homework problems became the center of attention of the class. As a result, the role of the professor was removed from the role of "curator of the dogma and arbiter of truth" [**7**, p. 100] and placed in the position of being a strong supporter of students developing their own understandings. Students, working in pairs and teams in a computer classroom equipped with Macintosh computers running *Mathematica*^{TM}, explored exercises designed to aid students in the acquisition of mathematical understanding through real-world application problems relating calculus concepts to other sciences [**32**]. The explorations were recorded in *Mathematica*^{TM} notebooks which in turn promoted the communication of students' mathematical ideas through writing. These compositions included graphical images, computations, and textual material comprised of informal language concerned with the conveyance of meaning over formal mathematical syntax and symbolism.

The traditional calculus curriculum was based upon Stewart's [**51**] *Calculus* text and focuses upon the development of student understanding of the central calculus concepts through formal introductions, skill development, and examination of applications [**51**]. The goals of this curriculum were to develop rigorous, formal understandings of calculus' central concepts and to utilize the methodologies of calculus to solve problems. The professor took on the more traditional role of instructor and facilitator of discussions. The students were taught to conceptualize calculus as an abstract mathematical discipline with modeling capabilities of business, science, and engineering applications [**51**]. Development of proficiency resulted from engaging students in solving multiple problems presented in varied formats. Technology, either calculator or computer based, was not permitted during assessments since the goal of the implemented *TRAD* curriculum was to have students quickly determine exact answers using by-hand methodologies. However, students of the *TRAD* curriculum were permitted to use calculators when completing homework exercises.

The content differences between the *C&M* curriculum and the *TRAD* curriculum appear to be numerous. The authors of the *C&M* curriculum wished to orient the curriculum away from an axiomatic system and toward empirical explorations [**7**]. The *C&M* goal was to present calculus as a measuring tool. As a result, formal definitions were eliminated from the *C&M* curriculum and replaced with active explorations which pointed to the essential components of those definitions. In addition, visualization became the general delivery system and algebra was relegated to serving as a means of convincing. Many of the well established traditional calculus topics, i.e., L'Hospital's rule, local extrema, infinite sequences and series, error terms for Taylor's series, convergence at endpoints, and individual partials, were eliminated from the *C&M* curriculum [**7**]. This was because either technology rendered them obsolete or they were simply devalued due to a desire to present calculus as a set of measuring tools useful in solving real-world problems. For example, since the indefinite integral has no measuring properties, it was not considered a reasonable topic in a *C&M* course primarily concerned with measurement.

Instruments and Administration

Three separate instruments were employed in this study and each of these were undergirded by the framework provided by Pirie and Kieren's model of mathematical understanding. This model was chosen because it correlated well with other characterizations of understanding and included elements such as multiple categories of understanding, mechanisms for overcoming cognitive obstacles, and systems for classifying and correlating students actions to levels of the model. As a result, the model's framework provided structure to the design of the instruments and aided the analysis of the information garnered from student responses to them. The extrapolated versions of the model explicating the various levels of understanding the concepts of limit, differentiation, and integration (see Appendix A) provided the opportunity to consider the amalgamation of responses provided by a student and then map the characterization of displayed understandings onto the model. Thus, the framework provided by Pirie and Kieren's model of understanding structured the design of the three instruments and the analysis of student responses to them.

As a result, the instruments were designed to not advantage either curriculum but rather to aid in ascertaining if students had developed formalized conceptualizations of the concepts of limit, differentiation, and integration. Formalized, as consistent with the position taken by Pirie and Kieren [**38**], does not mean the use of formal mathematical syntax or a definition logically equivalent to a concept's accepted mathematical definition. Here, formalized implies that the student provided evidence across all the instruments of an ability to articulate a description consistent with a concept's accepted mathematical definition and use the description to discuss the concept's implications.

The paper-and-pencil instrument, administered during the initial phase of data collection, consisted of ten open-ended assessment tasks (see Appendix B) adapted from studies examining understanding of the concepts of limits, differentiation and integration. The tasks broadly assessed calculus understandings of these concepts as well as examined a variety of possible influential factors on student performance. In particular, student performance influenced by specific concepts (i.e., limit, differentiation, or integration), understanding types, or presentation type was examined. The understanding types were segmented into two categories: conceptually-oriented and procedurally-oriented. Conceptually-oriented items focused upon conceptual understanding of a topic and typically required students to define a particular concept and to explain internal and external relationships impinging on the definition. Procedurally-oriented items, although containing conceptual aspects, required the sequential performance of particular mathematical skills or computations to obtain intermediary and a final result. The presentation types were either text-and-pictorial or text-only. For each of these, the item's written information may have been augmented with symbolic notation and tabular information although the text-and-pictorial items included pictorial representations, likely pertinent to the question's solution, and the text-only items did not contain such pictorial components. As a result, the paper-and-pencil instrument provided a rough estimation of student understandings of these concepts of calculus from a variety of viewpoints.

An expert panel comprised of mathematicians familiar with the *TRAD* and *C&M* curricula, mathematics educators, and psychometricians validated the paper-and-pencil instrument as well as the other instruments used in this study. The evaluation of the paper-and-pencil instrument primarily dealt with the content, wording, and reasonableness of the questions being delivered to third-semester honors calculus students of both curricula. The instrument, included as Appendix B, was administered to both groups of students over a fifty-minute class period during the early part of December, 1994. The items of the paper-and-pencil instrument were designed to be accessible without requiring technology and as a result, students were told not to use technology when answering the questions. All student responses were scored by a pair of raters using rubrics specifically designed for each item.

The second phase of the data collection took place over a period of a month between mid-February, 1995 and mid-March, 1995 and utilized the second and third instruments. For this second phase, five students of each curriculum were selected for participation. The methodology of selection involved partitioning student performances on the various subtests of the paper-and-pencil instrument (i.e., limit subtest, differentiation subtest, and integration subtest) with respect to the median performances on those subtests. The five students selected were chosen to reflect the diversity of performances displayed. In particular, students were selected to be representative of the performances displayed on the subtests with the group composition being held comparative by match pairing students from the two curricula based upon their performances on the subtests.

The instruments of the second phase of the study, a problem-solving interview (see Appendix C) and a understanding interview (see Appendix D), were individually administered and required approximately two hours to complete. The expert panel examined the interview instruments for appropriateness, content, wording, and format of the questions. The interviews were audio taped and student artifacts were collected at the conclusion. The audio tapes were transcribed and the transcriptions and artifacts were the basis for response analysis. The problem-solving interview was comprised of four "real-world" application tasks which required a little over an hour and unlike the administration of the paper-and-pencil instrument, $Mathematica^{\mathrm{TM}}$ was at the *C&M* students' disposal and the *TRAD* students were permitted to use a scientific or a graphing calculator of their choosing. The administration took place in a setting where the researcher could unobtrusively observe the students' solution processes used to make conclusions concerning the problem-solving tasks. These problem-solving tasks were open-ended and assessed students' abilities to utilize their understandings of differentiation and integration to solve cognitively complex, "real-world" application problems. In particular, the problems were presented in a text-only format, i.e., the task presentation included no pictorial component, and required either finding the maxima and minima of functions or determining and interpreting the area under a curve.

Approximately forty-five minutes of the two hours were dedicated to the understanding interview which consisted of a series of interview questions focused on conceptual understandings of the calculus concepts of interest to this study. Pirie and Kieren's model of understanding guided the design and interpretation of the interviews by framing the actions considered to necessary for evidencing operation at particular levels of the model. The table presented in Appendix A explicates the specific displayed actions and their connection to Pirie and Kieren's model described earlier in this paper. In addition, two final questions asked students to discuss the best aspect and worst aspect of the particular curriculum from which they studied in order to gather insight into their perceptions of the curriculum. The student responses to these questions provided invaluable insight into the students' perception of the curricular beneficial and detrimental factors.

Data Coding and Analysis

The student responses to the paper-and-pencil instrument were scored according to two analysis schemes: a wholistic scoring scheme (quantitative analysis) and a cognitive analysis scheme (qualitative analysis). In the quantitative analysis, each student's response was assigned a numerical score by raters according to researcher designed scoring guides consistent with the guidelines discussed by Lane [27]. The students' identities were unknown to the raters and a pair of raters scored all student responses to each task with inter-rater agreement ranging from 69.2% to 88.5% with a mean of 81.6%. Additionally, the researcher, besides adjudicating any discrepancies between rater scores, scored a third of the student responses and the rater to researcher agreement for these responses ranged from 71.4% to 100.0% with a mean of 80.7%. These quantitative scores formed the basis from which totals and sub-totals were developed and upon which six Kruskal-Wallis[1] tests were conducted. The information resultant from these tests answered the first research question by revealing whether there were significant between-group differences in performance on the paper-and-pencil instrument. In particular, the analysis sought to uncover between-group differences with respect to overall performance, performance with respect to the various concepts (i.e., limits [Items #1, 2, 3], differentiation [Items #4, 5, 6], or integration [Items #7, 8, 9]), to the understanding type (i.e., conceptually-oriented [Items #1, 3, 5, 7, 9] or procedurally-oriented [Items #2, 4, 6, 8, 10]), and to the task format (i.e., text-and-pictorial [Items #3, 5, 7, 8, 10] or text-only [Items #1, 2, 4, 6, 9]).

The qualitative analysis of student responses to the paper-and-pencil instrument helped answer the second research question concerning between-group cognitive similarities and differences when solving items of the paper-and-pencil instrument. Here, the analysis focused on four critical aspects of the student's response: solution strategies, mathematical errors, mathematical justifications, and modes of representation. Similar to the employment of raters to develop the quantitative scores, a pair of raters categorized components of student responses according to researcher-designed coding schemes. The inter-rater agreement ranged from a low of 71.4% to a high of 100.0% with the mean being 78.2%. Rater to researcher agreement was also examined for a third of the student responses. The rater to researcher agreement ranged from 71.4% to 100.0% with a mean of 80.4%. These analyses were descriptive in nature and Fisher-Irwin and Chi-Square tests[2] were used to examine if significant between-group differences existed.

In order to answer the third question concerning between-group differences in problem-solving components, the framework for the analysis of problem-solving protocols [47] was used to organize the analysis for particular aspects of the problem-solving process: global schema, problem-solving response, strategies, modes of representation, quality of mathematical justifications, and errors. In particular, the global schema, which was used to characterize the mode of entry and process toward solution, was adapted from research by Crocker [11]

---

[1]The Kruskal-Wallis test, a valid alternative to the ANOVA test, compares k distributions when the dependent variable is not normally distributed or sample size is not sufficiently large to apply the central limit theorem.

[2]The Fisher-Irwin exact test and Chi-Square tests are tests which examine differences in proportions. If the variable is dichotomous, then the Fisher-Irwin exact test, valid for small samples, can identify differences between expected distributions and collected samples. The Chi-Square test, also valid for small samples, identifies differences between proportions when the variable contains more than two categories.

and identified three general schemas: (a) *acting*—to first design a specific plan and then execute that plan, (b) *reacting*—to first design a general plan without specifying methodologies and then tour the problem space, and (c) *exploring*— to first develop a graphical image of the problem situation and then engage in either acting or reacting. The problem-solving responses of (a) non-response, (b) use of a single strategy, (c) use of multiple strategies without success, or (d) use of multiple strategies with success were adapted from categories used by Bookman and Friedman [5] and Crocker [11]. Each of the multi-step, problem-solving items used in this study required students to employ a variety of problem-solving strategies in order to accomplish the task although the use of multiple representations was not required. As a result, these qualitative descriptions identified the various types of responses exhibited by students as they solved the items and corresponded to the identification and usage of problem-solving strategies. The global schema and problem-solving response, along with focuses on strategies, errors, modes of representation, and quality of mathematical justifications, were used to detect similarities and differences between *C&M* and *TRAD* students' problem-solving methodologies and provide descriptions of these relationships.

The interview protocol for the understanding portion involved a structured interview where students were prompted for precise and reasonable definitions of statements dealing with the limit, differentiation, and integration concepts. Students were asked to provide formal definitions of these concepts and to discuss the meaning and the implications of the conditions impinging on these concepts. Furthermore, students were urged to name at least 5 mathematical topics which utilized the various concepts and, for each, to explain the utilization thereby providing insight into the students' conceptual webs of connection and the nature of those connections. The student responses to these questions (see Appendix D) were pooled with the information garnered from the student's responses to the paper-and-pencil instrument into a data base of displayed actions and verbalizations. This data base then was examined in light of requisite actions and verbalizations considered necessary evidence to be operating at any particular level of understanding in Pirie and Kieren's model of understanding (see Appendix A). The resultant codings indicate the generally consistent level of displayed understanding evidenced from the student's responses to the two instruments. The between-group comparison of the displayed understandings utilized these codings as the basis for qualitative descriptions. In addition, misunderstandings evident from student responses to the various instruments were discussed.

Results and Discussion

The results are reported in four different sections: the quantitative analysis of student responses to items on the paper-and-pencil instrument, the qualitative analysis of responses to the items on the paper-and-pencil instrument, the analysis of data obtained in the problem-solving interviews, and the analysis of data obtained in the understanding interviews. This order of reporting results corresponds to the four research questions at the heart of this investigation.

Quantitative Analysis of the Paper-and-Pencil Instrument

The quantitative analysis of the student responses to the questions of the paper-and-pencil instrument examined differences and similarities of the *TRAD* students' and *C&M* students' performances on the paper-and-pencil instrument as a whole and on various partitionings of the items. In particular, the instrument examined the performance similarities and differences with respect to the mathematical topics of limit, differentiation, and integration. The instrument's items permitted two other parsings: items presented in either a text-only or a text-and-pictorial format and items oriented toward either the examination of conceptual understanding or procedural knowledge.

Consistent with some of the previous research [**21**, **24**, **25**, **31**], the examination of student performance on the paper-and-pencil instrument as a whole found the two groups of students to have performed similarly. In particular, the Kruskal-Wallis one-way analysis of variance found the two groups to not be significantly different in terms of the overall performance on the calculus instrument ($H = 1.24$, $p > .05$).

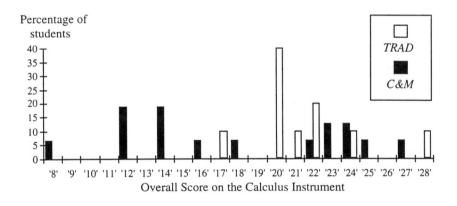

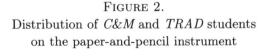

FIGURE 2.

Distribution of *C&M* and *TRAD* students
on the paper-and-pencil instrument

It was interesting, however, to notice that the distributions shown in figure 2 revealed the overall performance of the *C&M* students to be somewhat bimodal and that the performance of the *TRAD* students appeared clustered in the middle of the two modes.

The analysis of the student response in light of the concepts of limit, differentiation, and integration (see figure 3) found the *TRAD* students to have performed significantly better than the *C&M* students on the items associated with the limit concept ($H = 6.09$, $p < .0166$); however, with respect to differentiation and integration, the performance of the students from the two groups were similar ($H = 2.89$, $p > .0166$ and $H = 1.09$, $p > .0166$, respectively).

The result associated with limits was expected due to the lack of emphasis in the *C&M* curriculum on the formal definition of limit. Rather than defining the concept, as was the case for the *TRAD* curriculum, the *C&M* curriculum presented the limit concept through applications resulting in the developed perception that the concept was tied to specific situations and images rather than an abstracted conceptualization. In addition, the language utilized by the *C&M* curriculum to discuss the limit concept was informal thereby not adhering to the concept's precise nuances and resultant in case-restricted definitions not entirely consistent with the mathematical definition of the concept.

The format of presentation had a significant impact on performance displayed by the students of the two groups (see figure 4). There were two categories used to demarcate the distinction between presentation formats: text-and-pictorial and text-only. Text-and-pictorial items incorporate pictorial representations, typically pertinent to the solution of the question, and written information which may include symbolic notation and tabular information. Text-only items have written text as the dominant mode of presentation although symbolic notation and tabular information may augment the item.

The *TRAD* students performed significantly better than the *C&M* students on the items presented in a text-only format ($H = 6.08$, $p < .0166$). However, the performance of the two groups on the items presented in a text-and-pictorial format was similar ($H = 0.00$, $p > .0166$). Both groups of students performed better on the text-and-pictorial items in comparison to their performance on the text-only items. However, only the *C&M* students performed significantly better on the text-and-pictorial items compared to their performance on the text-only items ($\chi_r^2 = 14.06$, $p < .01$).

In light of the design of the two curricula, the affinity of the *C&M* students to items presented with a visual component was expected because of the amount of computer-rendered graphics incorporated into the curriculum. Hence, the combination of the administration constraint of no technological support and the presentation of tasks with no visual component appeared to negatively impact *C&M* students' performances. The *TRAD* students, on the other hand, did not appear to have such an attachment since they were showed no between-format performance differences. Two possible conclusions can be drawn from these results. The first could be that the *TRAD* students were more capable than the *C&M* students in solving tasks presented with or without a pictorial component. The second conclusion which could be drawn was that of the need for the inclusion of a pictorial component when *C&M* students are assessed using an instrument unsupported by technology. The restriction of technology and the lack of visual presentation of information acted as a double obstacle to students of the *C&M* curriculum. For instance, one *C&M* student, EP, stated the following about the authors of the *C&M* curriculum:

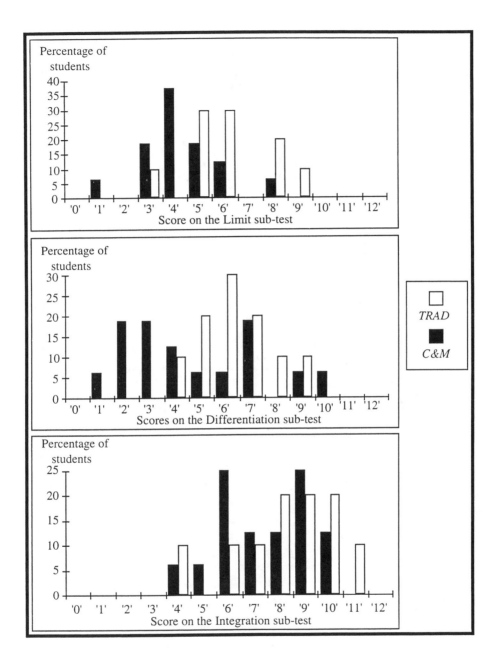

FIGURE 3.
Distributions of the *C&M* and *TRAD* students
on the concept sub-tests

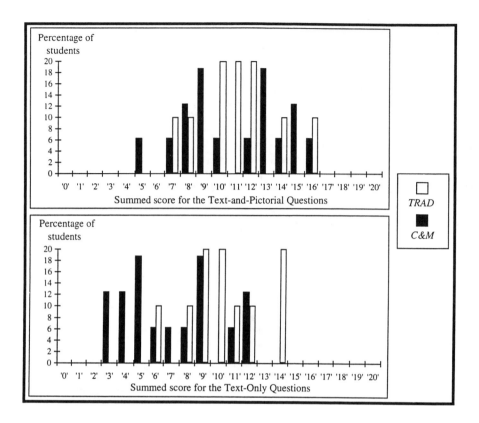

FIGURE 4.
Distributions of the *C&M* and *TRAD* students
on the Text-and-Pictorial and the Text-Only Items

. . . they don't want to make anything mathematical, they want it discovered on your own. So, you're not going to sit down and put it into simple, precise definitions. So, whenever I see them, they don't make any sense. I have to go through, from more I have to look at a picture at all the times it seems.

Here, the student indicated the curriculum presentation caused a need in the student to draw a clear relationship between the concepts and pictorial manifestations of the concepts.

Examinations of student performance on the conceptually-oriented items revealed an interesting result seemingly divergent from previous research comparing students of a computer-enhanced calculus curriculum and students of a traditional calculus curriculum. Several of the previous comparative studies [21, 36, 37, 49] examining student performance on conceptually-oriented tasks have reported that students of CAS-integrated calculus curricula displayed either similar or significantly higher levels of achievement on items examining conceptual understanding.

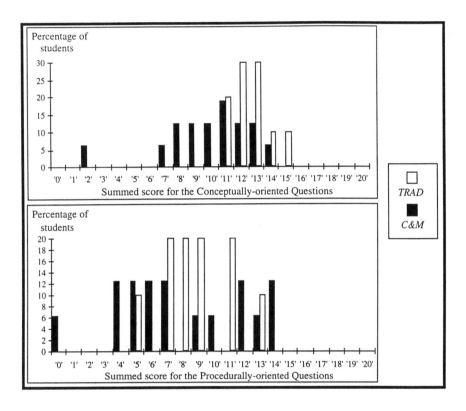

FIGURE 5.
Distributions of the *C&M* and *TRAD* students
on the Conceptually-oriented and the Procedurally-oriented Items

As can be surmised from figure 5, this study found that the honors students of the *TRAD* curriculum performed significantly better than the honors students of the *C&M* curriculum on the conceptually-oriented items of the paper-and-pencil instrument ($H = 6.68$, $p < .0166$). With respect to performance on the procedurally-oriented items, the two groups of students were found to have performed similarly ($H = 0.44$, $p > .0166$).

This study's administration constraint disallowing technological support was consistent with the conditions under which the previous studies were conducted. As a result, the differences may be attributed to the scoring guides used to rate the student responses to the items of the paper-and-pencil instrument. The

guides were designed to reward responses consistent with formalized conceptualizations of limit, differentiation, and integration. Such a reward advantage
for responses with greater compatibility to the formal mathematical definitions
was consistent with the framework upon which the instrument was based, i.e.,
Pirie and Kieren's model of understanding. Provision of case-restricted definitions was considered to be evidence of operation at the property noticing level
whereas generalized explanations consistent with the mathematical definitions
were indicative of formalized understandings of the concept. As a result, the
scoring guides reflected this difference by rewarding responses indicative of formalized understanding. It was interesting that some of the *C&M* students were
able to provide rich explanations utilizing informal language. The use of informal language was not the problem; rather, explanations tended to either contain
errors or only hold in some cases. The *TRAD* students, in contrast, discussed the
concepts with textbook language and their explanations better approximated the
accepted mathematical definitions even though some errors in expression were
made.

Qualitative Analysis of the Paper-and-Pencil Instrument

Rather than examining student responses wholistically, the qualitative examination focused on the strategies employed, the quality of mathematical justifications, and errors displayed. The qualitative analysis revealed many results
consistent with prior research on student understandings of central concepts of
calculus. For instance, student responses to task #1 of the paper-and-pencil
instrument, which asked students to translate a symbolic expression denoting
the limit of a sequence and then explain its meaning, were consistent with the
conclusions of previous studies examining student understandings of the limit
concept (e.g., [10], [13], [50], [52]). In each of these studies, the majority of
students when requested to explain the meaning of the expression,

$$\lim_{x \to a} f(x) = c,$$

produced a definition of the limit which captured its dynamism, i.e., $f(x)$ gets
close to c as x gets close to a. This explanation, although capturing an essential
characteristic of the limit concept, lacked some of the essential characteristics
delineating its nature, such as what it means when one states "gets close to" or
what the necessary and sufficient conditions are for having a limit.

The analysis of the student responses to tasks #2 and #3, also dealing with
the limit concept, revealed that some students of both curricula held a belief in
the sufficiency of examining a point or set of points "near" the point under consideration when finding the limit. For example, some student responses to task
#3 revealed a belief that virtual proximity would ensure accuracy in approxima-
tion of the limit even though the terms were generated by $a(n) = (-1)^n(\frac{1}{2} - \frac{4}{n})$.
This belief was indicated in response to the item and can be seen in the two
samples shown in figure 6.

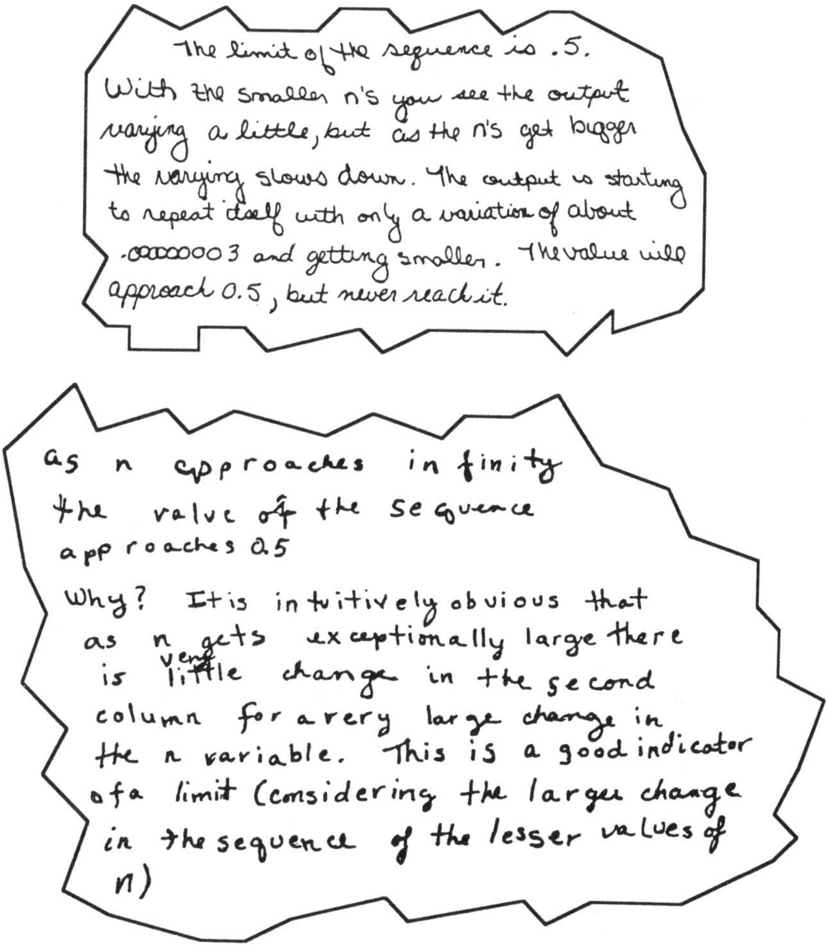

The limit of the sequence is .5.
With the smaller n's you see the output
varying a little, but as the n's get bigger
the varying slows down. The output is starting
to repeat itself with only a variation of about
.00000003 and getting smaller. The value will
approach 0.5, but never reach it.

as n approaches infinity
the value of the sequence
approaches 0.5

Why? It is intuitively obvious that
as n gets exceptionally large there
is very little change in the second
column for a very large change in
the n variable. This is a good indicator
of a limit (considering the larger change
in the sequence of the lesser values of
n)

FIGURE 6.
Sample student responses to Item #3

This propensity was commented upon by Williams [**57**] and attributed to a
faith that a few points could be used to develop a representative graph. This
graph was then thought to be sufficient to extrapolate all the particular nuances
and end behaviors of the "function" under consideration. Such a potentially
incorrect belief may be a result of limitations in the scope of examples and problems presented to the students. If the situations presented to students include
only particular characteristics, i.e., monotonically increasing or monotonically
decreasing functions, then students may extrapolate that these define the set of
possibilities and abstract a conceptualization consistent with the restricted range

of essential characteristics.

The *TRAD* student responses to the two of the three questions focused on the concept of differentiability (tasks #4 and #6) revealed a strong connection of differentiability with continuity. This connection was evident, although not as strongly, in the *C&M* students' responses to these same items. Students' explanations from both groups revealed a belief that continuity was considered a necessary and sufficient condition for deciding differentiability of a function. For example, in task #6 (see Appendix B), the function is continuous but contains a cusp at which point the derivative of the function does not exist. Many of the students, especially *TRAD* students, examined only the continuity of the component functions and this decision indicated a belief that the examination of continuity would be sufficient to ensure the existence of the derivative of the function. The two examples provided in figure 7 reveal how students exemplified this belief.

The mere examination of continuity would be beneficial when deciding the differentiability of a non-continuous function as was the case with task #4; however, it can act as an obstacle to obtaining the differentiability of a continuous function with a cusp.

The linkage of continuity to differentiability also was found in a study conducted by Artigue and Swed [2] on student understanding of graphical representations. In addition to the connection of continuity to differentiability, several students indicated a concern that the derivative function was not a function defined by a singular rule. From this, it appeared that some of these students have not been sufficiently exposed to piecewise-defined functions. Piecewise-defined functions model many real-world situations but they seem to have been neglected by the two curricula when discussing differentiability. In addition, the analysis of student responses to the paper-and-pencil instrument's other differentiation item (task #5), which was originally conceptualized and used by Orton [34], revealed that many of these third semester honors calculus students ignored the limit component of the differentiation formula and considered the formula to measure the average rate of change rather than the instantaneous rate of change. This result was consistent with Orton's study [34] which examined the understandings of differentiation held by first year university students.

The qualitative results of the integration questions (tasks #7, 8, and 9) revealed that the students of both curricula were adept at conceptualizing viable methodologies for improving the estimation of the area under a curve of a function which had no closed form antiderivative and at selecting and justifying a function which corresponded to a given derivative. In general, the students of each group proffered many reasonable methodologies to improve the approximation. These included increasing the number of segments, using midpoints instead of endpoints, using trapezoids rather than rectangles, averaging the sums found by using right-hand and left-hand endpoints, cutting the figure out and weighing it against a unital piece, and using an approximating function for the curve and

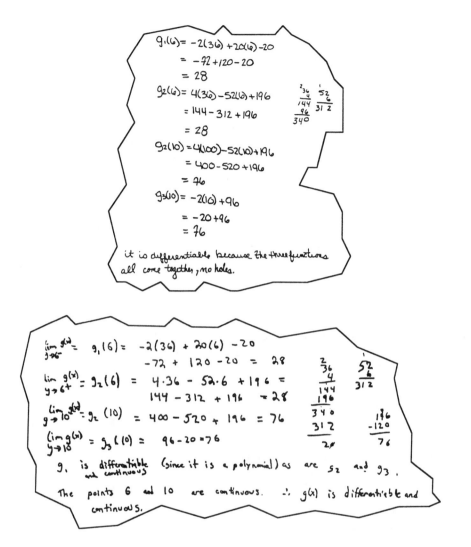

finding the area under that function.

When the focus of the items turned from methodologies to the three conceptualizations of integration, i.e., area under a curve, inverse operation of differentiation, and summation of infinitesimally small quantities, some students had difficulty in expressing their ideas. Such a difficulty also was found by Orton [35] when he examined first year university students' conceptualizations of integration. In addition, some students of both the *C&M* and the *TRAD* curricula indicated, incorrectly, the equivalence of the area under a curve conceptualization and the summation of infinitesimally small quantities conceptualization forgetting the constraint of the function being non-negative for the area under the curve interpretation. The *C&M* students appeared to rely primarily on informal discussions of the conceptualizations whereas the *TRAD* students tended to utilize more formalized terminology in their discussions but these contained either incorrect or incomplete components which may be attributable to either an incomplete command of the language or a lack of understanding of the concepts.

A glimpse at the problem-solving abilities of the students of the two curricula was provided through their responses to task #10 of the paper-and-pencil instrument (see Appendix B). Some internal differences, albeit not significant, indicated that the *C&M* students recognized the integral components necessary to solve this real-world application task more often than the *TRAD* students. For example, in the part A portion of the task, a considerably larger percentage of *C&M* students used the derivative to find the values of instantaneous rate of change of the two functions than *TRAD* students. In addition, the student examinations of the part B section, which required integration, revealed that a larger percentage of the *C&M* students utilized integration to find the total amount of oil saved by changing the consumption curve. It was interesting to find that a majority of students of both curricula indicated that if the two functions intersected then no between-function growth rate differences existed. Additionally, students of both curricula erroneously used pointwise differences to examine the accumulated difference over an interval.

Overall, the qualitative analyses of the student responses to the paper-and-pencil instrument revealed that the *C&M* students approached both the defining of the mathematical concepts and the provision of explanations with a tool kit of informal language and visualization. The *TRAD* students were more conversant with the precise symbolic formulations; however, in many cases the *TRAD* students fell back to discuss these formal definitions using informal language which had many of the same error characteristics associated with the *C&M* students' explanations.

Analysis of the Problem-Solving Protocols

The problem-solving interviews utilized four open-ended, quasi real-world application tasks designed to examine the implementation of the student's understandings of differentiation and integration. The focus was not necessarily what could be recalled but rather what could be applied to solve complex problems which have been mathematically modeled. The administration conditions of the problem-solving interviews provided the opportunity to examine students' problem-solving skills in a setting where technological tools that students were accustomed to using for problem-solving were allowed.

In response to each of the problem-solving tasks, the same number or a larger number of *C&M* students, in comparison to the number of *TRAD* students, attained the highest problem-solving response level (same on the first item and greater on the other three items). The highest problem-solving response level was achieved by attaining the correct solution and completely and correctly utilizing multiple strategies during the problem-solving process. These findings were consistent with the conclusions of a study by Bookman and Friedman [5]; however, unlike the technological allowance of this study, they did not permit technology use on their problem-solving instrument. The number of students attaining the highest level was small for each of the tasks except for the first task where all the students attained this level. There was only one student, a *C&M* student, who attained this highest problem-solving response level on all four of the tasks. In a study by Crocker [11], she examined student problem-solving capabilities and reported that the A-level students of her study had greater difficulty in problem-solving because of a lack of use of multiple strategies or lack of engagement. Although the number of honors students attaining the highest level of problem-solving response was low in this study, it was not because of the lack of use of strategies as Crocker [11] suggested. Rather, it appeared to be due to a tendency of some students to not completely come to an understanding of the task's conditions and requirements.

Examination of the problem-solving process associated with movement toward solution revealed that the *C&M* students utilized the technology, typically the CAS *Mathematica*^{TM}, to develop a means of extracting a plan by attempting a variety of attacks, examining the results from those attacks, and then deciding upon a direction which appeared to make the most sense. This process was seen primarily when students were unable to directly analyze the situation to develop either a global or specific plan or when the student encountered a result which ran contrary to expected outcomes. Such flexibility was aided by the CAS *Mathematica*^{TM}; however, flexibility did not always lead to correct solutions. Students were permitted to follow unwarranted and fruitless solution paths; but at the same time, the students were able to gather insight into the mathematical functions with which they were modeling the real-world phenomena. In light of the end results, the *C&M* students' greater adaptability created opportunities to reexamine their own thinking, to question if the line of thinking being used made sense in light of the resultant evidence, and to proceed further toward the solution.

The *TRAD* students appeared to be more rigid in their problem solving process because they tended to be less flexible in the selection of strategies. For example, once a strategy was chosen, the *TRAD* students tended to persistently utilize the strategy even when obtaining unreasonable results. This particular behavior may have been driven by either uncertainty in the correctness of the computational results or an incorrect belief that the strategy would produce the necessary result. A case in point was the strategy "differentiate and then set the result equal to zero" when confronted with the phrase "find the maximum of. . ." in problem solving task #3 (see Appendix C). Several of the *TRAD* students decided that the function describing the strength of reaction would need to be differentiated and the resultant function when set equal to zero would determine the dosage which maximized the sensitivity to the drug. The students should have recognized that the process provided the dosage which maximized the strength or reaction rather than the sensitivity. From the student responses to this and other questions, it was evident that the *TRAD* students tended to focus on a singular strategy and not consider questioning the validity of the strategy in light of the provided function and the desired outcome. This resistance to reconsider was evident even when students were directly confronted.

The discussion above by no means should be interpreted as implying that the *TRAD* students were the only ones who fell into the trap of using the strategy "differentiate and then set the resultant equal to zero." *C&M* students were not immune to this well intentioned but sometimes errant strategy. However, the primary difference between the *C&M* students and the *TRAD* students was the fact that many of the *C&M* students were able to reexamine the strategy by examining the problem situation from multiple perspectives, with or without prompting, and recognize that the strategy did not provide the needed information.

Therefore, what was seen from the problem-solving interviews was the rigidity of the *TRAD* students in their unwillingness to reevaluate their assumptions or conclusions. The *C&M* students were better equipped than the *TRAD* students to deal with complex problem situations where the solution process was not self-evident. This flexibility of using singular strategies to gain information on multiple topics and checking the validity of assumptions from multiple viewpoints may have been the result of curricular differences in the sense that the *C&M* students were provided with a technology which could easily generate graphical images, compute complex derivatives and integrals, and solve equations quickly. The *TRAD* students were not provided with the technology to accomplish these feats but were relegated to the use of at best graphical technologies and technology-supported, by-hand computations of derivatives and integrals. These restraints may have constrained the students' problem-solving processes and caused them to wonder more about computational error, a fear alleviated in the minds of the *C&M* students by the accuracy of the technology, over the possibility that the process itself was possibly flawed.

Analysis of the Understanding Protocols

The understanding interviews (see Appendix D) gathered additional information concerning student understandings of the concepts of limit, differentiation, and integration. Through the verbalizations and actions exhibited in response to the questions of the understanding interview and paper-and-pencil instrument, the selected students revealed their understandings. No student captured the entire essence of the limit concept and many of the responses revealed a dynamic view of the limit. Even those *TRAD* students, who provided reasonable approximations to the formal definition of the limit concept on the paper-and-pencil instrument, did not clearly delineate the limit concept's essential components and their linkages. As a result, all the selected students of both groups displayed actions consistent with the property noticing level, i.e., the learner is capable of integrating various images of the limit situation and has developed an intuitive casewise definition of limits based on a narrow repertoire of images.

Such a consistency across the two curricula with regard to displayed understandings of the limit concept appeared to be in contention with the significant between-group performance difference found on the limit questions of the paper-and-pencil instrument. This was especially intriguing when one remembers that the interviewed students were selected to be reflective of the range of exhibited performances. Thus, perhaps the most remarkable result was not that the selected students of each curriculum displayed actions which were similar in nature but rather that all five students of each curriculum displayed actions corresponding to the property noticing level.

In reference to student understandings of the concepts of differentiation and integration, the lack of significant differences found by the paper-and-pencil instrument was mirrored by the analysis of student responses to the items of the understanding interview. The groups displayed understandings which were generally equivalent although particular students provided unique insights. For example, JG, one of the *C&M* students, stated the following during the interview:

> . . . the integral and the derivative, the integral happens to measure something and the derivative happens to measure something else. One measures the accumulation of area which is defined as the sum of the rectangles of $f(x)$ and delta x and as delta x goes to 0, or delta x goes to 0 so it means dx. And the other case, the one that had the rate of change. The neatest things that is is the fundamental theorem of calculus which so happens, those two different functions which measure two different things are completely interrelated. And, . . . I guess that's one of the most important ideas that. Not only does something appropriate measure and say this this value between two things it measures, it gives, it allows you to think about things. When I mean the fundamental theorem of calculus, I mean something that's important, it allows you to think in terms of existent theoretical functions, that have theoretical derivative, if they are differentiable or integral and there is a relationship between that integral and that derivative. And derivative . . . if $f = dg/dx$ and the integral of that is equal to g. Having that theoretical function, that's helping in a lot of applications, that's, that's something that, anyway not only are measuring I can, can measure antiderivative. That constant, it's, it's as over looked as the number 0. Because just 0 is the function 0, it limits it limits the space. . . .

The above statements by JG, provided as a verbal response, conveyed the belief that integration was considered the summation of infinitesimally small rectangles and, perhaps more importantly, explicated the thematic connector between integration and differentiation.

The selected students of each group displayed actions predominantly associated with property noticing for both the concepts of differentiation and integration. However, the analysis of the understandings of integration indicated that greater numbers of students, in comparison to those displayed in conjunction with differentiation, displayed actions consistent with levels of understanding higher than property noticing. This result may have been a consequence of more recent exposure and work with integration or that the two curricula in calculus 3, in which the students were engaged, focused more on integration than differentiation in three dimensions. Either way, the results of the analysis of the student understandings of limit, differentiation, and integration displayed by the students were generally similar.

Analysis of the Ancillary Questions

The questions concerning the best and worst aspects of the student's curriculum were responded to with rich and insightful vignettes concerning impressions of the two courses. The ensuing discussion characterized some of these.

There appeared to be a positive sentiment exuded by the *TRAD* students that the mathematics they learned was "real" mathematics. These students were able to see calculus in the form of its original purpose. For instance, one of the *TRAD* students, MR, stated:

> Being as calculus is so direct, is calculus, well first off, from Newton's perspective, the only purpose to calculus is physics. But even from Leibniz perspective that calculus, I mean calculus, without, when you teach the physics along with it, it links mathematics to the real world, so that you can see, you can directly see the value of the mathematics.

Students commented on being glad to be learning mathematics and not computer programming. One of the *TRAD* students, JK, summarized this sentiment in the following statement:

> Well the best thing is that you don't have to worry about getting short changed in the learning . . . I think it's [traditional calculus] better because you know you're going to get the information because you're not learning any calculators or computers; you're only learning the information.

At the same time, students mentioned that the prohibition of technology was one of the worst aspects of the *TRAD* curriculum. Many of the *TRAD* students saw the restriction of technology as an undeserving hardship. For example, JK later went on to state:

> . . . because it's the traditional they don't allow you to use calculators which can be very annoying especially with all the revolutionary, the aspects of calculators where you can take a derivative, I mean a matrix that takes a year to multiply by hand, plug it into your calculator and get the answer in two seconds, more time typing into the calculator than to multiply them.

Some of the students reported being able to use technology in other non-mathematics courses and wondered why it was decided to disallow its use in the mathematics courses. According to Wilson and Kilpatrick [58], the disparity between the technological allowances of the traditional mathematics classroom and the world external to the school has a poignant impact on the students. The above quotation exemplified the fact that many of the *TRAD* students saw the incongruity between the world of school mathematics and the mathematics used in the world. In these *TRAD* students' minds, the technology could alleviate a computational burden which when released would allow the students to concentrate on solving the problems.

The *C&M* students felt that the best aspect of the *Calculus&Mathematica* curriculum was the tool, *Mathematica*^{TM}, with its graphical and computational capabilities. For example, one of the *C&M* students, JG, made the following comment:

> And the great thing about *Mathematica*^{TM} is that it helps you see a function graphically and it give you that abstraction that not too many calculus students see is that the function is not this, the function is this. . . . You are able to measure, algebra doesn't let measure only lets you determine this particular or this particular idea. And I think I got to that conclusion after I was exposed to so much plotting, it gives you a lot of sense for functions.

Another *C&M* student, EP, when discussing the best aspect of the *C&M* curriculum stated:

> . . . if I have a real life problem that I won't be able to do on paper or it would be just too time consuming, especially if it is integration, I can go down and get *Mathematica*^{TM} to solve it.

In addition to the technological advantages, the design of the curriculum and its focus on student developed understandings was mentioned by BC, a *C&M* student, in the following quotation:

> I found the best aspect to be the amount of self-learning occurs as you do like, like the way the structure for the class and everything you can't just go to lecture and you don't rely on the professor and you don't just memorize things. You have to come to your own understanding of the material.

Therefore, these students felt that the *C&M* curriculum fostered strong intuitions about calculus.

The *C&M* curriculum was not without some shortcomings. Students mentioned the loss of by-hand skills and reduced set of memorized rules and techniques for such things as differentiation and integration. This was poignantly etched on the minds of the *C&M* students, for three of the five selected *C&M* students mentioned it as one of the worst aspects of the *C&M* curriculum. One of the *C&M* students, TE, summed up this concern very well in the following quote:

> . . . I'm not as good in the areas of say integration especially because, I mean you learn integration more as just type in integrate and have it do this than you do all the techniques for integrating. And I think that's

something I'm having to catch up on now that I'm in Calc 4 than it's differential equations I've had to learn different methods. Not to say that I didn't learn them in *Mathematica*, it's just that I didn't, I didn't have to, actually I didn't learn some of them, but the ones I did learn, there wasn't enough, there wasn't as much a need to practice them and really learn them as there is in a traditional calc class.

This concern has been taken to another level by a different *C&M* student, BN, when he stated:

. . . once I got into it [*Calculus&Mathematica*] I was stuck in it because I didn't know or understand enough to jump into the traditional. And that it just kept getting worse and worse and here I am in Math 5 now and Math 25 and just like, blown away.

As can be seen, these comments were typically connected to allusions to needing these skills in traditionally taught upper division mathematics course. The *C&M* student, BC, who mentioned that student-developed understandings were beneficial, tempered his statement later in the interview when stating the following:

I guess the best thing about it [*Mathematica*^{TM}] is that it promotes creativity and the worst thing about it is that it promotes too much creativity and you start making up your own math. You know, making up your own mathematical rules and stuff that aren't really real. Like the things I say about functions.

Thus, a concern was raised concerning the pedagogical technique of placing the student as the builder of his or her own understanding without the provision of a mechanism to compare the developed understanding against a benchmark.

It was interesting to find that in contrast to the *TRAD* students' desires to have technology incorporated into the *TRAD* curriculum, *C&M* students were calling for the limitation of the integration of technology in calculus curricula. These comments were not necessarily a desire to return entirely to the traditional practice of disallowance of technology but rather a moderating of the infusion of technology into the *C&M* curriculum. In order to accomplish this, many of the *C&M* students echoed a call for *Mathematica*^{TM} to be only a part of the curriculum rather than the entire curriculum being built around it. Two of the *C&M* students, EP and BN, pointed to *Mathematica*^{TM} and stated that it should be used "more as a supplement than the whole course" or "in like recitation or a lab". They both felt, as was echoed in many of the *C&M* students comments, that a greater emphasis should have been placed on the development of by-hand skills. For instance, one of the *C&M* students made comments such as "I would have lectures and by-hand assignments. They are tedious usually but I think they help with the understanding." Thus, these students felt that the reduction of the status of technology would provide sufficient opportunity to engage in the activity of computing with by-hand methods and this practice would serve as a mechanism for the improvement of their "understanding" of the calculus concepts.

Conclusion

This study examined the differences in understandings and problem-solving abilities of third semester, honors calculus students from either a *C&M* curriculum or a *TRAD* curriculum as displayed in responses to three instruments. The calculus instrument allowed the researcher to gain a general feel for the understandings and capabilities of the students of the two curricula. Since the instrument was comprised of only ten items and the students were given just a class period to complete it, the responses could only provide a general sense of what the students understood concerning the calculus concepts of limit, differentiation, and integration. The results of the analysis of the student responses to this paper-and-pencil instrument revealed that with respect to overall performance no between-group difference was found. Analysis also revealed the two groups of honors students to be similar when the focus was on the differentiation concept, the integration concept, procedurally-oriented items, and text-and-pictorial items. However, when the scope of analysis focused on the limit concept, conceptually-oriented items, or text-only items, significant differences in performance were found between the two groups of honor students favoring the *TRAD* students. Some of these differences could have been a result of excluding the use of technology; however, the qualitative analysis of the student responses to the paper-and-pencil instrument indicated that the differences were more likely a result of differences in the depth, scope, and sequence associated with the presentation of the two curricula.

The problem-solving interviews provided the opportunity to examine student understanding and the application of the understanding to solve "real-world" tasks. This combination allowed one to see how the understanding was connected to the problem-solving process, to view the problem-solving process as an entity to itself, to trace student problem-solving processes, and to develop an understanding of the strategies and errors produced as part of the process. The analysis of the problem-solving interviews revealed that the *C&M* students were more successful and tended to be more flexible in solving problems than were their *TRAD* counterparts. The *TRAD* students appeared more rigid in their problem solving sessions because they examined the problem situations, developed either global or specific plans, and then proceeded through the computations associated with the plans. The *C&M* students, in comparison, tended to explore prior to developing global or specific plans which would utilize a multiplicity of strategies. This flexibility extended beyond the use of a multiplicity of strategies into the utilization of an implemented strategy for multiple purposes and was mostly seen when students encountered answers which did not correlate with expected results. The *TRAD* students would show more concern with computational aspects of a strategy than the validity of the strategy. The *C&M* students, on the other hand, utilized the multiple strategies to check the validity of their work by re-examining their assumptions. In particular, the *C&M* students used the graphical images they developed in *Mathematica*^{TM} to both make sense of the problem situation, gather data, and correlate computational results with intuitions developed from the images. Thus, the *TRAD* students' concern with the accuracy of the computations appeared to inhibit the development of flexibility and the provision of *Mathematica*^{TM} permitted the *C&M* students to be more flexible with their choice of available representations and techniques in solving application problems.

The understanding interview allowed greater insight into student understandings of the concepts of limit, differentiation, and integration than that which could be obtained from the calculus instrument and problem-solving interviews. This instrument provided the opportunity to develop a dialogue where the researcher could interact with the student and ensure that the interpretations of the student responses were consistent with the actual beliefs of the student. In particular, the understanding interview provided the opportunity for the student and the researcher to negotiate a common language which was satisfactory to both and from which interpretation of the student responses could occur. The analysis of the student responses to the understanding interview questions revealed that students of both curricula conceived the concepts of limit and differentiation in ways that did not capture their entire essence. However, with respect to integration, the students of both curricula appeared to display understandings compatible with understanding the formal definition of integration. So, in light of the student performance on the various instruments, it appeared to be the case that students of neither curriculum generally outperformed the students of the other one.

One is left with the question if either curriculum satisfied the needs of these honors calculus students. As the students pointed out in response to the final questions concerning the best and worst aspects of their curricula, each of the curricula was not without its problems. And, based upon the *C&M* students' comments, one might get the impression that the students were calling for the dismemberment of the *C&M* curriculum for a more traditional-like sequence of courses which incorporated *Mathematica*^{TM} as a purely problem-solving tool. Assuming this was the case, consider the reasons. In response to the best and worst aspects of the *C&M* curriculum, the worst aspect mentioned by the selected *C&M* students pointed to a piece of the *TRAD* curriculum either not incorporated into or de-emphasized by the *C&M* curriculum. The question which naturally flows from this observation: is "What aspect of the *C&M* students' mathematical experience would evoke such responses?"

In every case, the *C&M* student was engaged in an upper division mathematics course based upon the traditional classroom structure and philosophy. The honors students of *C&M* curriculum were therefore engaged in courses which de-emphasized technology and student-developed understandings in exchange for greater emphasis on by-hand skills and teacher-directed validations. The students appeared to have developed a perception that the *C&M* curriculum was not fully preparing them for reentering into a traditional-based mathematics course. This possibly was a self-fulfilling prophecy or a reality. Obviously the skills of a student from the *TRAD* curriculum would be different from the developed skills of a student from the *C&M* curriculum. For the honors *C&M* student, the various rules and techniques which were mediated through the computer were neither honed through by-hand skills nor necessarily committed to memory. The concerns of the *C&M* curriculum were to develop students with strong problem-solving skills and an understanding of the applications of calculus in the real-world with its complex problems. Therefore, it does not seem reasonable to expect the honors *C&M* students to be equipped to flourish in upper level mathematics courses which are incongruous with the philosophy of the calculus curriculum under which they have been trained. Especially poignant was the perceived devaluing of the skills developed as a result of the *C&M* curriculum and the resultant conclusion that the *C&M* curriculum must be adapted to address these needs.

The question which then comes to mind is not whether the *C&M* curriculum should be overhauled, although particular aspects could be reexamined, but rather why were honors *C&M* students shunted in traditional upper division courses? Consider, hypothetically for the moment, the soundness of the premise on which the reformed calculus curricula was built, what could this study imply about the construction of upper level mathematics courses? Perhaps one could conclude that the reform of undergraduate mathematics education for honors students has not gone far enough and upper division mathematics courses need to also reflect these ideals. The impact of reforming calculus may not be able achieve its maximum effect if upper level mathematics courses devalue the reform principles and dismiss skills honed by the *C&M* curriculum.

References

1. Artigue, M., *Analysis*. In D. Tall (Ed.), Advanced mathematical thinking, Kluwer, Dordrecht, 1991, pp. 167–198.
2. Artigue, M., & Swed, T., *Représentation graphiques*, IREM Paris Sud, 1983.
3. Bennett, E.M., Calculus students' concept images of functions in an environment of computer-generated animation of graphs of transformations of functions, Dissertation Abstracts International **55(1)** (1994), 58A.
4. Bivens, I.C., *What a tangent line is when it isn't a limit*, College Mathematics Journal **17(2)** (1986), 133–143.
5. Bookman, J., & Friedman, C.P., *A comparison of the problem solving performance of students in lab based and traditional calculus*. In E. Dubinsky, A.H. Schoenfeld, & J. Kaput (Eds.), Research in collegiate mathematics education. I, American Mathematical Society, Providence, RI:, 1994, pp. 101–116.
6. Bressoud, D.M., *How should we introduce integration?*, The College Mathematics Journal **23(4)** (1992), 296–298.
7. Brown, D., Davis, W., Porta, H., & Uhl, J., *Calculus & Mathematica*, Addison-Wesley, Reading, MA: 1992.
8. Brown, J.S., Collins, A., & Duguid, P., *Situated cognition and the culture of learning*. Educational Researcher, **18(1)** (1989), 32–42.
9. Brownell, W.A., *Psychological considerations in the learning and teaching of arithmetic*. In W.D. Reeve (Ed.), The Teaching of Arithmetic. Tenth yearbook of the National Council of Teachers of Mathematics, Columbia University, New York, New York, 1935, pp. 1–31.

10. Cornu, B., *Limits*. In D. Tall (Ed.), Advanced Mathematical Thinking, Kluwer, Dordrecht, 1991, pp. 153–166.

11. Crocker, D.A., *A qualitative study of interactions, concept development and problem solving in a calculus class immersed in the computer algebra system Mathematica*^{TM}, Dissertation Abstracts International **58(8)** (1992), 2850A.

12. Davis, R.B., *Learning mathematics: The cognitive science approach to mathematics education*, Ablex, Norwood, NJ, 1984.

13. Davis, R.B. & Vinner, S., *The notion of limit: Some seemingly unavoidable misconception stages*, Journal of Mathematical Behavior **5** (1986), 281–303.

14. Driver, R. & Easley, J., *Pupils and paradigms*, Studies in Science Education, **5** (1978), 61–84.

15. Dubinsky, E. & Tall, D., *Advanced mathematical thinking and the computer*. In D. Tall (Ed.), Advanced Mathematical Thinking, Kluwer, Dordrecht, 1991, pp. 231–248.

16. Ellison, M.J., *The effects of computer and calculator graphics on students' ability to mentally construct calculus concepts*, Dissertation Abstracts International **54(11)** (1994), 4020A.

17. Ferrini-Mundy, J. & Graham, K.G., *An overview of the calculus curriculum reform effort: Issues for learning, teaching, and curriculum development*, American Mathematical Monthly **98(7)** (1991), 627–635.

18. Friedman, M.L., *Research—The sparse component of calculus reform—Part I: An analysis of the reform effort*, Primus **3(1)** (1993), 4–10.

19. Ganter, S.L., *The importance of empirical evaluations of mathematics programs: A case from the calculus reform movement*, Focus on Learning Problems in Mathematics **16(2)** (1994), 1–19.

20. Greeno, J.G., *Number sense as situated knowing in a conceptual domain*, Journal for Research in Mathematics Education, **22(3)** (1991), 170–218.

21. Hawker, C.M., *The effects of replacing some manual skills with computer algebra manipulations on student performance in business calculus*, Dissertation Abstracts International **47(8)** (1987), 2934A.

22. Heid, M.K., *Resequencing skills and concepts in applied calculus using the computer as a tool*, Journal for Research in Mathematics Education **19** (1988), 3–25.

23. Hiebert, J. & Wearne, D., *Procedures over concepts: The acquisition of decimal number knowledge*. In J. Hiebert (Ed.), Conceptual and procedural knowledge: The case of mathematics, Erlbaum, Hillsdale, NJ (1986), pp. 199–223.

24. Judson, P.T., *Effects of modified sequencing of skills and applications in introductory calculus*, Dissertation Abstracts International **49** (1989), 1397A.

25. Keller, B.A., *Symbol sense and its development in two computer algebra system environments*, Dissertation Abstracts International **54(11)** (1994), 5704B.

26. Kieren, T.E., *Understanding for teaching for understanding*, The Alberta Journal of Educational Research **36(3)** (1990), 191–201.

27. Lane, S., *The conceptual framework for the development of a mathematics performance assessment instrument*, Educational Measurement: Issues in Practice **12(2)** (1993), 16–23.

28. Lienhardt, G., *Getting to know: Tracing student's mathematical knowledge from intuition to competence*, Educational Psychologist **23(2)** (1988), 119–144.

29. Mamona-Downs, J., *Pupils' interpretations of the limit concept: A comparison study between Greeks and English*, Proceedings of the 14th International Conference for the Psychology of Mathematics Education **1** (1990), 69–76.

30. Meel, D.E., *Understandings of the limit concept: Case restricted definitions, miss-connections within the formal definition, and levels*, University of Pittsburgh, Unpublished manuscript, 1994.

31. Melin-Conejeros, J., *The effect of using a computer algebra system in a mathematics laboratory on the achievement and attitude of calculus students*, Dissertation Abstracts International **53(7)** (1993), 2283A.

32. Michael, B.K., Manfredi, J. & Beatrous, F. *CALC-TECH: The western Pennsylvania calculus technology consortium*, University of Pittsburgh, Unpublished manuscript, 1993.

33. Nemirovsky, R. & Rubin, A., *Students' tendency to assume resemblances between a function and its derivative*, TERC Communications, Cambridge, MA., 1992 (ERIC Reproduction Service No. ED 351 193).

34. Orton, A., *Students' understanding of differentiation*, Educational Studies in Mathematics **14** (1983a), 235–250.

35. Orton, A., *Students' understanding of integration*, Educational Studies in Mathematics **14** (1983b), 1–18.

36. Palmiter, J.R., *Effects of computer algebra systems on concept and skill acquisition in calculus*, Journal for Research in Mathematics Education **22(2)** (1991), 151–156.

37. Park, K., *A comparative study of the traditional calculus course vs. the Calculus & Mathematica course*, Dissertation Abstracts International **54(1)** (1993), 119A.

38. Pirie, S.E.B. & Kieren, T.E., *A recursive theory of mathematical understanding*, For the Learning of Mathematics **9(3)** (1989), 7–11.

39. Pirie, S.E.B. & Kieren, T.E., *A recursive theory for the mathematical understanding— some elements and implications*. Paper presented at the Annual Meeting of the American Educational Research Association (1990), Boston, Massachussets.

40. Pirie, S.E.B. & Kieren, T.E., *A dynamic theory of mathematical understanding: Some features and implications*. Paper presented at the Annual Meeting of the American Educational Research Association (1991), Chicago, Illinois.

41. Pirie, S.E.B. & Kieren, T.E., *Watching Sandy's understanding grow*, Journal of Mathematical Behavior **11** (1992), 243–257.

42. Pirie, S.E.B. & Schwarzenberger, R.L.E., *Mathematical discussion and mathematical understanding*, Educational Studies in Mathematics **19** (1988), 459–470.

43. Ratay, G.M., *Student performance with calculus reform at the United States Merchant Marine Academy*, Primus **3(1)** (1993), 107–111.

44. Resnick, L.B. & Omanson, S., *Learning to understand arithmetic*. In R. Glaser (Ed.), Advances in instructional psychology (Vol. 3). Erlbaum, Hillsdale, NJ, 1987, pp. 41–95.

45. Saxe, G.B., *Studying working intelligence*. In B. Rogoff & J. Lave (Eds.), Everyday Cognition. Harvard University Press, Cambridge, MA, 1988, pp. 9–40.

46. Schneider, M., *On learning the rate of instantaneous change*, Educational Studies in Mathematics **23** (1992), 317–350.

47. Schoenfeld, A.H., *Mathematical problem solving*, Academic Press, Inc., Orlando, FL, 1985.

48. Schoenfeld, A.H., Dubinsky, E., Gleason, A., Harnisch, D., Kaput, J., Kifer, S., Moore, L., Newman, R., & Swafford, J., *Student assessment in calculus: A draft report of the NSF working group on assessment in calculus*, Unpublished manuscript, 1993.

49. Schrock, C.S., *Calculus and computing: An exploratory study to examine the effectiveness of using a computer algebra system to develop increased conceptual understanding in a first-semester calculus course*, Dissertation Abstracts International **50(7)** (1989), 1926A.

50. Sierpinska, A., *Humanities students and epistemological obstacles related to limits*, Educational Studies in Mathematics **18** (1987), 371–397.

51. Stewart, J., *Calculus*, Second Edition., Brooks/Cole Publishing Company, Pacific Grove, CA, 1991.

52. Tall, D.O., *Intuitions of infinity*, Mathematics in School **10(3)** (1981), 30–33.

53. Tall, D.O., *Building and testing a cognitive approach to calculus using computer graphics*, University of Warwick, UK. Unpublished doctoral dissertation, 1986.

54. Tall, D.O., *Inconsistencies in the learning of calculus and analysis*, Focus on Learning Problems in Mathematics **12(3 & 4)** (1990), 49–63.

55. Tall, D.O., Blokland, P. & Kok, D. *A Graphic Approach to the Calculus* (I.B.M. compatible software), Sunburst, Pleasantville, NY, 1990.

56. Tall, D.O. & Vinner, S., *Concept image and concept definition in mathematics with particular reference to limits and continuity*, Educational Studies in Mathematics, **12** (1981), 151–169.

57. Williams, S.R. (1991). *Models of limit held by college calculus students*, Journal for Research in Mathematics Education **22(3)** (1991), 219–236.

58. Wilson, J.W., & Kilpatrick, J., *Theoretical issues in the development of calculator-based mathematics tests*. In J. Kenelly (Ed.), The use of calculators in the standardized testing of mathematics, College Entrance Examination Board, New York, NY, 1989, pp. 7–15.

APPENDIX A

Level of Understanding	Actions associated with limits	Actions associated with differentiation	Actions associated with integration
Primitive Knowing	Cell 01	Cell 02	Cell 03
Image Making	Cell 04	Cell 5	Cell 06
Image Having	Cell 07	Cell 08	Cell 09
Property Noticing	Cell 10	Cell 11	Cell 12
Formalising	Cell 13	Cell 14	Cell 15
Observing	Cell 16	Cell 17	Cell 18
Structuring	Cell 19	Cell 20	Cell 21
Inventising	Cell 22	Cell 23	Cell 24

Contents of Cell 01

The learner would be assumed to be entering the situation with conceptions of things getting closer in value, convergence, asymptotes and informal terminology.

———————— ◇ ————————

Contents of Cell 02

The learner would be assumed to be entering the situation with understanding of functions, limits, tangents, secants, distance, velocity, acceleration and slope.

———————— ◇ ————————

Contents of Cell 03

The learner would assumed to be entering the situation with understandings of limits, functions, and area.

———————— ◇ ————————

Contents of Cell 04

The learner is able to find the solution to simple limit problems and apply mathematical language to explain the actions employed.

———————— ◇ ————————

Contents of Cell 05

The learner is able to compute the average rate of change of a function over a given finite interval and calculate derivatives of simple functions, complex functions, and implicit functions.

———————— ◇ ————————

Contents of Cell 06

The learner is able to compute the area under a curve for a function. The learner is able to determine the antiderivatives of particular functions.

———————— ◇ ————————

Contents of Cell 07

The learner is able to internalize multiple images of the limit situation although the pattern features of these images are not completely recognized (Case-wise conceptions have not been achieved).

———————— ◇ ————————

Contents of Cell 08

The learner is capable of interpreting the information provided by average rate of change and relate this to instantaneous rate of change. The learner can explain how scaling of a curvature can result in a segment of the curvature which looks like a line and what relationship the slope of the "line" has to the derivative.

———————— ◇ ————————

Contents of Cell 09

The learner is able to relate the integral and the original function.

———————— ◇ ————————

Contents of Cell 10

The learner is capable of integrating various images of the limit situation and developed an intuitive definition of limits (although possibly casewise and based on a limited repertoire of images).

———————— ◇ ————————

Contents of Cell 11

The learner is capable of extracting the salient features of differentiation as well as discuss the information which can be drawn from differentiation.

———————— ◇ ————————

Contents of Cell 12

The learner is capable of delineating the important properties associated with integration and determination of the area under a curve.

———————— ◇ ————————

Contents of Cell 13

The learner is capable of severing reliance on particular case-wise definitions and has developed a formal symbolic notion of limits.

———————— ◇ ————————

Contents of Cell 14

The learner is capable of providing and explaining the requirements associated with the formal definition of differentiation. The learner is capable of utilizing the formal definition of derivative to determine derivative formulas.

———————— ◇ ————————

Contents of Cell 15

The learner is capable of formally explaining the connection of the integral to various conceptualizations of the integral: the area under a curve, the inverse operation of differentiation, and the summation of infinitesimally small quantities.

———————— ◇ ————————

Contents of Cell 16

The learner is capable of generalizing and recognizing the limit as a mathematical entity which can be operated on.

———————— ◇ ————————

Contents of Cell 17

The learner is capable of observing differentiation as an operator which is used to extract information. The learner is capable of operating with different derivative definitions to determine the alternative derivatives of simple functions.

———————— ◇ ————————

Contents of Cell 18

The learner is capable of observing integration as an operator which is used to extract information. The learner is capable of discussing the relationship between the indefinite integral and the definite integral. The learner is capable of discussing the merits of various integration techniques: circumscribed, inscribed, midpoint, trapezoidal rules.

———————— ◇ ————————

Contents of Cell 19

The learner is capable of placing the concept of limits into the frame of reference of calculus, Banach Spaces, L^p Spaces, Real and Complex Analysis and Measure Theory.

———————— ◇ ————————

Contents of Cell 20
The learner is capable of determining the form and function of derivatives in contexts other than $\Re$, i.e., partial derivatives and complex derivatives.

———————— ◇ ————————

Contents of Cell 21
The learner is capable of examining integration problems where the conditions do not satisfy those required by Riemann integration and conceptualizing a methodology to overcome this short-coming (i.e., anticipate Lebesgue integration)

———————— ◇ ————————

Contents of Cell 22
The learner uses the structured knowledge as primitive knowing when extending to questions which cannot be answered by the topic which the structure contains however the structure is seen as a guide for answering the questions.

———————— ◇ ————————

Contents of Cell 23
The learner uses the structured knowledge as primitive knowing when extending to questions which cannot be answered by the topic which the structure contains however the structure is seen as a guide for answering the questions.

———————— ◇ ————————

Contents of Cell 24
The learner uses the structured knowledge as primitive knowing when extending to questions which cannot be answered by the topic which the structure contains however the structure is seen as a guide for answering the questions.

———————— ◇ ————————

APPENDIX B

1. Translate the symbolic expression,

$$\lim_{n \to \infty} a_n = L,$$

into words and then explain what the expression means.

2. Determine the answer to the following:

$$\lim_{(x,y) \to (0,0)} \frac{x^2 y}{x^4 + y^2}.$$

Explain or show how you found your answer.

3. A student has programmed a computer to print out the terms of a sequence. Here is an excerpt from what was produced:

n=1	3.5
n=2	-1.5
n=3	0.833333
n=4	-0.5
n=5	0.3
n=6	-0.166667
n=7	0.0714286
n=8	0.0
n=9	-0.0555556
n=10	0.1
n=100	0.46
n=10000	0.4996
n=1000000	0.499996
n=100000000	0.49999996

Explain what the student should conclude concerning the limit of the sequence being investigated and why.

4. A function f will be called $*$-differentiable at a if

$$\lim_{h \to \infty} \frac{f(a+h) - f(a-h)}{2h}$$

exists.

(Note: this is different than the definition of differentiation you learned in class)

(a) Determine whether the function

$$f(x) = \begin{cases} x^2 + 2x, & x < 2 \\ 10 & x = 2 \\ 6x - 4 & x > 2. \end{cases}$$

is $*$-differentiable at $x = 2$. Explain or show how you found your answer.

$f^*(2) = $ _____

(b) Is the function

$$f(x) = \begin{cases} x^2 + 2x, & x < 2 \\ 10 & x = 2 \\ 6x - 4 & x > 2. \end{cases}$$

ordinarily differentiable (i.e., differentiable in the manner that you learned in your calculus class) at $x = 2$? Explain or show how you found your answer.

$f'(2) = $ _____

(c) Compare and contrast the ordinary formula for differentiation and the $*$-differentiable formula.

5. The diagram below is one that is commonly used to introduce the following definition for derivative or differentiation,

$$\frac{dy}{dx} = \lim_{h \to 0} \frac{k}{h} :$$

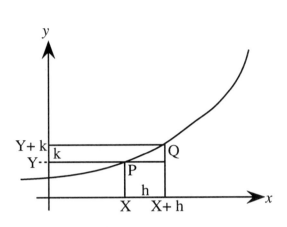

(a) At which point of the graph does the formula measure the rate of change?

(b) Explain why the formula defines this rate of change.

6. If the function $g(x)$ is defined in the following manner:

$$g(x) = \begin{cases} g_1(x) : -2x^2 + 20x - 20 & [0, 6) \\ g_2(x) : 4x^2 - 52x + 196 & [6, 10) \\ g_3(x) : -2x + 96 & [10, 18]. \end{cases}$$

Is the function $g(x)$ differentiable over its domain? Explain why or why not.

7. If one is attempting to improve an approximation to the area under a curve $y = f(x)$ for which no closed form antiderivative exists, what are <u>three</u> techniques which would improve the estimate developed by the technique depicted below? For each technique, explain why the technique would result in an improvement in the estimate.

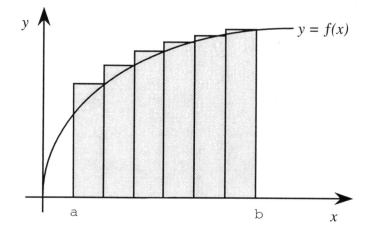

8. Graph 1 is the derivative $y = f'(x)$ of a function $y = f(x)$ defined for $0 \leq x \leq 13$.

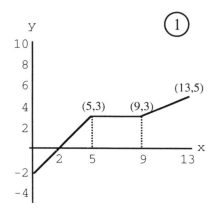

(a) Which of the graphs 2, 3, 4 could be the original graph $y = f(x)$?

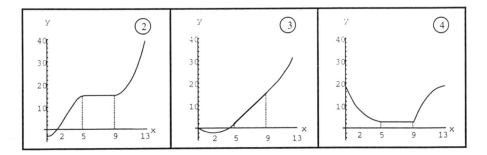

Graph # _____ could be the original graph $y = f(x)$

(b) For each of the two graphs you did not pick, explain why the graph could not be the graph $y = f(x)$.

9. There are three fundamental ways integration can be conceptualized:
   1. Area under a curve $y = f(x)$
   2. Differentiation's inverse operation
   3. The summation of infinitesimally small quantities

For each of these conceptualizations, explain what the conceptualization means and how the relationship between the integral and the conceptualization is formulated.

Area under a curve $y = f(x)$

Differentiation's inverse operation

The summation of infinitesimally small quantities

10. In 1974, the oil prices grew to a dramatic high. As a result, the rate of
consumption of world oil (in billion barrels of oil per year) changed from
$$R_1(t) = 16.1e^{0.07t}, \ t \geq 0 \qquad \text{(rate of consumption prior to 1974)}$$
to
$$R_2(t) = 21.3e^{0.04(t-4)}, \ t \geq 4 \qquad \text{(rate of consumption during and after}$$
1974)

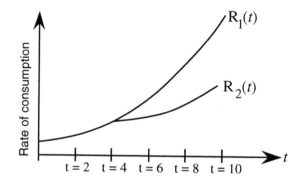

(a) What is the difference in growth rates for $R_1(t)$ and $R_2(t)$ at the beginning
of 1974?

(b) What is the total amount of oil saved between 1976 and 1980 caused by
the change in the rate of consumption initiated in 1974?

APPENDIX C

Problem-solving task #1

Deforestation is one of the major problems facing sub-Saharan Africa. Although the clearing of land for farming has been the major cause, the steadily increasing demand for fuel wood has become a significant factor. The World Bank conducted a study to estimate the rate of fuel wood consumption and the rate of new tree growth. They found the projected rate of fuel wood consumption (in millions of cubic meters per year) in the Sudan t years after 1980 would be approximately given by the function

$$c(t) = 76.2e^{0.3t}.$$

They also found the projected rate of new tree growth (in millions of cubic meters per year) in the Sudan t years after 1980 would be approximately given by the function

$$g(t) = 50 - 6.03e^{0.09t}.$$

Explain what is happening to the fuel wood supply in the Sudan between the years 1980 and 2000.

Problem-solving task #2

The government commissioned a study of the spread of a certain strain of influenza, INF-138. The members of the disease control conducting the study developed two models to describe the phenomena of the spread of INF-138 for a city of 10,000 where $N_i(t)$ is the number of people who will contract INF-138 within the first t weeks. The two models are described below:

$$N_1(t) = 54t^2 - 2t^3 \quad (0 \le t \le 18)$$

$$N_2(t) = \frac{6000}{1 + 119e^{-.453t}} \quad (0 \le t \le 18)$$

where t is the number of weeks after the initial diagnosis of a group of people having INF-138.

When approximately fifty people of a city of nearly 10,000 citizens contracted INF-138 and were diagnosed, the members of the disease control thought it was a perfect opportunity to examine the spread of INF-138 in realistic circumstances. What they wished to determine was which of the two models best described the spread of INF-138. In order to accomplish this, they conducted surveys and found the following information:

- approximately 57% of the community contracted INF-138 in the 18 weeks after the initial diagnosis of the original 50 people.
- The greatest number of people reported initial symptoms coming on during the 11th week.
- 480 people in the survey reported contracting the flu within the first 5 weeks.

Based upon this information, which model, $N_1(t)$ or $N_2(t)$, best describes the spread of the strain of influenza INF-138? Explain why you think this best describes the spread.

The model which best describes the spread of INF-138 _____

Problem-solving task #3

Doctors need to understand the characteristics of the drug they prescribe. For a given drug, there are two important aspects: the maximum allowable dose, C, and the patient's sensitivity to the drug. If x measures the dosage and $R(x)$ the strength of the reaction (change in body temperature, blood pressure, or some other measurable body function) then sensitivity tells the doctor (approximately) how much change to expect in R as a result of a unit change in the dosage, x. For a certain experimental drug, EXP-1001008, the strength of the reaction, R, is given by

$$R(x) = \frac{Cx^2}{9} - \frac{x^2}{9} \quad x < C.$$

Where R is the strength of the reaction, C the maximum allowable dose, and x the dosage given.

What dosage maximizes the sensitivity to the drug? _____.

How does that dosage relate to the dosage associated with the maximum strength of reaction?

Explain or Show how you found your answers.

Problem-solving task #4

A data processor keyboards registration data for college students from written forms to electronic files. The number of minutes required to process the kth registration form is estimated to be approximately given by the formula:

$$n(k) = 6(1+k)^{-1/3} \quad \text{(for an initial 8 hour shift)}$$

$$n(k) = 5.5(1+k)^{-70/243} \quad \text{(for each subsequent 8 hour shift)}$$

For any 8 hour shift of inputting registration data, the probability of reliably entering the kth registration form is estimated to be given by the formula

$$r(k) = (1.453x10^{-23})(k+8.5)^{35}e^{-3(k+8.5)}+0.79 \quad \text{for each subsequent 8 hour shift}$$

The college can hire one or two temporary data processors at \$6.00 per hour to enter the 2000 registration forms.

If the college wants to minimize the amount of money spent but maximize the average reliability of inputting the information, how many data processors should they hire?

They should hire _____ data processor(s).

In the space below, explain why you feel this is the best decision.

APPENDIX D

Interview Questions concerning limits:

1. Suppose $f : [a, b] \to \Re$ and $x_0 \in [a, b]$.

   Give a precise and reasonable definition of the statement

"the limit of f at x_0 is L"

(This information has been placed upon an index card for the subject's reference)

If an example or an informal definition is given . . .

1A. Ask the student . . .

If an example . . .

An interesting example. However, can you give me a precise and reasonable definition?

If an informal definition . . .

Can you give me a more precise definition?

If not, ask the student to explain what the meaning was for the individual pieces of the definition which was given.

If a formal definition is given . . .

1B. Ask the student . . .

Can you explain the meaning of the following:

For every $\epsilon > 0, |x - y| < \epsilon$.

(This information has been placed upon an index card for the subject's reference)

2. Name at least $\underline{5}$ mathematical topics which utilize the limit concept.

3. For each of the topics given, please explain how the limit is utilized.

Interview Questions concerning differentiation:

1. Suppose $f : [a, b] \to \Re$ and $x_0 \in [a, b]$.

   Give a precise and reasonable definition of the statement

   "the function f is differentiable at x_0"

(This information has been placed upon an index card for the subject's reference)

If an example or an informal definition is given . . .

1A. Ask the student . . .

   If an example . . .

   An interesting example. However, can you give me a precise
   and reasonable definition?

   If an informal definition . . .

   Can you give me a more precise definition?
   If not, ask the student to explain what the meaning was for the individual
   pieces of the definition which was given.

If a formal definition is given . . .

1B. Ask the student . . .

   Can you tell me what specific conditions must exist for a function
   to be differentiable at a point.

   If the subject has not already explained the reasons why, ask the following:

   Can you explain why each of these conditions are required?

   For every $\epsilon > 0, |x - y| < \epsilon$.

2. What are three things a derivative can tell you about a function?

3. Name at least $\underline{5}$ mathematical topics which utilize the derivative concept.

4. For each of the topics given, please explain how the derivative is utilized.

Interview Questions concerning integration:

1. Suppose $f : [a, b] \to \Re$ and $a < c < d < b$.

   Give a precise and reasonable definition of the statement

   "the function f is integrable over the interval $[c, d]$"

(This information has been placed upon an index card for the subject's reference)

If an example or an informal definition is given . . .

1A. Ask the student . . .

   If an example . . .

   An interesting example. However, can you give me a precise and reasonable definition?

   If an informal definition . . .

   Can you give me a more precise definition?

   If not, ask the student to explain what the meaning was for the individual pieces of the definition which was given.

If a formal definition is given . . .

1B. Ask the student . . .

   What property or set of properties must the function, f, have so

   $$\int_c^d f(x)\, dx$$

   corresponds to the area under the curve defined by $f(x)$ and bounded by x values of c and d?

   Explain why this property or set of properties is necessary.

2. Compare and contrast the definite integral $\int_a^b f(x)\, dx$ and the indefinite integral $\int f(x)\, dx$. Be sure to discuss how they are found and what information they provide.

3. Name at least $\underline{5}$ mathematical topics which utilize the integral concept.

4. For each of the topics given, please explain how the integral is utilized.

Ancillary Question: What do you think has been the best aspect of taking _____ and what do you think has been the worst aspect of _____?

UNIVERSITY OF PITTSBURGH

CBMS Issues in Mathematics Education
Volume **7**, 1998

Supplementary Methods for Assessing Student Performance on a Standardized Test in Elementary Algebra

ALVIN BARANCHIK AND BARRY CHERKAS

ABSTRACT.

This study investigates supplementary methods for assessing the performance of over 2,000 college students who took the 35-item Elementary Algebra Skills Test of the College Entrance Examination Board. Two approaches were used to assign partial credit to incorrect answers: expert judgment and a modification of a measurement technique known as empirical option weighting, the latter designed to illuminate errors made by higher scoring students. Of the 35 questions, experts were able to agree on partial credit distribution for only 20, thus creating a natural division of this instrument into two subtests. Factor analysis, used in part to evaluate subtest comparability, was found, on each subtest, to identify the same mathematical skills areas: (1) Early Skills, (2) Later Skills, and (3) Formulation. Formulation involved devising a solution strategy or recasting a problem in terms amenable to the direct application of the other two skills areas. Evaluating the quality of a student's incorrect answers in terms of the average partial credit earned per problem, it was found that both ways of assessing partial knowledge on the 20-question subtest were predictive of performance (in terms of number correct and of scores for each factor) on the 15-question subtest, even after controlling for the number correct score on the former. Partial credit was also effective in adding to the ability of number correct scoring to discover knowledge in each of the three mathematical skills areas. Among skills areas, the Later Skills score on one subtest was the most predictive of number correct performance on the other subtest. Empirical scoring was especially useful as an aid in analyzing distractors and ferreting out difficult-to-recognize partial understanding. Our main finding is that in using expert assessment, genuine partial understanding, which is relevant to student performance and is missed by number correct scoring alone, can be inferred from students' selections of certain incorrect alternatives.

* This research was supported (in part) by a grant from The City University of New York PSC-CUNY Research Award Program.

INTRODUCTION

Conventional number correct test scoring leaves many questions unanswered concerning the nature, quality, and quantity of mathematical understanding possessed by students. In this study, we explore alternative ways of scoring a standardized test in order to discover more about students' mathematical mastery. We take two different but complementary approaches: (1) on each question, we attempt to analyze and measure what students know as reflected by their incorrect responses and (2) over the entire test, we reconceptualize what can be measured coincidentally with traditional correct/incorrect scoring, using factor analysis to parse students' achievement into underlying components, each of which can be examined for possible mathematics interpretation. Our purpose is to investigate these methods for their ability to provide information about student understanding that extends beyond that obtained from the number correct score alone.

For our data, we study test results of college students on the standardized Elementary Algebra Skills Test developed by the College Entrance Examination Board (CEEB) [5]. This test was chosen for our investigation because: (a) we had a large and ethnically diverse pool of students from which to analyze data and (b) the test was written by professional test writers and its reliability had been established [6]. At the outset, we asked two college teachers with previous experience at giving partial credit on precalculus multiple-choice tests [3] to analyze the incorrect answers on the 35-item CEEB test and give partial credit based on their expert opinion. They found agreement on only 20 of the 35 items, raising the possibility that the 15 remaining questions might serve as an instrument in the evaluation of the nature and quality of the partial credit assigned on the 20 items. We used factor analysis to investigate the structural similarity of these two "subtests," comparing the individual factor structures of each to the factor structure of the full test.

In a recent study of tests and questionnaires from the National Educational Longitudinal Study of 1988, Kupermintz, Ennis, Hamilton, Talbert, and Snow used factor analysis in developing strong evidence that mathematics achievement is "multidimensional and should be treated as such" [14, p. 550]. Two factors, math knowledge and math reasoning, were found to be distinguishable at the two grade levels they studied: grades 8 and 10. In the spirit of Kuppermintz et al., and in order to enhance our assessment of student performance, we investigate what, if any, underlying mathematical meaning might be attached to the factors found in our study.

In terms of measuring incomplete knowledge structures, there is substantial research literature on partial credit scoring (for reviews and bibliographies of measurement articles, see [8] and [13]), but the results have been mixed. Among studies where partial credit scoring has been advantageous, two elements seem invaluable: (1) testing in subject areas where understanding is essential and (2) linking partial credit scoring with the diagnostic potential of incorrect answers.

For example, the study in vocabulary by Smith [23] and an earlier study in arithmetic by Davis and Fifer [7] display those features. In particular, Davis and Fifer developed multiple-choice questions on arithmetic reasoning where "Each distractor [*incorrect answer*] was the product of an incorrect chain of reasoning" (p. 160). Their scoring was based on a combination of expert judgment and a measurement scheme, originally due to Guttman [9], called empirical option weighting (described below in the Methods subsection, Empirical Partial Credit).

Analysis of distractors, which is an essential part of this study, has been found useful in other mathematics education research [3, 15]. For basic algebra, there is substantial cognitive research on errors and mal-rules that classifies incomplete knowledge structures [2, 4, 16, 19, 20, 22]. However, recognizing partial understanding in mathematics has largely been an art. Sternberg and Horvath [25], for example, have noted that novice teachers are less likely to be cognizant of student misconceptions than expert teachers. In fact even with experience, less expert teachers may not consistently know what to look for as evidence of partial knowledge. Given the difficulty our experienced college teachers had in valuation of partial credit here, we also develop an empirical expert-independent procedure. This technique is a modification of empirical option weighting and is based on giving greater credence to the incorrect responses of students who have higher scores under conventional number correct scoring. Its primary value may lie in its tendency to provide practitioners with information about the kinds of errors made by otherwise higher scoring students, who may be expected to make relatively more informed errors than lower scoring students. We therefore investigate the extent to which empirical scoring might provide insight when searching for and speculating about unanticipated partial understanding. We also consider the degree to which it might be a simulator of expert credit.

Both partial credit scoring techniques are designed to cull information about incomplete knowledge structures from incorrect student responses. To index the overall quality of partial credit assigned to a student, we compute each student's average expert and average empirical partial credit. These indices are used to evaluate the two methods of assessing credit in terms of their effectiveness in discovering additional (incomplete) knowledge. Further, to flesh out the nature of mathematical skills discovered by partial credit, we investigate the associations between these indices, number correct performance, and scores for the factors referred to above.

METHOD

Population.
Between 1991 and 1995, at an urban college with a diverse student body, 2,384 examinees took a multiple-choice test in basic algebra skills [5] for placement into a remedial or college level algebra course. Of these examinees, about 70% were female, a little over 50% were foreign born, and each of the ethnic groups—Asian, black, Latino, and white—contributed between 20% and 30% of the population.

Over 70% gave their first language: 63% reported English, 18% Spanish, 14% Chinese, and 5% French. Ages ranged from 17 to 68 with a mean of 23.8 and standard deviation of 6.6.

Instrument.

The Elementary Algebra Skills Test used in this study is a 30-minute timed test with 35 questions [**5**]. Each question offers four choices. CEEB investigated the reliability of the test ("the correlation between the students' scores on two different forms of a test (taken close enough in time so that no real learning or forgetting occurs)") [**6, p. 23**] in both a pilot study and an equating study, and estimated reliability coefficients to be .80 and .85, respectively. In addition, CEEB subdivided the test into four clusters, each with eight or nine questions: cluster A = operations with real numbers, cluster B = operations with algebraic expressions, cluster C = solutions of equations and inequalities, and cluster D = applications. The test was used to place students into a college precalculus course, which, in turn, was a prerequisite for entry into numerous science-related majors.

Scoring.

As previously noted, the two experts we used were in agreement on assigning partial credit for only 20 of the 35 test questions. Keeping track of this set of 20 questions, hereafter called Subtest 20, in one score, and the remaining 15 questions for which experts did not assign partial credit, called Subtest 15, in a second score, we rated students according to their number correct (NC_{20}, NC_{15}) on each subtest. Correct answers were worth 5 points.

Expert Partial Credit. Evaluating partial credit on a multiple-choice question, a priori, calls for insights into student thinking beyond that required to evaluate a comparable essay question since the written response is missing and must be inferred [**3**]. Experts were asked to analyze the incorrect answers and distribute partial credit integrally, totaling 3 points, over the three incorrect options. They were to base their valuation on the degree of student understanding inferred from the choice, similar to the way they would evaluate the same answer in the context of a written response to a comparable essay question. Under these rules, on each of the 15 questions in Subtest 15, the experts were either doubtful about which incorrect answers, if any, might reflect mathematical understanding, or were unclear about which of two incorrect choices reflected greater partial understanding. On each of the questions in Subtest 20, they found that only one of the three incorrect options merited partial credit. Although it was permitted, they found no question that warranted the point distributions {5, 2, 1, 0} or {5, 1, 1, 1}; they only used the allocation {5, 3, 0, 0}.

Empirical Partial Credit. The essential idea that motivates empirical option weighting [**9, 18, 24**] is to assign weights to each choice for a given question based on averaging "criterion" scores of all examinees selecting that choice, where the criterion scores come from some external or internal measure of all examinees.

Tests are then rescored and a composite score is calculated, consisting of the sum of these weights, thereby providing a fresh criterion that might be used to repeat the process any number of times. Several studies report stabilization of this process within a few iterations [11]. As our criterion for establishing initial option weights for each question, we selected examinees' percentage correct scores on the entire 35-question CEEB test.

To describe the modified version of empirical option weighting used here, we first discuss a standard method for generating empirical option weights from z-scores, which are computed as follows. For each question, on the first iteration let t_x represent the average percentage correct test score for all respondents selecting choice x, where x ranges over the four choices. The corresponding preliminary z-scores are given by the formula

$$z_x = \frac{t_x - \frac{1}{4}\sum_{j=1}^{4} t_j}{\sqrt{\frac{1}{3}\sum_{k=1}^{4}(t_k - \frac{1}{4}\sum_{j=1}^{4} t_j)^2}}.$$

The sum of a student's preliminary z-scores on the 35 test questions then provides a newly generated test score. On successive iterations, for each question replace t_x by the average previously generated test score for all respondents selecting choice x and repeat the processes of computing iterated z-scores and generating test scores. We carried out nine such iterations, observing little change to three significant digits over the last iterations. In what follows, the term z-score refers to any of the final iterated values of z_x.

All response choices (including correct responses as well) are assigned z-scores, which will vary in value from question to question. In keeping with the scale of expert partial credit scoring, the z-scores were used to distribute 3 points decimally over the incorrect choices by scoring the incorrect choices relative to their z-score weights. Specifically, for each multiple-choice question, we computed modified empirical partial credit scores according to the formula

$$m_x = 3\left(\frac{z_x - z_{min}}{\sum_{j=1}^{3}(z_j - z_{min})}\right),$$

where the subscripts x and j range over the three incorrect choices and z_{min} is the minimum of the question's z-scores. This yielded point distributions of $\{5, m_x, m_y, 0\}$, where $m_x + m_y = 3$ and $m_x, m_y \geq 0$. Since some practitioners prefer to compute the sample variance using the divisor 4 rather than 3, we note that the choice of divisor in the formula for the sample variance used in computing z_x above has no effect on the m_x score, since a scale change in the z-scores cancels out when computing m_x.

Partial Credit Indices.

To assess expert and empirical scoring, for each student (with at least one incorrect response) we define the *partial credit index* as the average partial credit score per incorrect response (omissions and correct responses are excluded). We use the notations EXP_{20} to refer to the expert partial credit index for Subtest 20, and EMP_{20} and EMP_{15} to refer to the empirical partial credit indices for Subtest 20 and Subtest 15, respectively.

Illustrative Examples.

To clarify our scoring methods, Figure 1 illustrates two questions, each of which is a "look-alike" to an actual question used on the test (the actual questions were not available for publication here, since the test is still in use; they may be seen in Form M-3LDT of [5]). Also shown are the distributions of student responses to the actual test questions and the expert and empirical partial credit assignments. Question 1 exemplifies the case in which the awarding of any differentiating partial credit was viewed by our experts, a priori, as problematic; we assigned it to Subtest 15, where no expert partial credit was given. This question is discussed further in the section below entitled Errors of Otherwise Higher Scoring Students.

On Question 2, choices A and B indicate that the examinee has selected the correct numbers to use in the factoring, but choice A is invalid due to an incorrect sign. The selection of choices C and D implies a basic misconception about the procedure for selecting the factors of 30 that will satisfy the problem since, while both 3 and 10 are factors, they cannot be combined, no matter what signs are tried, to yield the coefficient of the middle term, -1. Thus, from an instructional viewpoint, selection of answer A shows recognizable partial mastery of how to factor a quadratic equation and represents a discernible learning stage where attention to the last procedural detail is missing.

The last example also illustrates how empirical option weighting differs from a simple "majority rule" partial credit assignment since the most frequently selected incorrect answer, D, is assigned no empirical partial credit. Evidently, this answer with its factor of 10 (also a feature of the original CEEB item) was particularly popular with lower scoring students. The quality of the empirical scoring is considered further in the section Errors of Otherwise Higher Scoring Students.

RESULTS

Factor Analytic Study of the Instrument.

Similarity of Subtest Factor Structures. Since we wished to use Subtest 15 to evaluate the expert and empirical partial credit assigned on Subtest 20, and to use Subtest 20 to evaluate the empirical partial credit assigned on Subtest 15, we began an examination of subtest comparability using factor analysis. Scoring each question as correct or incorrect, a principal component factor analysis with varimax rotation was performed on: (a) all 35 questions (Full Test), (b) Subtest 20, and (c) Subtest 15. Kaiser's measure of sampling adequacy [10] demonstrated the appropriateness of factor analysis in each case, with the Full

Question/Choice	Mal-Rule/Error	Number of Respondents	Expert Scoring	Empirical Scoring
1. Which of the following is equal to $\dfrac{3^6}{3^3}$?				
(A) 1^3	$\dfrac{p^m}{p^n} = \left(\dfrac{p}{p}\right)^{m-n}$	788	0	1.98
(B) 3^{-2}	$\dfrac{p^m}{p^n} = p^{-\frac{m}{n}}$	59	0	0
(C) 3^2	$\dfrac{p^m}{p^n} = p^{\frac{m}{n}}$	296	0	1.02
(D) 3^3		1,069	5	5
Omits:		172		
2. Which of the following is a factor of $(x^2 - x - 30)$?				
(A) $x+6$	Sign Error	289	3	1.55
(B) $x+5$		1,126	5	5
(C) $x-3$	Procedural Error	263	0	1.45
(D) $x-10$	Procedural Error	476	0	0
Omits:		230		

FIGURE 1. Sample "Look-Alike" Test Questions

Test rating .91, Subtest 20 rating .87, and Subtest 15 rating .81. Based on the scree criterion, models with three factors were obtained for each. Table 1 gives the factor loadings for each question on the Full Test and on the corresponding subtest, along with a breakdown of questions by subtest, a specification of each question's content educed from CEEB's list of 26 content specifications [6], and CEEB's categorization into four clusters. For convenience, the items are presented by subtest and, within each subtest, are ordered by major factor loadings on the Full Test.

In terms of variance explained by each factor: factor 1 accounted for 9.0% of the variation on the Full Test, 10.5% on Subtest 20, and 12.0% on Subtest 15; factor 2 accounted for 8.4%, 10.8% and 11.1%, respectively; and factor 3 accounted for 6.7%, 7.9%, and 11.2%, respectively. We considered loadings as low as .30 in order to provide a stringent test of factor pattern consistency. Moreover, in studying an item that had two factors with loadings of at least .30, to substantiate comparable degrees of influence of each factor, we required that the contribution of the lower loading factor to the communality of the item (as measured by the square of that factor's loading—the communality itself is the sum of squares of the three factor loadings) was at least one-half that of the higher loading factor. Under this last criterion, item 16, with loadings of .33, .60, and .02 on the Full Test, was deemed to load on a single factor. All 28 items that loaded on a single factor on the Full Test also loaded on the same single factor on the corresponding subtest. Of the five items that loaded on two factors on the Full Test, four items (14, 15, 27, 33) loaded on the same two factors on the corresponding subtest, while the remaining item (32) concentrated its subtest loading on only one of the two factors. Of the two items that did not load on

TABLE 1. Full Test and Subtest Factor Loadings
and Multiple Choice Question Descriptors

CEEB Item No.	Full Test Factor Loadings			Subtest Factor Loadings			CEEB Cluster	CEEB Content Specification
	1	2	3	1	2	3		
Subtest 20								
23	.46	.02	.05	.47	.05	.09	C	Graphing linear equations
33[a]	.45	.36	.15	.45	.33	.22	B	Factoring $ax^2 + bx + c$ over integers ($a = 1$)
30	.44	.16	.07	.47	.13	.18	C	Graphing linear inequalities (one variable)
35	.43	.05	.03	.45	.03	.10	B	Positive rational roots
22	.38	.16	.14	.46	.11	.19	C	Solving linear inequalities (not involving multiplication or division by a negative)
32[a]	.38	-.05	.36	.24	.03	.51	D	Translating English phrases into appropriate algebraic expressions
24	.35	.21	-.08	.37	.21	-.09	B	Integer exponents applied to monomials
11	.34	.18	.09	.38	.21	.06	C	Solving linear inequalities (not involving multiplication or division by a negative)
12	.25	.63	.03	.24	.64	.02	B	Multiplication of polynomials
13	-.02	.49	.08	-.11	.63	.03	B	Addition and subtraction of polynomials
9	.29	.45	.08	.33	.48	.03	C	Solving linear equations
1	-.15	.40	.21	-.27	.52	.23	B	Distributive property in simplifying algebraic expressions
14[a]	.34	.39	.15	.39	.37	.21	A	Absolute value (numbers only)
15[a]	.34	.39	.09	.37	.38	.16	C	Graphing linear inequalities (one variable)
2	.19	.36	.09	.19	.44	.01	A	Subtraction of signed numbers
4	.11	.31	.05	.09	.32	.05	A	Multiplication and division of signed numbers
3	.05	.19	.50	.12	.14	.48	C	Solving linear equations
28	.17	-.06	.48	.05	-.05	.65	D	Translating English phrases into appropriate algebraic expressions
6	.00	.20	.45	-.01	.13	.63	A	Ordering signed numbers
7[b]	.09	.03	.03	.31	-.11	-.06	A	Order of operations
Subtest 15								
34	.49	.18	.13	.52	.26	.07	A	Integer exponents applied to numbers
25	.46	.07	.01	.58	.12	-.13	C	Graphing linear equations
20	.44	.06	.14	.56	.00	.19	D	Measurement (volume)
31	.43	.21	.14	.45	.34	.05	B	Monomial factors of polynomials of degree greater than 2
29	.43	-.08	.28	.57	-.07	.23	D	Measurement (volume)
16	.33	.60	.02	.29	.66	.03	B	Squaring a binomial
8	.12	.53	-.02	.05	.68	-.03	B	Factoring difference of squares
10	.16	.44	.15	.08	.58	.15	A	Substitution in algebraic expressions
5	-.05	.31	.27	-.04	.41	.21	A	Addition of signed numbers
26	.13	-.01	.59	.10	.03	.64	D	Data interpretation
21	.04	.09	.48	.26	-.03	.41	D	Translating English phrases into appropriate algebraic expressions
27[a]	.34	.05	.47	.39	.07	.45	D	Data interpretation
18	.06	.17	.39	.04	.18	.48	A	Square roots
19	.14	.15	.40	.15	.13	.48	D	Translating English phrases into appropriate algebraic expressions
17[b]	.07	.02	.29	-.11	.06	.51	D	Mean

[a] Question loaded on two factors
[b] Low factor loading

any factor on the Full Test, Item 7 did not load on its subtest, while item 17 did load on its subtest. In sum, the degree of agreement between each subtest and Full Test factor loadings suggested that the underlying factor structures of the subtests were similar.

Since the factor models in each of our three cases were obtained by varimax rotation, within each model the factors are independent of one another. From a construct validity perspective [**17**], if for each subtest the three factors were identifying the same constructs as the corresponding three factors for the Full Test (and, hence, the three factors on one subtest were identifying the same constructs as the three factors on the other subtest), we would not expect to see an item with a high Full Test loading on one factor and a low Full Test loading on another factor "switch" to a low/high pattern on the corresponding subtest factors. An inspection of Table 1 shows this is indeed the case for all items, even with the very broad criterion that identifies a high loading as one of value at least .30. A more complete investigation of construct validity issues, while in progress, is beyond the scope or purpose of this study.

As noted previously, the test was used for placement. Because of the importance of performing well in the subsequent course, which is a gateway course to science-related careers, a logistic regression was performed to relate success in that course (attaining at least a C grade) to the three factor scores. In this three factor model, each was significant with $P < .0001$. Even though, as reported above, the factors accounted for only a quarter of test performance variation, adding full test performance (as measured by total number correct) to the regression model did not improve predictivity ($P = .67$). Thus, whatever mathematical constructs the three factors represent, they appear to play pivotal roles in subsequent student success. We seek, therefore, interpretation of these three constructs, both out of curiosity, and in the hope that the constructs may shed some light on the nature of the knowledge that is discovered (or possibly missed) by the partial credit scoring methods.

Interpretation of Factors. Restricting our attention to the 33 items in Table 1 where the highest Full Test factor loadings were at least .30, we observed that among the eight items in CEEB cluster A (operations with real numbers) the maximal factor loadings spread over all three factors, and this was also the case for the eight items in CEEB cluster C (solutions of equations and inequalities). The nine items in cluster B (operations with algebraic expressions) spread their maximal factor loadings over factors 1 and 2, while the eight items in cluster D (applications) spread their maximal factor loadings over factors 1 and 3. For these reasons, it seemed apparent to us that one must reach beyond subject matter content alone to understand the constructs represented by the three factors.

In the detailed analysis to follow, we found that when comparing questions loading on factor 1 with those loading on factor 2, some qualitative differences seemed evident: questions loaded on factor 2 seemed somewhat more elementary and concrete in nature while questions loaded on factor 1 involved more advanced concepts and required that students be practiced in higher levels of mathematical abstraction. In effect, the two groupings suggested different levels in a student's mathematical development. From this perspective, the first two factors identified temporally ordered mathematical domains: Early Skills (factor 2) and Later Skills (factor 1). Factor 3, on the other hand, appeared to represent a different kind of skill, one of Formulation, which involved devising problem solving strategies or recasting problems in terms of a mathematical procedure or expression amenable to the application of skills grouped under the other two factors. Evidence for these interpretations rests on the following analysis.

We begin with the 28 items that loaded on a single factor. Items grouped by factor 2 (Early Skills) involved questions about arithmetic (items 2,4,5), combining arithmetic with rudimentary algebra (1, 10), or early topics in basic algebra (8, 9, 12, 13, 16). Items grouped by factor 1 (Later Skills) all involved skills acquired later in a student's mathematical education: graphing linear equations (23, 25), solving or graphing linear inequalities (11, 22, 30), spatial reasoning (20, 29), or exponents above order 2 (24, 31, 34, 35). Items grouped by factor 3 (Formulation) involved the necessity to reformulate a problem appropriately and often involved word problems or applications (19, 21, 26, 28), but involved non-word problems as well (3, 6, 18). To clarify how Formulation problems are different, we contrast item 3, a Formulation problem, with item 9, an Early Skills problem. Each of these items fit CEEB's content specification "solving linear equations." Item 9, which loaded on factor 2, is typical of the kinds of textbook exercises that students deal with in the early stages of learning how to solve a linear equation: a look-alike "stem" (the introductory part of a multiple-choice question without the alternative response choices [**12, 17**]) would be "If $6y = 18 - y$, then $y =$"; the fact that it involves an answer in fractional form (also a feature of the CEEB original item) requires that the student focus additionally on arithmetic skills to arrive at an answer. Item 3, which loaded on factor 3, is nonstandard in the sense that it is not based on how classroom mathematics is routinely taught: a look-alike stem would be "If $x - 3 = 8$, then $x + 3 =$". Given a linear equation in x, textbooks ordinarily ask a student to solve for x; here, the nonstandard counterpart asks, "$x + 3 =?$" Even though the given equation is simple (here, $x - 3 = 8$), there is an additional thought process involved: the student must reformulate a question of a type that may never have been seen before, in order to discover that the method inherent in solving item 9, can be adapted to solve item 3 as well.

The five items that loaded on two factors seemed to be explicable as a blend of the two factors. Of the three items that loaded on factors 1 and 2, item 14 required the addition of signed numbers (Early Skills) with absolute value (Later Skills), item 15 required using the number line (Early Skills, nowadays this is taught in K–6) in combination with inequality notation (Later Skills), and item 33 required arithmetic division of numbers (Early Skills) with exponents above order 2 (Later Skills). Items 27 and 32, which loaded on factors 1 and 3, each required abstract reasoning to devise a strategy to transform the given information (Formulation) into an algebraic expression or procedure (Later Skills) involving a given variable.

Lastly, we discuss items 7 and 17, which did not load on any factor. In the case of item 7, this is possibly due to the appearance of the uncommon division symbol, "÷", whose usage is relatively limited (compared with the slash "/" or horizontal line "—" symbols) and whose precise meaning may not readily be recalled, especially when alternative response choices provide plausible alternatives, as was the case on the original CEEB item. In the case of item 17, which "nearly" loaded on factor 3, the item depended on knowing the meaning of "average (arithmetic mean)" with its implied reformulation of the problem into one of sums and division; conceivably, many students were sufficiently practiced in problems involving averages, so that for them it was a standard problem, requiring no further formulation.

Correlation Analysis of Subtest Factor Scores. Student factor scores for Subtest 20 and for Subtest 15 were computed by applying the SCORE option in SAS PROC FACTOR [21] to the factors obtained on each subtest. Using these scores, comparability of the two subtests was examined further with Spearman (rank) correlations, which are reported in Table 2. Number correct performance on the two subtests had a correlation of .72, not unreasonably below the .80 and .85 reported in CEEB's reliability study [6] when two 35-item tests were considered. Measuring associations between factor scores on one subtest with factor scores on the other subtest, the greatest correlations occurred between corresponding factor scores, which is consistent with the factor identification between the two subtests.

Comparing factor scores with number correct scores, on each subtest the Later Skills scores were the most highly correlated with number correct performance (S20, .75; S15, .71), followed by the Early Skills scores (S20, .54; S15, .48), and then the Formulation scores (S20, .28; S15, .37). In terms of correlations between factor scores on one subtest with number correct performance on the other subtest, the Later Skills scores again yielded the highest correlations (S20 factor score with S15 number correct, .50; S15 factor score with S20 number correct, .48), followed again by the Early Skills scores (40; .46, respectively), and then by the Formulation scores (.25; .20, respectively).

Table 2 further emphasizes the distinction between Formulation and the other two factors. Indeed, the four lowest correlations in the table all involved the relationship of Formulation with the two domain-specific factors.

Comparing Partial Credit Indices On Subtest 20 and Subtest 15.

On Subtest 20, where both expert and empirical partial credit were applicable, the empirical method allocated partial credit more conservatively than the expert method: mean $EXP_{20} = 2.05$ ($s.d = .73$), mean $EMP_{20} = 1.77$ ($s.d. = .56$). (Here, $N = 2,283$ since the 101 examinees who had no incorrect responses on Subtest 20 were excluded.) A linear regression ($R^2 = .64$)

TABLE 2. Correlations Between Number
Correct and Factor Scores ($N = 2{,}384$)

| Scoring Rule | Subtest | Number Correct | | S20 Factor Scores | | |
		S20	S15	Later Skills	Early Skills	Formulation
Number Correct	S20		.722[a]	.751	.543	.278
Number Correct	S15	.722		.502	.402	.252
Later Skills	S15	.483	.709	.402	.213	.145
Early Skills	S15	.459	.483	.286	.394	.026
Formulation	S15	.203	.365	.067	.054	.259

[a] All Spearman (rank) correlations $> .1$ have P-values $< .0001$. The remaining three Spearman correlations $< .1$ have, in descending correlation order, P-values of .001, .009, and .210.

yielded $EXP_{20} = .19 + 1.05 EMP_{20}$, indicating that empirical scoring did, somewhat, mimic expert scoring, at least in terms of the amount of credit scored per item. Since students with higher NC_{20} scores had fewer incorrect responses over which to compute average partial credit, their indices tended to have greater variance. This lack of constant variance led us to prefer nonparametric analysis over regression analysis. All subsequent correlations are therefore based on ranks (Spearman r_s), with inference based on Mantel-Haenszel analysis [1]. Not surprisingly, rank correlations indicated that students with higher NC_{20} scores also tended to have higher partial credit indices: EXP_{20} ($r_s = .423, P < .0001$) and EMP_{20} ($r_s = .522, P < .0001$). In addition, EXP_{20} and EMP_{20} were themselves highly correlated ($r_s = .798, P < .0001$).

While expert scoring was not done on Subtest 15, applying empirical scoring to Subtest 15, we found that the mean EMP_{15} slipped to 1.29 ($s.d. = .56$, $N = 2{,}046$). This decline from the empirical score on Subtest 20, reported in the preceding paragraph as $EMP_{20} = 1.77$, is consistent with the difficulty experienced by our two experts in trying to identify any incorrect choices for questions on Subtest 15 that warranted expert partial credit.

Additional Knowledge Discovered by Partial Credit.

On both subtests, it was evident that incorrect responses were not completely random since, in that case, mean partial credit indices nearer to 1 would be expected because 3 points were distributed among the three incorrect choices. We therefore investigated the nature and quality of incorrect responses for each of the indices on Subtest 20 and Subtest 15, in terms of the following research questions:

(1) Is a high index on one subtest predictive of superior number correct performance on the other? If so, does the association remain statistically significant when controlling for the number correct score on the subtest for which the partial credit was earned?

(2) To what extent is partial credit on one subtest also predictive of the three factor scores on the other; that is, can the nature of the knowledge discovered by partial credit be described in terms of the mathematical

skills represented by these factors?

Regarding the second issue raised above in (1), Frary [**8**] has contended that number correct scoring does not leave partial information completely unrewarded. Moreover, when using the underlying number correct scores of the test as the criterion for option weighting the same test's questions, as we have done, Stanley and Wang have asked, "Does the test score itself already reflect the partial knowledge that the option weighting hopes to capture?" [**24, p. 28**]. We address these concerns in the context of the present study, using the Mantel-Haenszel correlation test to validate the positive association of partial credit on one (predictor) subtest to number correct and factor performance on the other (predicted) subtest, controlling for the number correct score on the predictor subtest [**21; CMH1 in PROC FREQ**]. Table 3 contains our results.

TABLE 3. Correlations of Partial Credit on Predictor
Subtest With Performance on Predicted Subtest

		Scores on Predicted Subtest			
			Factor Scores		
Partial Credit Index	Predictor Subtest	Number Correct	Later Skills	Early Skills	Formulation
Expert	Subtest 20	.380 (.0001)[a]	.224(.0001)	.267 (.080)	.104 (.0001)
Empirical	Subtest 20	.450 (.0001)	.260(.0001)	.325 (.0001)	.143 (.0001)
Empirical	Subtest 15	.249 (.0001)	.156 (.001)	.143 (.060)	.093 (.123)

[a] All Spearman (rank) correlations in this table have P-values $< .0001$. The P-values in parentheses are for the Mantel-Haenszel correlation test controlling for number correct on the predictor subtest. For predictor Subtest 20, $N = 2{,}283$ are included by virtue of having at least one incorrect answer; for predictor Subtest 15, $N = 2{,}046$.

Relating Partial Credit on Subtest 20 with Performance on Subtest 15. Both modes of scoring partial credit for Subtest 20 were positively associated with the number correct and factor scores on Subtest 15, with empirical scoring consistently showing higher correlations than expert scoring. When controlling for the number correct score on Subtest 20, we found that both modes of partial credit provided additional power in predicting Subtest 15 performance, except possibly for expert partial credit when predicting the Early Skills factor score (P-value $= .08$). Thus, although one might find fault with empirical scoring's item-by-item assessment (judgments based on student scores are not expected to coincide completely with expert value judgments), in its cumulative effect it is, if anything, more strongly associated with positive student performance than is expert credit.

Relating Empirical Partial Credit on Subtest 15 With Performance on Subtest 20. In the case of Subtest 15, where the experts could not decide upon partial credit, recall that the empirical scoring was far less generous than it was on Subtest 20. Correspondingly, correlations between Subtest 15 empirical scoring and Subtest 20 performance scores were weaker than the correlations between Subtest 20 empirical scoring and Subtest 15 performance scores. Additional predictive power to that of the number correct score on Subtest 15 was clear only when predicting the number correct and Later Skills factor scores on Subtest 20. This raised the possibility that empirical scoring may aid in identifying partial understanding—in the relatively important areas of Later Skills—which was either missed or undervalued by the experts.

Errors of Otherwise Higher Scoring Students.

As designed, empirical scoring recovers information about errors made by otherwise higher scoring students (by virtue of valuing their incorrect choices higher than those of lower scoring students). Thus far, we have seen that to a degree empirical scoring mimicked expert scoring. In this section, we explore the limitations and potential of empirical scoring in terms of the following questions:

(1) To what extent might empirical scoring be used as a substitute for expert scoring?

(2) Might empirical scoring be used retrospectively to discover unanticipated partial understandings that merit being quantified by some amount of expert partial credit?

Limitations of Empirical Scoring. Question 2 in Figure 2 is typical of many Subtest 20 items for which expert and empirical scoring were in close agreement. This, however, contrasts sharply with Question 2 in Figure 1, where there is a lack of agreement, since there is clearly no partial understanding to justify the 1.45 points given by empirical scoring to option C. This item, which was not an isolated instance, illustrates that empirical scoring, by itself, is not a sound nor a fair substitute for expert scoring, at least in terms of assessing genuine partial understanding.

Potential of Empirical Scoring. Using the empirical scores for Question 1 (a Subtest 15 item) in Figure 1 as a guide into the uncharted territory of student reasoning, we took a second look at option A. Conceivably, it was selected by higher scoring students because it exhibited a key feature of the correct rule, namely, subtraction of the downstairs exponent from the upstairs exponent. One of our experts admits to having been blinded by the serious nature of the mal-rule and noted, in looking back, that if experts had not been constrained by the rules of this study to distribute 3 full points, they might have given some lesser partial credit to option A, say, 1 or 2 points, since its selection implies that a previously unanticipated, but instructionally useful, stage of learning seems to have been reached. The fact that fewer than half the students correctly answered this question adds weight to the argument that option A, in comparison to the other incorrect options, is differentiating a step up on the learning curve for this kind of problem.

Empirical scoring on Question 1 (a Subtest 15 item) in Figure 2, which most students seemed to find easy (92% answered correctly), raised the following net-

Question/Choice	Mal-Rule/Error	Number of Respondents	Expert Scoring	Empirical Scoring
1. $\sqrt{1600} =$				
(A) 40		2,190	5	5
(B) 80	$\sqrt{100n} = \frac{1}{2}n\sqrt{100}$	24	0	.53
(C) 400	$\sqrt{100n} = 100\sqrt{n}$	136	0	2.47
(D) 800	$\sqrt{n} = \frac{1}{2}n$	27	0	0
Omits:		7		
2. $\sqrt{36y^{16}} =$				
(A) $6y^4$	$\sqrt{a^2x^{n^2}} = ax^{\sqrt{n^2}}$	1,616	3	2.83
(B) $18y^4$	$\sqrt{a^2x^{n^2}} = \left(\frac{1}{2}a\right)x^{\sqrt{n^2}}$	33	0	0
(C) $6y^8$		537	5	5
(D) $18y^8$	$\sqrt{a^2x^{n^2}} = \left(\frac{1}{2}a\right)x^{\left(\frac{1}{2}n\right)}$	29	0	.17
Omits:		169		

FIGURE 2

Sample "Look-Alike" Questions Involving Square Root Symbol

tlesome task for experts considering partial credit: in hindsight, does option C, which higher scoring "weaker" students (higher scoring amongst the 8% who found this easy question troublesome) valued highly, exhibit an instructionally sound learning stage that merits any partial credit? Option D shows a serious misunderstanding with no partial understanding in evidence; option B contains an element of understanding ($\sqrt{100} = 10$) mixed with the same serious misunderstanding seen in option D; while option C contains an element of understanding ($\sqrt{16} = 4$) with a comparatively less serious misunderstanding about how to deal with $\sqrt{100}$. Based on these considerations, there appears to be a degree of support for experts who might wish to give some minimal partial credit for option C, since it avoids the most common serious misunderstandings (which may, itself, hint at a degree of circumscribed understanding) while exhibiting a degree of partial understanding by getting a part of the question correct. In this regard, the pattern of student responses to incorrect choices suggests that the selection of option C was not completely random among the small group of students who got this question wrong.

SUMMARY AND CONCLUSIONS

In a search to discover more about what students know, a standardized test of elementary algebra skills was rescored using factor analytic and partial credit methods. Two ways of issuing partial credit were used to evaluate students' incorrect answers: expert judgment and a modification of the measurement technique known as empirical option weighting. The latter technique was studied for its potential as an aid to practitioners in illuminating errors made by higher scoring students. Of the 35 questions on this test, experts were able to agree on partial credit distribution for only 20, thus creating a natural division of the instrument into two subtests. The fact that experts did not find any alternatives on the remaining 15 questions that merited partial credit was not unreasonable since (a) the test was not designed for purposes of diagnostic value and (b) the rule to always distribute 3 points virtually eliminated questions with alternatives that only nominally exhibited partial understanding.

Factor analysis was used, in part, to assess the comparability of the two subtests and found three factors for each subtest that were comparable to those found for the full 35-item test. As further evidence of subtest comparability, the corresponding number correct and factor scores between subtests were positively correlated. The three factors were identified as mathematical constructs, representing: (1) Early Skills (arithmetic and rudimentary algebra), (2) Later Skills (subsequent algebra and a variety of skills involving mathematical abstraction), and (3) Formulation (either devising a solution strategy or reformulating a problem into a standard form that permits a solution using early or later skills). The Later Skills factor score emerged as the one most predictive of number correct performance.

Both assessments of partial knowledge on the 20-question subtest added to the ability of number correct scoring to predict performance, in terms of number correct and factor scores, on the 15-question subtest. The empirical procedure was also used to assign credit on the 15-question subtest, where it was—as if in agreement with the experts—far less generous than it was on the 20-question subtest, yet it still enhanced prediction of the number correct score and, most significantly, the Later Skills factor score on the 20-question subtest. This suggested the possibility that empirical scoring might ferret out information about student partial understanding on the more complex and relevant Later Skills that had been missed by experts. Generally, among the factor scores, both partial credit procedures were consistently informative about Later Skills but less consistent in their associations with Early Skills.

It should be noted that the associations between partial credit, number correct, and factor scores were all correlation-based and, thus, are scale invariant: they do not depend on the number of points of partial credit distributed per question. The choice of 3 points was simply intended to be a convenient number for the experts to distribute.

Empirical partial credit was found to be highly correlated (.798) with expert partial credit. Despite this, as Question 2 in Figure 1 illustrates, empirical partial credit is not a pedagogical substitute for expert partial credit. There were however, instances of items on the 15-question subtest for which empirical scoring provided a window into unanticipated selections of higher scoring students, showing where to take a second look for evidence of partial understanding. The empirical scoring prompted us to speculate anew about underlying student thought processes and unexpected stumbling blocks to learning. The examples of distractor analysis in this study suggest that empirical partial credit question scores might also be of instructional value for teachers, especially preservice and novice teachers of mathematics, in developing the art of recognizing students' partial understandings, learning to differentiate discrete learning stages, diagnosing student errors, and scoring expert partial credit.

In summary, we find that expert evaluation of distractors discovers genuine partial understanding, in addition to any found by number correct scoring. Specifically, this additional understanding is associated with the important Later Skills area as well as the ability to reformulate practical problems into mathematically solvable forms. Conceivably, this recovery of information that would be lost with simple number correct scoring could draw the scoring of multiple-choice questions one step closer to the richer scoring paradigm available when assessing performance with essay questions.

REFERENCES

1. Agresti, A., *Categorical data analysis*, Wiley & Sons, New York, 1990.
2. Cauzinille-Marmeche, E., Mathieu, J. & Resnick, L., *The integration of new knowledge: From arithmetic to algebra*, European Journal of Psychology of Education **2(1)** (1987), 41–56.
3. Cherkas, B. M. & Roitberg, J., *Humanizing the multiple-choice test with partial credit*, International Journal of Mathematical Education in Science and Technology **24(6)** (1993), 799–812.
4. Clement, J., *Algebra word problem solutions: thought processes underlying a common misconception*, Journal for Research in Mathematics Education **13** (1982), 16–30.
5. College Entrance Examination Board, *Elementary Algebra Skills*, a placement test in the series Descriptive Tests of Mathematics Skills, Educational Testing Service, Princeton, NJ, 1988.
6. College Entrance Examination Board, *Guide to the use of the descriptive tests of mathematical skills*, Educational Testing Service, Princeton, NJ, 1989.
7. Davis, F. B. & Fifer, G., *The effect on test reliability and validity of scoring aptitude and achievement tests with weights for every choice*, Educational and Psychological Measurement **19** (1959), 159–170.
8. Frary, R. B., *Partial-credit scoring methods for multiple-choice tests*, Applied Measurement in Education **2** (1989), 79–96.
9. Guttman, L., *Supplementary study B*, The Prediction of Personal Adjustment (P. Horst, ed.), Social Science Research Council, New York, 1941, pp. 251–364.
10. Hair, Jr., J. F., Anderson, R. E., Tatham, R. L., & Flack, W. C., *Multivariate data analysis*, Fourth Edition, Prentice-Hall, Englewood, New Jersey, 1995.
11. Hendrickson, G. F., *The effect of differential option weighting on multiple-choice objective tests*, Journal of Educational Measurement **8(4)** (1971), 291–296.
12. Hopkins, C. D. & Antes, R. L., *Classroom measurement and evaluation*, Third Edition, F. E. Peacock Publishers, Itasca, Illinois, 1990.
13. Hutchison, T. P., *Ability, partial information, guessing: Statistical modelling applied to multiple-choice tests*, Rumsby Scientific Publishing, Adelaide, South Australia, 1991.
14. Kupermintz, H., Ennis, M. M., Hamilton, L. S., Talbert, J. E., & Snow, R. E., *Enhancing validity and usefulness of large-scale educational assessments: I. NELS: 88 Mathematics Achievement*, American Educational Research Journal **32(3)** (1995), 525–554.
15. Marshall, S. P., *Sex differences in mathematical errors: An analysis of distractor choices*, Journal for Research in Mathematics Education **14** (1982), 325–336.
16. Matz, M., *Towards a process model for high school algebra errors*, Intelligent Tutoring Systems (D. Sleeman and J. S. Brown Eds.), Academic Press, New York, 1982, pp. 25–50.

17. Nitko, Anthony J., *Educational tests and measurement: An introduction*, Harcourt Brace Jovanovich, New York, 1983.

18. Patniak, D. & Traub, R. E., *Differential weighting by judged degree of correctness*, Journal of Educational Measurement **10(4)** (1973), 281–286.

19. Payne, S. J. & Squibb, H. R., *Algebra mal-rules and cognitive accounts of error*, Cognitive Science **14(3)** (1990), 445–481.

20. Payne, S. J. & Squibb, H. R., *Algebra mal-rules and cognitive accounts of error: Erratum*, Cognitive Science **14(4)** (1990), 641–642.

21. SAS Institute Inc., *SAS/STAT User's Guide, Version 6, Fourth Edition, Volumes 1 and 2*, SAS Institute, Cary, NC, 1989.

22. Sleeman, D., *An attempt to understand students' understanding of basic algebra*, Cognitive Science **8** (1984), 387–412.

23. Smith, R. M., *Assessing partial knowledge in vocabulary*, Journal of Educational Measurement **24** (1987), 217–231.

24. Stanley, J. C. & Wang, M. D., *Weighting test items and test-item options, an overview of the analytical and empirical literature*, Educational and Psychological Measurement **30** (1970), 21–35.

25. Sternberg, R. J. & Horvath, J. A., *A prototype view of expert teaching*, Educational Researcher **24(6)** (1995), 9–17.

DEPARTMENT OF MATHEMATICS & STATISTICS, HUNTER COLLEGE OF THE CITY UNIVERSITY OF NEW YORK

CBMS Issues in Mathematics Education
Volume **7**, 1998

Students' Proof Schemes: Results
from Exploratory Studies

GUERSHON HAREL AND LARRY SOWDER

1. Introduction

1.1 Literature Review.

Traditionally, the mathematics taught in school was divided into two topics, algebra and geometry, where algebra was considered as a branch that deals with quantities, measurements, numerical variables, and numerical operations, and geometry as a branch that deals with space, spatial measurements, and properties of spatial objects. The idea of proof, as a deductive process where hypotheses lead to conclusions, has traditionally been stressed in the teaching of geometry but not in the teaching of algebra. Davis and Hersh (1981) pointed out that "as late as the 1950s one heard statements from secondary school teachers, reeling under the impact of the 'new math,' to the effect that they had always thought geometry had 'proof' while arithmetic and algebra did not" (p. 7). The death of the "new math" almost put an end to algebra proofs in school mathematics. This asymmetrical emphasis on proof in teaching algebra versus geometry has an historical origin: while geometry has been taught according to the Euclidean tradition established in 300 B.C., not until the 1800s did deductive aspects of arithmetic began to be stressed in the teaching or in the development of new mathematics (Davis & Hersh, 1981).

Nevertheless, the learning of proof has been a major goal of mathematics curricula in many countries and for many generations. *The Curriculum and Evaluation Standards for School Mathematics* (National Council of Teachers of Mathematics, 1989) has reemphasized this goal and has recommended that proof

This framework presented here is part of the PUPA (Proof Understanding, Production, and Appreciation) Project, supported, in part, by the National Science Foundation. Opinions expressed are those of the authors and not necessarily those of the Foundation. We thank Sonia Hristovich, Jack Tedeski, and Cara Masson for their assistance, and James McClure for his comments on this paper.

should be taught to all students and in all mathematics courses, not just geometry:

> In grades 9–12, the mathematics curriculum should include principles of inductive and deductive reasoning so that *all* students can: make and test conjectures; formulate counterexamples; follow logical arguments; judge the validity of arguments; construct simple, valid arguments; and so that, in addition, college-intending students can: construct formal proofs for mathematical assertions, including indirect proofs and proofs by mathematical induction. (p. 143, emphasis added)

Despite the efforts made by mathematics educators over decades to promote students' conception of proof, only the ablest students have achieved an understanding of it (Williams, 1980). Usiskin (1987) studied 99 high school geometry classes in five states in the U.S. and found that at the end of their geometry course, 28% of the students couldn't do a simple triangle congruence proof, and only 31% of the students were judged to be competent in constructing proofs. Senk (1985) learned that only 30% of the students in full-year geometry courses that teach proof reach a 75% mastery level in proof writing. Lovell (1971) found that a high percentage of 14- to 15-year-old students derive the truth of a general statement from a sequence of particular instances. This also was the case with as many as 80% of preservice elementary school teachers (Goetting, 1995; Martin & Harel, 1989). Galbraith (1981) reported a study in which one third of 13- to 15-year-old students did not understand the role of counterexamples in refuting general statements. Porteous (1986) pointed out that a very high percentage of 11- to 16-year-old students do not appreciate the significance of deductive proof in geometry, algebra, and general mathematical reasoning. Fischbein and Kedem (1982) showed that high school students do not understand that mathematical proof requires no further empirical verification. Vinner's (1983) study supported this result and added that high school students view the general proof as a method to examine and to verify a particular case. Martin and Harel (1989) showed that college students believe that a proof of a general statement concerning a geometric object does not guarantee that the statement is true for all instances of that object; a proof only guarantees that the statement is true for those instances where objects are spatially similar to the figure referred to in the proof. Schoenfeld (1985, p. 173) pointed out that, for the most part, college students' perspective on the role of proof is either to confirm something that is intuitively obvious or to verify something that is already known to be true.

Many mathematics educators have criticized the current approaches to teaching proof in school, arguing that findings such as those just described are inevitable consequences of these approaches. Some of these educators have suggested new ways of teaching proofs. Alibert and Thomas (1991) believe that mathematics in general, and proof in particular, are presented as a finished product; the student is not a partner in the knowledge construction, but rather a passive receiver of knowledge. They pointed out that "the conflict between the practice of mathematicians on the one hand, and their teaching methods on the other, produces problems amongst students. They exhibit a lack of concern for meaning, a lack of appreciation of proof as a functional tool and an inadequate epistemology" (p. 215). Alibert and Thomas suggest that we consider these problems in the light of research which has been carried out, paying "particular attention to studies emphasizing the nature of proof as an activity with a social character, a way of communicating the truth of mathematical statement to other people, helping them to understand why it is true" (p. 216).

This suggestion is consistent with the view expressed by Usiskin (1980), who argued that "we seem to have failed in our teaching of proof, because we too often ignore when and why mathematicians do proofs, the variety of possible types of proof, and how mathematicians write down proofs" (p. 419). The impression students get from geometry classes—the only place where they are exposed to the idea of proof—is distorted, according to Usiskin. First, most of the mathematician's work is spent on exploring and conjecturing, not on searching for proofs of well stated propositions, and certainly not on obvious propositions, as is often done in geometry classes. Second, there is a great variety of proof types, not just geometry proofs; for example, "proofs using mathematical induction are different from proofs of trigonometric identities, which are different from epsilon-delta limit proofs, which are different from the proofs found in abstract algebra, and so on, with differences in every branch of mathematics" (p. 420). Third, mathematicians do not write proofs in two columns. Usiskin's recommendations were to delete "rigorous" proofs of obvious statements and allow informal proofs with less demand on formal ways of writing.

Motivated by the van Hiele model of levels of geometric thinking, Shaughnessy and Burger (1985) arrived at a similar conclusion: "Students' introduction to geometry should be informal, without formal proofs or axiomatic treatment, for at least one-half year. . . . Activities that encourage inference and deduction should also be included, but the writing of carefully structured formal proofs should be omitted" (p. 426).

This approach was recommended by others: MacPherson (1985) suggested that to develop the vocabulary and concepts needed for the development of proofs, students must be engaged first with informal geometry which is based on problem solving and hands-on activities. Semadeni's (1980) idea of "action proof" is in this direction as well: Students first prove for a specific case through manipulations, such as drawing pictures, then use more specific cases, and finally visualize the actions in their minds and generalize. Other recommendations, in line with those described here, were discussed by Hanna (1990). She indicated that the works by Leron (1983), Volmink (1988), Movshovitz-Hadar (1988), and Alibert (1988) suggest teaching approaches that do away with rigor and formality and focus on aspects of communication and social processes.

Our own research on the concept of proof corroborates many of the observations described here. For example, one of the conclusions coming from this

research is that a major reason that students have serious difficulties understanding, appreciating, and producing proofs is that we, their teachers, take for
granted what constitutes evidence in their eyes. Rather than gradually refining
students' conception of what constitutes evidence and justification in mathematics, we impose on them proof methods and implication rules that in many cases
are utterly extraneous to what convinces them. This begins when the notion of
proof is first introduced in high school geometry. We have demanded, for example, that proofs be written in a two-column format, with formal "justifications"
whose need is not always understood by a beginning student (e.g., Statement:
$AB = AB$. Reason: Reflexive Property). Also, we present proofs of well-stated,
and in many cases obvious, propositions, rather than ask for explorations and
conjectures. As a consequence, students do not learn that proofs are first and
foremost *convincing* arguments, that proofs (and theorems) are a product of
human activity, in which they can and should participate; that they are an essential part of doing mathematics. This is in essence the whole thrust of our
teaching treatments. The goal is to help students refine their own conception of
what constitutes justification in mathematics: from a conception that is largely
dominated by surface perceptions, symbol manipulation, and proof rituals, to a
conception that is based on intuition, internal conviction, and necessity.

1.2 Research Goals and Data.

The questions we are addressing revolve around the development of college students' proof understanding, production, and appreciation (PUPA). What are students' (particularly mathematics major students') conceptions of proof? What
sorts of experiences seem effective in shaping students' conception of proof? Are
there promising frameworks for teaching the concept of proof so that students
appreciate the value of justifying, the role of proof as a *convincing* argument,
the need for rigor, and the possible insights gained from proof? In answering
these questions, we hope, through an extended series of studies, to be able to do
the following:

(a) map students' cognitive schemes of mathematical proof,

(b) document the progress college mathematics students make in their conception of mathematical proof, in a typical undergraduate mathematics
program,

(c) offer developmental models of the concept of proof among mathematics
majors, in a teaching environment that is based on epistemological and
pedagogical principles advocated by the current research in mathematics
education, and

(d) offer principles for instructional treatments that facilitate proof understanding, production, and appreciation.

This paper is our first report on this broad investigation. The paper's main
focus is item (a)—students' schemes of mathematical proof—but inevitably it

touches upon the other three items as well. These schemes, or the lack thereof, were derived from the following sequence of teaching experiments:

NT: One-semester teaching experiment in elementary Number Theory taken by sophomore and junior mathematics majors ($N = 32$);

CG: One-semester teaching experiment in College Geometry taken by junior and senior mathematics majors ($N = 25$);

LA1,LA2:   Two consecutive one-semester teaching experiments in elementary Linear Algebra taken by sophomore mathematics majors ($N = 23$, $N = 27$, respectively);

LA3:   One-semester teaching experiment in advanced Linear Algebra taken by junior and senior mathematics majors ($N = 20$); and

EC: A case study of a precocious junior-high school student studying Euclidean Geometry and Calculus.

All these teaching experiments were taught by the first author of this paper. The data on NT, CG, LA3, and EC were collected from classroom observations in the form of field notes and retrospective notes, clinical interviews, team homework, individual homework, and written tests. The data in LA1 and LA2 were more extensive and included the following sources: (a) classroom sessions, which were all video-taped and transcribed; (b) classroom observations by graduate students, who recorded the classroom interactions, and small-group discussions; (c) 60-to-90-minute clinical interviews with students, which were all video-taped and recorded, and (d) students' homework, quizzes, and written tests.

The system of proof schemes reported in this paper has undergone numerous revisions dictated by the results from our qualitative analysis data, cross-checked through interviews of mathematics majors at a separate institution. The current version of this system's structure and components seems to have reached a stable stage. By this we mean in completing the analysis of about 50% of the data, we discovered no additional categories of proof schemes and none of the existent categories has been altered.

We characterize the results of this research as exploratory. The system of proof schemes described here must be validated by other researchers through multiple teaching experiments taught by various instructors in various institutions. Also, this report is not a full account containing all the empirical evidence, but one that sets the stage for such accounts by laying out the landscape and descriptive vocabulary. It is beyond the scope of this already lengthy paper to provide a detailed analysis of each category in this system of proof schemes. In this paper we restrict our report of the data to a collection of teaching experiment episodes, whose sole goal is to demonstrate the different categories of proof schemes we have observed.

We present a total of 24 episodes to describe a system of 16 subcategories of proof schemes which we observed with 128 students in 6 teaching experiments. These episodes are by no means isolated instances; each is an example of a phenomenon repeatedly observed in several teaching experiments. The detailed analyses of the exact quantitative accounts of each proof scheme are underway; we intend to provide them in a series of separate publications.

The reader has surely noticed the obvious paradox inherent to this research, namely, it applies empirical methods to validate the absence or presence of logico-mathematical reasoning.

2. The Process of Proving: A Definition

This section begins with a short sketch of the historical evolution of the concept of proof, followed by a cognitive analysis of this concept.

2.1 Proof: A Historical Perspective.

The view of what constitutes an acceptable mathematical proof has had many turning points. Babylonian mathematics is considered proof-free by current standards, because it does not deal with general statements, deduction, or explanations; rather, it prescribes specific solutions to specific problems.[1] The axiomatic method—that is, the notion of deductive proof from some accepted principles—was conceived by the Greeks. Its emergence is attributed to different factors (Kleiner, 1991): mathematical (e.g., resolving contradictory computational results obtained by earlier civilizations), social (e.g., Greek democracy required the skills of argumentation, which encouraged deductive reasoning), philosophical (Greeks' philosophical inquiries demanded the formulation of primitive assumptions and their logical implications), and pedagogical (the need to teach caused the Greeks to structure mathematics in a logical order).

The insistence of the Greeks on well-defined concepts and rigorous reasoning prevented them from using certain ideas, such as irrational numbers and infinity, which proved indispensable to the subsequent development of mathematics. This, in turn, was followed by a long period of mathematical activity with little attention to rigor. The most notable segment of this period is the sixteenth to eighteenth centuries, where symbolic notation and symbol manipulation were key methods of demonstration and discovery. These methods, despite their lack of rigor, led to major results which proved to be invaluable in solving physical problems and modeling physical phenomena. The application power of the results was a source of validity and legitimacy, and by implication the validity of the methods by which they were obtained (Kleiner, 1991).

---

[1] Bernal (1987) suggests that this characterization is indicative of the general "distancing" of Greek mathematics from Bablylonian mathematics. According to Bernal, this may in part be a reflection of mid-nineteenth and early twentieth-century historians' ethnic biases.

The end of this period may be marked by Fourier's "symbolic solution" to the Flow of Heat problem. Fourier reduced this problem to that of taking an even function and expressing it as an infinite sum of cosines, without attending to the meaning of infinite summation of functions. His solution led to observations which seemed at the time inconsistent with "regular" behavior of functions. This, in turn, fed by earlier doubts of the validity of ideas such as fluxions and infinitesimals (Boyer, 1989), led to thorough investigations into the assumptions of calculus and inspections of its structure, whereby the entire calculus was reconstructed into a new mathematical field, which now is called "analysis." With this reconstruction, the axiomatic method reemerged. Investigations into analysis led to questions on the foundations of real numbers. This in turn led to questions on the foundations of the positive integers, which were addressed in different ways in the late nineteenth century by Dedekind, Peano, and Frege (Boyer, 1989).

2.2 Proof: A Cognitive Perspective.

In what follows, we introduce the notions of "observation" and "certainty in an observation" to define "process of proving," "proof scheme," and a few other notions essential to our classification of proof schemes.

2.2.1 Observations.

Human beings live by the observations they make every moment they are conscious. An observation can be mere recognition ("It's raining now"), it may be based on a life-time of experience ("It always rains in the summer"), or it may take generation after generation to make ("Euclidean geometry is not an absolute truth"). For some observations, we still wonder, and may never know, whether they are true ("Every even number greater or equal to 4 is the sum of two prime numbers"). Despite any passive or sensory connotation of the term, observations are results of people's constructions, not mere preexisting, transmitted knowledge.

All observations—except possibly those which are simply a replay of past experience (i.e., recognitions)—are novel for the person who makes them. When an individual notices a relationship, it is a novel observation for her or him, because until then, he or she had never realized it. Observations do differ in three important characteristics: *originality, mode of thought*, and *certainty*. We briefly describe the first two and elaborate on the latter, which is the focus of our investigation.

2.2.2 Originality and Mode of Thought.

Originality refers to the following distinction: When a student solves a certain problem, it is one thing if he or she produces the solution on her or his own, and it is another if the student reproduces a solution that was communicated to her or him by others. Accordingly, some observations may be called *innovative*, others *imitative*. An observation is innovative if it originated with the observer (the person who made the observation), and it is imitative if it was communicated to the observer by others. This distinction must be tempered with what we know about ways of knowing: First, people make observations through interactions with their environments, which include social interactions; thus, no observation can originate with the observer alone. Second, and consistent with Piaget's theory, imitative observations are not copies of observations made by others, but the results of reconstructions by the individual (Piaget & Inhelder, 1967).

Mode of thought refers to how observations are made—for example, an observation can be made by abstracting a phenomenon from several empirical observations or by thought experiments with no mediation of empirical observations (e.g., Einstein's special theory of relativity).

2.2.3 Certainty.

Significant to this paper is not so much the kind of observations (originality) or how observations are conceptually made (mode of thought) but rather how observations are evaluated. An observation can be conceived of by the individual either as a *conjecture* or as a *fact*.

A conjecture is an observation made by a person who has doubts about its truth. A person's observation ceases to be a conjecture and becomes a fact in her or his view once the person becomes certain of its truth.

This is the basis for our definition of the *process of proving*:

By "proving" we mean the process employed by an individual to remove or create doubts about the truth of an observation.

The process of proving includes two subprocesses: *ascertaining* and *persuading*.

Ascertaining is the process an individual employs to remove her or his own doubts about the truth of an observation.

Persuading is the process an individual employs to remove others' doubts about the truth of an observation.

Central to this paper is the question:

How are conjectures rejected or rendered into facts?

Before we discuss this question, the following clarifications and qualifications to the above definitions are essential.

First, these definitions may imply that an observation remains a conjecture until the person reaches absolute certainty in its truth. It must be noted that conjectures are usually not viable without a certain degree of conviction in their truth. A person can be uncertain about, yet believe in, the truth or falsity of an observation. A student may be convinced about the truth of an observation, but not quite certain until, for example, her or his teacher has confirmed the observation, or until further evidence is provided. In some cases this evidence may look unnecessary to an outsider, but to the student it may be indispensable.

For example, Fischbein and Kedem (1982) noticed that students, even after producing a deductive proof of a given proposition, wished to check it in a few special cases, an indication that they continued to be uncertain about its truth.

Second, conjectures vary in the degrees of faith a person has in their potential truth. The amount of effort a person is willing to make in seeking evidence that would render the conjecture a fact (or refute it) is in some proportion to her or his faith in the truth (or falsity) of the conjecture. Also, if the person's faith in the truth of a conjecture is high, he or she would seek evidence to establish its certainty; conversely, if the person's faith is low he or she would seek evidence to refute the conjecture. This natural human behavior dictates the direction in which mathematicians choose to pursue their research. For example, one of the most famous, still open, problems of this century states: Does every bounded linear operator on a complex Hilbert space of dimension greater than 1 have a non-trivial closed invariant subspace? Halmos tells in his autobiography how his presumption about the solution of this problem affected his direction of research:

> I . . . conjectured that [quasitriangular] operators . . . all have invariant subspaces. . . . The Rumanian school . . . proved that the non-quasitriangular operators . . . [have] invariant subspaces; if my conjecture turns out to be right, then the invariant subspace problem is solved affirmatively. I admit that that rocked me. Since I am convinced that the solution of the invariant subspace problem is negative, I abandon my conjecture, and shall proceed instead to search for a quasitriangular counterexample. (Halmos, 1985, pp. 320-321)

Similarly, Lobachevsky wrote on his motives in doubting Euclidean geometry which until his time was a fact for the mathematics community for over two thousand years:

> The futile efforts since Euclid's time on throughout two thousand years have compelled me to suspect that the concepts themselves do not contain the truth which we have wished to prove. . . . (quoted in Alexandrov, 1963, p. 101)

Third, the proof schemes held by an individual are inseparable from her or his sense of what it means to do mathematics. If, for example, a student holds the view that mathematics is just a collection of truths, then he or she is likely to ascertain herself or himself and persuade others of the truth of an observation by an appeal to authority, such as a textbook or a teacher.

Last, and most importantly, as defined, ascertaining and persuading are entirely subjective and can vary from person to person, civilization to civilization, and generation to generation within the same civilization.

As was mentioned earlier, the methods of ascertaining and persuading employed in the Babylonian mathematics are strikingly different from those employed in Greek mathematics. While the former consists of specific prescriptions for specific problems, the latter is characterized by its attention to rigor. The European mathematics of the sixteenth and seventeenth centuries, on the other hand, employed methods that are far less rigorous than those employed by the Greeks. Within the Western culture, the methods of proof of the sixteenth to eighteenth centuries are markedly different from those of the nineteenth and twentieth centuries.

Methods of proof may differ even within the same culture during the same period. The emergence of formalism and constructivism—the two main competing mathematical philosophies of this century—attests to this fact. Constructivism, founded by Brouwer, views the natural numbers as the fundamental objects that can not be reduced to further basic notions, and so any meaningful mathematical proof must ultimately be based *constructively* on the natural numbers. An example of a corollary of this premise is that one cannot establish the truth of an argument by showing that its negation leads to a contradiction, for no construction that is based on the natural numbers is involved in such a demonstration. Formalism, founded by Hilbert, offers mathematical certainty by turning mathematics into a meaningless game. Any proof must start with undefined terms and accepted statements (axioms) about these terms. The meaning that one may assign to these terms and axioms is irrelevant to the subsequent logical deductions (theorems) from them. As the undefined terms and axioms, the theorems too, as far as mathematics is concerned, have no content until they are supplied with an interpretation.

In this paper we are interested mainly in how individuals prove or justify; more specifically, in how students ascertain for themselves or persuade others of the truth of a mathematical observation. In this regard, we assert that a person's ascertaining and persuading processes for an observation may be based on logical and deductive arguments, empirical evidence, intuitions, personal beliefs, an authority (e.g., an opinion is true because the teacher said so), social conventions, or any other knowledge the person considers as relevant to the truth of the observation. Further, a person can be certain about the truth of an observation in one situation, but seek additional or different evidence for the same observation in an another situation. For example, long before students learn geometry in school, they are convinced, based on personal experience and intuition, that the shortest way to get from one point to another is through the line segment connecting the two points. Later, as participants in an Euclidean geometry class, an instantiation of this observation—stated in the theorem "The sum of the lengths of two sides of a triangle is greater than the length of the third side" —may become a conjecture for the students until they find evidence that would be accepted by their class community or their teacher. The kinds of evidence the students may look for are based on whatever conventions are accepted in their class as evidence for a geometric argument. These conventions may differ from one class to another; for example, what might be accepted as evidence in a standard high school Euclidean geometry class is likely to be insufficient evidence for a college class studying axiomatic geometry.

In short, people in different times, cultures, and circumstances apply different methods to remove doubts in the processes of ascertaining and persuading. Accordingly:

> A person's proof scheme consists of what constitutes ascertaining and persuading for that person.

3. Classification of Proof Schemes

Our definitions of the process of proving and proof scheme are deliberately psychological and student-centered. In the remainder of this paper, *the verbs "to prove" and "conjecture" and the nouns "proof," "conjecture" and "fact" will always be used in this (subjective) sense and according to the definitions stated above*.[2] This interpretation is essential in order to understand what we intend to communicate to the reader.

Each of the categories of proof schemes in our classification represents a cognitive stage, an intellectual ability, in students' mathematical development, and all were derived from our observations of the actions taken by actual students in their process of proving.

Thus, this classification is *not* of proof content or proof method, such as the classification made by Usiskin (1980)—geometry proofs versus proofs by mathematical induction, versus proofs of trigonometric identities versus epsilon-delta limit proofs versus abstract algebra proofs, and so on. Nor is this classification a priori, such as that suggested by Hanna (1990), who distinguished between "proofs that explain versus proofs that prove," and according to whom proof by mathematical induction, for example, is a proof that explains, not a proof that proves. Such an a priori determination is not based on the individual's conception of what constitutes proofs and what constitutes refutations.[3] In contrast, it is the individual's scheme of doubts, truths, and convictions, in a given social context, that underlies our characterization of proof schemes. Nor is the classification about philosophical stands, though different proof schemes may be suggestive of various mathematical philosophies. The question of the alliance between our proof scheme system and the historical epistemology of the concept of proof (e.g., as in Kleiner, 1991) is beyond the scope of this paper, and it will not be addressed except for brief mentions in what follows.

Three categories—each with several subcategories—of proof schemes are the product of the work so far (Figure 1). It is important to note that these schemes are not mutually exclusive; people can simultaneously hold more than one kind of scheme.

---

[2]This restriction applies to other similar terms, such as "to justify," "to show," "justification," "verification," etc.

[3]We recognize, however, the importance of the pedagogical implication alluded to by Hanna's distinction. It conveys the message that a proof must be a convincing argument, not just a sequence of logically-inferred statements.

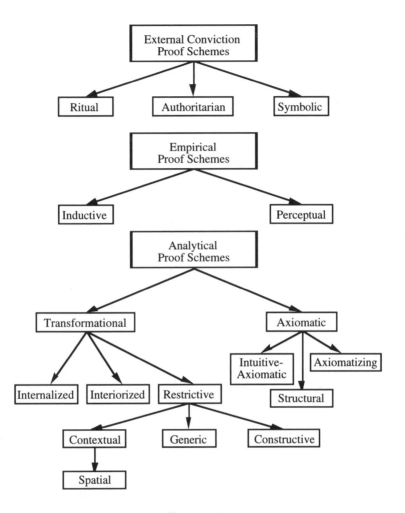

FIGURE 1

3.1 External Conviction Proof Schemes.

When formality in mathematics is emphasized prematurely, students come to believe that ritual and form constitute mathematical justification. When students merely follow formulas to solve problems, they learn that memorization of prescriptions, rather than creativity and discovery, guarantee success. And when the teacher is the sole source of knowledge, students are unlikely to gain confidence in their ability to create mathematics. These learning habits are believed to lead to the formation of *external conviction proof schemes*—schemes by which doubts are removed by (a) the ritual of the argument presentation— the ritual proof scheme, (b) the word of an authority—the authoritarian proof scheme, or (c) the symbolic form of the argument—the symbolic proof scheme.[4]

3.1.1 Ritual Proof Scheme.

Martin and Harel (1989) addressed the question: "Are students' judgments of an argument influenced by its appearance in the form of a mathematical proof—the ritualistic aspects of proof—rather than the correctness of the argument?" (p. 42). They addressed this question by examining students' responses to a false-proof "verification" that looked like a deductive proof of a certain mathematical statement. They found that "many students who correctly accepted a general-proof verification did not reject a false-proof verification; they were influenced by the appearance of the argument—the ritualistic aspects of the proof—rather than the correctness of the argument" (p. 49).

Accepting false-proof verifications on the basis of their appearance is a severe deficiency in one's mathematical education, which is possibly attributable to the over-emphasis in schools on proof writing prior to and even in place of proof understanding, production, and appreciation. The ritual proof scheme, however, does not need to manifest itself only in this severe behavior of judging mathematical arguments on the basis of their surface appearance. For example, often during the beginning period of a teaching experiment, either in a class discussion or in a personal exchange, students have asked whether a certain justification is considered a proof. When asked to explain the motivation for their question, the students indicate that although they are convinced by the justification, they have doubts whether it counts as a mathematical proof, for "it does not look like a proof." Typically, such doubts are raised when the justification is not communicated via mathematical notations and does not include symbolic expressions or computations, such as in the following episode from LA1, which took place shortly after the unit on linear independence was completed.

Episode 1. In response to a test question,

A, B, C, D, E are linearly dependent. If we add a new vector S to this set of vectors, would the vectors A, B, C, D, E, S be dependent or independent?

Andy wrote:

Adding a new vector S to a set that is currently linearly dependent will not change the dependency of the entire set. The set will remain linear[ly] dependent. This is because one vector can be expressed as a linear combination [of the other vectors] in the set (by definition), therefore the entire set remains linear[ly] dependent due to this fact.

Following this test, during an interview with this student, he expressed concern about the fact that his proof did not include any symbolic expressions and therefore he had doubts whether it is mathematically valid, for, according to him, it

---

[4]A tendency to form external conviction proof schemes may also reflect certain basic psychological tendencies of an individual of the sort discussed by Frid (1994), who found that some students tended to "learn" mathematics by collecting "isolated, relatively unconnected mathematical statements, rules, and procedures" (p. 77).

didn't look like a proof. The possibility that this student's concern was the level of formality of his proof is dismissed on the grounds that his other justifications which included symbolic expressions were acceptable to him as proofs despite their lack of formality and generality.

3.1.2 Authoritarian Proof Scheme.

Why do so many students lack the intellectual curiosity to wonder why a theorem or a formula is true? We believe the answer to this question lies in the fact that current mathematics curricula emphasize truth rather than reasons for truth. This begins with elementary mathematics where children are rushed into using mathematical prescriptions to solve arithmetic problems (Harel, 1995) and continues with secondary and postsecondary mathematics where instrumental understanding rather than relational understanding is emphasized throughout the curriculum.[5] As a consequence, students build the view of mathematics as a subject that does not require intrinsic justification. Although students understand that the mathematics they do must be true, they are not concerned with the question of burden of proof; their main source for conviction is a statement appearing in a textbook or uttered by a teacher. Such a conception of proof we call *authoritarian*. We observed five different kinds of manifestations of the authoritarian proof scheme in students' mathematical behavior. The first and most common expression of this proof scheme is students' insistence on being told the procedure to solve their homework problems, and when proofs are emphasized, they expect to be told the proof rather than take part in its construction. *The underlying characteristic of this behavior is the view that mathematics is a collection of truths, with little or no concern and appreciation for the origin of the truths.* The following examples demonstrate that memorizing and applying ready-made formulas are what students expect to do in mathematics.

Episode 2. During the first week in the Teaching Experiment LA3, the students were assigned to prove "$Null(A) \subset Null(B)$ for any two matrices A and B for which the product is defined." In the class session that followed, three students who worked as a group on this assignment complained that they went through all their notes, including relevant material in their textbook and notebook from their previous linear algebra class, but found no theorem that could tell them how to prove this statement.

Episode 3. In one of the class sessions in LA3, toward the end of this course, the students were asked to complete the proof of a certain proposition by justifying some of its steps. In the class session that followed, Bob, one of the students in this class, asked the instructor to show how to complete these steps. The instructor responded by asking Bob to first share with the class his thoughts on the problem and his attempts to solve it. It turned out that neither Bob nor any

---

[5]The notions of "instrumental understanding" and "relational understanding" are from Skemp (1978). The former means knowing the "how" whereas the latter means knowing both the "how" and the "why."

one else in the class had worked on this assignment. The instructor, therefore, declared that the discussion of this assignment would be postponed to the next class session after the students have tried completing the proof on their own. Bob expressed his dissatisfaction with the instructor's decision by saying that he does not understand what difference it makes if he was told the proof or if he found it on his own; the end result in both cases is the same: he would know the proof.

The second expression (and consequence) of the authoritarian proof scheme is this: It is not uncommon that students ask for help on a certain problem without first making a serious effort to solve it on their own. Often in such cases, after a brief discussion of the problem the students realize that they in fact were capable of solving it on their own, but needed the presence and confirmation of an *authority* to arrive at their solutions, as in the following episode.

Episode 4. In the teaching experiment LA3, a student came to consult with the instructor of the class about a homework problem requiring her to generate examples of non-diagonal diagonalizable matrices of different sizes. The student complained that the method we had established in class did not work, for each time she took a diagonal matrix Λ and an invertible matrix S, the product $S\Lambda S^{-1}$ resulted in the same diagonal matrix Λ she began with. After a very short conversation, she realized on her own the reason for the outcome; namely, that she had been choosing matrices Λ with equal entries on the diagonal. This by is no means an exceptional case. If anything is exceptional about it, it is the fact that this student had traveled quite a distance from her home to campus, exclusively—as she had indicated—to consult with the instructor about this problem.

The third expression of the authoritarian proof scheme was first observed in LA1. It demonstrates the mystical power of the term "theorem" on students' process of proving.

Episode 5. Consistent with the instructional perspective on the concept of proof introduced earlier is the stand that a mathematical relationship should not be formulated as a "theorem" until it has been motivated, debated, and applied— a standard practice of the teaching experiments. In LA1 we first noticed that until a mathematical relationship is declared a theorem, the students continued— either voluntarily when they needed to use the relationship or upon request—to justify it. But once the relationship was stated as a theorem, there seemed a reduced effort, willingness, and even ability with some of the students to justify it. It seems as though, for these students, the label "theorem" renders the relationship into a formula—something to obey rather than to reason about. The fourth manifestation of the authoritarian proof scheme is an extension of the former. Often students prove a certain statement by rephrasing it into a statement that for them is a fact. Consider the following two episodes:

Episode 6. Lee, a student in LA1, was given the following problem:

M, N, K, R, V are linearly dependent.
(a) If we remove two of these vectors, say M and N, would the remaining vectors be dependent or independent?
(b) If we add a new vector S to this set of vectors, would $\{M, N, K, R, V, S\}$ be dependent or independent?

Lee responded:

(a) They would be dependent because you could express these vectors as linear combinations of each other.
(b) The vectors would be dependent because you could express S as a linear combination of the others.

The following additional episode of the authoritarian proof scheme is particularly interesting; it justifies a conjecture by simply saying its contrapositive.

Episode 7. Don, a student in LA2, responded to the question,

"Why must $rank(A) = rank([A|b])$ for any system $AX = b$ that has a solution?"

by saying:

$rank(A) = rank([A|b])$ because otherwise our system would be inconsistent. If a system is inconsistent it can't have a solution. Therefore, a system must be consistent to have a solution.

A fifth manifestation of the authoritarian proof scheme is the reluctance of students to ask questions about the instructor's motivation and the reason for his thinking, or to challenge his assertions even when they suspect them to be incorrect, as Episode 8 demonstrates. This occurred despite the major effort on the part of the instructor to establish a classroom atmosphere that was conducive to open discussion and questioning.

Episode 8. In one of the class sessions in teaching experiment LA2, while reviewing a set of problems in a preparation for the midterm exam, the following problem was discussed:

"Find a vector e that is not in the span of

$$a = \begin{bmatrix} 1 \\ -2 \\ 3 \\ 1 \\ -5 \end{bmatrix}, \quad b = \begin{bmatrix} -5 \\ -21 \\ 13 \\ -11 \\ 5 \end{bmatrix}, \quad c = \begin{bmatrix} -9 \\ -1 \\ -2 \\ -4 \\ 12 \end{bmatrix}, \quad d = \begin{bmatrix} -52 \\ -22 \\ 14 \\ 71 \\ 51 \end{bmatrix}.$$

Eric, one of the students in this class, suggested first row-reducing the matrix $A = [a\, b\, c\, d]$ into a row-reduced echelon form R, and then choosing a vector e that is *not* in the span of the columns of R. The instructor reiterated Eric's "solution" while computing R with MATLAB,[6] but gave no indication or gesture about its falsity. None of the students rejected Eric's solution or raised any question about its validity. At this point he asked the class to discuss Eric's solution in their working groups. In the class discussion that followed, Jon, one of the students in the class, said that he was not sure that Eric's solution was correct because he did not think that row operations preserve the span of the columns. He then went on and suggested checking his hypothesis on a specific example. The example he suggested (a 3×2 matrix, which he seemed to choose at random) showed that indeed row operations do not necessarily preserve the column space. Following this, another student, Mathew, indicated that he had suspected that Eric's solution was incorrect but he accepted it because the instructor did not reject it. At this point, the instructor asked the class, How many students doubted the correctness of Eric's solution prior to Jon's example? Over 50% of the class raised their hand. And when he asked the class, "Why didn't you express your doubts?" the answer, which all seemed to agree with, was: "Because you (the instructor) appeared to agree with Eric's solution."

The authoritarian proof scheme is both pervasive and difficult to relinquish. Students' most common questions during the first part of the teaching experiments have been about "how" rather than "why." Further, it is rather difficult to establish a new "didactical contract" (à la Brousseau, 1986) in which the concern is with both kinds of questions and in which they, the students, must participate in the search for answers to such questions. It is this latter demand that is so difficult for students to accept, for they view the instructor as the sole source for answers and believe that it is the instructor's responsibility to tell them the needed knowledge. To extinguish this belief, students' questions, both how and why, are seldom answered directly in our teaching experiments; rather, they are brought to reason together among themselves and with the instructor about the questions and the search for their answers. For further discussion, see the papers by Arcavi et al., Santos, and Schoenfeld (this volume).

3.1.3 Symbolic Proof Scheme.

Thinking of symbols as though they possess a life of their own without reference to their possible functional or quantitative reference, we call symbolic reasoning. As discussed below, symbolic reasoning can either be superficial and mathematically vacuous, or a very powerful technique. A symbolic proof scheme is a scheme by which mathematical observations are proven by means of such symbolic reasoning. Consider the following episode:

Episode 9. In his attempt to prove that any homogeneous system of linear equations $AX = 0$ is consistent, Hugh, a student in LA2, said:

---

[6]A computer display system was present in all the linear algebra teaching experiments. The computer package MATLAB was used during the class sessions to perform tedious computations (e.g., row reducing a matrix) and, in particular, to make and test conjectures, empirically verify proven results, etc.

Take, for example, $x_1 A_1 + \cdots + x_n A_n = 0$. If we want to find x_1 and we have some values $x_2, \ldots, x_n$ and $A_1, \ldots, A_n$, by moving the known values to the other side of the equation, we can solve x_1. This is the same for $x_2, \ldots, x_n$. Hence, this demonstrates that a homogeneous system has solution. [In giving this explanation, Hugh wrote $x_1 = \dfrac{x_2 A_2 + \cdots + x_n A_n}{A_1}$.]

When he was asked what dividing by A_1 means, he replied:

It is just this [pointing to the numerator of his fractional expression] is over this [pointing to the numerator of his fractional expression]. It is just like one over x.

The main characteristic of the symbolic reasoning is the behavior of approaching the solution of a problem without first comprehending its meaning, that is, without building a coherent image of the problem situation. Consider the following episode:

Episode 10. In teaching experiment NT, the instructor observed students' immediate actions when they were given a problem to solve individually (either in a class setting or an interview). Many of the students read the problem only once and haphazardly began manipulating the symbolic expressions involved in the problem, with little or no time spent on comprehending the problem statement. Hence, many approached the solution without knowing the meaning of some of the terms used in the problem statement, and many others were unable to articulate the exact task they were to accomplish.

Symbolic reasoning is a habit of mind students acquire during their school years—from elementary school to secondary and post secondary school—a habit that is very persistent and extremely difficult to relinquish. For an analysis of the consequences of symbolic reasoning on students' mathematical development, particularly on the development of multiplicative reasoning and algebraic reasoning see Harel (1995, in press).

Against this devastating reasoning, we shall point to a different, essential practice of symbolic reasoning. The definition of symbolic reasoning we gave earlier may have evoked with the reader a different image from the one revealed in Hugh's responses. For, relative to the reader's practice of mathematics, it is not uncommon that symbols are treated as if they possess a life of their own, and, accordingly manipulated without (necessarily) examining their meaning. Historically, this practice of symbolic reasoning played a significant role in the development of mathematics. For example, during the nineteenth century an enormous amount of work was done in differential and difference calculus using a technique called the "operational method," a method whose results are obtained by symbol manipulations without account of their possible meanings, and in many cases in violation of well-established mathematical rules. (See, for example, how the Euler-MacLaurin summation formula for approximating integrals by sums was derived [Friedman, 1991, pp. 176-178].) It was only with the aid of functional analysis, which emerged early in the twentieth century, that mathematicians were able to justify many of the techniques of the operational method.

3.2 Empirical Proof Schemes.

In an empirical proof scheme, conjectures are validated, impugned, or subverted by appeals to physical facts or sensory experiences. We distinguish between two kinds of this scheme: The *inductive* empirical proof scheme and the *perceptual* empirical proof scheme.

3.2.1 Inductive Proof Scheme.

When students ascertain for themselves and persuade others about the truth of a conjecture by *quantitatively evaluating*[7] their conjecture in *one or more* specific cases, they are said to possess an inductive proof scheme. Every teacher has likely observed the dominance of this scheme among students, and research into the concept of proof corroborates this observation (see, for example, Chazan, 1993). Martin and Harel (1989) studied how prospective elementary school teachers judged whether particular arguments were mathematical proofs. The arguments were either inductive (based on specific instances) or deductive (assertions via general statements). More than 80% of the 101 prospective teachers considered inductive arguments to be mathematical proofs. Their conviction about the truth of the conjecture became particularly strong when they observed a pattern suggesting that one can generate as many examples as wanted in support of the conjecture. In Goetting's study (1995), almost 40% of her advanced undergraduates used examples as a basis for judging the truth of a divisibility question (p. 43).

Since people's evaluation of hypotheses in everyday life is probabilistic in nature (Anderson, 1985), the use of inductive evidence is only natural. Moreover, the initial application of inductive reasoning in mathematical activities is in most cases essential. So the concern is not that college students think inductively; rather, the concern is that their proof schemes do not develop beyond the empirical proof schemes. This retarded development should not be a surprise when mathematics instruction in both the elementary and secondary levels is dominantly inductive in its best forms, and authoritarian, ritual, or symbolic in its worst forms.

Despite its dominance, the inductive proof scheme phenomenon is not entirely understood. Evidence exists to indicate that students—at least adult students—are aware of the limitations of an inductive scheme. Chazan (1993), for example, has shown that high school students who thought examples were sufficient proof "understood some of the limitations inherent in the use of examples, and had strategies for minimizing these limitations" (p. 370). Yerushalmy (1986), also with high school geometry students and in a computer environment inviting inductive work, noted that "throughout the (year-long) course the students'

---

[7]E.g., direct measurements of quantities, numerical computations, substitutions of specific numbers in algebraic expressions, etc.

appreciation of data as a source of ideas grew, while their appreciation of data as an argument declined" (p. vii). Our teaching experiments corroborate Chazan's and Yerushalmy's observations but reveal further complexity.

3.2.2 Proof By Example and Counterexample.

The issue of "proof by examples" was discussed with the students in our teaching experiments. In this discussion the instructor showed his students examples of mathematical statements that are true for numerous cases but untrue for *all* cases.[8] By doing this, he intended to convince the students that inductive verifications are insufficient to validate a conjecture. Although in these discussions the students seemed to understand the limitations inherent in the inductive method, their subsequent behavior was not consistent with this impression. Specifically, we observed the following behaviors:

a) students continued to prove mathematical statements by examples;

b) students did not protest when they were presented with an inductive proof;

c) students' inductive proofs mostly consisted of *one* example, rather than a multitude of examples.

When the instructor confronted his students with their contradictory behavior by directly asking them why they used proof by examples when they agreed that counterexamples may be found, they typically said something like the following:

d) The inductive method had always been used by their instructors in previous mathematical classes—typically they mentioned calculus classes; and

e) even if a counterexample to the statement is found, the statement stands, because the counterexample is just an exception.

In addition to these observations, here are some other related observations:

f) Students seldom used proof by counterexample and

g) they did not seem to be convinced by it;

h) nor were they convinced by proof by contradiction; further,

i) students confused the admissibility of proof by counterexample with the inadmissibility of proof by example(s); and

j) the use of inductive proofs diminished as students developed advanced proof schemes.

To explain these behaviors, we suggest that there are four combined cognitive forces influencing students' thinking with respect to inductive proofs. They interact in powerful ways, as discussed below.

---

[8]E.g., the conjecture, $\sqrt{1141y^2 + 1}$ is an integer, is false for $1 \leq y \leq 10^{25}$. The first value for which the statement is true is $30,693,385,322,765,657,197,397,208$ (see Davis, 1981).

The first cognitive force is the psychologically natural tendency to evaluate conjectures probabilistically and hence the readiness with which this mode of evaluation is accepted as a mode of mathematical reasoning. This force accounts for students' use of specific examples to verify a general statement. But, against one's expectation, very often students use just *one* example, rather than a multitude of examples to prove their conjectures (observation *c*). As we have looked at this phenomenon more closely, we offer this as the reason: The students believed that since the single example was chosen randomly and it conformed to the general statement, the statement must be true. The single example is taken as representative of all cases. Even when a counterexample to the statement is found, the statement still stands in the students' eyes, because the counterexample is just one exception to the general rule (observation *e*). This argument is consistent with the fact that the first author's students seldom used proof by counterexample (observation *f*) and they did not seem to be convinced by it (observation *g*). The second author's students, on the other hand, often sought counterexamples first, as did Goetting's subjects (1995), although many of her interviewees were not certain whether a counterexample gave a proof. Whether this seeming difference from the first author's students is a fact or an happenstance of either the particular interviewees or the curricula at the different universities, we do not know. This, together with Balacheff's (1991) finding that younger students (junior-high school students in France) do react to counterexamples in various ways, requires a further look at college students' conception of proof by counterexample.

The second cognitive force fostering an inductive proof scheme is the effect of the authoritarian proof scheme discussed in the previous section. Combined with the first force, it explains why students do not protest when they are presented with an inductive proof (observation *b*), since other mathematics teachers, both in high school and college, have used inductive proofs regularly (observation *d*), as the students have explicitly indicated.

The third cognitive force is students' difficulty understanding proof by contradiction (Tall, 1979; Thompson, 1996), where they may believe the proof assumes what is to be proved (see Episode 22 below). This belief accounts for observation *h*. In a deeper sense this difficulty with proof by contradiction may also account for students continuing to prove mathematical statements by examples (observation *a*) despite instructor warnings, with which they seemed to concur. The instructor's attempt to convince the students of the invalidity of proof by example is based on proof by contradiction, which is a method of proof the students have never accepted.

The fourth cognitive force is in fact an absence of one, namely students' lack of advanced proof schemes other than the external conviction proof schemes and the empirical proof schemes. Students justify their conjectures by these proof schemes simply by default—these are the only schemes they possess. One of the most positive results of our teaching experiments is that the use of the empirical and external conviction proof schemes diminished as students developed more advanced proof schemes (observation j).

As students begin to acquire these alternative proof schemes, they begin to appreciate proof by contradiction and proof by counterexample. But the impact of the second force—the authoritarian proof scheme—forces them to accept these modes of proof before they have completely internalized them. The result is a confusion between the admissibility of proof by counterexample with the inadmissibility of proof by example(s) (observation i), as the following episode demonstrates.

Episode 11. Andy, a student in the teaching experiment LA1, protested the grade he received on one of the test problems, where he proved a certain statement inductively, by saying,

> I am confused. Sometimes you can prove things by examples and sometimes you can't.

When asked to indicate a case where a proof by an example was accepted, he mentioned a case where the instructor demonstrated the falsity of a certain statement by pointing to a single counterexample of the statement. The statement he referred to was: If two matrices are different from zero, then their product is different from zero. This statement was refuted by the counterexample:

$$A = \begin{bmatrix} 1 & 2 \\ 2 & 4 \end{bmatrix}, \qquad B = \begin{bmatrix} -2 & 1 \\ 1 & -0.5 \end{bmatrix}, \qquad AB = \begin{bmatrix} 0 & 0 \\ 0 & 0 \end{bmatrix}.$$

3.2.3 Perceptual Proof Scheme.

Perceptual observations are made by means of rudimentary mental images—images that consist of perceptions and a coordination of perceptions, but lack the ability to transform or to anticipate the results of a transformation. The important characteristic of rudimentary mental images is that they *ignore transformations on objects or are incapable of anticipating results of transformations completely or accurately.* "Such images constitute an imitation of actions that can be carried out in thought (e.g., rotations of objects) . . . [but they] cannot be adequately visualized all the way to [their] ultimate conclusion before [they have] actually been performed" (Piaget & Inhelder, 1967, p. 295). A full mental image (as opposed to a rudimentary mental image), on the other hand, is "a pictorial anticipation of an action not yet performed, a reaching forward from what is presently perceived to what may be, but is not perceived" (Piaget & Inhelder, 1967, p. 294).

One might look at the triangle ABC in Figure 2 and perceptually observe two equalities: that sides AB and AC are of the same length and that angles ACB and ABC are of the same size. If this observation is merely perceptual, the observer will not see a causality relationship between these two equalities (i.e., that one equality causes the other). On the other hand, in an observation that involves transformations, the same figure can be viewed as one out of many possible outcomes of transformations on the figure's parts. For example, the isosceles triangle ABC in Figure 2 can be seen as a special state—in which the angles opposite AC and AB are congruent—among all the possible states resulting from varying the point A on the half circle with center C and radius AC—in which the angles opposite AC and AB are not congruent. The following episodes demonstrate students' perceptual proof schemes.

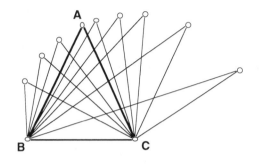

FIGURE 2

Episode 12. In the teaching experiment CG, while discussing the homework problem, "Prove that the midpoints of any isosceles trapezoid form a rhombus," the instructor drew a figure on the board similar to Figure 3.

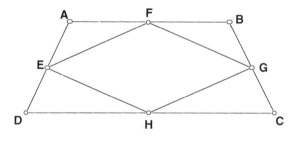

FIGURE 3

Melissa presented her proof of this proposition, saying that she first proved that FH is congruent to EG by showing that $\triangle FEH$ is congruent to $\triangle HEG$. During her presentation, she kept looking at the figure she drew in her notebook, matching the letters in her figure to the letters in the figure the instructor drew on the board. Melissa's attempt to prove that the midsegments FH and EG are congruent was driven by her perceptual observation of the figure she drew, in which the midsegments indeed looked congruent. She was concerned with this specific case only, unaware of the variability of the trapezoid's shape.

Interestingly, the class discussion that followed did not address Melissa's proof per se; rather, it centered on the plausibility of such a "proof." The students argued that "there is no chance that Melissa can prove that the midsegments are congruent," for the trapezoid can vary, and among its variations it can be narrow and long, in which case the midsegments FH and EG would not be congruent. This is an example of how transformations are applied for evaluation and control purposes (Schoenfeld, 1985).

There is no doubt that Melissa was capable of varying the trapezoid (e.g., imagining how it can be stretched along the midsegment EG or FH to get different trapezoid shapes). Indeed, Melissa did understand the argument made by her classmates and fully agreed to it. The question, however, is whether Melissa was capable of initiating such transformational reasoning[9] on her own. An indication that Melissa did not possess such a cognitive ability can be found in her response to a similar problem on a written test that she took five days later. The problem was:

> A, B, C, D are the midpoints of the four sides of a parallelogram. The quadrilateral $ABCD$ is ALWAYS a: (a) parallelogram; (b) rectangle; (c) rhombus; (d) square; (e) none of the above. Justify your answer.

Melissa drew a parallelogram $TRPS$ which looked like a square (Figure 4) and argued:

> "by Pythagorean theorem $AB \cong BC$ in $\triangle ARB$ and $\triangle CPB$. By the same reason, $AD \cong DC$ in $\triangle TAD \cong \triangle DSC$"

and concluded that $ABCD$ must be a square.

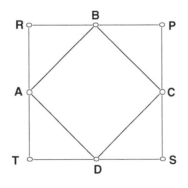

FIGURE 4

Again, Melissa's reasoning was based on the particular figure she drew, not the possible variation of the figure.

Students apply perceptual proof schemes in algebraic situations as well:

Episode 13. Don was asked to determine whether the following vectors are linearly dependent or independent:

$$u = \begin{bmatrix} \sqrt{3} \\ \sqrt{5} \end{bmatrix}, \qquad v = \begin{bmatrix} -\frac{7}{10} \\ \frac{1}{\sqrt{2}} \end{bmatrix}, \qquad x = \begin{bmatrix} \sqrt{61} \\ 103 \end{bmatrix}.$$

He responded:

I conclude u, v, and x are linearly independent by observation. My observation being one vector can not be written as a linear combination of the others.

Piaget's observations of different conservation tasks (Piaget, 1983), Steffe's research on children's counting schemes (Steffe, Cobb, & von Glasersfeld, 1988), and even Kitcher's philosophical outlook (1983) suggest that, epistemologically, the perceptual proof scheme is children's first source of internal conviction. This scheme continues to play an important role throughout students' mathematical education. In learning fractions, for example, children's early judgments of the order relation between fractions are merely perceptual (e.g., 2/3 is smaller than 3/4 because it looks so). The above two episodes demonstrate that even in advanced topics such as geometry and linear algebra, the perceptual proof scheme remains for many students a source of conviction and persuasion.

3.3 Analytical Proof Schemes.

Simply stated, an analytical proof scheme is one that validates conjectures by means of logical deductions. By this, however, we mean much more than what it is commonly referred to as the "method of mathematical demonstration"—a procedure involving a sequence of statements deduced progressively by certain logical rules from a set of statements accepted without proofs (i.e., a set of axioms). Our characterization of the analytical proof schemes category is best described by its subcategories: the transformational proof scheme and the axiomatic proof scheme.

3.3.1 The Transformational Proof Schemes.

Transformational observations involve operations on objects and anticipations of the operations' results. The operations are goal oriented. They may be carried out for the purpose of leaving certain relationships unchanged, but when a change occurs, the observer intends to anticipate it and, accordingly, intends to apply operations to compensate for the change. We call them "transformational" because they involve *transformations* of images—perhaps expressed in verbal or written statements—by means of deduction. By "images" in this context we mean the ones which Thompson (1994), based on Piaget (1967), has characterized as images that "support thought experiments and support reasoning by way

of quantitative relationships" (p. 230). The following two episodes demonstrate
this characterization of the transformational proof scheme.

Episode 14. Amy, one of the students in teaching experiment CG, demonstrated to the whole class how she imagines the theorem, "The sum of the measures of the interior angles in a triangle is 180°." Amy said something to the
effect that she imagines the two sides AB and AC of a triangle $\triangle ABC$ being
rotated in opposite directions through the vertices B and C, respectively, until
their angles with the segment BC are 90° (Figure 5a, b). This action transforms
the triangle ABC into the figure $A'BCA''$, where $A'B$ and $A''C$ are perpendicular to the segment BC. To recreate the original triangle, the segments $A'B$ and
$A''C$ are tilted toward each other until the points A' and A'' merge back into
the point (Figure 5c). Amy indicated that in doing so she "lost two pieces" from
the 90° angles B and C (i.e., angles $A'BA$ and $A''CA$) but at the same time
"gained these pieces back" in creating the angle A. This can be better seen if
we draw AO perpendicular to BC: angles $A'BA$ and $A''CA$ are congruent to
angles BAO and AOC, respectively (Figure 5d).

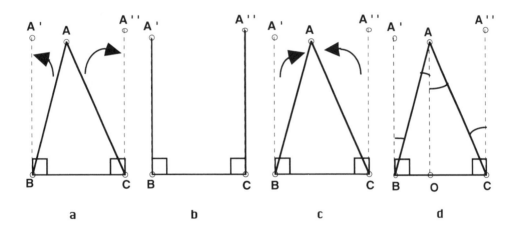

FIGURE 5

The focus of this episode is on Amy's way of thinking about the relationship
stated in the theorem. Amy views a triangle as a dynamic entity; it is a product
of her own imaginative construction, not of a passive perception. Her operations
were *goal oriented* and intended the *generality* aspect of the conjecture (rather
than a particular figure as in Episode 12). She *transformed* the triangle and
was fully able to *anticipate* the results of the transformations, namely, that the
change in the 90° angles B and C caused by the transformations is compensated
for by the creation of the angle A. All this leads to her *deduction* that the sum
of the measures of the angles of the triangle is 180°.

Episode 15. In teaching experiment CG, while discussing the relationship between an inscribed angle AHB and the angle between the chord AB and the tangent line AN (Figure 6a), Jeff argued that the two angles are congruent, because when H moves along the arc ATH (drawing a figure like Figure 6b on the board), a sequence of inscribed angles AH_1B, AH_2B, AH_3B, ..., is formed. All these angles, including all angles AXB where X is on the arc ATH, are congruent by a known theorem. The point A is one of these X's. When X coincides with A, the angle AXB becomes BAN. Therefore, the angles BAN and BHA are congruent.

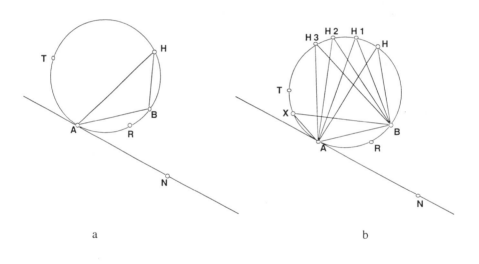

a   b

FIGURE 6

In this episode, we see how Jeff *varied* the position of point H for the *purpose* of evaluating the relationship between and the inscribed angles that result, and how he was able to *anticipate* the outcome of the variation: *deducing* the size of the angle. This ability is essential in viewing geometric objects as loci of points (e.g., a circle consists of all points whose distance from a given point is fixed; an angle bisector consists of all points whose distances from the angle rays are equal) rather than static figures.

Students apply perceptual proof schemes in algebraic situations as well:

Episode 16. Ed (in Case Study EC) explained his solution to the problem: Prove that for $x \geq 0$, $\log(x+1) \leq x$. He first converted this inequality into the form $x + 1 \leq e^x$, then he said:

> Both functions [$x + 1$ and e^x] are increasing but e^x goes faster. At zero they are equal, so e^x must be greater.

When Ed was asked to explain the mathematical meaning of his statement, "e^x goes faster [than $x + 1$]," he did so in terms of the concept of derivative.

Episode 17. When Ed was a high school student he took a college linear algebra course. The instructor asked him: If an $n \times m$ matrix transformation A is one-to-one, is A "tall" ($n > m$), "short" ($n < m$), or square ($n = m$)? Ed's answer was this:

> It can't be short because if you look at the system $AX = 0$, you would have free variables, which means the null-space of A contains a non-zero vector. This would destroy the definition of one-to-one, because you would have more than one vector going to zero.

In a follow-up discussion, shortly after this response, he added: "If the matrix is short, then it [the transformation] would run out of 'space'." The instructor learned that this latter metaphoric statement represented Ed's image of one-to-one matrix transformations. That is, when A is one-to-one, different vectors in R^m would correspond to different vectors in R^n. Since R^m is "larger" than R^n, there wouldn't be enough vectors, so to speak, in R^n to correspond to vectors in R^m. It must be mentioned that Ed understood the notion of R^m being "larger" than R^n in terms of dimensions, not cardinality. He brought up the concept of dimension when the instructor presented the following "counterexample" to his statement:

> The function $f(x) = \arctan(x)$ is one-to-one [a fact Ed agreed to by saying "Yes, it is an increasing function, so it must be one-to-one"] and maps a "larger" interval, $(-\infty, \infty)$, onto a "small" interval, $(-\pi/2, \pi/2)$, but it doesn't run out of space.

Ed even constructed his own "counterexample" that involves a linear transformation. He pointed out that one can map a "large" interval into a "small" interval by a linear function, by simply taking a straight line that goes through zero and with a slope less than 1.

3.3.1.1 Cognitive Levels of the Transformational Proof Scheme. To recapitulate, the transformational proof scheme is characterized by (a) consideration of the generality aspects of the conjecture, (b) application of mental operations that are goal oriented and anticipatory, and (c) transformations of images as part of a deduction process. These characteristics do not provide a complete picture of the transformational proof scheme, for they neither capture its inherent limitations, nor do they express its different cognitive levels. In the next two sections, we discuss two levels of the scheme: the internalized proof scheme and the interiorized proof scheme (cf. Steffe, Cobb, & Glasersfeld,

1988). Following this, we address the restrictions presumed by students on the transformation proof scheme.

3.3.1.1.1 Internalized Proof Scheme. An internalized proof scheme is a transformational proof scheme that has been encapsulated into a proof heuristic—a method (of proof) that renders conjectures into facts. For example, to prove two segments in a given figure are congruent, students commonly look for two congruent triangles that respectively include the two segments. This proof heuristic is abstracted by the students from repeated application of an approach they have often found to be successful. Here is another example of the internalized proof scheme pertaining to elementary mathematics. Students who were taught to think of fractions transformationally, not just symbolically, abstract different methods of comparing the order relation between fractions. For example, in many cases, when asked to compare the order relation between two given fractions, they respond by comparing the complements of the fractions to the whole (e.g. $7/8 < 8/9$ because $7/8$ is $1/8$ away from 1 whereas $8/9$ is only $1/9$ away from 1). An indication that the "comparing-to-the-whole" approach is an internalized transformational proof scheme rather than a ready-made formula is that the students apply it selectively, that is, only when they recognize its efficacy (for example, they may not apply it in comparing $2/5$ and $2/7$ or $5/11$ and $6/11$).

In teaching experiments LA1 and LA2 most of the students internalized the matrix row reduction process as a method of proof. That is to say, row reduction became for these students a spontaneous conceptual tool for conjecturing and evaluating conjectures. This way of thinking is demonstrated in the following episode.

Episode 18. Lee, a student in LA2, was asked,

Let A_1, A_2, ..., A_m be different vectors in R^n. If $m > n$, are these vectors linearly independent?

Lee began by writing

$$\# \text{ equations} < \# \text{ unknowns},$$

then she wrote:

The vectors are dependent because there are more unknowns than equations. So you will have some free variables. These free variables will be linear combinations of the independent vectors so the vectors are dependent.

Implicit in Lee's solution is the translation of the problem at hand into a system of linear equations. This was evident in her solution to the problem that immediately preceded the previous one:

Determine whether the following vectors are linearly dependent or independent:

$$A_1 = \begin{bmatrix} 0.2 \\ 0.4 \\ 1.6 \\ 4 \end{bmatrix}, \qquad A_2 = \begin{bmatrix} 0.9 \\ 3 \\ 12 \\ 0.8 \end{bmatrix}, \qquad A_3 = \begin{bmatrix} 0.03 \\ 535 \\ 97 \\ 1 \end{bmatrix},$$

$$A_4 = \begin{bmatrix} 7 \\ 4 \\ 68 \\ 175 \end{bmatrix}, \qquad A_5 = \begin{bmatrix} 68 \\ 890 \\ 4 \\ 2 \end{bmatrix}, \qquad A_6 = \begin{bmatrix} 69 \\ 20 \\ 9 \\ 0 \end{bmatrix}.$$

Lee wrote:

> If we consider the dependency equation $xA_1 + yA_2 + zA_3 + wA_4 + vA_5 + uA_6 = 0$. If we wrote this out as a system of equations we would get 4 equations with 6 unknowns. 4 equations is not enough to [uniquely] determine 6 unknowns since the system is homogeneous and hence consistent, we know there are an infinite number of solution because we will have 2 free variables. Hence the vectors are linearly dependent.

Also implicit in Lee's solution is the image she had of the reduced row echelon form of a matrix and its implications to solution existence. Her next solution to another problem gives some hints of the structure of this image: Lee was asked to solve a specific non-homogeneous linear system $AX = b$ of four equations and five unknowns, then was asked to look at the relation between $rank(A)$, the number of unknowns, and the number of spanning vectors in the solution set (that is, the basis of the solution space of the corresponding homogeneous system), and to prove that that this relation holds for any system that has a solution. Lee responded:

> Want to show that: number of unknowns— $rank(A)$ = # spanning vectors. The number of unknowns will determine how many columns are in the matrix. The $rank(A)$ (reduced row echelon form of A) corresponds to the number of non-zero rows which in reduced form correspond to the pivot variables [paraphrasing: $rank(A)$ corresponds to the number of non-zero rows in $rref(A)$, which, in turn, corresponds to the number of pivot columns]. So if we subtract the pivot variables from the number of unknowns the resulting columns are the free variables which form our spanning vectors [paraphrasing: If we subtract the number of pivot columns from the total number of columns, we get the number of the non-pivot columns, or the number of free variables, which is the number of spanning vectors in solution form of the equation]. Thus it follows: number of unknowns— $rank(A)$ = # spanning vectors.

The development of this way of reasoning was a result of our effort to eradicate students' external conviction proof scheme by helping them develop alternative, transformational proof schemes. We engaged students in numerous analyses of linear algebra questions in terms of systems of linear equations and, in turn, in terms of the meaning of row operations on the system's equations. As a result, students built images of the structure of the rref (reduced row echelon form) of a matrix and the meaning and implications of row reduction in questions of existence and uniqueness of solutions of linear systems and in questions of linear independence and span.

Further, some students have even discovered important theorems by analyzing the situation in terms of row operations, the most notable of which were the Rank Theorem (the row rank of a matrix equals its column rank) and the Fundamental Theorem of Linear Algebra ("Nullity($A_{m \times n}$) + Rank($A_{m \times n}$) = n"). The students' thinking was along these lines: Let A be a matrix and let r and c be its row-rank and column-rank, respectively. By definition, r and c are the maximum number of linearly independent rows of and the maximum number of linearly independent columns of A, respectively. Both r and c are invariant under row operations. Thus r is the number of non-zero rows in $rref(A)$ and c is the number of pivot columns in $rref(A)$. Based on their image of what the structure $rref(A)$ must be, they concluded that $r = c$, for each non-zero row in $rref(A)$ corresponds to exactly one pivot column in $rref(A)$.

A particularly important instance of the internalized proof scheme lies in the transformational use of symbols. To prove or refute a certain conjecture, the conjecture may be represented algebraically and symbol manipulations on the resulted expressions are performed, with the intention to derive relevant information that deepens one's understanding of the conjecture, and that can potentially lead to its proof or refutation. In such an activity, the individual does not necessarily form specific images for some or all of the algebraic expressions and relations that result in the process. It is only in critical stages in this process—viewed as such by the individual—that he or she intends to form such images.

Students should develop this scheme during their early experiences with algebra word-problems and especially through activities in analytic geometry. Despite this, we found that the scheme was largely absent with among students, at least during the first part of the teaching experiments. It was not that these students were unable to understand a symbolic translation of a verbal conjecture when it was presented to them, but that such an approach was seldom initiated by them. For example, in discussing the conjecture $Null(A)$ is orthogonal to $Rowspace(A)$, none of the students in LA3 suggested analyzing the conjecture by first representing it symbolically (e.g., $A_{m \times n} x = 0 \Leftrightarrow \sum_{i=1}^{n} x_i A_{j,i} = 0, \quad j = 1, \ldots, m$). This observation is worth mentioning because mathematics instructors usually take this scheme of transforming verbal statements into symbolic statements for granted, perhaps believing students' mathematical education in high school guarantees its acquisition.

3.3.1.1.2 Interiorized Proof Scheme: The Case of Mathematical Induction. An interiorized proof scheme is an internalized proof scheme that has been reflected upon by the person possessing it so that he or she becomes aware of it. A person's awareness of the proof scheme is usually observed when the person

describes it to others, compares it to other proof schemes, specifies when it can
or cannot be used, etc. As an example of this scheme, we illustrate with the
case of mathematical induction. By definition, the interiorization process cannot occur unless the internalization process has taken place. In what follows we
will describe briefly how students internalized and then interiorized the principle of mathematical induction. This process is divided into three stages: The
construction stage, the internalization stage, and the interiorization stage.

3.3.1.1.2.1 The Construction Stage. We investigated the concept of mathematical induction in the teaching experiment NT. As a result of previous pilot experiments we hypothesized that students' difficulties with the principle of mathematical induction can largely be attributed to two factors: (a) the formal expression
of this principle is hastily introduced to students, and (b) the kinds of problems typically introduced to students in their first experience with mathematical
induction are cognitively inadequate in the sense we will explain below. Accordingly, students in the NT teaching experiment were engaged for a relatively long
period of time—before the principle of mathematical induction was explicitly
mentioned—in working on problems typified by:

1. Find an upper bound to the sequence $\sqrt{2}$, $\sqrt{2 + \sqrt{2}}$, $\sqrt{2 + \sqrt{2 + \sqrt{2}}}$, ...

3. Three pegs are stuck in a board. On one of these pegs is a pile of disks
   graduated in size, the smallest being on top. The object of this puzzle is to
   transfer the pile to one of the other two pegs by moving the disks one at a
   time from one peg to another in such a way that a disk is never placed on
   top of smaller disk. Prove that this can be done for 31 disks in 2,147,483,647
   moves. Generalize the problem and your solution accordingly.

This kind of problem, which we call construction-stage problems, led students
to focus on the relationship between consecutive items in the sequence. Thus,
for example, in working on Problem 1 in small groups, students first conjectured
that 2 is an upper bound—typically by finding the calculator values of several
items in the sequence. Then they explained that the third item is less than 2
because it is the square root of a number that is smaller than 4 (this number
being the sum of 2 and a number that is smaller than 2). They repeated this
argument several times by applying it to the next few items in the sequence,
and concluded that all the items in the sequence must be less than 2 because
the same relationship exists between any two consecutive items in the sequence.
The students' conviction through the latter argument was in the ascertainment
level rather than the persuasion level, so the instructor focused their attention
on proving—persuading him, that is—that indeed the relationship they had observed holds for any consecutive items of the sequence. This stage of development
may be viewed as students' construction of a transformational proof scheme for
mathematical induction.[10]

---

[10]For a different view, see Dubinsky, 1986, 1989.

3.3.1.1.2.2 The Internalized Stage. After repeated applications of this way of reasoning in solving problems such as Problems 1 and 2, and of the formulation and proving of the general relationship between consecutive statements, and the establishment of the first statement in the sequence, we introduced a different kind of problem typified by this one:

3. Prove that for any positive integer $n \geq 1$,

$$\frac{1}{1 \cdot 2} + \frac{1}{2 \cdot 3} + \cdots + \frac{1}{n \cdot (n+1)} = \frac{n}{n+1}.$$

At first, the students did not appear to see any relation between this kind of problem, which we call internalized-stage problems, and construction-stage problems; their main attempts were to calculate a closed form for the summation on the left-hand side of the equality. It turned out that the students did not interpret the problem in terms of a sequence of statements (that is, as a proposition-valued function), so we worked on this way of interpretation. Problem 3, for example, was reformulated into:

3′. Find the general pattern in

$$\frac{1}{1 \cdot 2} = \frac{1}{1+1}$$

$$\frac{1}{1 \cdot 2} + \frac{1}{2 \cdot 3} = \frac{2}{2+1}$$

$$\frac{1}{1 \cdot 2} + \frac{1}{2 \cdot 3} + \frac{1}{3 \cdot 4} = \frac{3}{3+1}$$

$$\vdots$$

At this stage, many students realized that for this new breed of problems they could use reasoning similar to that used for construction-stage problems. Our interpretation is that this is a stage where the related transformational proof scheme built in the construction stage has been internalized and become a method of proof for these students, but they were not aware of it as a method of proof. This took place in a subsequent stage.

3.3.1.1.2.3 The Interiorized Stage. At this stage we introduced interiorized-stage problems, which are typified by these:

4. Prove that for any positive integer n,

$$\log(a_1 a_2 \cdots a_n) = \log a_1 + \log a_2 + \cdots + \log a_n$$

5. Prove that for any positive integer $n \geq 4$, $2^n \leq n!$

Before we continue, a brief analysis of these three stages of problems is in order. Textbooks typically present their problems on mathematical induction in an order that is almost opposite to ours: They usually present internalized-stage problems and interiorized-stage problems first, leaving construction-stage problems to the end. Presumably, their order is based on the view that problems of the latter kind are harder than the former kind. In our teaching experiments, we were concerned about which problems fit what stage of students' mathematical development rather than about the (subjective) order of difficulty of the problems. Based on previous experience, we found that interiorized-stage problems were inadequate to introduce the principle of mathematical induction. Students felt no need to search for a relationship between consecutive items of the given sequence because they could easily find "alternative" ways of solving them. Problem 5, for example, was viewed by the students as completely trivial (i.e., for any integer $n \geq 4$, all but one factor in $n!$ is greater than or equal to the corresponding factor in 2^n); similarly, they solved Problem 4 by a repeated application of the formula $\log xy = \log x + \log y$, and saw no need to look for an alternative proof, certainly not a proof by mathematical induction.

It was this simplistic aspect of interiorized-stage problems that posed a challenge to some of the students in the NT teaching experiment. They sensed the underlying structure of the three sets of problems and began to see how the same method of proof could be applied to all. They had to deny their natural inclination to solve these problems with a simple method and look for a different way to apply the method they used in the construction and internalized stages. This forced them to be explicit about the method of proof they had internalized in the second stage and to examine its applicability to the new set of problems. Indeed, we found that most of the students who had internalized the principle of induction in the internalized stage were able to formulate it explicitly and apply it to solve interiorized-stage problems. Thus, these students had interiorized the principle of mathematical induction as a method of proof.

It should be clearly stated that the interiorization stage does not (and it did not in the case of our students) imply the understanding that mathematical induction is essential in proving proposition-valued statements whose domain is the positive integers. Indeed those students who successfully proved interiorized-stage problems by mathematical induction continued to believe that mathematical induction is not necessary in the case of problems such as Problems 4 and 5, for "easier" proofs do exist. We did not expect our students to reach this level of understanding based on the instructional program of the teaching experiment. We believe that a full appreciation of mathematical induction—specifically this level of understanding—can only be reached when the *axiomatic* proof scheme (to be defined below) is built.

3.3.1.2 Restrictive Characteristics of the Transformational Proof Scheme. We found that many of our students who were able to think transformationally presumed certain restrictions on either the context of the conjecture, the generality of the justification, or the mode of the justification. Accordingly, a transformational proof scheme that involves any one of these restrictions is called a *restrictive* proof scheme, and depending on the kind of the restriction, it may be called a *contextual*, *generic*, or *constructive* proof scheme, respectively.

3.3.1.2.1 Contextual Proof Scheme. Researchers (e.g., Lave & Wenger, 1991) have addressed the importance of the broad context in which a particular activity takes place. As can be seen from the discussion below, our interest is more narrow than this broad level of contextualization. We are interested in the specific interpretations students give to mathematical assertions in the process of their justification in collegiate mathematics settings.

In a contextual proof scheme conjectures are interpreted, and therefore proved, in terms of a specific context. For example, a student might interpret and prove the *general* statement "$n+1$ vectors in an n-dimensional vector space are linearly dependent" in the *specific* context of R^n. One reason for this is that the only linear algebra "world" the student has ever "lived" in is R^n, and so he or she has not yet abstracted the concept of "linear independence" beyond this specific context.

Another example of the contextual proof scheme comes from students' inability to deal with any geometric structure but the one that deals with their spatial imageries. One of the questions we asked in the CG teaching experiment was: Can students (in this teaching experiment) think in terms of abstract structures, namely, that the axioms in geometry require no specific interpretation? In particular, can they consider their own imaginative space as a specific system which may or may not satisfy the structure at hand?

Students' responses in an extensive set of interviews conducted at the end of the instructional unit that dealt with axiom systems revealed three categories of proof schemes: The *perceptual* proof scheme (discussed above, where students are unable to reason about the problem situation unless it is present perceptually, in which case their justification is solely based on their particular perception), the *spatial* proof scheme, which is a particular case of the contextual proof scheme (where students are able to think of the problem situation only in terms of their imaginative space), and the *axiomatic* proof scheme (to be discussed below, where students can think of the axioms in general structures, see below). The decisive majority of the students resided in the first two categories. Examples of the perceptual proof scheme were presented earlier; the following interview episode demonstrates the spatial proof scheme.

Episode 19. In the Teaching Experiment CG we introduced a hypothetical participant, who was called Mr. or Ms. Smart. This participant is an intellectually able creature with whom the students can communicate in their own natural language, including the language of basic set theory, but possesses none of the physical senses, such as visual and tactile perceptions. The class is presented with the task of communicating to Mr. or Ms. Smart geometric concepts, conjectures, propositions, and justifications they have formed intuitively and transformationally. The idea is to bring the students to realize that in order to facilitate such a communication, they must formulate certain "agreements" with Mr. or Ms. Smart. These agreements amount to a system of axioms. In the beginning, the instructor played the role of Mr. or Ms. Smart, but gradually the students took on her or his persona.

Prior to the following interview, the class discussed finite geometries, where the notions of "line" and "parallel" were defined for Mr. or Ms. Smart set theoretically.

I[11]: Consider the following model: The points are: A, B, C, D, E, F, G, and the lines are: $\{A, B, F\}$, $\{A, C, E\}$, $\{A, D, G\}$, $\{B, C, D\}$, $\{B, E, G\}$, $\{C, F, G\}$, $\{D, E, F\}$. Determine whether the following property holds in this model. "Given a line and a point NOT on the line, there is a line which contains the given point and is parallel to the given line."

Duane: If I were to take line ABF which of course contains those points ... no because one of those points [pointing to A, B, F] appears ... in each of the other lines so there won't be a line parallel to that.

I: You said the line ABF contains those points. Do you mean consists of these points?

Duane: I guess I don't understand the difference between contain and consist.

(The interviewer explains the difference between these two terms.)

Duane: There are other points on that line [line ABF]. Even if A, B, and F are consecutive points if it is defined as a line and that line will continue in each direction, so there has to be an infinite number of points on one line.

I: In this problem each line is defined to be consisting of exactly three points. There are no points on this line [pointing to $\{A, B, F\}$] other than the points A, B, and F.

Duane: To have a line that only contains A, B, F?

I: Yes.

Duane: It would be a segment with three points.

I: But a segment too contains infinitely many points.

Duane: ... To say a line consists of only three points is impossible because there should be an infinite number of points.

I: How did we define a line for Mr. Smart?

Duane: We defined the line for Mr. Smart as a set of consecutive points and that's all I can remember.

I: In terms of Mr. Smart's definition of a line, is there a model where the following property does not hold: "Between two points there exists a line, and such a line is unique," and (b) "Given a line and a point NOT on the line, there is a line containing the given point and is parallel to the given line."

Duane: No, because that defines the line on a plane. Between two points there exists a line and such a line is unique. . . . We defined a line as uh a line can be drawn, a unique line can be drawn between any two points in space. . . . And then for the second one we also defined the plane as ... The first one will have, would have to hold. And the second one, ... yeah, that would have to hold. I can't think of any alternatives.

(At this point the interviewer explained again to Duane that by a line it is not meant a Euclidean line, that is, his spatial imagery line, but a line as a set of objects, such as in Problem 1.)

I: Do you now understand the question?

Duane: Yeah I understand the question. I'm trying to think about different situations you can encounter. I think it's gonna go. OK. If I was given two points and I want to construct a situation where the two points cannot be joined by a line, is that what you're saying? ... No for number one I cannot think of anything ...

I: How about the possibility that you have more than one line going between two points? Duane: Uh that's not possible is it? . . . No you cannot have ... you can label it as two different lines but it's the same line.

I: OK. What if Mr. Smart took two lines ABC and ABD. Line ABC is a set consisting of three objects labeled A, B, and C, and a line ABD is also a set of objects labeled A, B, D. These objects Mr. Smart calls points. According to Mr. Smart, he has two lines that go through different points, A and B.

Duane: Well, I would have to, I would try to show him [Mr. Smart] that if we have two lines ABC and ABD ... and I would have to try to explain to him by the fact that uh A, B, and C are first line and A, B, and D are second line contain[ing] two common points. Therefore, since they contain two common points they have to lie on the same line or the same, ... it would be easier probably here to demonstrate it, to demonstrate them as two different rays. The line, a singly line ...

I: Let's say I am Mr. Smart, and I am telling you that what I mean by a line is just a set of three objects, no more and no less. This is what I call a line. The objects I call points.

Duane: Only a set of three points.

I: Yes. Would you then agree with Mr. Smart that between two points there is more than one line.

Duane: ... Why would he, Mr. Smart, define the lines as only three points. It has to be all the points contained [between] those three points.

I: What can't he?

Duane: Because if you have three points there, it can be named by those three points but not defined by those three points. Three points, you can only define three points as three points. If they're three non-collinear points then we can define a plane. If they're three collinear points you can define a line. But there has to be an infinite number of points between them.

This excerpt demonstrates Duane's inability to represent the geometric properties stated, in any context but his own imaginative space. Textbooks in axiomatic geometry, on the other hand, usually begin with finite geometries as a preparation for non-Euclidean geometries, not taking into account the impact of the spatial proof scheme. The idea that geometric properties are not supposed to evoke spatial imagery properties is a relatively new concept in mathematics; it was born at the turn of this century with the publication of Hilbert's *Grundlagen*. Poincaré, in his review of the *Grundlagen*, saw a need to point to this seemingly self-evident feature of the *Grundlagen*:

> ... the expressions "lie on," "pass through," etc., [in the *Grundlagen*] are not intended to evoke images; they are simply synonyms of the word "determine." The words "point," "straight line," and "plane" should not produce any sensible representation in the mind. They could with indifference designate objects of any nature whatever, provided that one can establish a correspondence among these objects so that there corresponds to each system of two of the objects called points one and only one object called a line [and so on]. (quoted in Mueller, 1981, p. 5)

So judging from the historical development of geometry, we believe that the spatial proof scheme is epistemologically inevitable. What surprises us is its robust influence on students in an advanced stage in their mathematics education.

3.3.1.2.2 Generic Proof Scheme. In a generic proof scheme,[12] conjectures are interpreted in general terms but their proof is expressed in a particular context. This scheme reflects students' inability to express their justification in general terms, as is demonstrated in the following episode.

Episode 20. In teaching experiment NT, several students proved the statement, "If a whole number is divisible by 9 then the sum of its digits is divisible by 9," by taking a specific whole number, say 867, and saying something to the effect: This number can be represented as $8 \times 100 + 6 \times 10 + 7$, which is $(8 \times 99 + 6 \times 9) + (8 + 6 + 7)$. Since the first addend, $8 \times 99 + 6 \times 9$, definitely is divisible by 9, the second addend, $8 + 6 + 7$, which is the sum of the number's digits, must be divisible by 9. Some of these students indicated, in addition, that this process can be applied to any whole number. In so doing, the students were utilizing a generic proof scheme.

The generic proof scheme was particularly apparent in students' justifications of statements involving the reduced echelon form of a matrix. Here is an example:

Episode 21. In response to the problem,

> Is the following statement true? "If $rank(A)$ is smaller than the number of unknowns in the system $AX = b$, then the system has infinitely many solutions."

Adam, a student in teaching experiment LA2, wrote:

> For this to be true the system must be consistent. Assuming consistency this [is] true because if the rank of A is less than # of unknowns one or

---

[12]Consistent with Tall's (1979), following Steiner (1976), notion of a generic proof. See also Harel and Tall (1991).

more free variables will exist. These free variables can be any constants and are part of the spanning vectors in the solution. Therefore the solution will either [be] a line, plane, etc. and have an infinite # of solutions.

Apparently Adam sensed that his answer was not completely convincing because his main argument, "if the rank of A is less than # of unknowns one or more free variables will exist," was not justified, and so he continued:

$$\left[\begin{array}{ccc|c} 1 & 0 & a & b \\ 0 & 1 & c & d \\ 0 & 0 & 0 & 0 \\ 0 & 0 & 0 & 0 \end{array}\right].$$

For this general system, $rank(A) = 2$, there are three unknowns.
The solution is: $[x \quad y \quad z] = [b \quad d \quad 0] + z[-a \quad -c \quad 1]$.

We consider this latter part of Adam's response as an indication of a generic proof scheme, because his concept of rank—as we knew it from other instances—included the idea of rank of a matrix being the number of non-zero rows in the reduced echelon form of the matrix. So the matrix he presented is a representation of a "general system" as he had explicitly indicated.

3.3.1.2.3 Constructive Proof Scheme. In the constructive proof scheme, students' doubts are removed by actual construction of objects—as opposed to mere justification of the existence of objects. (This scheme is reminiscent of the constructivist mathematics philosophy founded by Brouwer at the turn of the 20th century.) Just as was the case historically, a manifestation of this proof scheme is students' dislike of proof by contradiction, as it is seen in the following episode.

Episode 22. In teaching experiment EC, Ed's proof of the theorem,

> A segment k emanating from the midpoint of AB in a triangle ABC and parallel to BC bisects AC.

was this:

> Let D and E be the midpoints of AB and AC, respectively, and assume DE is different from k. By previous result, DE must be parallel to AB. So DE and k have the point D in common and both are parallel to BC—a contradiction to the parallel postulate.

The instructor presented this proof in class during the CG teaching experiment. Dean, a student in this class, responded by saying,

> I really don't like proof by contradiction. I have never understood proofs by contradiction, they never made sense. You are assuming what was required to prove. Could you please give us a different proof?

3.3.2 Axiomatic Proof Schemes: Intuitive, Structural, and Axiomatizing.

When a person understands that at least in principle a mathematical justification must have started originally from undefined terms and axioms (facts, or statements accepted without proof), we say that person possesses an *axiomatic* proof scheme.

Such a person is necessarily aware of the distinction between the undefined terms, such as "point" and "line," and defined terms, such as "square" and "circle," and between statements accepted without proof and ones that are deducible from other statements.[13] He or she, however, may be able to handle only axioms that correspond to her or his intuition, or ideas of self-evidence, such as "for any a and b in F, $a + b = b + a$" in relation to her or his experience with real numbers, or "one and only one line goes through two points" in relation to her or his imaginative space. Such an axiomatic proof scheme we call an *intuitive-axiomatic* proof scheme.

Historically, one of the philosophical distinctions between Euclid's *Elements* and Hilbert's *Grundlagen* is that while the former is restricted to a single interpretation—that its content is a presumed description of human spatial realization—the latter is open to different possible realizations—such as the Euclidean space, the surface of a half sphere, the ordered pairs (x, y) and triples (x, y, z), where x, y, z are real numbers, etc.—including the interpretation that the axioms are meaningless formulas. In both cases special attention is paid to the formulation of undefined terms and accepted statements as the basis for any justification in mathematics, and therefore both are consistent with the axiomatic proof scheme. However, while the axioms in the *Elements* describe intuitively grasped truth—and therefore are consistent with the intuitive-axiomatic proof scheme[14]—the axioms in the *Grundlagen* characterize a *structure* that fits different models (Mueller, 1981). This obviously is not unique to geometry. In algebra, a group or a vector space is defined to be any system of objects satisfying certain axioms that specify the structure under consideration. Accordingly, we define a *structural* proof scheme as an axiomatic proof scheme by which one thinks of conjectures and theorems as representations of situations from *different* realizations that are understood to share a common structure characterized by a collection of axioms.

In the structural proof scheme, the axioms that define the structure are permanent, and the focus of the study is on the structure itself, not on the axiom system; so, for example, one studies real analysis on the basis of the axioms of

---

[13]Evidence exists to indicate that the distinction among the concepts of "definition," "axiom," and "theorem" is far from simple even for college students (see Vinner, 1977).

[14]The *Elements* is consistent with the intuitive proof scheme but does not entirely satisfy its definition, for proofs of some propositions are not grounded in the stated axioms. For example, the proposition that triangles which agree in two sides and the enclosed angle are congruent is proved by using the idea of motion and superimposition of figures, not the stated axioms.

a complete ordered field, or studies the theory of vector spaces on the basis of the vector space axioms, etc. We speculate that the structural proof scheme is a cognitive prerequisite to the *axiomatizing* proof scheme—a scheme by which a person is able to investigate the implications of varying a set of axioms, or to axiomatize a certain field.

The structural proof scheme is essential in studying many undergraduate mathematics topics, such as the theory of vector spaces, group theory, real analysis, etc. Without it, one cannot understand, for example, the need for the completeness axiom in real analysis or the need for the vector space axioms in linear algebra. In teaching experiment LA1 we found that most of the students viewed the vector-space axioms—as well as the basic properties that they imply—as a collection of trivial statements, which deserve no attention, as it is seen in the following episode:

Episode 23.

Interviewer: Consider the statement, "If x be an element of a vector-space V, then $(-1)x = -x$." Your friend complains to you that he does not understand the point made by this statement. Explain to your friend the argument made by this statement.

Student: To tell you the truth, I too think this is a ridiculous statement. Of course, negative one times x is negative x!

Further conversation with this student revealed that he restricted the context of the conjecture ("If x be an element of a vector-space V, then $(-1)x = -x$") to the context of R^n and was unable to think of it in general terms. Further, at the time of the interview, he was familiar with the operations in R^n and had experienced the fact that $(-1)x = -x$ for x in R^n and so he viewed this statement as self evident in this context. This phenomenon, which is another manifestation of the contextual proof scheme, hindered students appreciating the non-triviality of the statement, namely, that the product of the scalar -1 by any vector x produces the additive inverse of x. Evidently, students' past mathematical experiences were insufficient to build the structural proof scheme, which we believe is needed to cope with the theory of vector space.

An important distinction between the structural proof scheme and the intuitive proof scheme is the ability to separate the abstract statements of mathematics (e.g., $1 + 1 = 2$) from their corresponding quantitative observations (e.g., 1 apple + 1 apple = 2 apples), or the axiomatically-based observations from their corresponding visual phenomena. As an example of the latter, consider many students' difficulties in appreciating the need to prove the Intermediate Value Theorem in real analysis once they have formed its pictorial meaning. Finally, in our view the axiomatic proof scheme is epistemologically an extension of the transformational proof scheme. One might mistakenly think of the axiomatic proof scheme as the ability to reason formally, that is, to apply rules of inference to meaningless formulas. In fact, no philosopher of mathematics of the twentieth century seems to have maintained this position about formalism. Even Hilbert, the founder of the formalist movement, "looked on formalization as a means of solving certain mathematical questions, notably the question of consistency, but he regarded mathematics itself as the study of ideal objects created by the intellect to simplify treatment of the empirically and intuitively given" (Mueller, 1981, p. 7).

4. Recapitulation and Concluding Remarks

4.1. Recapitulation.

Studies of university students' understanding of mathematical proof have shown serious deficits. These findings are not surprising if collegiate mathematics instruction assumes on the part of entering students a general understanding of proof and its roles in mathematics, since studies of high school students have shown that only a limited number of them acquire a respectable degree of proof understanding and proof-writing ability during their high school mathematics. Thus for most university students, including even mathematics majors, university coursework must give conscious and perhaps overt attention to proof understanding, proof production, and proof appreciation as goals of instruction.

Accordingly, knowing what is guiding students' thinking about mathematical proof is essential. The notion of a psychological *proof scheme* has been very valuable to us in thinking about students' reactions in mathematical settings. The phrase "proof scheme" refers to what convinces a person, and to what the person offers to convince others. "Proof scheme" as used here refers to justifications in general, so it should not be interpreted narrowly in terms of mathematical proof in its conventional sense. One's proof scheme is idiosyncratic and may vary from field to field, and even within mathematics itself.

The classes of proof schemes offered here is based largely on extensive work with college mathematics majors and includes three major categories: *External conviction proof schemes*, *empirical proof schemes*, and *analytical proof schemes* (see Figure 1). Justifications under an external conviction proof scheme might depend on an authority such as a teacher or a book (the *authoritarian proof scheme*), on strictly the appearance of the argument (the *ritual proof scheme*), or on symbol manipulations, with the symbols and/or the manipulations having no meaningful basis in the context (the *symbolic proof scheme*). The latter two proof schemes are direct results of faulty instruction and have little to recommend them, since they lead to the endorsement or rejection of an argument solely on its appearance, or to presenting an argument based on the plausible-looking symbol manipulations, as in $\log(x+y) = \log x + \log y$. A dash of the authoritarian proof scheme, on the other hand, is not completely harmful and perhaps unavoidable, and people may use this scheme to some extent when they are sampling an area outside their specialties. In two of its worst forms, however, either the student is helpless without an authority at hand, or the student regards a justification of a result as valueless and unnecessary.

Empirical proof schemes are marked by their reliance on evidence from examples (sometimes just one example) of direct measurements of quantities, substitutions of specific numbers in algebraic expressions, etc. (the *inductive proof scheme*), or perceptions (the *perceptual proof scheme*). These proof schemes are commonly observed with mathematics students, perhaps partly because natural, everyday thinking utilizes examples so much. As with the authoritarian proof scheme, despite its grave limitations in mathematical proof,[15] the empirical proof scheme does have value. Examples and nonexamples enrich one's images and can help to generate ideas or to give insights, for instance. The problem arises in contexts in which a mathematical proof is expected, and yet all that is necessary or desirable in the eyes of the student is a verification by one or more examples.

The final categories—the *analytical proof schemes*—encompass mathematical proof, although again the emphasis is on the student's thinking rather than on what he or she writes. Key to the analytical proof schemes is the *transformational proof scheme*: the creation and transformations of general mental images for a context, with the transformations directed toward explanations, always with an element of deduction. At some point, a collection of cues and transformations may be chunked into a heuristic, yielding an *internalized (analytical) proof scheme*. Ideally an internalized proof scheme becomes itself an object of reflection (an *interiorized (analytical) proof scheme*), allowing comparison and contrast with other heuristics and usually giving greater insight into the context and/or the heuristic. Transformational proof schemes may be unnecessarily but unconsciously limited by the owner, either because of her or his restriction of the images to a familiar but narrow setting (e.g., an argument in R^3 for an R^n situation), or because of her or his use of a specific case in a generic way (e.g., a justification based on a specific or even a general 3×3 matrix in an $n \times n$ setting), or because of a need for an envisioned step-by-step creation of a result (e.g., a distrust of a proof by contradiction).

Axiomatic proof schemes, the second category of analytical proof schemes and an epistemological extension of the transformational proof scheme, involve an awareness of an underlying formal development. Although many undergraduates reach a point at which they can utilize an axiomatic proof scheme, their thinking may be grounded solely in familiar examples for very general ideas—e.g., the real numbers for a field, or $(Z_5, +)$ for a group, or a Euclidean line for a line, or a continuous real-valued function for a function—giving an *intuitive-axiomatic proof scheme*. With the realization that definitions and axioms about "fields," "groups," "lines," and "functions" can be applied very generally and can assume the central roles, one's proof scheme becomes a *structural axiomatic proof scheme*. An occasional undergraduate reaches this last stage and may then even reach a higher stage where he or she appreciates the possibility of alternate axiomatic developments for the same body of results—giving an *axiomatizing proof scheme*.

---

[15] "Mathematical proof" means a proof at the level of the analytical proof scheme.

4.2 Concluding Remarks.

By their natures, teaching experiments and interview studies do not give definitive conclusions. They can, however, offer indications of the state of affairs and a framework in which to interpret other work. The following comments and speculations should be read in that spirit.

The current analysis of proof schemes is no doubt not the last word on the typology. The analysis has been based mainly on work with students at one site, so it naturally describes their behaviors well. It has, however, also been tested to a degree by its adequacy in interpreting the work of mathematics majors at another university. Further validations should be done and will likely lead to a refinement of the categories.

It is important not to regard the taxonomy in a hierarchical, single-niche sense. A given person may exhibit various proof schemes during one short time span, perhaps reflecting her or his familiarity for, and relative expertise in, the contexts, along with her or his sense of what sort of justification is appropriate in the setting of the work. Although the authoritarian and empirical proof schemes have value, we feel that mathematics majors in particular should also eventually show evidence of the analytical proof schemes.

Although we prefer to speak of an individual's proof schemes in the plural so as to recognize that one might operate differently in different contexts, within a particular context there is often at least a partially hierarchical nature implicit in the categories. For example, in the analytic proof schemes, it is plausible if not definitional that the structural proof scheme is a cognitive prerequisite to the axiomatizing proof scheme, and we hypothesize that the transformational proof scheme is a necessary prerequisite to building an axiomatic proof scheme. On the other hand, we do not believe that the external proof schemes are essential in the development of the analytic proof schemes. The external authoritarian scheme and the empirical schemes should for mathematics students at some stage fill only confirming and conjecturing roles. van Dormolen (1977) hypothesized that the development of proof ideas in a given domain might follow a developmental sequence. With our terminology, this sequence might begin with a dependence on external schemes (e.g., the professor's assertions) and/or empirical schemes (e.g., studying examples) but grow gradually into analytic schemes; students in the teaching experiments have followed such paths. But it would be sobering if one must follow this crawl-before-walk-before-run in each domain, sobering because instruction may begin at the run stage, so to speak. Some description of student understanding of proof other than ours, however, might better describe a developmental sequence. All this conjecturing is provoked by the work of the van Hieles (cf. Fuys, Geddes, & Tischler, 1988), who identified different levels of understanding of geometric topics by precollege students. Their claim that students necessarily have to go through all the levels has some research support (summarized in Clements & Battista, 1992). Hence, instruction that begins at an advanced level might well not register with any students who are at earlier levels. In the proof schemes context, this hypothesis could mean, for example, that proofs at an axiomatic level for some topic might indeed be "over the head" of students whose proof schemes are at less sophisticated levels. Experienced students do recognize that there is an expected type of justification even though they might not be able to give it; we have often heard in the interviews statements like "I know this isn't a proof, but here is what I would do."

As is noted in section 2.1, the empirical proof scheme is not well understood. For example, our work at two different sites has given different impressions of students' comfort with the use of counterexamples. Is this an artifact of the limits of teaching experiments and interviews, or might some difference in the college (or precollege) curricula experienced at the two locations account for the contrast?

The importance of the setting in which the justification takes place naturally leads to implications for instruction. An awareness that there are different proof schemes, some unsophisticated, is important for the instructor. The dependence on the authoritarian and empirical proof schemes by most students must be a consideration in planning our teaching. We may, for example, be fostering the empirical proof schemes *through* our teaching: During instruction, empirical justifications themselves serve as examples of arguments given by mathematicians, and may inadvertently sanction the empirical proof scheme as a mode of justification fully acceptable in the mathematical context. Psychologists have found that some examples of natural concepts are psychologically more representative of the concepts than others are (cf. Mervis & Rosch, 1981). It may be that mathematics students who hear the word "proof" only in the presence of a certain form of argument may then generate their representative exemplar of proof on that basis and be guided by these aspects, perhaps ritualistic ones, in judging whether other arguments are proofs.

One role of our instruction is to exemplify or educe more powerful and logically sound proof schemes, and to make the case for their necessity and their value. The usual lecture-textbook method does appear to suffice for some students, but other students apparently only grudgingly "play the game" without a genuine conviction that mathematical proof is really necessary or personally goal-worthy. Students might mouth, for example, that examples do not give a "proof," but then offer only examples as justifications. To be fair, some explain that they can offer only examples because they do not know how even to start a mathematical proof, as Moore (1994) noted with his majors.

Writing a mathematical argument appears to require instruction; Wilf is convinced that there is a pay-off in devoting the "first few class hours" of his junior level analysis course to students' writing and critiquing proofs of familiar results from outside analysis (1996). In our teaching experiments, we adopted the proof-writing refinement-through-reflection approach, where students refine their own writing after they have reevaluated the meaning of their own proof from the perspective of another reader. Often students' written proofs include the right idea

but are very difficult to understand because of inadequate wording and poor
self expression. In many of these cases the instructor meets with the student
individually to discuss the written proof. The goal is to bring the student to
realize that her or his writing did not convey to an outsider the meaning he or
she originally meant to convey, either because it is incomprehensible or because
it conveys different meanings. While this approach appeared to be effective,
it demanded from the instructors, as was expected, enormous amounts of time
outside the regular classroom hours.

In the hope of fostering the transformational proof schemes, the teaching experiments have focused on the following technique. A carefully chosen problem,
which might be called a "proof-eliciting problem" (a suggestive description due to
R. Lesh, 1995), is presented to the students. They work on the problem, sometimes in groups, sometimes as individual homework or team homework. The
students are then encouraged to express in their own words their justification
for any conjecture. This ascertainment phase of the proof scheme—convincing
oneself—is followed by the persuasion phase—convincing others—where the justification is examined by the whole class. Once the justification is accepted,
the teacher usually gives a further assignment whose goal is to bring students
to reflect upon the justification for further learning. Here is an example of a
proof-eliciting problem.

Episode 24. At the beginning of the first lesson on modular arithmetic in
teaching experiment NT, the class worked in groups on the problem: "Find the
remainder when $(107)^4 + (107)^3 \times 2346 - 2376 \times 3475$ is divided by 5." One of the
students, Laura, suggested her solution to her group-mates, who seemed to be
satisfied with the solution. The instructor asked Laura to present her solution
to the whole class. She presented her solution as follows: Laura first pointed to
the addend, 2376×3475, arguing that its remainder, when divided by 5, is 0
because this product results in a number with unit digit 0. Then she looked at
2346 and argued that its remainder is 1 because its unit digit is 6. Next, Laura
argued that the remainder for $(107)^3$ is 3. To defend her argument she wrote
$(100 + 7)^3$ below the expression $(107)^3$, and said that she will be looking at 100^3
and 7^3 [sic]. She continued by arguing that the remainder for $(107)^3$ is 3 since
the remainder for 100 is 0 and the remainder for 7^3 which is 343 is 3. Laura then
indicated that in a similar way she computed the remainder for $(107)^4$ which
she argued was 1 because the remainder for 100 is 0 and the remainder for 7^4,
which is 2401, is 1. Lastly, Laura concluded the remainder for the expression
when divided by 5 is $1 + 3 \times 1 + 0$, which is 4.

In the class discussion that followed, there were some students who agreed
with Laura's actions and there were others who raised questions about their
mathematical legitimacy. The instructor saw this as an opportunity for a possibly fruitful debate about properties of modular arithmetic operations. He asked
the whole class to express the general statements that they believed constituted
Laura's steps, in order to evaluate their correctness. After some discussion within

each of the working groups, many students stated the general relationships believed to be implicitly used in Laura's actions. These statements then stood for evaluation by the whole class. Those which were later found to be true were declared as theorems. *Since these theorems originated from the students' own actions, they were better appreciated by them. More importantly, because of the uncertainty the students initially had about the truth of their statements, they saw a real need to seek justifications.* With shaping by the instructor in the choice of initial problems and sometimes in the provision of further test cases for conjectures or steps like Laura's erroneous $(a+b)^3 = a^3 + b^3$, students are led away from both an authoritarian proof scheme and a complete reliance on examples. When the classroom authority remains silent (see the account of the Schoenfeld course, this volume) and when the shortcomings of examples are accepted, the classwork leads naturally toward a search for a method of justification based on transformations of images and companion deductions.

The education of students toward transformational reasoning must not start in college. Years of instruction which focus on the results in mathematics, rather than the reasons behind those results, can leave the impression that *only* the results are important in mathematics, an opinion sometimes voiced even by mathematics majors. We argue that instructional activities that educate students to reason about situations in terms of the transformational proof schemes are crucial to students' mathematical development, and they must begin in an early age (see Harel, in press, for more details). Exciting projects in which children in even the primary grades routinely expect to give explanations for their thinking (e.g., Ball, 1993; Cobb et al., 1991; Lampert, 1990), show that the precollege mathematics curriculum can indeed promote proof schemes beyond the authoritarian and empirical ones.

Until such background is common among our college students, we can think about what proof schemes we are cultivating in our courses. When we go beyond authoritarian or example-based stances, will it be appreciated why the mathematical proofs we call for or give are needed? Should our lectures be a recitation of what we are writing on the chalkboard, or a "thinking out loud" which exemplifies transformational reasoning? With students' likely proof schemes in the back of our minds, is a transition course with a central concern the development of more sophisticated thinking about proof a necessity? If we are relying on a transition course, or on a discrete mathematics course, to bring students' proof production, understanding, and appreciation to a higher state, is the course accomplishing that goal? Finally, the difficulty of students in reaching a structural axiomatic proof scheme (cf. Episode 19) suggests that a capstone course including some attention to metamathematics as a topic might be of value to mathematics majors. As Babai notes, "One of the most remarkable gifts human civilization has inherited from ancient Greece is the notion of mathematical proof" (1992). Our students should share in this gift.

REFERENCES

1. Alexandrov, A. D. (1963). Non-Euclidean geometry. In A. D. Aleksandrov, A. N. Kolmogorov, & M. A. Lavrent'ev (Eds.), *Mathematics, its content, methods, and meaning, vol. III* (pp. 97–189) (K. Hirsch, Trans.). Cambridge, MA: M.I.T. Press.

2. Alibert, D. (1988). Towards new customs in the classroom. *For the Learning of Mathematics, 8*, 31–35.

3. Alibert, D., & Thomas, M. (1991). Research on mathematical proof. In D. Tall (Ed.), *Advanced mathematical thinking* (pp. 215–230). Dordrecht, The Netherlands: Kluwer.

4. Anderson, J. R. (1985). *Cognitive psychology* (2nd ed.). New York: W. H. Freeman.

5. Babai, L. (1992). Transparent proofs. *Focus. 12*(3), 1–2.

6. Balacheff, N. (1991). Treatment of refutations: Aspects of the complexity of a constructivist approach to mathematics learning. In E. von Glasersfeld (Ed.), *Radical constructivism in mathematics education* (pp. 89–110). Dordrecht, The Netherlands: Kluwer.

7. Ball, D. L. (1993). Halves, pieces, and twoths: Constructing and using representational contexts in teaching fractions. In T. P. Carpenter, E. Fennema, & T. A. Romberg (Eds.), *Rational numbers: An integration of research* (pp. 157–195). Hillsdale, NJ: Lawrence Erlbaum Associates, Inc.

8. Bernal, M. (1987). *Black Athena: The Afroasiatic roots of classical civilization.* New Brunswick, NJ: Rutgers University Press.

9. Boyer, C. B. (1989). *A history of mathematics* (2nd edition). New York: Wiley.

10. Brousseau, G. (1986). Basic theory and methods in the didactics of mathematics. In P. F. L. Verstapen (Ed.), *Proceedings of the Second Conference on Systematic Co-operation Between Theory and Practice in Mathematics Education* (pp. 109–161). Enschede, The Netherlands: NICD.

11. Chazan, D. (1993). High school geometry students' justification for their views of empirical evidence and mathematical proof. *Educational Studies in Mathematics, 24*, 359–387.

12. Clements, D. H., & Battista, M. T. (1992). Geometry and spatial reasoning. In D. Grouws (Ed.), *Handbook of research on mathematics teaching and learning* (pp. 420–464). Reston, VA: National Council of Teachers of Mathematics.

13. Cobb, P., Wood, T., Yackel, E., Nicholls, J., Wheatley, G., Trigatti, B., & Perlwitz, M. (1991). Assessment of a problem-centered second-grade mathematics project. *Journal for Research in Mathematics Education, 22*, 3–29.

14. Davis, P. J. (1981). Are there coincidences in mathematics? *American Mathematical Monthly, 88*, 311–320.

15. Davis, P., & Hersh, R. (1981). *The mathematical experience.* Boston: Birkhauser.

16. Dubinsky, E. (1986). On the teaching of mathematical induction. *Journal of Mathematical Behavior, 5*(3), 305–17.

17. Dubinsky, E. (1989). On the teaching of mathematical induction II. *Journal of Mathematical Behavior, 8*, 285–304.

18. Fischbein, E., & Kedem, I. (1982). Proof and certitude in the development of mathematical thinking. In A. Vermandel (Ed.), *Proceedings of the Sixth International Conference of the Psychology of Mathematics Education* (pp. 128–131). Antwerp, Belgium: Universitaire Instelling Antwerpen.

19. Frid, S. (1994). Three approaches to undergraduate calculus instruction: Their nature and potential impact on students' language use and sources of conviction. In E. Dubinsky, A. H. Schoenfeld, & J. Kaput (Eds.), *Research in collegiate mathematics education I* (pp. 69–100). Washington, DC: Conference Board of the Mathematical Sciences.

20. Friedman, B. (1991). *Lectures on applications-oriented mathematics.* New York: Wiley.

21. Fuys, D., Geddes, D., & Tischler, R. (1988). *The van Hiele model of thinking in geometry among adolescents* (JRME Monograph No. 3.). Reston, VA: National Council of Teachers of Mathematics.

22. Galbraith, P. (1981). Aspects of proving: a clinical investigation of process. *Educational Studies in Mathematics, 12*, 1–29.

23. Goetting, M. M. (1995). The college student's understanding of mathematical proof (Doctoral dissertation, University of Maryland, 1995). *Dissertations Abstracts International,*

56-A, 3016, Feb., 1996.

24. Halmos, P. (1985). *I want to be a mathematician*. New York: Springer-Verlag.

25. Hanna, G. (1990). Some pedagogical aspects of proof. *Interchange, 21*, 6–13.

26. Harel, G. (1985). *Teaching linear algebra in high school*. Unpublished Doctoral Dissertation, Ben-Gurion University of the Negev, Israel.

27. Harel, G. (1995). From naive interpretist to operation conserver. In J. Sowder & B. Schappelle (Eds.), *Providing a foundation for teaching mathematics in the middle grades* (pp. 143–165). New York: SUNY Press.

28. Harel, G. (in preparation). Symbolic reasoning and transformational reasoning and their effect on algebraic reasoning. In James J. Kaput (Ed.), *Employing children's natural powers to build algebraic reasoning in the content of elementary mathematics*.

29. Harel, G., & Tall, D. (1991). The general, the abstract, and the generic. *For the Learning of Mathematics, 11*, 38–42.

30. Kitcher, P. (1983). *The nature of mathematical knowledge*. New York: Oxford University Press.

31. Kleiner, I. (1991). Rigor and proof in mathematics: A historical perspective. *Mathematics Magazine, 64*(5), 291–314.

32. Lampert, M. (1990). When the problem is not the question and the solution is not the answer: Mathematical knowing and teaching. *American Educational Research Journal, 27*(1), 29–63.

33. Lave, J., & Wenger, E. (1991). *Situated learning: Legitimate peripheral participation*. New York: Cambridge University Press.

34. Leron, U. (1983). Structuring mathematical proofs. *American Mathematical Monthly, 90*, 174–185.

35. Lesh, R. (1995). Personal communication.

36. Lovell, K. (1971). The development of the concept of mathematical proof in abler pupils. In M. Rosskopf, L. Steffe, & S. Taback (Eds.), *Piagetian cognitive-development research and mathematical education* (pp. 66–80). Washington, DC: National Council of Teachers of Mathematics.

37. MacPherson, E. D. (1985). The themes of geometry: design of the nonformal geometry curriculum. In C. Hirsch & M. Zweng (Eds.), *The secondary school mathematics curriculum*, 1985 Yearbook (pp. 65–80). Reston, VA: National Council of Teachers of Mathematics.

38. Martin, G., & Harel, G. (1989). Proof frames of preservice elementary teachers. *Journal for Research in Mathematics Education, 20*(1), 41–51.

39. Mervis, C. B., & Rosch, E. (1981). Categorization of natural objects. *Annual Review of Psychology, 32*, 89–115.

40. Moore, R. C. (1994). Making the transition to formal proof. *Educational Studies in Mathematics, 27*, 249–266.

41. Movshovits-Hadar, N. (1988). Stimulating presentation of theorems followed by responsive proofs. *For the Learning of Mathematics, 8*, 12–19.

42. Mueller, I. (1981). *Philosophy of Mathematics and Deductive Structure in Euclid's Elements*. Cambridge, MA: MIT Press.

43. National Council of Teachers of Mathematics. (1989). *Curriculum and evaluation standards for school mathematics*. Reston, VA: Author.

44. Piaget, J. (1983). Piaget's theory. In P. H. Mussen (Ed.), *Handbook of Child Psychology* (4th ed., pp. 103–128). New York: John Wiley & Sons.

45. Piaget, J., & Inhelder, B. (1967). *The child's conception of space*. New York: W.W. Norton & Company.

46. Porteous, K. (1986). Children's appreciation of the significance of proof. *Proceedings of the Tenth International Conference of the Psychology of Mathematics Education* (pp. 392–397). London, England.

47. Schoenfeld, A. (1985). *Mathematical problem solving*. Orlando, FL: Academic Press.

48. Semadeni, Z. (1980). Action proofs in primary mathematics teaching and in teacher training. *For the Learning of Mathematics, 4*, 32–34.

49. Senk, S. L. (1985). How well do students write geometry proofs? *Mathematics Teacher, 78*(6), 448–456.

50. Shaughnessy, J. M., & Burger, W. F. (1985). Spadework prior to deduction in geometry. *Mathematics Teacher, 78*(6), 419–428.

51. Simon, M. A. (1996). Beyond inductive and deductive reasoning: the search for a sense of knowing. *Educational Studies in Mathematics, 30*, 197–210.

52. Skemp, R. R. (1978). Relational understanding and instrumental understanding. *Arithmetic Teacher, 26*, 9–15.

53. Steiner, M. (1976). Mathematical explanation. Mimeographed notes, Columbia University.

54. Steffe, L., Cobb, P., & von Glasersfeld, E. (1988). *Construction of arithmetical meanings and strategies.* New York: Springer-Verlag.

55. Tall, D. O. (1979). Cognitive aspects of proof, with special reference to the irrationality of $\sqrt{2}$. *Proceedings of the Third Conference of the Psycology of Mathematics Education* (pp. 203–205). Warwick, England.

56. Thompson, D. R. (1991, April). *Reasoning and proof in precalculus and discrete mathematics.* Paper presented at the meeting of the American Educational Research Association, Chicago.

57. Thompson, D. R. (1996). Learning and teaching indirect proof. *Mathematics Teacher, 89*, 474–482.

58. Thompson, P. W. (1994). Images of rate and operational understanding of the Fundamental Theorem of Calculus. *Educational Studies in Mathematics, 26*(2–3), 229–274.

59. Usiskin, Z. (1980). What should not be in the algebra and geometry curricula of average college-bound students? *Mathematics Teacher, 73*, 413–424.

60. Usiskin, Z. (1987). Resolving the continuing dilemmas in school geometry. In M. M. Lindquist & A. P. Shulte (Eds.), *Learning and Teaching Geometry, K–12, 1987 Yearbook* (pp. 17–31). Reston, VA: National Council of Teachers of Mathematics.

61. van Dormolen, J. (1977). Learning to understand what giving a proof really means. *Educational Studies in Mathematics, 8*, 27–34.

62. Vinner, S. (1977). The concept of exponentiation at the undergraduate level and the definitional approach. *Educational Studies in Mathematics, 8*, 17–26.

63. Vinner, S. (1983). The notion of proof: Some aspects of students' view at the senior high level. *Proceedings of the Seventh International Conference of the Psychology of Mathematics Education.* Rehovot, Israel: Weizmann Institute of Science.

64. Volmink, J. (1988). The role of proof in students' understanding of geometry. Paper presented at the annual meeting of the American Educational Research Association, New Orleans.

65. Wilf, H. S. (1996). Epsilon sandwiches. *Focus. 16*(2) 24–25.

66. Williams, E. (1980). An investigation of senior high school students' understanding of the nature of mathematical proof. *Journal for Research in Mathematics Education, 11*(3), 165–166.

67. Yerushalmy, M. (1986). Induction and generalization: An experiment in teaching and learning high school geometry. Doctoral dissertation, Harvard University.

Purdue University, West Lafayette, IN

San Diego State University, San Diego, CA

CBMS Issues in Mathematics Education
Volume **7**, 1998

Students' Use of Diagrams to Develop Proofs in an Introductory Analysis Course

DAVID GIBSON

ABSTRACT. This study investigated the strategy of drawing diagrams to develop proofs. Task–based interviews with students in an introductory analysis (advanced calculus) course revealed that these students used diagrams to perform the following subtasks of proof development: (a) understand information, (b) judge the truthfulness of statements, (c) discover ideas, and (d) write out ideas. Typically, using diagrams helped students complete subtasks that they were not able to complete while working with verbal/symbolic representations alone. Diagrams aided students' thinking by corresponding more closely to the part of their understanding with which they were operating at the time and by reducing the burden that proving placed on their thinking.

I arrived at the idea for this study through my experience as a graduate mathematics student. Like most students in graduate mathematics programs, I spent the majority of my time studying and developing proofs. And, like many students, I found the process of developing proofs difficult. Researchers have found that, in general, students' difficulties with mathematical proof are related to the following factors: (a) understanding of the rules and nature of proof [15, 27]; (b) conceptual understanding [10, 17]; (c) proof techniques and strategies [16, 26]; and (d) cognitive load [2, 17].

While I was student, I was not aware of such research. Therefore, I determined from my own experience factors that helped me to develop proofs. My attempts to overcome my difficulties usually involved applying a common strategy used to solve mathematics problems in general — drawing a diagram [21, 26]. After receiving an assignment, some of my classmates and I often met in an unused classroom. In these sessions, we spent much of our time drawing pictures on the chalkboard as we searched for the solutions to our proofs. Also, the work I did on my own and the help I received from more experienced students frequently involved using diagrams. These experiences motivated me to more closely examine the role of diagrams in proof development. In this paper, I describe what

I found out about how students use diagrams in their proof attempts and why diagrams can help students develop proofs.

Diagrams and Verbal/Symbolic Representations

Before proceeding further, I will address how diagrams fit in the scheme of representations in general. According to Hiebert and Carpenter [11, p. 66], "to think about and communicate mathematical ideas, we need to represent them in some way." These representations of ideas can be internal and/or external. In order to think about ideas, they must be represented internally within a person's mind. The nature of internal representations, however, is unclear because they are not observable. The need to communicate gives rise to the need for external representations of ideas. As a necessity, external representations are observable.

Winn [33] offers a scheme to classify both internal and external representations. According to Winn, forms of representation fall along a continuum. Realistic pictures fall at one end of the continuum because they possess considerable resemblance to what they represent. Written language, on the other hand, occurs at the other end of the continuum because the symbols of language are a matter of convention and do not ordinarily coincide at all with what they represent. Charts, graphs, and diagrams fall in the middle of the continuum—they coincide to a degree with what is being represented, yet do no appear exactly as what they represent.

The present study focuses on three types of external representations. Mathematical proofs almost exclusively involve the first two, words and symbols. These two types of representations fall at the abstract end of Winn's [33] scheme. Therefore, I will consider them together since neither serves as a close resemblance of the concepts they represent. I will refer to these representations as verbal/symbolic representations. I will refer to the third type of external representations, which include any drawing done by the students, as diagrams. These representations fall in the middle of Winn's scheme.

To apply these ideas to a mathematical concept, consider the concept of onto function. When students learn this concept, they form an unobservable internal representation of onto function. Their internal representation could include the definition and a mental picture, perhaps of circles, dots, and arrows. In communicating the concept, students could externally represent the concept by either writing a definition (does not embody characteristics that coincide with the concept) or by drawing a diagram (embodies characteristics that coincide with the concept).

Diagrams and Mathematical Tasks

Endorsements for the use of diagrams appear frequently in the mathematics education literature. Using visually represented information has been advocated for all levels of mathematics, including fractions [5], algebra [18], calculus [29], and college–level proofs [1, 3, 12]. Rationale for these endorsements focus on the benefits that thinking visually can bring to understanding mathematical concepts and to performing mathematical tasks. For example, Dirkes [5, p. 28] concludes, "Many students who make drawings understand mathematical operations better than those who use only symbols." In regards to proof, Zimmerman adds, "There is no doubt that diagrams play a heuristic role in motivating and understanding proofs" [34, p. 132].

Although many authors advocate using diagrams to perform mathematical tasks, little is known about the effectiveness of this strategy at the college level. Studies [19, 31, 32] of elementary students indicate that these students can improve their mathematical problem solving performance after being taught to use diagrams. Such results suggest that the problem solving activity of developing mathematical proofs may also benefit from the use of diagrams.

However, research related to whether diagrams might help college students create proofs is scarce. In fact, students' thinking as it relates to college level mathematical proofs and the use of diagrams was not found to be the central focus of any study. Therefore, the purpose of this study was to begin to describe and explain students' use of diagrams as they develop proofs. In particular, this study aimed to answer the following questions:

1. How willing are students to use diagrams in proving situations?
2. When or under what conditions do students use diagrams?
3. In what ways do students use diagrams while proving?
4. Why might diagrams help students with their proofs?

The answers to the first two questions require discussion beyond what is practical for this paper and can be found elsewhere [8]. An additional concern, again beyond what can be practically addressed in this paper, is the potential difficulties that using diagrams can create for students [25, 29]. How this issue relates to the findings of this study are also discussed in [8]. This paper will describe the ways students used diagrams and the reasons why diagrams helped students as they developed their proofs.

Procedure

The subjects of the study were all 12 students who completed a first semester introduction to analysis course at a state university in the Southeastern United States. This course was selected for the study because it included a heavy emphasis on students constructing their own proofs and the subject matter was conducive to being represented by diagrams. The title of the course was Advanced Calculus, and the textbook was Introduction to Analysis by Gaughan [7]. It should also be noted that although the instructor of the course implied that diagrams were important by using them regularly, he never provided outright instruction on them, and he never overtly suggested that the students use them.

Because the purpose of this study was to describe and explain students' use of diagrams to create proofs, I used task–based interviews to obtain detailed information about how the students acted and thought as they developed their proofs. I asked the students to "think out loud," and I recorded the interviews on audio tape. Each student participated in three task–based interviews. Proofs that had been assigned as homework provided the tasks for these interviews. These tasks were as follows:

Interview 1. For functions $f : A \to B$ and $g : B \to C$, prove or disprove the following two statements:
a. If f and g are onto then $g \circ f$ is onto.
b. If $g \circ f$ is onto, then g and f are onto.

Interview 2. Let $\{x_n\}_{n=1}^{\infty}$ be a sequence and set $S = \{x_n : n \in \mathbb{N}\}_{n=1}^{\infty}$. Suppose $A = \sup(S)$ and $A \notin S$. Prove that there is a subsequence of $\{x_n\}_{n=1}^{\infty}$ which converges to A.

Interview 3. Let $f : \mathbb{R} \to \mathbb{R}$ be continuous at c and suppose that $f(c) > 0$. Is there a neighborhood, N, of c such that $f(x) > 0$ for all $x \in N$? Prove your assertion.

In order not to bias students towards using diagrams, neither I nor the instructor told them the specific aim of the study. Directing students to make diagrams or directly questioning them about their use of diagrams may also have biased students' behavior and comments regarding diagrams. Therefore, data about their use of diagrams were obtained indirectly by observing their behavior and by asking them about their proving processes in general. In particular, before each task-based interview concluded, I asked the students to reflect on their work with the following two questions: "What do you think helped you make progress on the proof?" and "What do you think hindered your progress on the proof?" I did ask students about their use of diagrams in response to their answers to these questions. For example, if a student answered that making a diagram helped them make progress on the proof, then I would follow with a question like, "How did you use the diagram to help you?" In keeping with the implicit investigation of diagrams, I asked students to elaborate on their answers whether or not they pertained to diagrams.

Copies of the students written work during the three task–based interviews (including their diagrams) and the transcripts of the interviews provided the primary data of the study. A final interview, conducted at the end of the course, provided further insight into the students' proving processes. In this interview, I asked students to reflect on their proving practices in the course but did not ask them to develop a proof. Furthermore, in order to understand the context in which the students were taught, I observed all class meetings of the course.

I analyzed the interview transcripts generated in this study using a qualitative methodology. The method of analysis, influenced by Strauss and Corbin [28], involved inductively deriving the descriptions and explanations of how the students used diagrams. During this inductive process, I accumulated examples of students' uses of diagrams as well as their comments about using diagrams. Then, I categorized these examples into topics. Using related behaviors and comments within a topic, I wrote descriptions of the students' use of diagrams. These descriptions formed the findings of the study.

However, because of the nature of this type of analysis, the findings presented here depict only one possible interpretation of the data. The data include only external representations of students' ideas. The findings, especially those related to why diagrams helped students, include inferences about students' internal representations. I relied on two inferences in particular. One is when students used visual language, I inferred that they were operating with the visual part of their understanding. Also, when students claimed that using diagrams reduced the burden on their thinking, I inferred that this corresponded to what was actually occurring in their brains. Since internal mental processes are not observable, other inferences, and thus other interpretations of the data, are possible.

Findings

Typically, students began their proof attempts using only verbal/symbolic representations. However, after running into difficulty or becoming stuck, they often turned to the strategy of drawing a diagram. Students used diagrams to try to help themselves become unstuck in four general activities: (a) understanding information, (b) judging the truthfulness of statements, (c) discovering ideas, and (d) writing out their ideas. This section describes how students used diagrams in these activities. It also describes, for each activity, how diagrams helped complete the activity and why diagrams helped students' thinking in that activity.

Understanding Information.

Creating proofs involves understanding the information in the proofs. For example, students must understand the definitions of the terms in both the hypothesis and conclusion of the statement to be proved in order to know what must be shown in the proof. In this study, students sometimes used diagrams after they had become stuck trying to understand definitions and other information related to the proof.

For example, during Interview 1, Steve looked up the definition of onto function in the textbook but had difficulty understanding it. So he made a diagram (see Figure 1) to help him "remember how [onto] worked." (The book did not contain a diagram of onto function). More than this, he expressed his understanding of onto in visual terms.

Steve: I was thinking since every point that was in here in this white spot.
   I: OK. Every point in the far right circle.
Steve: And, uh, you could get back. Every point in there could get back to a point in the one before it.

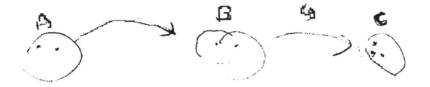

FIGURE 1.   Steve's diagram used to understand onto function.

I: OK.

Steve: That's onto. That's what I think's onto.

I: OK.

Steve: And, uh, I was just trying to remember how that worked. (Int 1)

To Steve, a function was onto when "every point in [the far right circle]" (elements of the codomain) "could get back to a point in the one before it" (an element of the domain).

Students indicated that diagrams helped them understand information by appealing to their natural thinking. They said that diagrams seemed to coincide with the way their "minds work" and that information represented visually seemed easier or clearer than verbal/symbolic representations.

Nick: It just kinda gives me a better understanding. I don't exactly know why. Maybe it's just because of the way my brain works. I don't know, but it does help me to be able to see a picture or have a diagram. (Int 2)

Agnes: There's something about looking at a picture that makes things more clear than looking at words. (Final Int)

Sally: If you can't understand the words, then the picture makes it easier. (Final Int)

Students revealed two characteristics of visually represented information that appealed to their natural thinking. First, students found them more concrete than verbal/symbolic representations. In other words, students found information more understandable when they could think about it in physical terms. Second, students reported that diagrams reduced the burden proving was placing on their thinking.

Nick's comments illustrate both of the characteristics of diagrams that appealed to students' thinking. These comments refer to the diagram (see Figure 2) that he used to understand information from the statement to be proved in Interview 3.

I: For what purposes did you use the picture?

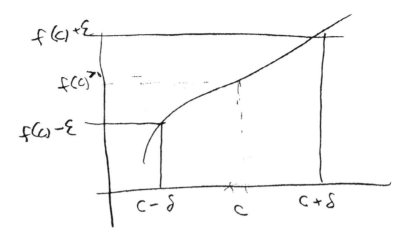

FIGURE 2.   Nick's diagram that helped him understand information
because it was concrete and it reduced mental strain.

Nick: To try to help me think about it....I looked at it to use it to conceptualize the fact that f of c is bigger than zero, and then I can actually
physically see my neighborhood, instead of having to think about it in
my head. I can say well here's a neighborhood of c and I can physically
see myself putting some x in that neighborhood and think well f of x
would be greater than zero too for all x in that neighborhood. Yeah, I
just basically used it to help me see what would be happening in that
situation. (Int 3)

He wanted to "see what would be happening in that situation." According
to Nick, the diagram helped him understand the information because he could
think about it "physically" and because he did not have to "think about it in
his head." In other words, diagrams appealed to his natural thinking because
they were more concrete than verbal/symbolic representations and because they
caused less mental strain than verbal/symbolic representations.

Diagrams produced less mental strain than information in verbal/symbolic
form for two reasons. Drawing diagrams reduced the burden on students' thinking because putting information down on paper freed their minds from spending
energy on retaining the information and, in turn, allowed more mental energy
to be used on understanding the information.

Carl: So I thought, well, just let me draw them out so I can quit thinking
about that, and I can think about, I can just look at it. I don't know.
I think it's just less work if I have them sitting in front of me. I don't

have to think about picturing them. I just have to look at them. And
it makes it easier I think. (Int 1)

Also, in situations where information represented in verbal/symbolic form was
difficult to monitor, diagrams allowed students to think about more information
at one time.

Agnes: When I read the definitions you can't think about the whole thing at
once, but when you have a picture you can. (Final Int)

Frequently, as with Steve above, the understanding that students obtained
by using diagrams possessed visual attributes. Students exhibited the visual
attributes of their understanding by expressing it in visual terms rather than
verbal/symbolic terms. This visual aspect of students' understanding was important because, as will be seen in the descriptions of the other activities, students often developed their proofs relying on the visual part, rather than the
verbal/symbolic part, of their understanding of the information in the proofs.

Judging Truthfulness.

A second way students used diagrams was to judge the truthfulness of statements. For a proof to be valid, the mathematical statements and logical connections within the proof must be true. Therefore, creating a proof requires
that the truthfulness of mathematical statements be evaluated. When students
had difficulty evaluating the truthfulness of statements, they sometimes made
diagrams to help them make these judgments.

The following two examples describe instances where Alice used diagrams
to help her judge the truthfulness of statements. In each, she had difficulty
judging the truthfulness of statements represented in verbal/symbolic form and,
in response, had made a diagram. These examples show that she used diagrams
to help her judge the truthfulness of statements and show how and why diagrams
helped her make these judgments.

Alice used a diagram (see Figure 3) to judge the truthfulness of the statement
to be proved in Interview 1. She decided that it was true that the composition
of onto functions must itself also be onto.

Alice: I'm going to draw some pictures. Maybe that will help. OK. If I let the
elements be in C, then there has to be, there has to be elements in A
that maps to those. So, if I start off with having elements in C, then
I'm going to have that. All the elements in C would come from A. OK,
when I look at this picture, then I know that it's true.

(Later in the same interview)

I: What helped you come to that conclusion?

Alice: In my picture, all these elements mapped to B and all these elements in
B mapped to C. And so, when I think of surjective, I think of all the

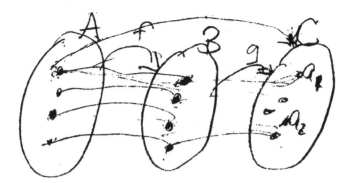

FIGURE 3. Alice's diagram used to judge whether the composition of onto functions is also an onto function.

elements are used.

I: OK.

Alice: And in my picture, they all are. And so that makes me think that g of f is surjective. (Int 1)

Alice based her decision on whether her criteria for the condition of onto function had been met. Her criteria were visual. Alice viewed a function as onto if all the elements in the codomain "are used." So to judge whether $g \circ f$ was onto, she checked to see if all the elements of C were used. When her picture showed that they were, she concluded that $g \circ f$ was onto (surjective).

In the third interview, Alice again had difficulty determining if the statement to be proved was true. She could not decide if there existed a neighborhood of point c which would always produce positive functional values (given f continuous and $f(c) > 0$). In response, she decided to make a diagram (see Figure 4).

After drawing, Alice judged that there was, in fact, a neighborhood on which f was always positive, and again she based her decision on visual criteria.

Alice: By looking at the picture I can tell it, it just depends on how small you make the neighborhood of c. Eventually, it's going to be so close that it has to be positive.

I: What has to be positive?

Alice: Any x in that neighborhood causes f of x has to be positive when it gets really really close to c if f of c is always positive.

(Later in the interview)

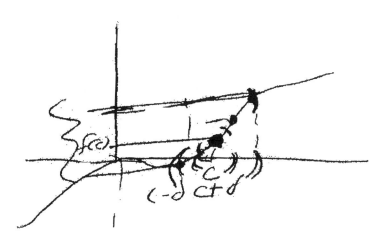

FIGURE 4.   Alice's diagram used to judge whether there was a neighborhood of c in which f would always be positive.

I: And you think it's true?

Alice: Yes, I think it's true.

I: What caused you to think it's true?

Alice: Well, mainly the picture because even though I showed that this one is negative in spots around c, if I make epsilon small enough, delta small enough, then eventually anything else inside that neighborhood is going to be positive. (Int 3)

Alice based her judgment on two visual criteria, closeness and aboveness: "By looking at the picture I can tell it, it just depends on how small you make the neighborhood of c. Eventually, it's going to be so close that it has to be positive." Her criteria were closely tied to her graph. Her criterion for a neighborhood of a point was closeness to that point, and her criterion for functional values to be positive was that the graph of the function be above the x–axis. Therefore, since the points were "so close" to c, her condition for a neighborhood had been met, and since the graph of the function was above the x–axis at these points, her condition for positive functional values had been met. As a result, she concluded that the statement was true.

As in Alice's examples, diagrams helped students judge the truthfulness of statements by helping them evaluate whether the criteria upon which they were basing their judgments had been met. The primary reason why diagrams helped students evaluate whether their criteria had been met was because information represented visually corresponded more closely to the criteria than did information in verbal/symbolic form. As mentioned earlier, students often expressed their understanding in visual terms. Similarly, students' criteria for making judgments often possessed visual attributes. Therefore, if students believed that their visual conditions had been met, then they believed that the statement they were examining was true. Because students did not usually think of their criteria in terms of the formal definitions, their ability to decide whether their criteria had been met was hindered when they worked with information represented in only verbal/symbolic form. On the other hand, since diagrams more closely matched the visual criteria students used to make their judgments, they could more easily decide from diagrams whether or not their criteria had been met.

Discovering Ideas.

In addition to understanding information and judging the truthfulness of statements, students also used diagrams to make discoveries. Proving a theorem requires discovering a logical argument that shows that the conclusion of the theorem will be true whenever the hypothesis of the theorem is true. Because an argument is a sequence of connected ideas, creating an argument requires determining appropriate ideas and connections between ideas in order to form the argument. Since complete algorithms for developing the arguments of proofs do not exist, students must "come up with" or discover ideas to use in their proofs. When students had difficulty finding ideas for their proofs, they sometimes used diagrams to help themselves discover these ideas.

The following comments indicate how diagrams helped students make discoveries—they could obtain ideas more readily from diagrams than they could from verbal/symbolic representations.

Bill: You see, if I have the picture in front of me, I can look at the picture, and I can see things that otherwise I might not think of. (Int 1)

Alice: When I can't get any more ideas from just the definitions, then I draw a picture. (Int 3)

When attempting to make discoveries, students must search for appropriate ideas. During this search, initial ideas are evaluated and either accepted or discarded. Since students obtained ideas more readily from diagrams and, therefore, had more ideas to evaluate, they were more likely to find ones suitable for their proofs.

The reasons why diagrams helped students obtain ideas more readily were that diagrams more closely corresponded to students' thinking, were alterable, and reduced the burden on students' thinking. As suggested by Agnes' comments below, the main reason students could obtain ideas more readily from diagrams than from verbal/symbolic representations was that diagrams more closely corresponded to the way students were thinking about the information in the problem. Again, students often operated with the visual part of their understanding of the information in the proofs. When they were thinking about information in this way, students had difficulty obtaining ideas from information represented in verbal/symbolic form. On the other hand, since diagrams more closely matched the way they were thinking, they could more easily obtain ideas from the problem information when it was represented in visual form.

For example, Agnes used a diagram (see Figure 5) to discover an ϵ that would make $f(c) - \epsilon > 0$ when $f(c) > 0$.

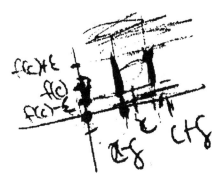

FIGURE 5.   Agnes' diagram used to discover that when $f(c) > 0$, then choosing epsilon to be one half of $f(c)$ makes $f(c) - \epsilon > 0$.

Looking at the diagram helped Alice make herdiscovery because it more closely matched the way she thought about the meaning of greater than zero.

Agnes: Because looking at the picture, I could easily visualize an epsilon between zero and f of c. You know, I could find an epsilon that I wanted. I was looking for an epsilon, and I don't know if it was right or not. But, I was trying to find an epsilon. And so I said let epsilon equal f of c over two. And seeing that helped me see that the distance, you know, that I could take half of that, and it would still be greater than zero. (Int 3)

Agnes thought about the meaning of greater than zero in visual terms: $f(c)$ greater than zero meant that $f(c)$ was some distance above the x–axis. Seeing that distance in her diagram helped her discover that she could "take half of that" distance ("let epsilon equal f of c over two") and still be some distance above the x–axis. Because $f(c) - \epsilon$ was still some distance above the x–axis, Agnes knew that $f(c) - \epsilon$ was greater than zero, and, thus, she had found the epsilon for which she had been searching.

Another reason diagrams helped students obtain ideas more readily was because they were alterable. In their search for ideas, students added to, subtracted from, and redrew their diagrams. Altering diagrams allowed students to explore possible scenarios within the problem situation and, as a result, come up with ideas. Roger's two diagrams in Figure 6 provide an example of obtaining an idea by altering a diagram.

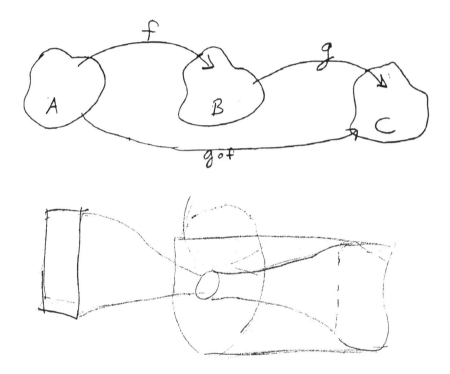

FIGURE 6.   Roger's original diagram and altered diagram used to discover how f could not be onto even though g of f was onto.

The first diagram in Figure 6 is a diagram typical of representing the composition of two functions. Roger made this diagram first and used it to help his understanding of the definitions of onto function and function composition. Later in his proof attempt, when he was trying to discover how f could not be onto when $g \circ f$ was onto, Roger redrew this diagram in an atypical fashion. Set B was at the heart of this discovery.

Roger: So, what I'm trying to think of is any kind of set where I can go from a set and either shrink it down into smaller sets and expand to C, or have B, or at least a subset of B, so that it just takes one chunk out of B as we go through with the compositional function.

For the composition function $g \circ f$ to be onto, g did not need to map the entire set B onto set C; only the image of f needed to be mapped onto C. Therefore, the image of f did not have to equal B (f did not have to be onto) for $g \circ f$ to be onto. Roger discovered this idea through his diagram by having f "shrink" A into a subset of B so that f would not be onto, and then g "expand" that subset of B back out to cover C so that $g \circ f$ would be onto.

Students also indicated that they obtained ideas more readily from diagrams because diagrams helped reduce the heavy mental burden that developing proofs placed on their thinking. Diagrams have already been shown to have helped reduce the burden on students' thinking as they tried to understand information. In this case, diagrams allowed students to spend less mental energy retaining information and also permitted them to think about more information at one time. These same two factors helped students reduce their mental burden as they tried to make discoveries.

Diagrams allowed for less mental energy to be consumed on retaining information leaving more energy to be spent on discovery.

> Jack: Why always keep the picture in your mind when you can have it on the paper allowing you to focus more on how to get to the end of the proof instead of always having to always recall the picture in each individual step? (Int 1)

Drawing a diagram of information allowed Jack not to have to keep bringing that information to mind. The mental energy that would have been spent on retaining information could then be spent on discovering ideas for his proof.

Being able to think about more information also helped students obtain ideas.

> Roger: I'd have a proof that wasn't working out. So I'd write down everything that I knew, and I'd be able to see each piece individually. But I'd want to see them all at once, and the picture would help me.
> (later in same interview)
> I: And the picture does what?
> Roger: It gives you a broad overview, kinda like an aerial view. You don't get details but an idea of where everything is in relation to everything else.
> I: Once you have this overview what do you do with it?
> Roger: Try and see if it leads me anywhere. Maybe it won't look complete, and I'll try and plug in more facts. Or maybe, it will suggest connections between two or three theorems. (Final Int)

As a result of being able to think about more information at once, Roger acquired an overview of this information and, consequently, was able to obtain ideas about how the different pieces of information in the problem related to each other.

Writing Out Ideas.

Once students discovered ideas for their proofs, they needed to write these ideas into their proofs. However, students often had difficulty expressing their discoveries in the appropriate words and symbols. When they had difficulty writing their ideas into verbal/symbolic form, students sometimes used diagrams to help them express their ideas. One student, Laura, was very successful using diagrams in this manner. For example, she used a diagram to write out her entire proof in Interview 3 (see Figure 7).

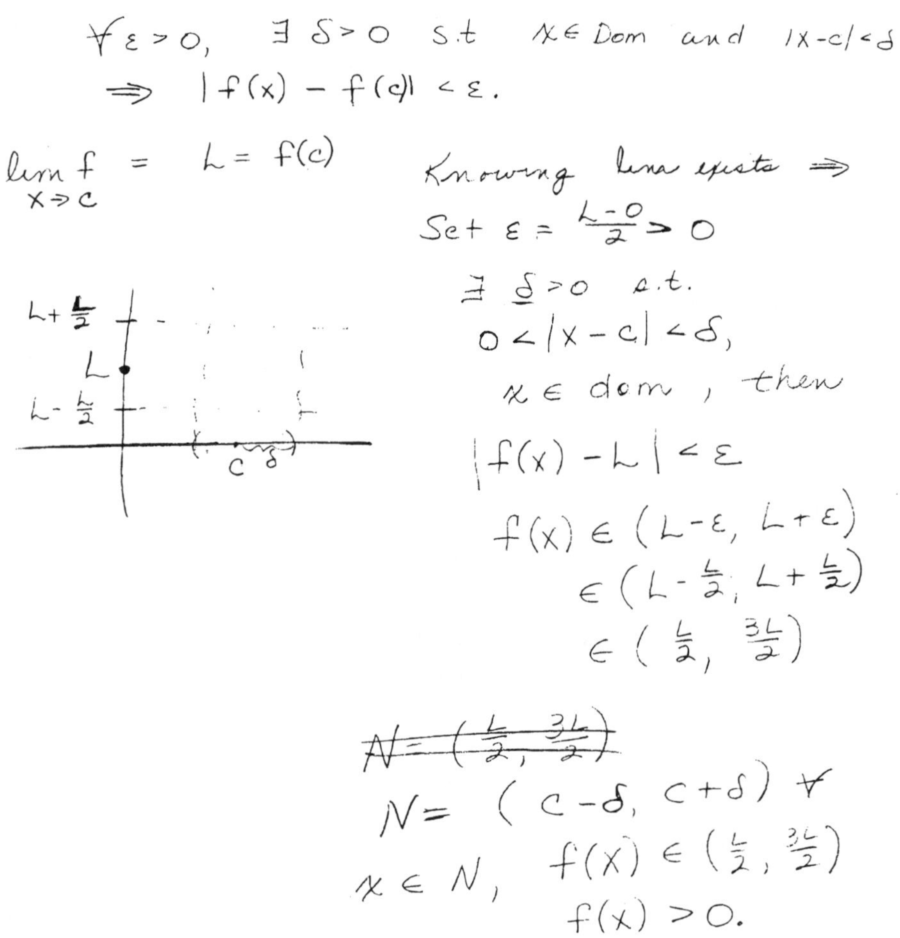

FIGURE 7.   Laura's proof and the diagram she used to write out her proof.

Diagrams helped Laura write out her ideas by helping her connect her ideas to verbal/symbolic representations of these ideas.

> Laura: I've got to be able to turn in the assignment by getting what's going on up here down loaded onto paper for [the instructor]. So probably, that's a kind of an intermediary step. I see it up here, and then I have to draw what I see. And then, I have to translate that into words for when I turn it in. (Int 1)

Laura tried to write her ideas on paper in a form appropriate to submit for homework. To this end, she used diagrams to link the ideas which she had in her mind to verbal/symbolic representations of these ideas. In other words, diagrams served as an intermediary representational form between the ideas in Laura's mind and verbal/symbolic representations of these ideas. Therefore, diagrams helped Laura write out her ideas by helping her "translate [her ideas] into words."

Laura offered two reasons why diagrams helped her link her ideas to verbal/symbolic representations. First, diagrams more closely matched her ideas than did verbal/symbolic representations.

> Laura: What you are trying to do when you write a proof is to put into words what you're visualizing so someone else can read your words and visualize the same thing. It's the intermediate step, down loading your understanding. And by getting it into a picture form, it's closer to what you are seeing, and that can help you translate it into words. (Final Int)

Laura operated with the visual part of her understanding of mathematical ideas. Therefore, diagrams were "closer" to her thinking than were verbal/symbolic representations. Because diagrams more closely corresponded to the ideas in her mind, Laura could more easily represent her ideas with them. Consequently, she represented her ideas visually first. From this intermediate step, she then translated her ideas into verbal/symbolic form.

A second reason diagrams helped Laura connect her ideas to verbal/symbolic representations was because they reduced the burden proving placed on her thinking. Reducing the burden on students' thinking has already been shown to have helped them understand information and obtain ideas. In the case of Laura, using a diagram to reduce the burden on her thinking was instrumental in allowing her to think about how to write out her ideas.

> Laura: Yeah, it's, maybe it's like you can't chew gum and walk at the same time. When all of that is going on in your head, you need to down load that picture on here so that you can touch it and then allow your brain to think about the words you need to say. (Int 3)

While Laura's ideas remained only in her mind, "all that was going on in her head" burdened her thinking to the point that she could not write her ideas into verbal/symbolic form. However, by making a diagram, Laura reduced her mental burden by taking ideas she was trying to retain in her mind and putting them on paper. This allowed her "to think about the words she was going to say" and thus, helped her connect her ideas to verbal/symbolic representations of these ideas.

Summary of Findings.

The findings related to the ways students used diagrams, the means through which diagrams helped students complete these activities, and the reasons why diagrams helped students in these activities are summarized in Table 1. It should be noted that the phrase "reduced mental burden" is used in the table for the sake of brevity. This phrase should be understood to include both the point that diagrams reduced the amount of information students needed to retain in their minds and the point that diagrams allowed students to think about more information at one time.

TABLE 1. Activities in which students used diagrams along with how and why diagrams aided students' thinking in these activities.

Activity	Diagrams Helped Students:	Diagrams Helped Because They:
Understand information	Appeal to their natural thinking	Were concrete & reduced mental burden
Judge truthfulness of statements	Evaluate their criteria	More closely corresponded to students' criteria
Make discoveries	Obtain ideas more readily	More closely corresponded to students' understanding of information, were alterable, & reduced mental burden
Write out ideas	Link their ideas to verbal/symbolic representations	More closely corresponded to ideas & reduced mental burden

Discussion

This study addresses one of the most frequently suggested strategies for solving problems: drawing a diagram [21, 26]. In this study, students dealt with the problem of verifying the truth of mathematical statements. Students sometimes used the strategy of drawing diagrams as they attempted to find solutions (mathematical proofs) to these problems. Perhaps most importantly, this study describes and explains specific characteristics of students' use of diagrams. Because particular attention was paid to students' processes while they were actually developing their proofs, the study's findings convey more than just general notions concerning whether or not diagrams might help students be more successful. In particular, the findings reveal ways students used diagrams to perform specific subtasks of proof development, how diagrams helped them complete the activities, and why diagrams helped their thinking.

Diagrams Used to Complete Subtasks.

The fact that students used diagrams for particular subtasks of proof development suggests a basis for judging the effectiveness of using diagrams. A natural criterion for judging the effectiveness of a strategy would be a finished, correct proof. On occasion, students who had become stuck trying to complete proofs did successfully finish their proofs after they had used diagrams (Laura's proof in Figure 7 for example). However, in light of the ways students used diagrams, and in light of the one hour time constraint on the task–based interviews, completed proofs may not be the most appropriate basis for judging the effectiveness of using diagrams. In this study, the effectiveness of using diagrams is probably best judged in relation to the subtasks of proof development for which students used them.

Students used diagrams after they had become stuck trying to understand information, discover ideas, judge the truthfulness of statements, and write out ideas. Using diagrams almost always helped students successfully complete these subtasks when they were not able to do so while working with only verbal/symbolic representations. Such was the case for each of the diagrams presented in the findings of this study. In fact, in 18 out of the 22 interviews in which students used a diagram, they were able to complete at least one subtask that they were unable to complete before drawing. Therefore, that drawing a diagram can be an effective strategy for developing proofs may best be seen in the students' ability to progress further on their proofs by using diagrams to complete subtasks that they were not able to complete otherwise.

The result that students benefited from using diagrams was not guaranteed. In fact, some research [14, 24] indicates that the opposite might have occurred. In these studies, students preferring nonvisual methods for working mathematical problems tended to outperform those preferring visual means. However, the present study coincides with what has been found concerning elementary students and word problems. Namely, that when attempting to solve unfamiliar problems, students can benefit from using diagrams. Drawing diagrams has helped elementary students solve word problems [19, 31, 32] and now has been shown to help college students further their progress when constructing proofs.

How Diagrams Helped.

The means through which diagrams helped students complete their subtasks appear in the second column of Table 1. For example, diagrams helped students understand information by appealing to their natural thinking. Interestingly, it may be students' use of diagrams to understand information that also enabled them to complete the other activities. Other research on proof has shown that the ability to complete proving activities is often dependent on sufficient conceptual understanding. Hart [10] found that each aspect of developing a proof is strongly tied to students' conceptual understanding. For example, students in Hart's study needed to link their proving strategies to the specific concepts in the proofs (make them domain–specific) before the strategies could be used effectively. Similarly, Moore [17] found that students' conceptual understanding was related to their ability to use definitions in proof development. For example, students needed sufficient conceptual understanding to be able to use the definitions of the concepts to determine the general structure of their proofs.

More than this, Moore [17] explains how the students in his study developed sufficient conceptual understanding.

> The students' ability to use the definitions in the proofs depended on their knowledge of the formal definitions, which in turn depended on their informal concept images. The students often needed to develop their concept images through examples, diagrams, graphs, and other means before they could understand the formal verbal or symbolic definitions. (p. 262)

Therefore, when the students in the present study used diagrams to understand information, they may have also been developing the conceptual understanding they would need to be able to evaluate their criteria, obtain more ideas, and link their ideas to verbal/symbolic representations. For example, Roger used the first diagram in Figure 6 to understand information. The conceptual understanding built there may have been necessary for him to then later use the second diagram in Figure 6 to obtain an idea for his discovery.

Why Diagrams Helped.

Other important characteristics of students' use of diagrams include the reasons why these representations benefited students. An examination of Table 1 reveals two strands that run through the column describing the reasons why diagrams helped students. One is that diagrams more closely corresponded to the part of their understanding with which students were operating at the time.

The other strand is that diagrams reduced the burden on students' thinking. These characteristics are consistent with what others have reported concerning students' thinking.

Several aspects of students' behavior indicated that visual representations corresponded more closely to the way they thought about the concepts. One was that in each of the situations where students used a diagram to complete a subtask, they first tried to complete the subtask using only verbal/symbolic representations but were unable. Another was that as students thought out loud they used visual language such as "shrink it down," "could get back to," and "gets really close." In addition, students made direct references to diagrams being "easier," "more clear," and coinciding with the way their "minds work."

Tall and Vinner's [30] idea of concept image reveals that in students' thinking much more is associated with a concept than the mathematical definition of that concept. In fact, it is normal for students to operate with parts of their concept images other than the definitions. Students in the present study frequently operated with visual parts of their concept images. That students would operate in this manner and that such behavior might be of benefit is reasonable when one considers the nature of the concepts in the proofs together with the students' experiences as visual beings and the physiology of their brains.

First, many calculus concepts possess visual characteristics (distance, function, and increasing for example). Therefore, at least some of the meaning of these concepts can be displayed directly in diagrams. On the other hand, although verbal/symbolic representations can be used to represent the same information, they will not directly display the visual characteristics [33]. Also, as mobile and visual creatures, human beings have built up a lifetime of experience dealing with spatial matters. The outcome of such experience is a natural and powerful way of thinking about physical and visual objects [4]. More than this, some of the neural processes associated with mental imagery are the same as those that process information received from the eye [13]. Therefore, it makes sense that students would tend to operate and operate successfully with visual parts of their concept images of the concepts in this study.

The burden that proving puts on one's thinking has been found to affect high school students [2], college students [17], and mathematicians [9]. Students in this study reported that diagrams helped ease that burden in two ways: first, by freeing their minds to deal with other matters and second, by allowing them to think about more information at one time. Phillips [23] agrees with the first in the following explanation of the value of representing information visually.

> Why does it help us to present the information in a graphical form? When the information is spread out in front of us in a graph or a diagram, there is no longer any need to store the raw information inside our heads. The limited capacity of working memory ceases to be a serious limitation on human thinking. The graphical image becomes a kind of memory store. (p. 54)

Nunokawa [20, p. 34] provides another reason why a diagram can be helpful, "Its usefulness lies, we think, in the fact that it can show relationships among elements in the problem clearly." Agnes' and Roger's discoveries (see Figures 5 & 6) give validity to this claim that diagrams are helpful because they present information in a manner which exhibits relationships within the information. However, it may be the second way that diagrams in this study helped ease students' mental burden that allows students to take advantage of such displays. Phillips [22] puts it this way:

> The visual image passes through many stages of parallel processing within the brain, and it seems that this visual information is encoded in a way that allows us to move our attention rapidly between different details of the display, and so to see patterns and relationships in a large mass of complex data. (p. 54)

In other words, it may be the brain's ability to process visual information in parallel (think about more things at one time) that allows students to become cognizant of the relationships exhibited by the diagram. That is, through the combination of exhibiting relationships and increasing processing capabilities, diagrams may allow students to gain an overview that they could not acquire from verbal/symbolic representations alone.

Implications for Teaching.

The students in this study were not explicitly instructed on how to use diagrams. Yet, students often benefited from using them. However, in many cases students could have profited even more from using diagrams. Therefore, there is the potential that appropriate instruction could help students use diagrams to an even greater advantage. Knowledge of the specific characteristics of using diagrams described in this study could inform such instruction. This knowledge is important if instructors and students are to be able to understand and take advantage of the practical aspects of the strategy of using diagrams to develop mathematical proofs.

Teaching a problem–solving strategy is generally more effective when students are told not just to use a strategy but are also told specific situations in which they might want to apply it. For example, if students are only told that drawing diagrams can help them with their proofs, then they may have difficulty identifying appropriate occasions in which to apply the strategy and, thus, limit its effectiveness. However, if students are told specific subtasks in which diagrams may help them, such as understanding information or writing out ideas, then they should have a better chance of being able to more purposely, and therefore more successfully, apply the strategy.

The effectiveness of a strategy should also be enhanced if instructors and students know the means through which the strategy works. This information is important because it provides a signal that it is time to apply the strategy. For example, the means through which using diagrams helped students make discoveries was by helping them obtain ideas more readily than they could from verbal/symbolic representations. Students who are aware of this fact will be prompted to draw diagrams when they realize that they are having trouble coming up with ideas.

In addition, knowledge of why diagrams helped students can give instructors a better understanding of some general aspects of students' thinking. For example, the fact that students often operated with the visual part of their understanding indicates that even students in advanced undergraduate mathematics courses can profit from thinking concretely. In particular, they possess visual resources that can be exploited for their benefit. Another important aspect is that in order to operate effectively, students often need to reduce the burden that performing complex tasks places on their thinking. Knowledge of these aspects of students' thinking should help teachers make instructional decisions that can benefit their students.

Conclusion

Most students find developing mathematical proofs to be a difficult task. Similar to my experiences as a student, the students in this study overcame some of their difficulties with proof by drawing diagrams. Paying careful attention to students' processes while they were actually developing their proofs revealed specific characteristics of how students used diagrams in the context of college level mathematical proofs. In particular, more is now understood about the subtasks of proof development in which students may use diagrams, the means through which diagrams can help students complete these subtasks, and the reasons why diagrams might benefit students' thinking while performing these subtasks. Although this study involved only a small sample of students working in a limited context, the findings are significant enough to warrant that instructors of courses involving proof try to facilitate their students' use of diagrams and that further research on proofs and diagrams be conducted.

REFERENCES

1. Barwise, J., and Etchemendy, J., *Visual information and valid reasoning*, Visualization in Teaching and Learning Mathematics, (MAA Notes Number 19), (W. Zimmerman and S. Cunningham, eds.), Mathematical Association of America, Washington, DC, 1991, pp. 67–76.

2. Bell, A. W., *A study of pupil's proof–explanations in mathematical situations*, Educational Studies in Mathematics 7 (1976), 23–40.

3. Davis, P., and Anderson, J., *Nonanalytic aspects of mathematics and their implication for research and education*, SIAM Review 21 (1979), 112–127.

4. Davis, R., *Learning mathematics: The Cognitive Science Approach to Mathematics Education*, Ablex, Norwood, NJ, 1984.

5. Dirkes, M., *Draw to understand*, Arithmetic Teacher 39 (1991), 26–29.

6. Fischbein, E. and Kedem, I., *Proof and certitude in the development of mathematical thinking*, (ERIC Document Reproduction Service No. ED 226 943), 1982.

7. Gaughan, E., *Introduction to analysis*, Brooks/Cole, Pacific Grove, CA, 1993.

8. Gibson, D., *Advanced Calculus Students' Use of Visual Representations in the Creation of Mathematical Proofs*, (unpublished doctoral dissertation) (1996), University of Kentucky, Lexington, KY.

9. Hadamard, J., *The psychology of invention in the mathematical field*, Dover, New York, 1954.

10. Hart, E., *A conceptual analysis of the proof–writing performance of expert and novice students in elementary group theory*, Research Issues in Undergraduate Mathematical Learning, (MAA Notes Number 33), (J. Kaput and E. Dubinsky, eds.), Mathematical Association of America, Washington, DC, 1994, pp. 49–62.

11. Hiebert, J. and Carpenter, T., *Learning and teaching with understanding*, Handbook of Research on Mathematics Teaching and Learning (D. Grouws, ed.), National Council of Teachers of Mathematics, Reston, VA, 1992, pp. 65–97.

12. Kline, M., *Logic versus pedagogy*, American Mathematical Monthly 77 (1970), 264–281.

13. Kosslyn, S., and Koenig, O., *Wet Mind: The New Cognitive Neuroscience*, Free Press, New York, 1992.

14. Lean, G., and Clements, M., *Spatial ability, visual imagery, and mathematical performance*, Educational Studies in Mathematics 12 (1981), 267–299.

15. Martin, G. and Harel, G., *Proof frames of preservice elementary teachers*, Journal for Research in Mathematics Education 20 (1989), 41–51.

16. Marty, R., *Getting to eureka: Higher order reasoning in math*, College Teaching 39 (1991), 3–6.

17. Moore, R., *Making the transition to formal proof*, Educational Studies in Mathematics 27 (1994), 249–266.

18. Morelli, L., *A visual approach to algebra concepts*, The Mathematics Teacher 85 (1992), 434–437.

19. Moses, B., *Visualization: A different approach to problem solving*, School Science and Mathematics 82 (1982), 141–147.

20. Nunokawa, K., *Improving diagrams gradually: One approach to using diagrams in problem solving*, For the Learning of Mathematics 14 (1994), 34–38.

21. Polya, G., *How to solve it: A new aspect of mathematical method.*, Princeton University, Princeton, NJ, 1971.

22. Phillips, R., *Computer graphics as a memory aid and a thinking aid*, Journal of Computer Assisted Learning 2 (1985), 37–44.

23. Phillips, R., *Graphs and Diagrams*, Mathematics Teaching 111 (1986), 53–54.

24. Presmeg, N., *Visualization and mathematical giftedness*, Educational Studies in Mathematics 17 (1986), 297–311.

25. Presmeg, N., *Prototypes, metaphors, metonymies, and imaginative rationality in high school mathematics*, Educational Studies in Mathematics 23 (1992), 595–610.

26. Schoenfeld, A., *Mathematical problem Solving*, Academic, Orlando, 1985.

27. Seldon, A., and Seldon, J. (1987), *Errors and misconceptions in college level theorem proving*, Proceedings of the Second International Seminar on Misconceptions in Science and Mathematics, Cornell University (Vol. III), 1987, pp. 457–470.

28. Strauss, A. and Corbin, J., *Basics of qualitative research: Grounded theory procedures and techniques*, Sage, Newbury Park, CA,1990.

29. Tall, D., *Intuition and rigor: The role of visualization in the calculus*, Visualization in Teaching and Learning Mathematics, (MAA Notes Number 19),(W. Zimmerman and S. Cunningham, eds.), Mathematical Association of America,Washington, DC, 1991, pp. 67–76.

30. Tall, D. and Vinner, S.,*Concept image and concept definition in mathematics with particular reference to limits and continuity*, Educational Studies in Mathematics 12 (1981), 151–169.

31. van Essen, G., and Hamaker, C. H. , *Using self–generated drawings to solve arithmetic word problems*, Journal of Educational Research 83 (1990), 301–312.

32. Yancey, A., Thompson, C., and Yancey, J.,. *Children must learn to draw diagrams*, Arithmetic Teacher, 36, (1989), 15–19.

33. Winn, B., *Charts, graphs, and diagrams in educational materials*, The Psychology of Illustration: Basic Research Vol. 1, (D. Williams and H. Houghton, eds.), Springer-Verlag, New York, 1987, pp. 152–198.

34. Zimmerman, W., *Visual Thinking in Calculus, Visualization in Teaching and Learning Mathematics*, (MAA Notes Number 19), (W. Zimmerman and S. Cunningham, eds.), Mathematical Association, Washington, DC, 1991, pp. 127–137.

DEPT. OF MATHEMATICS AND STATISTICS, MURRAY STATE UNIVERSITY

CBMS Issues in Mathematics Education
Volume **7**, 1998

Questions Regarding the Teaching and Learning of Undergraduate Mathematics (and Research Thereon)

ANNIE SELDEN AND JOHN SELDEN

Conference on Research in Collegiate Mathematics Education
Central Michigan University, September 5–8, 1996

What follows is an assortment of questions which arose during the above RUMEC-sponsored[1] Exxon-funded conference, attended by some 150 mathematicians, mathematics educators, and mathematics education researchers. Highlights of the conference are described in "Enthusiasm for Research in Collegiate Math Ed Grows," *Focus: The Newsletter of the Mathematical Association of America*, February 1997.

Questions, and commentaries thereon, were gleaned from remarks made by various speakers and participants. These have been attributed to specific persons, where possible, but the exact wording or interpretation is our own. Apologies to those whose contributions we may have forgotten or misrepresented.

We hope these questions will stimulate research, as well as promote discussion about the nature of mathematics, its teaching and learning, the nature of research in the area, and how such research might prove useful in teaching.

---

[1]RUMEC is an acronym for Research in Undergraduate Mathematics Education Community, a group of interested college mathematics teachers working together to produce research in this area.

Questions about the nature of
mathematics and its teaching and learning:

1. What is the nature of mathematical definitions? Do they describe (mentally) pre-existing objects, such as rectangles, or do they bring objects, such as vector spaces, into existence? How do students cope with definitions at various levels, K–12 through college? What is the best way to introduce definitions at various levels? Via examples? Via informal descriptions? Via formal descriptions?

In his plenary address, Richard Noss of University of London suggested that mathematical definitions pose an epistemological dilemma: Mathematical definitions, by themselves, supply few meanings. Meanings derive from properties. Properties, in turn, depend upon definitions.

2. What is the epistemological status of examples in college mathematics texts?

When describing her research on introductory linear algebra, Anna Sierpinska of Concordia University noted that, in introducing concepts, textbook authors can go either the synthetic or the analytic route. In the former, one describes an object which already exists, whereas in the latter, one creates an object via the definition. The status of these two kinds of definitions is very different. Some authors follow the didactic principle of going from the "concrete to the abstract" when giving introductory examples. Such authors are in the analytic mode from the beginning—that's why they speak of "examples." She suggested that typical North American students operate in the synthetic mode and are consequently "taken for a ride." How do such presentations affect students' learning?

3. What is the nature of abstraction in the learning of mathematics? Why is it that some students focus on the situation and others focus on the math?

Richard Noss, University of London, saw this as a pedagogical dilemma: Concrete thinking is both a prerequisite for abstract thinking and an impediment to it. Others suggested that abstraction might consist of ignoring details when you don't know enough, or perhaps, in suppressing them when you know a lot, or a combination of both. Abstraction might also be regarded as a relationship between a person and an object about which he or she is thinking.

4. What is the nature of transfer? Does it exist? What is transferred from a (mathematical) learning situation to other contexts? Is all knowledge situated? If transfer exists, of what does it consist?

5. What do we know, and what must we learn, in order to achieve, in the teaching and learning of mathematics, the kind of organic and integrated use of language that is manifest in the culture of mathematics as a discipline?

In posing this question, Hyman Bass of Columbia University noted that "language is central to the progress, communication, and understanding of mathematics," by which he meant "not only conventional text, but also symbolic notation, formulas, and even some imagistic and diagrammatic representations." Mathematicians have learned to deal with vast numbers of ideas, resting on centuries of research, discovery, and conceptual synthesis, through the use of a very sophisticated and compressive language. But herein lies an educational dilemma. On the one hand, the language of mathematics is a sophisticated conceptual tool containing expressions which are abstract, iconic, and remote from what they signify. On the other hand, to convey an authentic sense of contemporary mathematics to students, they need some fluency in its use.

6. What is the nature of mathematical understanding?

[David Tall, Warwick University]

The difficulty with such general questions is that they are almost impossible to answer. One needs to generate corresponding operational formulations, as well as consider appropriate frameworks within which to gather evidence, so a convincing case can be made for one's proposed answer. In his own research, Tall began by considering the nature of students' understanding of continuity, infinity and limit process. He subsequently considered visualization using the computer – this led him to thinking about the symbolism of arithmetic, algebra, and calculus, and eventually to the notion of "procept."

Questions (which could be refined) for research:

7. We need to know more about the kinds of mathematical understandings that matter in teaching, how to help teachers develop those understandings, and how to help teachers learn mathematics in, and from, their daily practice.

Specifically, how do we design curriculum materials so teachers are levers for math? How could student comments be used by teachers for learning? What might preservice teacher education do to help people learn specific mathematics and also to help them learn more math on their own?

[Deborah Ball, University of Michigan]

8. What is the nature of student learning and teaching in a technology-intensive environment, focused on function as an introductory and organizing theme? What influences a student's choice of representations?

[M. Kathleen Heid, Pennsylvania State University]

9. What happens to teachers as they learn a new curriculum? What are their mathematical understandings? What are their views of their understandings?

[M. Kathleen Heid, Pennsylvania State University]

10. What's the culture of the university mathematics classroom? What are the interactions? What can be said about the contexts of universities and colleges (where the learning takes place)?

These questions parallel those currently being asked at the K–12 level. Deborah Ball indicated a need for "disciplined inquiry" into the professional development of college teachers (like that done on K–12 teachers). She stated, "It's not adequate to just understand what students' think. What do teachers do with this knowledge?"

11. What kind of classroom micro-culture is conducive to the emergence of shared mathematical meanings?

12. How do students come to understand statistical concepts? What is the epistemological and psychological nature of statistical knowledge? What pedagogical strategies are effective for guiding students to construct their knowledge of statistics?

[Georgia Tolias, Purdue University Calumet]

13. How does one learn the concept of proof? In teaching, which aspects of proof should one focus on? Students' perceptions? Teachers' perceptions?

[Celia Hoyles, University of London]

When speaking of students' lack of precise language skills, Hyman Bass mentioned entering college students' inability to cope with sentences involving two or more quantifiers—a condition that handicaps serious levels of conceptual understanding of much of college level mathematics, and their construction of mathematical proofs.

How does one best learn about quantification? Is the separation of logic, and other aspects of abstract mathematics, into "bridge" courses effective?

14. What effect do writing projects have on students' understandings of mathematics?

[Annalisa Crannell, Franklin and Marshall College]

15. What types of informal knowledge do students bring to class?

[Albert Otto, Illinois State University]

Questions about RUME and how one does it:

16. What, if anything, is special about research in undergraduate mathematics education (RUME)? What's the reason for considering it a separate topic, rather than seeing it as a continuation of research into the teaching/learning of school mathematics?

                              [Celia Hoyles, University of London]

What are the positives/negatives of treating RUME as a separate field? Does this have an epistemological aspect? What is the nature of the change in going from K–12 to college to graduate school?

                              [Ed Dubinsky, Georgia State University]

What insights might we gain from the K–8 curriculum?

                              [Albert Otto, Illinois State University]

17. What can research about collegiate mathematics education teach us?

                              [Ed Dubinsky, Georgia State University]

18. How can RUME flourish, grow, and relate positively to the rest of the (mathematical) community?

                              [Ed Dubinsky, Georgia State University]

19. How does one judge research in mathematics education? Mathematics Departments struggle with this.

                              [Jim Leitzel, University of New Hampshire]

There was also concern about how to convince university mathematics faculty that RUME is a legitimate area of research that should not be "downgraded" as low quality.

20. What role do practitioners (regular college mathematics faculty) have in a research field like RUME?

21. What experiences are necessary for preparing researchers in UME?

22. What makes a good research question? Which research paradigm would be a sensible one for my purposes? Which research methods should I use? What is the process of looking at data?

Questions of practitioners (college mathematics teachers):

23. What are some effective ways to help math Ph.D. students reflect on their teaching (often developmental math or college algebra) in positive and progressive ways?

24. How can we help, support, and encourage college mathematics teachers to think about student learning, the nature of mathematics, and the implications of mathematicians' "ways of knowing" on teaching and learning? In particular, how can non-tenured faculty be encouraged to try novel approaches to teaching that would improve student understanding of mathematics, and at the same time, not be threatened by the effects of poor student evaluations?

25. What purposes are served by the expository lecture?

26. How can we motivate our students and help them overcome their difficulties in reading and understanding mathematical concepts?

27. How can we help students move readily between the numerical, visual, and symbolic domains?

  Presenting multiple representation approaches does not, in itself, seem to ensure this.

28. How much emphasis on skills is enough? How does one make optimal use of class time?

29. What are some effective ways of teaching mathematics to a diverse student population?

30. What is the best learning environment I can provide my students given the particular constraints of the course, e.g., a large section with 300–600 students?

[Eric Muller, Brock University]

DEPT. OF MATHEMATICS, TENNESSEE TECHNOLOGICAL UNIVERSITY, COOKEVILLE, TN

MATHEMATICAL EDUCATION RESOURCES COMPANY, COOKEVILLE, TN

RESEARCH IN COLLEGIATE MATHEMATICS EDUCATION

EDITORIAL POLICY

The papers published in these volumes will serve both pure and applied purposes, contributing to the field of research in undergraduate mathematics education and informing the direct improvement of undergraduate mathematics instruction. The dual purposes imply dual but overlapping audiences and articles will vary in their relationship to these purposes. The best papers, however, will interest both audiences and serve both purposes.

CONTENT.

We invite papers reporting on research that addresses any and all aspects of undergraduate mathematics education. Research may focus on learning within particular mathematical domains. It may be concerned with more general cognitive processes such as problem solving, skill acquisition, conceptual development, mathematical creativity, cognitive styles, etc. Research reports may deal with issues associated with variations in teaching methods, classroom or laboratory contexts, or discourse patterns. More broadly, research may be concerned with institutional arrangements intended to support learning and teaching, e.g. curriculum design, assessment practices, or strategies for faculty development.

METHOD.

We expect and encourage a broad spectrum of research methods ranging from traditional statistically-oriented studies of populations, or even surveys, to close studies of individuals, both short and long term. Empirical studies may well be supplemented by historical, ethnographic, or theoretical analyses focusing directly on the educational matter at hand. Theoretical analyses may illuminate or otherwise organize empirically based work by the author or that of others, or perhaps give specific direction to future work. In all cases, we expect that published work will acknowledge and build upon that of others—not necessarily to agree with or accept others' work, but to take that work into account as part of the process of building the integrated body of reliable knowledge, perspective and method that constitutes the field of research in undergraduate mathematics education.

REVIEW PROCEDURES.

All papers, including invited submissions, will be evaluated by a minimum of three referees, one of whom will be a Volume editor. Papers will be judged on the basis of their originality, intellectual quality, readability by a diverse audience, and the extent to which they serve the pure and applied purposes identified earlier.

SUBMISSIONS.

Papers of any reasonable length will be considered, but the likelihood of acceptance will be smaller for very large manuscripts.

Five copies of each manuscript should be submitted. Manuscripts should be typed double-spaced, with bibliographies done in the style established by the American Mathematical Society for its CBMS series of volumes (an example style sheet is available from the editors on request).

Note that the *RCME* volumes are produced for electronic submission to the AMS. Accepted manuscripts should be prepared using AMS-TeX 2.1 (the macro packages are available through e-mail without charge from the AMS). Illustrations should also be prepared in a form suitable for electronic submission (namely, encapsulated postscript files).

CORRESPONDENCE.

Manuscripts and editorial correspondence should be sent to one of the three editors:

Ed Dubinsky
Department of Mathematics, Statistics,
    & Computer Science
Georgia State University
Atlanta, GA 30303-3083
edd@cs.gsu.edu

James Kaput
Department of Mathematics
University of Massachusetts at Dartmouth
North Dartmouth, MA 02747-2300
jkaput@umassd.edu

Alan Schoenfeld
School of Education
University of California at Berkeley
Berkeley, CA 94720-1670
alans@socrates.berkeley.edu